KENYA

Taking Liberties

July 1991

An Africa Watch Report

485 Fifth Avenue
New York, NY 10017-6104
Tel: (212) 972-8400
Fax: (212) 972-0905

1522 K Street, NW, Suite 910
Washington, DC 20005-1202
Tel: (202) 371-6592
Fax: (202) 371-0124

90 Borough High Street
London SE1 1LL
United Kingdom
Tel: (071) 378-8008
Fax: (071) 378-8029

Library of Congress Catalog Card No.: 91-074109.
ISBN 1-56432-036-7

Cover design by Dan Neiss.

CONTENTS

ACKNOWLEDGMENTS

Africa Watch expresses its gratitude to the many Kenyans who provided us with invaluable information and material for this report. While most of them requested anonymity, we pay tribute to their individual courage and their determination to ensure respect for human rights in Kenya. In addition, we thank the many knowledgeable people who assisted us, especially Sue Fletcher.

ACRONYMS

AP Administration Police
CID Criminal Investigation Department
CITES Convention on the International Trade and Endangered Species
CPK Church of the Province of Kenya
DC District Commissioner
DO District Officer
GEMA Kikuyu, Embu and Meru cultural association
GSU General Service Unit
IBA International Bar Association
ICRC International Committee of the Red Cross
IUS International Union of Students
KADU Kenyan African Democratic Union
KASA Kenya African Socialist Alliance
KANU Kenyan African National Union
KBC Kenya Broadcasting Corporation
KCA Kikuyu Central Association
KCPU Kenyan Coffee Planters Union
KPF Kenya Patriotic Front
KPU Kenya Peoples Union
LSK Law Society of Kenya
NCCK National Council of Churches of Kenya
NEP North Eastern Province
NFD Northern Frontier District
NGO Nongovernmental Organization
NORAD Norwegian Development Agency
NUSO Nairobi University Students Organization
OAU Organization of African Unity
OCS Officer in Charge of Station
PCEA Presbyterian Church of East Africa
SNM Somali National Movement
SONU Student Organization of Nairobi University
SPLA Sudan People's Liberation Army
SPM Somali Patriotic Movement
SRC Student Representation Council
UNHCR United Nations High Commission on Refugees

INTRODUCTION

Kenya presents a series of contradictions. It has a lively civil society; yet civil freedom has been increasingly circumscribed. Many take the rule of law seriously; yet the independence of the judiciary has been all but extinguished and that of the Bar is seriously threatened. While demands for democratic government are expressed ever more urgently by an ever wider segment of the population, those demands are increasingly resisted by a head of state whose claim to personify the state is reflected in his bestowal of his own name on many of its institutions and artifacts.

Kenya is a nation that has largely avoided the violent ethnic strife that is tearing countries apart all over the world; yet ethnic persecution has been institutionalized and the government's ostensible efforts to suppress ethnic politics may contribute to some future explosion. Above all, Kenya is a nation in which hopes for establishing a decent society that respects the rights of all its citizens have not been crushed—as in several nearby countries—by war, famine and disintegration; yet one wonders how long those who seek respect for human rights can sustain their struggle in the face of harassment and persecution.

This report by Africa Watch is an attempt to provide a comprehensive assessment of the current human rights situation in Kenya. Because of the contradictions and complexities, we have considered it necessary to closely examine the record and to provide substantial detail. We have looked at those aspects of the human rights record that are ordinarily the focus of international attention: that is, the struggles of Nairobi-based journalists, lawyers, clergy and political figures to promote democratic government, freedom of the press and the rule of law. We have also examined many aspects of the human rights record that have received scant international attention, and of which even the international community concerned with human rights has been largely oblivious. These include the arbitrary, punitive and cruel measures by the Kenyan government against rural and urban squatter communities; the miserable conditions of confinement for those charged with common crimes as well as for those held for political and security offenses in Kenya's police detention facilities and its prisons; the gross violence in the implementation of emergency powers in the North Eastern Province; the "screening" of ethnic Somalis; and the treatment of refugees from Kenya's war-torn neighbors.

Some of Africa Watch's findings about the human rights situation in Kenya include:

- The process of consolidating power in the office of the president has been progressive in Kenya, beginning under President Kenyatta and continuing under President Moi. Political opposition is not tolerated; no political rivals have been permitted to emerge; political pluralism is anathema to the government. Those who have challenged one-party, one-man rule have been accused of "treason" or labelled "subversive." Detentions, criminal prosecutions, publication bans and violent harassment have all been employed against those who have attempted to speak out against the monopolization of the political process.

- Freedom of speech, freedom of the press and freedom of assembly have been seriously undermined in Kenya. To the extent that anyone is able to speak out critically or to publish dissenting views, it is because the state determines at a particular moment when to tolerate a measure of dissent, perhaps because it is in its own interest to avoid international condemnation. To dissent, however, is always to risk persecution. It is not only by means of prosecutions, detentions and banning that the government limits dissent; it also systematically applies economic pressure against critics and critical publications.

- The year 1990 saw a marked deterioration of human rights in Kenya as the government employed its emergency powers and security forces in an attempt to crush a growing popular movement for political reform. The murder in February of Foreign Minister Dr. Robert Ouko sparked demonstrations that were met with lethal force by the security services. A large number of people were detained, including many children.

- As the demands for political pluralism grew, the government responded with a campaign to intimidate opponents. Many were detained or threatened. Two politicians, Kenneth Matiba and Charles Rubia, articulated popular discontent in demanding a multiparty system. Their efforts to register a new party were frustrated, and days before their attempt to hold a public meeting in July 1990, they were detained. When large crowds gathered on July 7 (Saba-Saba), despite the government ban, the official response was indiscriminate violence. Evidence obtained by Africa Watch indicates that the official figure of twenty deaths is a gross underestimate. At least one hundred people were killed in various locations, and over 1,000 detained, some for such offenses as shouting for the release of Matiba and Rubia or flashing a two-finger salute (symbol of the demand for two parties).

- During the crackdown that began in 1990, one of the most sinister developments was the intensified use of the sedition charge by the government against suspected political opponents. Among those charged are George Anyona, Augustine Kathangu, Edward Oyugi and Ngotho Kariuki, all arrested in July 1990 and sentenced on July 11, 1991 to seven years imprisonment for holding a "seditious meeting." Earlier that year, Rev. Lawford Indege Imunde was brought to trial after a long period in police custody. The basis of his alleged crime was an entry in his personal diary; the alleged proof of his guilt was a confession obtained under torture. In this and other cases, incriminating evidence was also "planted" by the security forces. These cases illustrate the impunity with which the government manipulates the legal system to obtain criminal convictions against political dissidents in violation of the most basic standards of due process and judicial procedure.

- Political manipulation of the judiciary is at the heart of Kenya's human rights crisis. The government uses an array of administrative procedures and the appointment of compliant judges, particularly British expatriates who serve on contract, to undermine the independence of the judiciary and to mold a system to its liking. Few defendants have access to lawyers; law reports are not published; the government removed tenure for judges (though later reinstated it); economic pressures are brought to bear on lawyers' private practices; and lawyers have been detained without trial or forced into exile.

- Torture continues to be used in Kenyan prisons and detention centers, in flagrant violation of Kenya's international legal obligations. One of the facilities used for systematic torture is Nyayo House, a prominent high-rise building that houses government facilities in the center of Nairobi. The torture is carried out both in underground cells and interrogation rooms on the twenty-fourth floor. Physical methods of torture involve beating, rape, the flooding of cells and starvation. Psychological methods to disorient prisoners or terrify them are also employed. "Confessions" obtained under torture are commonly admitted in evidence in court as proof of guilt. The level of chronic brutality by the police is such that ordinary citizens are deterred from bringing complaints to them, for fear of detention and abuse.

- Kenya's prisons, confining some 60,000 prisoners, suffer from severe overcrowding. Food is poor, and medical facilities are often nonexistent. Brutality and deliberate efforts to degrade and humiliate prisoners are commonplace.

- A proliferation of security forces wields increasing power in Kenya. This includes the Special Branch, which answers directly to the president, the Criminal Investigation Department, the General Service Unit (a para-military wing of the police), and others with special mandates, such as protection of wildlife. The security forces are permeated by their own culture of corruption and contempt for the law.

- Violent abuses by the government have been most prevalent in the North Eastern Province, a large semiarid area inhabited by ethnic Somalis. Since independence in 1963, the government has asserted wide-ranging emergency powers in the province which remain more than twenty years after the end of the insurgency that ostensibly justified their imposition.

Campaigns against alleged bandits, smugglers and poachers are often no more than punitive measures taken against ordinary civilians. These emergency powers form the basis for arbitrary rule throughout Kenya. Kenyan Somali citizens have been subject to discrimination and harassment by what are, in effect, forces of occupation, often degenerating into violence and at times into large-scale massacre. Africa Watch has obtained evidence which suggests that the civilian death toll at the hands of the security forces at Wajir in 1984 totalled more than 2,000—well in excess of the fifty-seven acknowledged by the government.

This episode is the bloodiest in post-independence Kenya of which Africa Watch is aware. It was such a gross violation of human rights that, even though seven years have elapsed, Africa Watch calls on the Kenyan government to conduct a public inquiry in which testimony from survivors and other witnesses would be taken and a good faith effort would be made to identify, prosecute and punish those responsible.

- One of the most blatant examples of discrimination against an ethnic minority was the "screening" introduced in 1989 of all Kenyan Somalis. Without legal or constitutional basis, the government ordered all Kenyan citizens of Somali ethnicity to obtain a special "pink card" by showing proof of citizenship, or face deportation to war-torn Somalia, although many had no connections with Somalia and did not even speak the language. The "screening" became an exercise in mass forcible expulsion on the basis of ethnicity. Thousands of Kenyan Somalis, with full documentary proof of citizenship, were expelled from Kenya. Families were separated, violence was used, and many people lost their livelihoods.

- In 1988, Kenya annexed 14,000 square kilometers of disputed land on the border with Sudan and Ethiopia. In their efforts to exert control, security forces massacred several hundred people belonging to semi-pastoralist communities.

- An important way that the government of Kenya's disregard for human rights affects ordinary citizens is through the issue of land. Farm land, pasture and building land are essential to the livelihoods of most Kenyans, but it is a scarce resource. The government has consistently put its own interests (and those of its senior members) before the land rights of farmers, pastoralists, shantytown dwellers and vendors in the informal economy. Mass evictions, often involving force, have resulted. Africa Watch has gathered evidence of killings and other abuses by government forces in a case of rural land expropriation in Trans-Nzoia district and in a campaign to "clean up" shantytowns and informal markets in and around Nairobi during 1989 and 1990. Squatters have been summarily evicted without notice in a number of recent episodes, and their meager possessions have been destroyed, causing great hardship to tens of thousands of Kenyans.

- Kenya has repeatedly refused entry to bona fide refugees from Uganda, Rwanda, Ethiopia and Somalia fleeing persecution and violence in their troubled homelands. They have been subjected to harassment and refoulement, in contravention of international law. Africa Watch documents a variety of abuses against refugees, mainly from Uganda, Rwanda and Somalia.

- Until recently, the West's criticism of Kenya's human rights record was generally nonexistent, and at best private and muted. Kenya has long been a close ally of the West, particularly the U.S. and Britain, and has been willing to allow foreign investment on favorable terms and the use of military bases. As a result, Kenya has received generous development and military assistance. Recent calls by the U.S. and Britain for democracy to be a precondition for aid have led to the beginnings of a new course by the U.S., with the Ambassador to Kenya making strong representations to the government on certain rights issues. The British government has yet to alter its policy of uncritical support.

Africa Watch calls on the international community to pay heightened attention to all aspects of the human rights struggle in Kenya. Again, despite the abuses documented here, Kenya is not a country where all hope has been lost. Its citizens have demonstrated fortitude and determination in seeking democratic development and respect for human rights. Not only is international support crucial for them to succeed but it is essential if Kenya, as the commercial and communications capital for a large region, is to point the way for its troubled neighbors.

Kenya stands at an important crossroad. The need to explore strategies that will avoid the cycle of violence plaguing several of its neighbors has never been more urgent. In recent months, the government has taken a number of welcome moves, including the release of political detainees whose names were gazetted in Kenya,[1] the restoration of security of tenure for judges and the establishment of the KANU Review Committee which allowed citizens to air their views on matters of national importance. But this is not enough if Kenya is to avoid becoming another international symbol of human misery.

---

[1] The term gazette in this context, refers to an official log that records decisions regarding prisoners.

1
BACKGROUND

The geographical and political entity which corresponds to Kenya today, did not exist prior to the nineteenth century. Within its modern boundary there lived a variety of people, most of whom practiced a mix of agriculture and herding and lived in societies with varying social and political structures. On the coast, there was an established trading civilization, primarily urban and linked to Arabia and the Indian subcontinent. This fell to Portuguese conquest in the sixteenth century, was replaced by the Omani Sultanate, then yielded to British colonial rule in the nineteenth century. Throughout this period, there was limited interaction between the coast and the interior, apart from trade caravans which brought ivory, minerals and slaves from the hinterland.

In the 1880s and '90s, the societies of Kenya were more firmly incorporated into the wider world, first economically under the commercial activities of the imperial British East Africa Company after 1885, and then politically when formal colonial status was declared at the beginning of this century.

Britain appeared to colonize Kenya more by accident than by design. It controlled the east African coast through the Zanzibar protectorate, but also sought control of the Nile headwaters in Uganda. Once the Suez Canal opened in 1869, it was vital to gain access to the source of Egypt's lifeline. Using laborers imported from India, a railway was built between Mombasa on the coast and Uganda. One of the railway's wayside stops, Nairobi, was to become the administrative headquarters and later, the national capital. It lay just at the foot of the fertile highlands which were judged suitable for European settlement. There was a new determination to turn Kenya into a "white man's country," and a program to attract European farmers from Britain and South Africa was introduced. It gathered momentum at the end of the First World War, when British war veterans went to Kenya to acquire land at concessionary rates. Close to seven million acres of African land were expropriated for European settlement. This meant that Africans, particularly the Maasai and Kikuyu communities, lost large tracts of land to the settlers.

The origins of European settlement in Kenya arose out of ruthless suppression of indigenous people. Local resistance was overcome by a series of violent massacres, communal punishment and confiscation of livestock—the most valued asset of both farming and pastoral groups.

LAND AND LABOR UNDER COLONIAL RULE

During the first half of this century, Kenya was dominated by a small but immensely wealthy and powerful settler class that originated in Britain and South Africa. Beneath them in the social pyramid were Indians—mostly traders and shopkeepers whom the British kept out of agriculture by law—and in the early colonial period, some Africans, mainly Swahilis, Somalis and Sudanese, who served as policemen and military auxiliaries. They were elevated or dispatched according to the demands of the colonial rulers.

For the vast majority of Africans, colonial rule meant a rapid disruption of their way of life and the denigration of local cultural norms. Western, Christian social values were accorded respect and superiority, while African institutions and cultures were dismissed as superstitious and viewed undesirable by the colonialists. This view was held both by the Christian missionaries and the settlers. Despite this negative attitude, Christian missionaries provided modern education and medicine long before the colonial government. The Anglican, Presbyterian and Roman Catholic churches built schools and produced the educated African elite which was—after several decades—to spearhead the nationalist movement.

The colonial administration introduced two measures that were particularly loathed by local residents and which the nationalist elite exploited. One was the alienation of land, the origins of which have already been mentioned. A succession of land regulations between 1899 and 1915 expropriated much of the best land in the central highlands, and reserved it for white settlers. A huge number of Kikuyu farmers, as well as the Giriama, Kamba and some of the Nyanza peoples, were deprived of their livelihoods. At the same time, the pastoralists, particularly the Maasai, were deprived of most of their seasonal pastures which the British settlers regarded as "unoccupied land." In precolonial times the Maasai ranged as far north as Lake Turkana. Two agreements which were fraudulently coerced from their leaders in the first decade of this century, restricted them to what had previously been just the southern corner of their land.

The second and widely resented measure was the hut tax. Under this legislation, Africans were required to pay an annual tax (then set at two shillings [8 cents] per hut). It had a dual purpose. The first was to raise taxes to run the colonial government. Africans paid more in taxes than the wealthier Europeans throughout most of the colonial period but received proportionately fewer public services in return. The second objective was to force Africans to work either in the settler farms or in the new towns. After the initial period, taxes were paid in cash, which made it obligatory for Africans to work for wages at least for part of the year.

Deprived of their livelihood, and faced with the hut tax, many farmers and some pastoralists had no choice but to become laborers on white farms. In addition, the administration introduced the *kipande* system, under which each laborer was required to carry a "passbook" showing a person's current employment: it allowed travel from designated "native reserves" to places of employment. Akin to the pass system enforced in South Africa, the kipande system generated deep-seated resentment. In 1922, following a move to reduce African wages, a group of demonstrators converged outside Nairobi Central Police Station demanding the end of the kipande system and the release of Harry Thuku, one of the first African nationalist leaders. Panicking, the police shot dozens of innocent demonstrators in what came to be known as the Thuku Riots. Harry Thuku was exiled to Kismayu until 1907.

White farmers had almost unlimited powers over their laborers, punishing their workers for petty offenses with floggings or detention. Though it was technically illegal, one punitive measure often adopted or threatened was the tearing up of a worker's kipande, thus making it impossible for the worker to stay in the area or find work elsewhere. The European-dominated courts treated white farmers with indulgence on the rare occasions such transgressions were brought before them. One such incident involved a leading settler, Colonel Grogan, who flogged three African men outside the High Court in 1931 with complete impunity.

The colonial administration used the institution of chieftainship to enforce laws and forced labor at the African "reserves." Many of the peoples of Kenya had not had chiefs in the manner the colonial government defined them. In reality, many chiefs wielded no real power; nor did they have local legitimacy. Chiefs were invented, imposed, and vested with a range of administrative and magisterial responsibilities. Previously fluid ethnic lines hardened into "tribes"; previously flexible social systems were turned into an unchanging hierarchical order.

While the farmers and herders of the highlands found themselves faced with alien fences keeping them away from land to which their ancestors had enjoyed customary rights, the pastoralists of the northern and eastern peripheries found themselves faced with the equally alien concept of international frontiers, drawn through the middle of their territories. The colonial cartographers divided the Oromo people between Ethiopia and Kenya, and the Somali between four different empires, including those of France, Italy, Ethiopia and Britain. "Pacification" of the nomadic population was a constant colonial preoccupation, usually carried out with a combination of the punitive patrol and a measure of autonomy under a government-appointed chief.

NATIONALISM AND REVOLT

In Kenya, national sentiment first arose in the highlands, coalescing around the issue of land alienation and a defense of Kikuyu cultural practices such as female circumcision.[1] In the 1920s, the Kikuyu Central Association (KCA) led the struggle for African political rights, fighting for an end to land alienation and emphasizing the need for greater educational opportunities for Africans. In due course, other ethnic-based movements like the Kavirondo Taxpayers Association, the Akamba Members Association, Teita Hills Association and others took up the same causes. Johnstone "Jomo" Kenyatta became the General Secretary of the KCA in 1928 and gave the movement new vigor. He testified for African rights in the Hilton Young Commission of 1927 and travelled to England in 1929 to represent the African case to the imperial government.

By the early 1950s, the land question and the lack of political progress directly led to the Mau Mau insurrection from 1952 to 1959. Using Kikuyu cultural symbols, the Mau Mau guerrillas waged a bloody war against the established order. Over 11,000 people, most of them Kikuyus, were apparently killed. Sixty-three Europeans members of the security forces were also killed, and thirty-two white settlers. The government responded with a fierce counterinsurgency campaign: one million Kenyans of the Kikuyu, Embu and Meru districts were forcibly resettled in protected villages, 90,000 were detained in camps, and all

---

[1] These issues are powerfully evoked in the novel by Ngugi wa Thiong'o, *The River Between* (Oxford, U.K.: Heinemann, African Writers Series, 1965).

political activity was banned.[2] In 1953, Jomo Kenyatta was convicted of involvement in the Mau Mau insurrection (on the basis of what was later established as fabricated evidence) and imprisoned until 1961. After the declaration of the state of emergency in 1952, the Kenya Federation of Labor under Tom Mboya became the vanguard of political activism until 1955, when limited, district-level political organization was allowed in the non-Kikuyu areas.

The colonial government introduced two major reforms to defeat the Mau Mau. One was a program of land reform. In 1955, the Swynnerton Plan, first implemented in the Central Province, gave African farmers in the highlands land titles for the first time, and created an African elite with a vested interest in the economic status quo. The other was a belated move to give Africans representation in national politics. After the suppression of the insurrection, political activity was legalized in stages. The Kenyan African National Union (KANU) was formed in March 1960, and Jomo Kenyatta became its leader upon his release from prison in 1961. Other prominent KANU members included Tom Mboya and Jaramogi Oginga Odinga.

KANU took a radical nationalist stand and drew membership from the groups most affected by colonial rule, such as the Kikuyu, Luo, Kamba, Taita and Kisii. The Kenyan African Democratic Union (KADU) was created in 1960, headed by Ronald Ngala, Daniel arap Moi and Masinde Muliro. KADU was more conservative and had closer links to the colonial establishment. It was seen as a vehicle for representing the interests of smaller ethnic groups.

KANU won an overall majority of seats in elections to the newly-created National Assembly in 1963 and led the country to independence in December 1963. Kenyatta was then sworn in as prime minister and became president the following year when Kenya became a republic.

THE KENYATTA ERA

Jomo Kenyatta was regarded as the father of the nation, and enjoyed enormous prestige and respect. However, the government he

---

[2] See *Kenya: A Country Study* (Washington, D.C.: American University Foreign Area Studies, 1984).

presided over soon became highly centralized and authoritarian, particularly after 1966, when it faced political opposition from the Kenya Peoples Union (KPU) party.

At independence, the constitution gave considerable powers to autonomous regions—in part to placate the minority ethnic groups associated with KADU. This system was soon replaced with a centralized government, and regional powers were abolished. Before long, the new government faced an irredentist movement from the Somali peoples of the North East Province, wishing to join the new Somali Republic. The independent government's policy toward the Somali minority was not very different from that of its colonial predecessor. There was intense fighting in February 1964, which resulted in widespread extrajudicial killings and other human rights abuses in the North East Province.

In 1964, KADU voluntarily dissolved itself and its members joined KANU, creating de facto one-party rule. This was a result of political pressure and promises of power sharing. But as soon as unity was achieved, differences arose between the left wing of KANU led by Oginga Odinga, and the right wing—now reinforced by KADU—led by Jomo Kenyatta and Tom Mboya. In 1966, the left broke away from KANU to form KPU. The KPU leaders were harassed, refused permission to meet and denied public services. In 1966, the government passed legislation permitting detention without trial in cases where security was threatened. Many ethnic Somalis and KPU members were imprisoned under this measure. That same year, the government changed the electoral laws so that any member of parliament who crossed the floor and joined an opposing party had to seek the voters' mandate anew under sponsorship of the opposition. When the "little general election" (KANU v. KADU) was called in June 1966, only Odinga and six of his KPU colleagues were returned.

In July 1969, Tom Mboya was assassinated. Details of the plot to kill him were never ascertained, but President Kenyatta took the opportunity to use the communists and the KPU as scapegoats, accusing them of being subversive and tribalist. In October 1969, the KPU was banned after a violent anti-Kenyatta demonstration in Kisumu in which eleven men were shot at close range by police. No inquest or trials were held. Instead, the government immediately banned the KPU and detained its leading officials including Odinga, Ochieng Oneko (who was jailed with Kenyatta for involvement in the Mau Mau insurrection in 1953) and Wesonga Siyjeyo. With the tumultuous events of October 1969, parliamentary opposition in Kenya came to an end. Even though Odinga was released in 1971, no effective opposition party was subsequently registered. Kenya became a de facto one-party system, but refused to legislate for a one-party state.

In the 1970s, Kenyatta became more remote. Attorney General Charles Njonjo and his trusted colleague, Daniel arap Moi, were increasingly in control. There was continuing political violence, including a crackdown after an alleged coup attempt in 1971 and strikes in 1974. In March 1975, an outspoken government critic and member of parliament, Josiah Kariuki, was murdered. The government clumsily interfered with the investigation into the killing, raising suspicions of its own involvement. A parliamentary inquiry was instituted thereafter; its report established that senior police and administrative officials in the government may have had a hand in the assassination of J. M. Kariuki.

THE ASCENDANCY OF PRESIDENT DANIEL ARAP MOI

In 1977, President Kenyatta's succession had been contested by the "Change the Constitution Group," a combination of wealthy individuals from Kenyatta's homeland allied with leaders from other communities, under a Kikuyu, Embu, Meru cultural association known as GEMA. Their efforts were halted by a coalition of Daniel arap Moi, as vice-president, Charles Njonjo and President Kenyatta. Despite this, and efforts to physically prevent him from reaching State House on the day of President Kenyatta's death, Daniel arap Moi assumed the presidency on the death of President Kenyatta in August 1978.

President Moi initially assumed the presidency for a three month interim period while KANU proceeded with nominations and election preparations. During this time, he capitalized on a politically bland and unassuming image to bring in charismatic and influential figures to create the power base he lacked—namely Charles Njonjo and Mwai Kibaki. He harnessed posthumous reverence for Kenyatta by stressing a theme of "continuation," calling it "Nyayoism" or "footsteps." By the time KANU elected President Moi as its leader, there had been no serious contest of power, only the formalizing of his presidency. Kibaki, popular among the large Kikuyu community, became vice-president, and the most influential men under former President Kenyatta retained their seats.

Stepping Out

Former President Kenyatta's steps had to be followed with caution, however, as factional exercise of power had stirred resentment, particularly toward the end of his reign. Kenyatta was intolerant of critics, had rejected political pluralism, and—after the events of 1969—used a Kikuyu power base. His policies and his status as the first president of independent Kenya was a powerful legacy which has indelibly shaped Kenyan politics. Many Kenyans argue that popular fear of a return to disproportionate privileges for the large Kikuyu community still tempers dissatisfaction with President Moi. The president has used this fear of tribalism as a central focus; a member of the minority Kalenjin community, he has emphasized a popular anti-tribalist rhetoric. Initially, President Moi's policy was "open door" in as much as the main requirement was personal loyalty to him. By 1990, however, most of the senior positions in government, the military, security agencies and state-owned corporations were held by Kalenjin and old KADU allies, and the president was increasingly accused of tribalism.

Soon after he came to power, President Moi released twelve political detainees who remained in detention, including former M.P.s Martin Shikuku, George Anyona and J. M. Seroney, the writer Ngugi wa Thiong'o, and Wesonga Siyjeyo, an ex-KPU leader detained in 1964.

The release of all the detainees in December 1978 gave President Moi a boost in popularity. Students at the University of Nairobi marched in the city to demonstrate their support. He also introduced a series of populist measures to benefit the less advantaged communities, including the provision of milk to children in schools, the increase of employment possibilities and the building of schools and roads in some pastoral districts. Gradually, he brought in popular nationalists like Waruru Kanja, who had a reputation for radical nationalism as an ex-Mau Mau fighter and colonial detainee; and former vice-president, Jaramogi Oginga Odinga.[3] Odinga was soon out in the cold again after calling Jomo Kenyatta's reign "malevolent" and "land-grabbing."

However, President Moi's new "open door" policy was not a genuine liberalization of KANU, but a means of promoting disintegration of existing power blocs by playing various politicians and factions one

---

[3] The idea of bringing in these leaders who had run afoul of the Kenyatta government was to undermine GEMA and the old Kikuyu guard.

against the other. President Moi shared Jomo Kenyatta's dislike of dissent. A fear of communism was used in its broadest sense to carry on a witch-hunt of the left as well as government critics. Many of those termed "radical" he initially courted: Waruru Kanja, for example, was used to undermine the influential Mwai Kibaki and was rewarded with a cabinet post until he was sacked and expelled from the party in 1990. Ex-detainees such as George Anyona and Martin Shikuku were welcomed to the party, later to be either detained or ousted. After the 1979 general election, President Moi moved his political supporters into government positions—Nicholas Biwott is just one example—and used G. G. Kariuki as well as then immensely powerful attorney general, Charles Njonjo, as his closest confidants. In 1983, both were accused of conspiring to oust President Moi (see below).

Part of President Moi's success in playing off competing factions lay in the generally-accepted view that his was essentially a caretaker government. The more assertive and influential politicians scrambled to line up in what they mistakenly perceived to be a vacuum. It was commonly believed that President Moi had been promoted by Jomo Kenyatta because he posed no threat. His political career was not dynamic, but he was one of Kenya's most experienced politicians. As Home Affairs minister, he became closely acquainted with departments which were later to prove invaluable to him as president, including the police, immigration, intelligence, revenue and licensing, and the prison system. These departments were later skillfully used to eliminate political opposition and peaceful dissent.

Dealing with Opposition

Serious economic decline in the early years of his presidency was accompanied by political discontent. Faced with the threat of opposition groups, President Moi responded with a severity that surprised even Kenyans who had been critical of President Kenyatta's increasingly intolerant policies. While President Kenyatta had tolerated some degree of free expression in parliament, his successor considered parliamentary opposition tantamount to treason. His stern public warnings against "traitors" and "dissidents" were issued against all groups perceived as "hostile." He banned all tribal unions, such as the Luo Union and the powerful GEMA and used the security apparatus to put down strikes and demonstrations. He closed the University of Nairobi repeatedly (in 1979, 1981 and 1982) whenever students made anti-government statements. His willingness to use tough measures and his skill at balancing parliamentary power drew increasingly obsequious pledges of loyalty from M.P.s—a hallmark of his style of government.

In 1981 and 1982, fear of "the enemy" focused on the university, which he monitored through informers. Many academics, students, lecturers and writers were arrested, interrogated, detained or exiled as a result. Detention without trial was brought back by mid-1982, when Stephen Muriithi, a former Deputy Director of Intelligence and a business associate of the president was detained because he challenged, in court, an order transferring him from the police to the chairmanship of the state-owned Uplands Bacon Factory. His lawyer, John Khaminwa, was also detained without trial, as was George Anyona who openly opposed the legislation in favor of a one-party state, introduced in May 1982. By the following month, as a result of this determination to crack down against all opponents, real and imaginary, six academics had been arrested and detained without trial allegedly for teaching subversion.[4]

Rewriting the Rules: Kenya Becomes a One-Party State

The June 1982 legislation making Kenya a de jure one-party state, by a constitutional amendment, was hastily pushed through parliament to forestall the registration of a new political party to be formed by George Anyona and Jaramogi Oginga Odinga. The new party, the Kenya African Socialist Alliance (KASA) intended to have a socialist agenda. Fear of KASA precipitated the president's move against all political opposition. There was no debate on the bill. A cowed parliament silently sat and approved the amendment as it was read by Charles Njonjo through the three stages. The whole process took twenty minutes. It was the first of many constitutional amendments curtailing civil rights which the government introduced in this manner between 1982 and 1989. Shortly before the amendment, Anyona and Odinga were expelled from KANU. Just before their expulsion, they had called a press conference and denounced the government's economic policies and the ceding of new semi-secret military base facilities to the United States.

The declaration of Kenya as a one-party state created a tense political climate. Anyona joined six other M.P.s, lecturers, lawyers, journalists and civil servants detained without trial. At least ten other

---

[4] See Africa Watch, *Academic Freedom and Human Rights Abuses in Africa* (New York: Human Rights Watch, April 1991).

academics and students were arrested and served between five and ten year prison sentences on political charges. Odinga was forced to leave Nairobi for the relative safety of western Kenya after threats on his life. During the same period, three truckloads of armed police bulldozed the education center and community theater in the hometown of Ngugi wa Thiong'o.

Though the 1982 amendment arguably only sanctified what already existed in practice, it nevertheless radically changed Kenyan politics in "legitimizing" the ban on all opposition parties. It effectively licensed the persecution of opposition groups by criminalizing them and creating an "underground" context. Advocates of pluralism dismiss the amendment as unconstitutional in that it was imposed without debate, and that it contradicts the provision of freedom of assembly and association guaranteed otherwise by the constitution.

The 1982 Coup Attempt

On August 1, two months after Kenya officially became a one-party state, there was an unsuccessful attempt to overthrow the government by junior officers of the Air Force. They seized several strategic positions in Nairobi including two air bases, the international airport, the post office and the radio station. Broadcasts denounced corruption, nepotism, economic chaos and the "dictatorial regime of Daniel arap Moi." After some hesitation, forces loyal to the president retook the main rebel positions in Nairobi by noon, but fighting continued for several days at Nanyuki Air Base near Mount Kenya, and there were reports of nationwide unrest. Looting, rape and acts of brutality were committed by soldiers in Nairobi's shantytowns—including Mathare, Kibera and Kawangware—for two days before the government could restore order. Army troops were ordered to shoot looters on sight. The government admitted to 159 dead, but unofficial tallies put the death toll between 600 and 1,800.[5]

The Asian community was targeted in the looting. This has been attributed to resentment felt by lower-income and unemployed Africans who took advantage of the disorder to attack successful Asian businesses, and was capitalized on by a government which has frequently played the xenophobic card. Asian women were reported to have been raped by

---

[5] See Norman Miller, *Kenya: The Quest for Prosperity* (Boulder, Colorado: Westview Press, 1984).

marauding looters and security personnel broke into private houses of the poorer Asians who lived in areas close to the slums like Ngara and Eastleigh.

Several hundred airmen were tried by military courts, receiving sentences of up to twenty-five years. Eleven enlisted men were sentenced to death. The two alleged leaders of the coup—Hezekiah Ochuka and Sgt. Ogidi Obuon—were extradited from Tanzania, where they had fled in the late hours of August 1, 1982, in a commandeered plane. They were courtmartialled, convicted and were hanged, after the Kenyan government gave assurances that they would not be killed.

The aftermath of the coup resulted in persecution and witch-hunts in which many people were imprisoned or implicated, including opponents, prisoners, lawyers and detainees, like Oginga Odinga's son, Raila Odinga. The pattern of the subsequent trials set the pace for what has followed ever since. After intimidation and torture in police custody, an accused person would be produced in the court of the senior resident magistrate, briefly and without legal representation. The charge would be read and the person would immediately plead guilty in fulfilment of prior promises of a light sentence. The accused would ask for leniency because of illness or family circumstances. Then a heavy sentence would be pronounced.

The fallout from the coup attempt was also used to remove from his post the powerful Attorney General Charles Njonjo, whom President Moi had come to regard as a potential challenger. Njonjo's accumulation of personal power was so great that by then, many Kenyan observers perceived him to be effectively running the country. The president's move against Njonjo began with a reference by President Moi to a "traitor" in the cabinet. The calls to "smoke the traitor out" began immediately. New pledges of loyalty from the remaining players were made to the president. Foreign Minister Elijah Mwangale (now Minister of Agriculture) then named Njonjo in parliament as the "traitor." Despite his denial and appeal for evidence and a fair trial—which he had consistently denied others—Njonjo's days were numbered. KANU expelled him in June 1983 and Njonjo resigned from parliament. He became the subject of a judicial inquiry in 1984 and was found guilty of subverting the state and bypassing the legal order. He was never charged in court. Instead, President Moi pardoned him in 1984. Njonjo declined the pardon but after that, his political career was finished.

After President Moi secured his position in the 1983 general elections, a campaign was initiated to increase membership of the party.

The party was increasingly projected as a "mass political movement."
Mass recruitment drives were organized while at the same time a greatly
strengthened security apparatus was being built, which gave increased
pre-eminence to the Special Branch.

KANU: THE MACHINERY OF CONTROL

Mass Recruitment and Party Powers
     Recruitment for the party was carried out by force in some cases
by the provincial administration and the administration police. Police
routinely asked individuals for their official identity and party
membership cards. If they had neither, they would be booked into police
cells for vagrancy. The local and district branches also enroled members
in a competition encouraged by the government. By 1988, the number
of party members had risen from several hundred thousand to eight
million, although critics of the government believe that these statistics are
exaggerated.[6]
     This massive recruitment drive peaked in 1985. Its objectives
were by then achieved largely by depriving nonmembers of certain basic
rights, such as access to rural produce markets, to trading licenses, to
education, land and administration services. Failure to produce a party
card was effectively criminalized as nonmembers were made increasingly
vulnerable to police harassment. Political suspicion of nonmembers was
encouraged by repeated calls from the president to demonstrate loyalty
to himself and to the party, and thus to the nation. Certain procedures
were decentralized to branch level to facilitate mass recruitment.
Recruitment drives held by local and district officials became organized,
flamboyant displays of loyalty to the president and party. Wherever
President Moi went, wealthy people stepped forward proclaiming loyalty
and paid the obligatory 10,000 shillings ($385).[7]
     More often, however, officials met their quotas through strong-
arm tactics. Youthwingers and security personnel intimidated people into
enrolling by threatening nonparty members; KANU membership became

---

[6] *Weekly Review*, (Nairobi), October 21, 1988.

[7] The exchange rate of 26 shillings per dollar used in this report is current
as of July 29, 1991. Kenya Tourist Office, New York.

necessary as a protection card to the average citizen and as insurance against intimidation by unruly KANU youthwingers and the police.

KANU Youthwingers: Party Police

Crucial to the creation of KANU's mass base was the rise of the party youthwingers. President Moi repeatedly asked for youthwingers to look out for "anti-party elements." Often they did more than that. They are known for their indiscriminate violence, thuggery and extortion. Youthwingers act as the party police but have no legal mandate to do so. One veteran parliamentarian explained the role of the youthwingers in the following terms:

> ...the party doesn't even know what they should do and shouldn't do; but we do know they're responsible for a lot of killings. But they also get murdered because they create a lot of fear and hate among the people. I get a lot of complaints that they prevent market women from selling their goods unless they produce a KANU membership card or pay a fine. They put a rope across the market and stop the women—that way, they get a lot of money.

Kenyan political analysts believe President Moi was influenced by his visit to the People's Republic of China in his use of KANU youthwingers as personal guards and party police. There were also strong links with former President Ceausescu of Romania, who sent members of the Securitate to train Kenyans at home, as well as a number of Kenyans who traveled to Romania for training purposes.

KANU was increasingly promoted as a mass political movement and periodically restructured to increase party power. Youthwingers are increasingly used to intimidate rival politicians as well as the public, and were used extensively in the rigging of the 1988 general elections. In 1988, the *Weekly Review* reported that on President Moi's return from China:

> ...the president spelt out what may turn out to be the beginning of yet another new direction for Kenya's sole legitimate political party....The party's ambit will be nationwide as the party delegates were exhorted by the

President to get involved in every sphere of both public and private life of every Kenyan.

The President went on to urge the delegates to be at the forefront in protecting the country and ensuring the security of the people. "You are the ones to ensure that people with ill intentions do not roam around," the President told them. With the President's address, KANU acquired yet another image and the change was well-nigh instantaneous. According to one delegate who requested not to be named, "When I returned home, I realized just how powerful I was."[8]

Strengthening the Disciplinary Machinery
    By 1986-87, the KANU code of discipline had been revised and strengthened, empowering the KANU Disciplinary Committee to deal with broad and loosely defined acts of "misconduct." This included criminal charges. The committee was also given powers to withdraw "the protection, rights and privileges" of persons established by the committee to be "an offender" even when not a member of the party. Trade licenses and land deeds have been withdrawn as a result of the committee's action against nonmembers, and has resulted in imprisonment and police harassment.
    Despite taking on the mantle of a judicial body, the Disciplinary Committee employed no legal expert. The committee could recommend "offenders" be taken to a court of law if the charges were criminal in nature, which it never did. But it was entitled to take action outside the judicial system. There were no provisions for an accused person to appear with legal representation. Although a person could technically appeal to the national executive or the national governing council, victims have had neither the faith nor the confidence to refer to a higher body, nor have decisions been reversed.
    This system became open to abuse by influential party members, who used it to victimize their political opponents. It was also used to dispose of rival politicians and government critics. The definition of misconduct included "undermining" the following institutions: the presidency of KANU, the head of state, the party constitution, the

---

[8] Ibid.

country's constitution, the KANU government and party activities. The committee also acted against any party members who violated party rules or "act in manner prejudicial to the reputation of the party." Disciplinary action included caution, severe reprimand, prohibiting the offender from contesting or holding any public office for a defined period; suspension or expulsion from the party (indefinitely or for a stipulated period). By mid-1987, the committee began to summon members of parliament for "discipline" whenever they spoke in the chamber in a manner it deemed contrary to party policy. Such action contradicted the principle of parliamentary supremacy and violated the immunities accorded members of parliament by the constitution for statements made in the course of parliamentary debates.

In September 1987, however, the committee was disbanded by President Moi as suddenly as he had created it. At a speech at Jomo Kenyatta Airport upon his return from a trip abroad, he accused the committee of challenging his authority by abrogating too much power. The attack came after the committee had summoned then minister of Labor, Peter Okondo, for criticizing its chairman, David Okiki Amayo, in parliament. Summoning a cabinet minister was seen to bring the question of supremacy of party over parliament too much to the fore. Oginga Odinga attacked the committee, saying it was unable to be an impartial arbiter of party conflicts when members held party posts, and that its effect was to stifle the concept of constructive debate and freedom of expression. By 1987, the committee practically determined the fate of politicians, according to an ill-defined interpretation of the Code of Discipline. M.P.s taken before the committee had variously been suspended or expelled for "troublemaking," "retarding development," "not raising hands in support of the queuing method and thereby showing disrespect for the party and the president," "not substantiating claims made in parliament," "not recognizing a leader elected by the people and nominated by the president, thereby challenging the intelligence of the electorate and that of the head of state" and amongst other accusations, "causing divisions among people."

The committee was also criticized for expelling on "serious security grounds" without referring to a court of law. In Tana River District, five members were brought before the committee for allegedly "obstructing the administration and security officials in their efforts to deal with the *shifta*[9] menace in the area" when they were supposed to have accused the provincial administration and security forces of collaborating to exterminate their ethnic group, the Wardey. The members reportedly wrote letters to senior members of the party and government officials apologizing "for claiming that the administration and the KANU branch officials were harassing, oppressing and frustrating them and members of their ethnic group."[10] Little publicity was given to the case, despite the very serious nature of the charges.

In spite of the abolition of the national KANU Disciplinary Committee, party branches continued to meet and "discipline," by expulsion or suspension, any leader or private citizen whose conduct was considered "disloyal" to the party. In many cases, the charges were vague. In others, they were criminal in nature and presumably they could have been handled through the courts. In one sense, therefore, the party was dispensing extrajudicial sentences with far-reaching consequences without any backing in law. Such was the case when parliamentarians lost their seats, and ministers their portfolios, after expulsion or suspension by KANU. In June 1990, for example, Maina Wanjai lost his cabinet seat after the Nairobi KANU branch convicted him of preaching "tribalism" (see chapter fourteen).

THE DEMISE OF PARLIAMENT

Parliament's independence has deteriorated significantly under President Moi. According to veteran M.P.s, there is noticeably less debate in parliament than during former President Kenyatta's rule. Lack of quorum was such a chronic problem that in April 1991, the party newspaper, the *Kenya Times*, began printing a list of M.P.s in the house as a way of embarrassing the absentees. One former M.P. told Africa Watch:

> Deterioration really set in in 1982, by which time there was no freedom of debate for fear of falling foul of the party. The days are gone when you could stand up and

---

[9] *Shifta* literally means "bandit," and was used as a derogatory name for ethnic Somalis in the secessionist movement during the 1960s.

[10] *Daily Nation*, (Nairobi), August 28, 1987.

discuss what is on your mind—now its considered "subversion" and treachery. If an M.P. says something unacceptable, he will immediately be summoned by his own district party subcommittee for disciplinary action, which we have to assume is expulsion. In fact, parliament is now treated as a livelihood and it's done for the money—if you're loyal, you can get a lot of money. The *wananchi* [people] feel no one takes their complaints to parliament any more—but they have so many complaints. Unemployment, education, high cost of living, harassment by the police, land—you hear it all the time. And you know the card-carrying members of KANU are a minority, so what is there for the majority non-card carrying [citizens]? There should at least be a parliament.

Africa Watch interviewed one former M.P. just after he had been expelled for remarks made in parliament. He argued that "discipline" went beyond the official action taken by the party. He anticipated financial ruin and constant surveillance by the Special Branch. He said the suspicion and disapproval leading up to his expulsion had been "tremendous—almost enough to make you resign to get away from it. I was living under a burden everyday." After expulsion, the government frequently revokes trading licenses, forecloses on debts, pressures prospective employers, and maintains constant surveillance. The feeling of persecution is evident: this former M.P. was convinced his phone was tapped, and said he felt as much fear at home as he did in public. Describing the expulsion, he said some of the charges were "laughable":

Why am I sacked if this government calls itself democratic; why am I sacked if there is room for expressing views? There has to be room in government for criticism. I am a debater, I like debate—it is the function of a parliament. I don't have to agree but I do appreciate a debate. That's all gone now. I've seen very, very great change in parliament, especially over the last three or four years. There's nothing wrong with the system itself, the written constitution, but with the way it's applied. The KANU machinery has become impossible—take my example. The KANU district branch tried me in absentia...and found me guilty on charges

made at a different meeting. The only organ of the party
where I personally appeared was KANU headquarters
executive committee. Under a normal judicial system, if
a magistrate's court and a high court hasn't tried
you—how does the appeal court then find you guilty?

The subdued nature of parliament is illustrated by the way vital
constitutional amendments have been rushed through parliament without
any debate (see appendix D). As mentioned earlier, in 1982, parliament
passed legislation making Kenya a de jure one-party state without a
single M.P. speaking out. Similarly, in 1986 another constitutional
amendment was passed without debate, dispensing with the security of
tenure for the attorney general, the comptroller and the auditor
general—as was the 1988 amendment removing security of tenure for
judges,[11] and empowering the police to hold people suspected of capital
offenses for fourteen days instead of twenty-four hours.

There has been speculation that the National Assembly (Powers
and Privileges) Act itself will be unanimously amended. When Charles
Njonjo was attorney general, he reportedly proposed that the
government introduce a bill curbing the immunity M.P.s enjoy against
anything said in parliament.[12] Such immunities are now effectively a
dead letter; they are only applicable against M.P.s who use their privileges
to make attacks in parliament on targeted individuals. There have been
a number of occasions where KANU has taken disciplinary action (see
above) against parliamentarians for what they have said in parliament,
even though the charges laid against such M.P.s are usually irrelevant to
the actual "crime." Waruru Kanja, for example, was sacked from the

---

[11] Restoration of the security of tenure for judges was announced by the
president in 1990, shortly before the results of the KANU Review Committee
became public, which recommended that they be restored.

[12] According to the National Assembly (Powers and Privileges) Act, subsection (4): "No civil or criminal proceedings shall be instituted against any
member for words spoken or written in a report to the assembly or a committee,
or by reason of any matter or thing brought by him therein by petition, bill,
resolution, motion or otherwise." Subsection (12) states that: "No proceedings or
decision of the assembly or the committee of privileges acting in accordance with
this act shall be questioned in any court."

cabinet and expelled from the party in 1990 after he suggested in parliament that the murder of Foreign Minister Dr. Robert Ouko had been one in a trend of political killings: but he was ostensibly expelled on charges of "interfering" in the politics of a number of constituencies and making "derisive comments" about President Moi's burning of ivory.[13]

Major parliamentary decisions are preceded by a meeting of the KANU parliamentary group, whose function, according to the KANU constitution, is to be "responsible for tactics and programs within parliament." The role of the group was laid down before Kenya became either a de facto (1969) or de jure (1982) one-party state, and was designed to lay out party strategy before meeting the opposition. After 1969, it was simply used to direct M.P.s to support the government on crucial issues. This has gained more significance in strangling debate under the present government, now that the role of KANU has been so enormously expanded.

Another former M.P., who was "rigged out" in the 1988 elections (see below), told Africa Watch he believed the "real turning point" came around 1986. Before that, he said, dissent was disliked but not pursued. According to this M.P.:

> If, for example, an M.P. disagreed with a policy or a paper, President Moi would frequently be heard to complain that we should all speak with one voice. He didn't like it, but people were not actively persecuted. Then around 1986 came the rise of the youthwingers who became the party police for government critics.

By acting as a police force within the party, the M.P. believed the youthwingers got "out of hand":

> M.P.s started to become persecuted to a point of making them fearful and it stopped all debate as such in the House. It is not actually just losing your seat, it is fear for what they can do to you. First of all, you are expelled

---

[13] This is a reference to a widely publicized incident in which President Moi publicly burned ivory worth a great deal of money as a way of demonstrating his commitment to the preservation of wildlife.

> from the party, then they take your business license and
> make sure all your debts are called in. They speak to the
> banks, they get your car, they go for your home. The
> police will just come and demand your business license or
> your employment card, and that's it, you're finished.
> They also take passports. They can even rob you, crash
> your car or beat your family. Moi, well, I believe Moi has
> bad advisers and won't admit to his mistakes. He relies
> on security men now too much as advisers.

President Moi has been single-minded in using parliament as a
rubber stamp for advice received from an inner circle of trusted security
officials and ethnic kinsmen. In a particularly open demonstration of this,
in April 1989, Vice-President J. N. Karanja (who had repeatedly praised
President Moi and backed the 1988 constitutional amendments) was
removed from his post after parliament had passed a motion of no
confidence in him. He was not given a chance to respond to the charges
which included "arrogance," "disrespect," "corruption" and "conspiring with
Uganda." (He is married to a Ugandan.) The orchestrated "debate"
violated all the standing orders of parliament which the speaker
consistently ignored.

During President Kenyatta's era, M.P.s Martin Shikuku and J.
Seroney were arrested and subsequently detained during full
parliamentary session. Despite isolated incidents, for the most part,
critical M.P.s were relegated to the back benches where they often
remained vocal in opposing government policies.

FOLLOWING THE LINE: RIGGING ELECTIONS

Queue-voting replaced the first round of voting in the secret
ballot in the 1988 general elections. In the new procedure, anybody
obtaining 70 percent of the votes at the queue-voting nominations went
on unopposed. Ostensibly used to improve the participation of a largely
illiterate population—who were counted by a government administrative
official—queue-voting proved infinitely more susceptible to "rigging" than
the secret ballot. Intimidation tactics and corruption ensured that party
faithful were returned to parliament. People were threatened and cajoled
into standing in the line of the government candidate. In some

constituencies, "head counts" declared a government candidate the winner in blatant contradiction to the size of the lineups.

In many cases during the 1988 elections, officers announced figures which were at variance with the actual tally in the lines, inflating those of government favorites and decreasing those of critical politicians. The Nairobi Starehe constituency was a seat previously held by Charles Rubia. The Nairobi Provincial Commissioner, Fred Waiganjo, announced the statistics which showed that Rubia would have proceeded to the run-off round of the top two candidates. Rubia complained that the figures were fraudulent. The Provincial Commissioner in his capacity as the returning officer subsequently revised the figures, increasing the number of votes supposedly received by Rubia's rival, Kiruhi Kimondo, to over 70 percent of the total votes cast. As a result, Rubia was denied the chance to be an M.P. for another four years. In 1989, Dr. J. G. Kiano was declared the loser in the Kiharu by-election even though he had defeated his rival, Gidraph K. Mweru, by a landslide.

In an "Election Special" issue from March 1988 of the church magazine *Beyond*, the editor wrote:

> What really came out to be the worst enemy of the people's democratic right is the way the administration conducted itself. In most areas, the administration terrorized citizens. There were countless glaring examples of the use of force. What has now emerged from the queuing form of nomination is that wananchi's [people] right and power to vote for a candidate of his or her choice was taken away by force by the administration....
>
> It must be concluded that elections by queuing were not fair. Consequently democracy in Kenya has slipped a step downward, putting the country onto the path of self-destruction which many African countries have followed.
>
> If Kenyan leaders have any regard for every citizens' feelings, then there is need to re-do a fair election....

The leaders took note of this by banning the magazine (see chapter twelve). The same magazine carried the testimony of a former councillor, John Kihoro, who was eliminated during the nominations and was later obstructed and physically abused by the administration for supporting the wrong candidate. Kihoro was interrogated and whipped by the District Officer and Administration Police, leaving injuries of "blackened flesh which had healed where he had been lashed with a whip....Six days after the beatings the body was still sore and some swellings had not completely abated." On the day of nominations, Kihoro said people had been openly barred from standing behind the line of a candidate who had been labeled by the government as anti-Nyayo (anti-government): "When we took our agents to polling stations, they were all chased away by the Assistant Chiefs and youthwingers....The DC [District Commissioner] has completely refused to show me the results of the nominations up to this day."[14] In the Nyandarua South constituency, Kimani wa Nyoike, an independent and popular M.P., was held up by the police until the lining up process was over.

Many people complained of being intimidated, threatened and physically abused during the elections and most of the more popular parliamentarians declared they had been rigged out. Youthwingers and armed Administration Police played a central role in policing the queues. Women reported they were threatened with eviction from their village plots and with beatings from their husbands; voters were told they could lose land, licenses and housing if they failed to vote for the "Nyayo" candidate. There were also reports of deaths after voters were attacked by supporters of rival candidates, and of serious acts of brutality by youthwingers and administration officials.[15]

One former M.P. told Africa Watch he believed he was rigged out to make way for a candidate with powerfully placed relatives:

> They went round all the major businesses and made it clear who they wanted. In fact, election officials since have told me that they were instructed to get [the opponent] elected. We had been told the counting would start at midday but they had escorted people to [the opponent's] queue since morning. They used trucks to go and get people, they brought them food and drink. They did everything possible to make his queue longer—they

---

[14] *Beyond*, Election Special, March 1988.

[15] *The Guardian*, (London), February 24, 1988.

brought in plainclothes *askaris* and even schoolchildren who had no ID.[16] But these people weren't even questioned so the queue swelled. Once the queue gets that long, people fear anyway, so they went to that queue. It is very obvious which queue you should be in. Some people did stand for me, my closest associates, but everyone who came to my queue was screened very thoroughly. You had to be very brave. Even if one letter was different in their name on their ID they were thrown out. Some were even arrested. But anyone could stand in [the opponent's] queue.

Sixty M.P.s went to parliament unopposed on the 70 percent rule, and many other M.P.s claimed decisive victories despite having produced poor results in previous elections. Daniel arap Moi was returned unopposed as president by the party, with a parliament purged of critics and bolstered by the most faithful and sycophantic. More than half of his supporters were returned unopposed, including his leading ministers.[17]

On April 3, President Moi banned all public discussion of the new queuing system and declared himself satisfied with the results, saying they had been carried out in accordance with the democratic traditions of the country.

The 1988 riggings ousted a group of respected liberals who were painfully aware of the consequences to the country of its deteriorating international image. In prosecuting his own fear of opposition, President Moi inadvertently created a threat which, in many ways, proved more real than that of the radicals and supposed communists. Kenneth Matiba, who resigned his cabinet position after the election and rigged-out politicians like Charles Rubia had always been prominent establishment figures who used their wealth, extensive business interests and their public status to make a significant mark on the political map. Their quarrel with the government was primarily its failure to establish workable economic policies and the deterioration of education facilities and employment opportunities. They also expressed concern for the increased deterioration of human rights in Kenya— although most of this

---

[16] Identification certificates are issued to all Kenyans 18-years-of-age or older.

[17] *The Guardian*, March 23, 1988.

liberal faction would have been aware that Kenya's human rights record had always been poor, despite its international profile. By alienating this influential sector, President Moi created an opposition group which ultimately found its political impact was greater outside parliament than in, and provided the most serious focus for discontent since the 1982 coup attempt.

MYSTIFICATION OF THE PRESIDENCY: RISING ABOVE THE PARTY AND THE NATION

President Moi has developed a personal cult. No direct criticism is expressed publicly, and a pervasive inhibition to do so even privately has made his name virtually taboo. He is usually referred to, if it is unavoidable, as "the big man" or "the man himself." The only recent publicized criticism of President Moi was during the multiparty debate in 1990, when some people were charged with sedition (see appendix C) after "shouting abusive words" about President Moi. One man was charged with breach of the peace for removing a portrait of President Moi from the wall. Even the sharpest critics of the government prefer to criticize the president by implication only. It is very often done by quoting the "wisdom" of the president's words and then the way in which they are "abused," thereby contrasting the reality with the rhetoric.

President Moi's omnipresence is reinforced by portraits in every building and on the national currency. His name is found on stadiums, schools, streets and hospitals. Nyayo badges and portrait pins are worn on the lapels of all important civic leaders and administrative officials; schools sing songs in praise of him wherever he goes; mass choirs exalt him on national holidays; the national radio plays music in his honor after every newscast; the Kenya Broadcasting Corporation TV News always begins with the activities of "His Excellency the President, Mr. Daniel arap Moi...." The party newspaper writes about his historical achievements, in comparison with his predecessor; and since 1988, a huge sculpture of black marble and steel in central Nairobi honors the president.

The result of this cultivated reverence is that President Moi's powers are considered supreme and his exercise of them wise; yet, at the same time, he is distanced from the abuses of the state. This is done by attributing all excesses to his "bad advisers." Protecting the image of the president in this way has been assisted by Western governments and diplomats, who take the attitude that President Moi is probably unaware of the extremes of, for example, police brutality and prison conditions. Yet the same diplomats are plainly aware of his power to transform any situation by a mere word.

Legalistically, the office of the president remains grounded by the rules laid down by the constitution and the party, but this mystification of President Moi has effectively removed him from written or legal constraints. Various amendments to the constitution have increased the powers of the president (see chapters seven and fifteen) and removed the need for parliamentary approval. Under the rules of the constitution, however, freedom of expression means criticism of the president is not a criminal offense in itself, and can only legally be seditious if used to deliberately agitate others into rebellion against the state.[18] Nevertheless, politicians have been expelled and persecuted in the party for implying criticism of the president, and people jailed for the same reason.

Unlike his predecessor, President Moi regularly tours the country. He uses public rallies to hand out thousands of land titles, and collects millions of shillings for variously named presidential charities, whilst warning the people he is watching them and encouraging them to watch each other. Demonstrations of his unlimited presidential powers, including threats to detain people and his public accusations and condemnations of individuals contradict the rights guaranteed by the constitution. Presidential addresses often touch on issues which are sub judice, thus prejudicing many pending trials.

Without ever having been elected president by direct popular mandate—he has always been elected by the party—the necessity to coerce respect through cult and mystification is clear. The president's image, however, has struggled to live up to the myth he attempts to build. One of President Moi's best known speeches exhorted people and politicians to "sing like parrots" to demonstrate their loyalty to him:

> I call on all ministers, assistant ministers and every other person to sing like parrots. During Mzee Kenyatta's period I persistently sang the Kenyatta tune until people said: This fellow has nothing except to sing for Kenyatta. I say: I didn't have ideas of my own. Why was

---

[18] See chapter eight for details of the case of Rev. Lawford Ndege Imunde.

I to have my own ideas? I was in Kenyatta's shoes and therefore, I had to sing whatever Kenyatta wanted. If I had sung another song, do you think Kenyatta would have left me alone? Therefore you ought to sing the song I sing. If I put a full stop, you should also put a full stop. This is how this country will move forward.[19]

On August 21, 1990, former Attorney General Matthew Muli, declared President Moi above the law: "I wish to state that no one except the president is above the law. Kenya believes in the rule of law and everyone is equal before the law."[20] The constitution of Kenya, however, is unequivocal in declaring that the powers of the president must be exercised "subject to and in accordance with the Constitution" and other laws, despite holding certain privileges and immunities.[21]

---

[19] September 13, 1984, on President Moi's return from Addis Ababa.

[20] *Daily Nation*, August 21, 1990.

[21] Constitution of Kenya, Section 4.

2
DEADLY VERDICT
THE MURDER OF FOREIGN MINISTER
DR. ROBERT OUKO

The events of 1990 proved to be a watershed in Kenyan politics. In February, the Minister for Foreign Affairs and International Cooperation, Dr. Robert Ouko, was found murdered, shot in the head and his body charred almost beyond recognition. Public demands for an impartial investigation into what was commonly believed to be a political killing exploded into demonstrations and riots. This unrest led to a nationwide political crackdown by the government against well-known government critics and "rumormongers"—a euphemism for speculation about the murder of Ouko (see chapter three). The evident sensitivity of the government provoked louder, more tenacious calls for a new political system from a population who suddenly saw President Moi uncharacteristically vulnerable and exposed. A new boldness to voice discontent grew, without any real focus other than a desire for a new political system and a new leadership. For the first time since President Moi came to power, demonstrators demanded his resignation.

RUMORMONGERING AND RIOTING

The partially-burned body of Dr. Robert Ouko was found in a field four miles from his home in western Kenya, two days after his family had reported him missing on Wednesday, February 14, 1990. The body was discovered by a herdsboy who was taken into police custody. Ouko's family said they had last seen the Foreign Minister alive early on Tuesday morning when he left his farm in Koru, near Lake Victoria; they reported him missing on Wednesday morning when he failed to return home or contact the family. Other reports said that Ouko had been driven away in a white car at about 3:00 A.M. that Tuesday on what was assumed to have been official business.

Immediately after Ouko's body was found, President Moi issued a statement saying that the circumstances suggested "foul play" and that "no stone will be left unturned" in the search to bring his killers to justice. Ouko was first appointed Foreign Minister in 1979, then served in other cabinet posts between 1983-88, and was reappointed Foreign Minister in 1988. He was widely seen as one of the few politically skilled and capable ministers left in President Moi's government. President Moi called him "a brilliant leader, an articulate and courageous spokesman of this country and a loyal servant of his people."

News of Ouko's death triggered massive anti-government demonstrations and riots in Nairobi and the provincial capital of Nyanza Province, Kisumu. Contradictory statements issued by official sources fueled the belief that Ouko's killing was a political assassination, especially when there was a suggestion that Ouko had committed suicide. Crowds openly called for the resignation of senior government members, including the president. There were student demonstrations in Kisumu where riot police descended on Siriba Teachers College to "avert a demonstration" and prevented about 400 students from leaving the college. On February 23, 1990, the *Daily Nation* reported: "The officer commanding Maseno Police Station, Mr. W. M'Mbijiwe, who led the riot police, told the students in a brief address that the Government had banned the wave of student demonstrations in the country." It also reported clashes between students and police at Egerton University, Njoro, and Jomo Kenyatta University College of Agriculture and Technology. Students marching down the Thika highway called for the resignation of the Commissioner of Police, Philip Kilonzo, and the Director of the Criminal Investigations Department, Noah arap Too, and for a review of all the security personnel.

Demonstrations by students during the week of February 19 were initially peaceful, and police escorted the demonstrators from the university grounds in Nairobi. However, rioting broke out when the paramilitary General Service Unit (GSU) used brutal tactics to disperse the crowds. Armed with riot shields, batons, tear gas, pistols and guns, the GSU attacked innocent bystanders as well as demonstrators. Eyewitness accounts described GSU officers beating women and men standing nearby—some at bus stops attempting to get out of the city—and dragging people out of cars. People were beaten down with riot batons and rifle butts and kicked in the head and back. According to hospital reports, over one hundred people were seriously injured, some sustaining broken limbs, deep cuts and severe bruising of the body and internal organs. One man died from bullet wounds; another was found with both legs broken after the crowds had finally dispersed.

In Kisumu, Ouko's constituency, there was even more violence with five people reported shot dead after GSU and riot police fired repeatedly over and into the crowds. Tear gas canisters were fired into houses to clear them of demonstrators who had taken refuge from the shooting.[1] Eyewitnesses described how riot police and GSU arrived in trucks and steel-sided vans, gun barrels protruding from the sides, and shot live ammunition and tear gas canisters directly into the crowd. Friends and relatives had to drag the injured away from further assault. No official numbers were released of those seriously injured or hospitalized, but national newspapers catalogued the injuries suffered by an estimated 100-150 people, and denounced the violent tactics used by GSU.

During the height of the demonstrations, recordings taken of comments by the crowd illustrate the extent of both the anger and panic:

> The government has killed him politically. He was becoming too powerful—of course, he was known worldwide. That is why Ouko is killed, because of his influence, and we know it here. But we cannot say it because we are *oppressed!*—because if I say in front of them, I'll be *in*! But we, Ouko's constituency, know exactly how he passed away. We should not be cheated—we want the full speech he gave in Washington, D.C., and why he was left behind.

Dr. Ouko's death was compared to political murders in Jomo Kenyatta's time— especially given his political prominence as a Luo. Tom Mboya, also a Luo, was an influential leader in the struggle for independence and a founding member of KANU. Originally a loyal ally of Jomo Kenyatta, he openly disagreed with the former president's centralizing elitism—known as the "Kikuyuization" of the bureaucracy—and his autocratic control of the economy. He had a great deal of popular support and was perceived by President Kenyatta as a potential threat to his presidency. He was assassinated on July 5, 1969, in Nairobi.

---

[1] *International Herald Tribune*, February 24, 1990.

After Ouko's body was discovered, many people from western Kenya claimed "influential Luos" were deliberately eliminated by the ruling powers:

> It is now one week and we still are given no results. He was killed by the government—everybody knows! It's like Tom Mboya...just like how Mr. Mboya was killed.

> Some other politicians have been killed the same way, among our people, the Luos, you see they don't want our people to grow. This is the third political murder—we think Oyugi should resign.[2] And the president. And the matter should be checked properly. Why should he bring in Scotland Yard? This is a rubber stamp. They are going to do nothing important. They know exactly how Ouko has been killed.

Most of the violence was triggered after Ouko's body had briefly been on view at Moi Stadium in Kisumu, with only a small part of his badly disfigured face visible. Many believed his face had been reconstructed—some refused to believe it was really his body. Thousands of mourners had lined up to view the body, but the occasion was brought to an end after only ninety minutes, and the majority of people were turned away:

> We have tried, but we have not seen the body, we have seen a statue! Something that has been made!

> Kisumu people and people as a whole are very angry about the death of Ouko, the way he has been killed. Some of these powerful M.P.s have been killed because they are led by those who are not fully educated. It will happen more—more of us will pass away. J. M. Kariuki,[3] Tom Mboya, Pinto Gama; and now we are

---

[2] Hezekiah Oyugi, Head of Internal Security, Office of the President.

[3] An outspoken and popular critic of Jomo Kenyatta's regime, murdered after being taken from a Nairobi hotel by senior police officers in March 1975.

burying Ouko tomorrow in a very horrible state. British
should think twice, and Americans—and worldwide! And
his speech in Washington, D.C., please send it to Kenya
to verify, or analyze, exactly what he gave to the press
conference because that is the main point why Ouko has
been killed. Because of the influence he had worldwide.

Calls for President Moi to resign led to speculation that he would
be unable to attend the funeral. In fact, he did, but under extremely
tight security. There were also demands for the resignation of Hezekia
Oyugi, Head of Internal Security, and President Moi's closest political
allies, including Minister of Energy Nicholas Biwott:

Everybody should resign. We don't fear *anybody* any
more, because this Kenya government is running by lies.
The murderer of Mr. Ouko is one of the government.
We know this because how can someone like a minister,
an elder statesman being guarded all the time by the
government, be killed just like that?

As GSU and riot police fired point blank into the crowds, two
people fell dead immediately, others who were badly wounded were
dragged from the crowd by friends and relatives. There was panic in the
crowd and increased outrage against the government:

It's his stomach. He was shot by a policeman just five
minutes ago—they were firing bullets at people. This man
was just standing in the crowd, he wasn't doing anything.
They just shot him—they were just firing at anything.

One woman, bleeding profusely from her head, was unable to get
the necessary medical attention as the security forces continued their
attack. People who dragged her to safety were weeping in anger and
despair:

This is the work of the police; this is what they have done
to her.

They are using their clubs on women. South Africa and
Kenya governments are the same in police action—we are

very unhappy. When police just pile on to that woman, well it appears we don't have a democracy. It's so wrong; they even shoot at women. When the police give you a direct attack like that, it means there is no democracy.

They have murdered, and now they continue to murder. Why? Tonight we still expect them to come for us.

Accusations made against the government and calls for resignations were accompanied by demands for a new and more democratic system:

Kenyans want to have the truth. We want the government to tell us the truth, or otherwise, if there is no truth in it, all we want is a democracy. A multiparty system in Kenya where the party that forms the government can be overseen by other parties, whose members are representative, so that their mistakes can be pointed out and corrected. But here is a place where, when the mistakes are pointed, the following day you are picked up. We want democracy. There is no real democracy, its not there in practice.

Fears that Ouko's funeral to be held the following day would lead to more violence and unrest were met by a public appeal for peace by his widow. There were no further demonstrations as the funeral ceremony and presidential address took place under full police guard. Police and GSU encircled the participants at gun-point. In the evening, after the international press and most local journalists had returned to Nairobi, GSU and police turned again on Kisumu residents. Patrolling residential areas, they ransacked houses for what they claimed to be goods stolen by rioters. Local residents say the security forces forced entry without warrants, arbitrarily confiscated household items—including television sets, stereos and furniture—and made violent threats. Many people were interrogated and arrested and taken from their house on charges of "breach of the peace" and "taking part in a riot." People found on the streets in the evening were beaten by the GSU with batons and rifle butts.

The government attributed the unrest and rioting to "drug addicts and hooligans," and Assistant Minister in the Office of the President John Keen said the GSU and police "handled the situation very well." He said the demonstrations were caused by "a couple of hundred unemployed youths taking advantage of the situation."

In the days following the riots and demonstrations, seventy-eight people were brought to court and charged with "taking part in a riot and destroying property." The majority of them were schoolchildren (see appendix B):

> Most of the schoolchildren aged between thirteen and seventeen were barefoot. They looked frail, dirty and hungry. Some of them said in mitigation that they were misled by colleagues to take part in the riots. Others claim they were severely beaten by armed GSU men who broke into their houses...[4]

None had legal representation. Ten denied the charge and were released after they had paid a bond of 5,000 shillings ($192). Thirty-six of the families concerned were unable to raise the 800 shillings ($31) fine, and the children were given two month jail sentences instead. Despite their youth and the fact that they were first time offenders, the magistrate justified the court's decision on the basis that "the offence was serious and should be discouraged through a deterrent sentence." He ordered twelve others too young to stand trial to be caned by the police. Given the harshness of prison conditions (see chapter ten), there must be concern for the effect these sentences had on young children.

Others accused included an old man, who protested he was dragged off by GSU officers as he was going to the hospital to visit his sick wife.

INVESTIGATING THE CASE

The government launched two investigations in response to public demands for the truth. Neither investigation has produced results of any significance, and at the time this report was written, many Kenyans did not feel they were any nearer the truth than they were in February 1990.

---

[4] "Kisumu Riots: 78 Appear in Court," *Daily Nation*, February 27, 1990.

Scotland Yard responded in its capacity as a private agency to the request from the Kenya government, and sent two detectives to Kisumu to investigate the Foreign Minister's death. This meant Scotland Yard was under no obligation as a representative of the British government to produce the findings of the report: any pressure brought to bear through government or parliamentary channels to reveal its contents was effectively blocked. During the 110-day investigation, led by Inspector John Troon, the detectives became increasingly less responsive to the media. According to journalists, the detectives were unhappy with the level of corruption they encountered, and with having to work closely "with the very officials we should be investigating." When the British pathologists' report confirmed that Ouko had been murdered, Troon initially refused to acknowledge the findings, saying he was "the man in the field" and would continue to investigate the case as a "death in suspicious circumstances." During the first few weeks of the investigations, hundreds of people were questioned and their statements recorded—from Ouko's house staff, his drivers and acquaintances—but there was no investigation, as far as the public was aware, into the possible implication of senior government officials or politicians.

Troon completed the written report in the U.K. and presented it to the Kenyan government. There were delays when Matthew Muli, then attorney general, intially insisted that the report must be handed over by Troon himself. Amidst much excitement in anticipation of its release, the Kenya government reneged on its promise that "the government [would] make further information known to the public about the circumstances pertaining to the death...as this information [became] known"[5] by refusing to release the full report to the public. It was partially released. The government said the report did not reveal who the killer or killers were and would therefore serve no good purpose for the public. Foreign correspondents were surprised, after being told by Troon—who took one hundred days to write it—that the report would "have something." A statement by the Church of the Province of Kenya said that the "failure to publish the Ouko report would be the very cover-up the Kenyans have been told there will not be." It went on to say the government could not expect to inspire confidence if it "keeps on dishonoring its promises and obligations, both legal and moral."

---

[5] Statement issued by President Moi on February 16, 1990.

Disappointment and continuing public suspicion about the involvement of senior politicians in Ouko's death, spurred President Moi into appointing a judicial commission of inquiry which began its work on October 26, 1990, eight months after the actual murder.

The Commission of Inquiry was chaired by Justice John Evans Gicheru. The other appointed commissioners were Justice Richard Otieno Kwach and Justice Akilano Akiwumi. The Deputy Public Prosecutor, Bernard Chunga, assisted the inquiry.

The initial stages of the inquiry were dominated by questions and statements on Ouko's movements just before his death, including those of his driver and his two official bodyguards. Paul Shikuku, the young herdsboy who discovered the body, was questioned at length then released along with various members of Ouko's staff and household. However, when Ouko's younger brother, Barrack Mbajah, was summoned before the commission, he fled to the United States and was given refuge on the grounds he feared for his life.

Despite the substantial coverage of the commission by the national papers, and considerable expectations of the public, nothing significant has come of the inquiry to date. Fear prevented Barrack Mbajah from testifying, and there is no indication that people are more willing to open up to a government-appointed commission than they were to the original investigators. The only significance of the commission seems, therefore, to have been its ability to dissipate people's passion and disappointment over the affair by saturating them with details of the inquiry. Public opinion remains the same—that Ouko's murder was a political assassination and that the government is effecting a cover-up—but, generally, expectations of finding out the supposed truth have been replaced with resignation that it will never be known.

The impact of Dr. Robert Ouko's murder nevertheless continued in the form of anger and disaffection that carried into more determined demands for political reform.

3
THE GREAT DEBATE
CALLING FOR POLITICAL PLURALISM

The debate began with Rev. Timothy Njoya's 1990 New Year sermon calling for reflection on the experiences of Eastern Europe and the need for political pluralism. Njoya told Africa Watch that he was heartened particularly by the downfall of the Ceausescu regime in Romania during the previous two weeks. In Njoya's view, Eastern Europe demonstrated that one-party dictatorships that had appeared invulnerable to change could be replaced by democracies without cataclysmic struggles.

In Kenya, the calls for greater democracy and a multiparty system that followed were not inspired by Eastern Europe, as it has so frequently been claimed, but emboldened. There have been calls for political pluralism during both President Kenyatta's and President Moi's rules, but they have gone unheeded and unpublicized. The difference of the 1990s was that intellectuals, the church, the lawyers and the activists seized the opportunity to put their appeal in an international climate uniquely tuned to the collapse of one-party states. Critics could challenge the West on its continuous support of the single-party state in Kenya.

Immediately after Dr. Robert Ouko's funeral, several hundred people were interrogated[1] by the Special Branch as part of an intense political crackdown. The questioning of a few high-profile public figures in Nairobi preoccupied the national and international media; but most of those interrogated and harassed were students, teachers, former civil servants and government officials, administration staff, businessmen and churchmen from western Kenya— Ouko's home region—and the central provinces. The crackdown in the latter was interpreted as government fear of Kikuyu-based discontent.

In the vast majority of cases, no charges were filed. People were typically taken away by plainclothes Special Branch officers for two or three hours, and grilled about their educational background, employment, travel and beliefs, colleagues, and whether they associated with dissidents.

---

[1] Information gathered by Africa Watch in western Kenya, Nyanza and the central provinces.

The security forces were given a mandate by the president to apprehend people, ostensibly over rumormongering, which meant speculations about Ouko's murder. However, interrogations appeared to have nothing to do with the killing.

According to one academic in Nairobi:

> The crackdown in Kenya at the present time appears to be in similar pattern to the crackdown in Kenya in 1975 and 1976 after the assassination of J. M. Kariuki. Following the death of Kariuki, there were very intensive and extensive demonstrations by both students and other people who felt horrified by that kind of political murder. Now similar demonstrations, but on a smaller scale, accompanied the killing of our former foreign minister, Dr. Robert Ouko, and after the demonstrations there appears to be a crackdown similar to the one in 1976—maybe to cool down the kind of hope and excitement that was being shown by the demonstrators in Ouko's case. So I think there appears to be a determination on the part of the government to again stifle all forms of expression. In fact, there was an explicit statement by the President banning all kinds of demonstrations after Ouko's death.

"Rumormonger" was soon used as a blanket term for anyone the government considered critical. Political repression seemed to be directed in particular at the Kikuyu community, chastised in parliament as being "traditionally hostile" to the president. The Nakuru District KANU branch chairman, Wilson Leitch, warned that MwaKenya[2] could have been involved in the murder in a political climate which looked set to whip up a witch-hunt similar to the MwaKenya crackdown in 1986-87. Reports of seditious pamphlets circulating in the provinces led to the arrest of a number of people on charges of sedition; they were later released. Roundups and arrests were facilitated by typically spurious charges of

---

[2] MwaKenya is a small underground movement that surfaced in the 1980s whose professed goal is the violent overthrow of the government. There was an intense crackdown against it in the mid-1980s and it has commonly been used by the government as a scapegoat.

disturbing the peace, drunk and disorderly behavior and prostitution—their political role being all the more transparent in the sudden proliferation of reports of such incidents in the newspapers. Police became diligent in preventing so-called illegal meetings, which is any gathering of more than three people.

In Nyamira District scores of women were injured, some seriously, when administration police broke up a cooperative society election meeting. In Kisumu, Special Branch officers were reported holding more than thirty people for allegedly spreading destructive rumors after launching an "intensive one-week anti-rumor exercise." A Special Branch spokesman told the press that "among them [is] a man who had been imprisoned as a member of the MwaKenya clandestine movement and a councillor of Kisumu."[3] In Nyeri, Hudson Njihia Kimani, a clerk with a branch of the Farmers' Cooperative Society, was charged with "uttering works likely to endanger public order and safety." The words were not specified in the charge, but, as is typical in politically motivated cases, the state prosecutor opposed bail on the grounds that the case "touched on national security" and asked the court to remand Kimani in custody as "investigations were not yet complete."[4]

Public fear became pronounced in what turned out to be only the beginning of a highly repressive phase. President Moi told security police they were allowed to go into any club and any bar for as long as necessary "to do their duty." KANU Secretary General, Joseph Kamotho, called on all KANU youthwingers, leaders and national branches, to "unearth those bent on undermining the government and poisoning the political climate"; telling them to arrest the rumormongers, he justified his orders by telling the press they would work closely with legitimate security forces.[5] The press reported at least forty-five people from the Nyanza Province and central provinces as having been convicted of "behaving in a manner likely to cause breach of the peace" (see chapter eight). In Nyeri alone, over one hundred people were picked up and held for interrogation. Calib, unemployed and from Nyeri town, said:

---

[3] *Daily Nation*, March 8, 1990.

[4] Ibid.

[5] *Kenya Times* (Nairobi), March 6, 1990.

Some people were just picked for a few hours, then
released, others were inside for some days, and some
"disappeared." It's different for people in Nairobi who
have lawyers and publicity, but in Nyeri,[6] there is
nothing we can do.

Prominent personalities detained for questioning by the Special
Branch were accused of being against the one-party state. Derogatory and
accusatory observations made in parliament about the fact that all those
interrogated were Kikuyu, were further inflamed by sections of the
national press speculating about a Kikuyu conspiracy. One local journalist
described it as a "sinister development":

I find it extremely difficult to understand or even
rationalise the current crackdown because the foreign
minister was murdered out in Nyanza Province—the
people who have been picked up are people from central
province, and say they have not been asked any questions
on Dr. Ouko's murder. So it is quite difficult to
understand or explain this crackdown. In parliament it
was held by a senior politician that the crackdown was
directed towards a particular community because they
have never supported the President. Now that's raised
quite a storm, because it is dangerous of course to
suggest an entire tribe has not supported the President.
That kind of allegation does not have any basis on fact.
Unfortunately most of those who have been picked are
prominent members of the Kikuyu tribe, and there is the
feeling that it's directed at the Kikuyu tribe. Before that
there was the screening of the Kenyan Somalis...but the
constitution specifically forbids the treatment of people
on a discriminatory manner purely on the basis of their
tribal origins or the color of their skin.

Among those interrogated were:

---

[6] 150 kilometers north of Nairobi.

Kenneth Matiba: Detained without trial three months later, Matiba said the Special Branch questioned him about whether he had intentions to form another party in Kenya, and grilled him about his movements both within the country and abroad since the beginning of the year.

Ben Gethi: Kenya's Commissioner of Police from 1978 to 1982, he was dismissed in August 1982 during the crackdown following the abortive coup attempt. He was detained until late 1983. At the end of February 1990, he was interrogated and released after a search of his house by a heavily-armed police contingent. He issued a statement to the press describing his arrest and the search of his house as "a contravention of his constitutional rights."

Dr. Josephat Karanja: Vice-president between April 1988 and May 1989, Karanja was removed from office through an orchestrated campaign to politically discredit him. Parliament passed a vote of no confidence against him without providing any opportunity to answer the numerous charges.

Andrew Ngumba: Former assistant minister from 1977 to 1983 and mayor of Nairobi, he fled the country in 1985 to escape what he considered a politically-motivated prosecution, following the collapse of the bank he chaired, the Rural Urban Credit Finance Company. He was expelled from KANU in absentia. After four years in exile in Sweden —during which time he announced he was willing to lead an organized political opposition against the government—he returned to Kenya under a general presidential amnesty declared for all self-imposed exiles. In spite of assurances that he was free to return to live as a normal citizen, he was under constant surveillance. Rev. Timothy Njoya was criticized by the government for welcoming Ngumba into his congregation. President Moi publicly denounced Ngumba as "going around to various hotels to say filthy words, including those relating to murder or anything."

James Mungai: Former Assistant Commissioner of Police for the Rift Valley Province, Mungai was earlier sentenced to nine months in prison, allegedly for burning a neighbor's field. The conviction was set aside on appeal by the High Court. On March 6, 1990, he issued a press statement vehemently denying having any involvement with spreading rumors or being engaged in any anti-government activities. President Moi proceeded to attack Mungai in public for "infiltrating deep inside" after "he had harassed people in Nakuru and fled before anybody could touch him, went to Europe and elsewhere....The police will now embark on them properly...."

Stanley Munga Githunguri: Former executive chairman of the National Bank of Kenya, he has been the subject of several highly publicized but unsuccessful prosecutions by the state. His fall from favor was generally believed to have come from his close association with former cabinet minister, Charles Njonjo, and charges made against him were seen as politically motivated. The former chief justice, the late C. B. Madan, halted the prosecutions, but President Moi's political allies have continued harassment by trying to sell off some of Githunguri's property. President Moi used the crackdown to strike out at Githunguri's Lilian Towers multistory complex as a hotbed of rumormongering, along with the Silver Springs Hotel and the Muthaiga Club.

Wangari Maathai: Head of the Green Belt Movement, former chair of the Kenya National Council of Women and an internationally recognized, award-winning environmentalist, Maathai has been harassed and victimized on account of her outspoken opposition to government plans to construct a sixty-story complex in Nairobi's largest remaining public park, Uhuru Park. She was picked up in early March and interrogated by the police for rumormongering. She was later asked if she thought she had been picked up as a prominent Kikuyu:

> I really have no idea whatsoever. I know that I am a Kikuyu and I haven't done anything that warrants anything but commendation. I would have expected my government to be applauding me for using my education and my energy and enthusiasm to do something that is positive and to work for my country...
>
> I don't know what the rumors are because they just say people are rumormongering. If rumormongering means speculations as to why and how Dr. Robert

Ouko died then every person who is capable of understanding what that kind of death meant is wondering, and so everybody is therefore a rumormonger, including the politicians themselves because much of what we hear and read about in the newspapers is actually what the members of parliament are saying. They are the ones who are feeding us what they are calling rumors. So I would say they are the initial rumormongers; and then they go around trying to pick a few individuals whom they think are vulnerable, like me. Nobody's going to be overly surprised because people like me are already being hunted. When they are picked, and therefore threatened, people are going to keep quiet. Well, I wasn't talking about who cut up Dr. Ouko, I don't know anything except what I read in the newspapers and what I hear in the Voice of Kenya.

The investigations are still going on. Most of us are very happy that the government—it is saying that it is doing everything possible to unravel the mystery and of course anybody of goodwill hopes that we shall eventually know who killed him. But I really think that perhaps the government is scared of something.

I think picking me at this time was not so much to link me with the death of Dr. Robert Ouko as to continue intimidating and harassing me and therefore ensuring that I will be so intimidated that I will never raise my voice again for environment or for anything else. They also hope that people will ostracize me. This is something that is very common in this country —once the government is picking you out, they attack you in parliament, they abuse you in public, they make people feel that they should not associate with you because you are dangerous, you are anti-government, you are a "bad guy." When they do that they hope they have ostracized you enough to make you completely ineffective. Whatever the government is doing towards me it is definitely geared towards silencing my voice....

Among those threatened with arrest were:

Gibson Kamau Kuria: Kenya's best-known human rights lawyer and a former political detainee. He was forced to flee the country three months later. Special Branch officers came to his office on April 3 before he had arrived. Kamau Kuria issued a press statement immediately, identifying three reasons why he believed the security forces were persecuting him again—his defense of clients charged with political offenses, including representation of three former political prisoners who have sued the government for damages for torture and illegal detention; his criticism of government interference in recent law society elections; and his outspoken criticism of Kenya's one-party system:

> I have argued...that there cannot be democracy in a
> one party state. Kenya's experience is a good example
> of the manner in which a single party can be
> manipulated by those in control of it to perpetuate
> themselves in power....So far the debate has been one
> sided and limited to those speaking in favor of the one
> party....Those arguing in favor of the one party do not
> wish to accord those of a different view an opportunity
> to be heard.

Mohamed K. Ibrahim: A lawyer, later detained, who refused to be screened when the government required all ethnic Somalis to present themselves for a special identity verification card (see chapter sixteen). His public refusal to be screened and his willingness to represent clients affected by the exercise resulted in his being served with two notices to report to the Special Branch. Ibrahim argued the offenses in the notices—"misconduct of good behavior" and "matters related to state security"—did not exist under the country's constitution, but a suit submitted to the high court requesting permission not to attend was dismissed (see chapter seven). He was interrogated by Special Branch officers on April 19 for three and a half hours. Ibrahim was not allowed to have his lawyer present, Dr. John Khaminwa—also detained later—and the interrogation focused on his consistent refusal to be screened.

Gitobu Imanyara: Journalist, lawyer and editor of the *Nairobi Law Monthly* (see chapter twelve for details about the case of the *Nairobi Law Monthly*).

"IT'S ONE PARTY OR WE PERISH"

The debate on multiparty politics was generally restricted to a chorus from M.P.s and KANU faithfuls on the need for a one-party state. Those willing to make public their desire for a multiparty system found no open channel in which to put forward their point of view. Instead, they discovered their opinions were progressively criminalized by the government who denounced them as anti-Nyayo, subversive and enemies of the state. At no time during the debate was there a free and equal exchange of ideas in the public forum; only a constant denunciation of multiparty advocates who remained invisible, aside from reports of their interrogation by the Special Branch. The one publication, the *Nairobi Law Monthly*, which did carry articles from proponents of political pluralism, was condemned as subversive. Its editor, Gitobu Imanyara, said in an interview in April 1990 that there was no real debate taking place:

> ...all we ask is that we can debate on the merits and demerits of the multiparty system. We want people to speak freely on the reasons given by the politicians as to why the one-party system is the best....
>
> I think the debate that is now taking place, which is very, very one sided, is designed to forestall free and open debate on the merits and demerits of a multiparty system of government. But I do not see how we can hold the clock; I do not see how we can avoid taking stock of what is taking place in the rest of the world....We feel we are not unique. We live in a world that is changing and that these changes could affect us as much as they are affecting the Soviet Union, Eastern Europe, Latin America and other countries in the world....

Prominent figures like Gibson Kamau Kuria, found no other publication or newspaper willing to publish statements in defence of advocates of pluralism. According to KANU, proponents of a multiparty system were inviting tribalism and chaos. "IT'S ONE PARTY OR WE PERISH" read a headline in the *Kenya Times*:[7]

> ...More support for the one-party system poured in yesterday with leaders in various parts of the country saying a multiparty system would spell doom for the young Kenyan nation....

Two cabinet ministers condemned the advocates of multiparty systems and described them as prophets of doom, hatred, tribalism and sectionalism.   Professor Ongeri (Technical Training and Applied Technology) said: "I will support President Moi until I go to the grave and those who are out to form a second political party will face the law and we send them to where they belong." He added that Kenyans "thinking they will change the Kenyan leadership through a second party or clandestine movement are daydreaming and instead should dig for their own grave and wait for another Government in hell."
Minister William Ntimama, echoing similar statements said the second party would pave the way for tribalism, sectionalism, hatred and petty politicking, factors which would hurt general development.
The Kisii KANU district chair also strongly castigated those who were calling for a second political party and said they would "not be tolerated in the peaceful Kenya...."[8]

DISCUSSING THE DEBATE

The argument of tribalism was rejected by multiparty advocates. One lawyer, in a press interview, called the argument of tribalism shallow:

> I personally do not believe in a one-party system you cannot have tribalism. We have seen tribalism in this country during the time of President Kenyatta when senior positions were held by people from a particular

---

[7] *Kenya Times*, April 7, 1990.

[8] Ibid.

division of one district. Now that is tribalism within a
one-party state. I'm not so sure we can say that currently
all tribes in Kenya have equal opportunities, have equal
chances of employment—and yet we're in a one party
state.

I think it is ridiculous to suggest that the existence of
more parties will destroy the nation because this is a
country of more than 40 tribes...it's essential for any
particular community to seek the support of others in
order to form a critical government. At the time we had
multiparty politics in this country at independence those
parties were not tribal. KADU was not tribal, KANU was
not tribal, KPU was not a tribal party. The tribal parties
are the ones which are dead, and any attempt to form
one would surely fail because we have developed to such
a stage that nobody would be taken in to such an extent
by purely tribal considerations.

Although support for a multiparty system appeared to come
almost exclusively from prominent churchmembers and the legal
community, as well as from a few former members of parliament, a
willingness to openly criticize the one-party state was broadening. People
who had suffered the consequences of convictions or detention during
other political crackdowns became bolder in expressing their
dissatisfaction. One such man, who had been tortured by the Special
Branch when he was a student, said he thought many people wanted
some sort of a change because there was too much general intimidation
by the police. He said he felt great fear during the ongoing crackdown as
he knew he was a target for the security forces.

It seems as though the Kenyan security officers have
greater interest in people who have had political
problems in the past with the Kenyan government and
I am quite apprehensive as to my own safety [see
appendix A]. People are being picked up in Nyeri over
flimsy charges, they would be put in for a bit of time and
then later released. Many of those picked up have since
been released; they were put in and interrogated on

various issues and later many of them were released. They had no access to counsel.

But right now, Nyeri is not so bad—people are not being picked up as much as just after the death of Robert Ouko; but there are a lot of accusations of seditious leaflets being circulated.

My life has always been made difficult by them, so I'm sure they want to take the opportunity to pick me too. I don't think I can carry on with the things I want to do because the government is still keeping all my documents and is denying me my right to work and my right to complete my education and even my right to move out of this country to pursue my academic studies outside. My life can never be normal unless all those rights have been restored.

I think very many people would like to see a multiparty system here because they're dissatisfied with the present one-party state—I personally feel the one-party state has been made into a dictatorship which has alienated many of the people.

RUBIA AND MATIBA CALL FOR REFERENDUM

On April 23, 1990, Dr. Henry Okullu, Bishop of the Maseno South diocese, issued a statement saying it was a mistake to make Kenya a de jure one-party state. He called for the decision to be reversed and for presidential tenure to be limited to two terms. Okullu suggested a representative committee be appointed to look into what political and economic systems Kenyans wanted, saying that the present debate was not allowing sufficient freedom of expression. Citizens, he said, "are forced by fear to withdraw into their professional ghettos" and that many Kenyans feared expressing views different from KANU because they would be victimized.[9]

---

[9] *Daily Nation*, April 24, 1990.

Threats were issued by a number of politicians and KANU branches not to "push [President] Moi too far" and for the population to ignore the calls for a new political system. But former cabinet ministers, Charles Rubia and Kenneth Matiba, brought forth the challenge by demanding the immediate dissolution of parliament, repeal of the 1982 constitutional amendment, new elections and a public referendum to decide the country's political future. They charged that inflexibility and indifference to demands for public accountability by the single party system was at the root of many of the country's problems: "Tribalism should not be used as an excuse to sustain a system that deprives people of their rights and freedoms."

CRIMINALIZING CRITICISM

After Rubia and Matiba presented their demands, events moved rapidly. The tension created in a society normally regulated by secrecy and caution was explosive as critics tried to push the government toward open political debate. President Moi publicly denounced the former cabinet ministers as "tribalists" and "puppets of foreign masters" and reiterated the argument that political pluralism would turn into chaos and bloodshed. Matthew Muli, then attorney general, said the constitution did not provide for holding a referendum on political issues and that Matiba and Rubia were part of "another misguided and ungrateful change-the-constitution group which is out to cause chaos in the country." Calling multiparty advocates "disloyal," he said they were "not welcome in the country."[10]

On May 11 at Kerugoya Stadium, Kirinyaga District, President Moi said Matiba and Rubia and "a section of the Church Province of Kenya" were part of a plot to murder government officials and blame the deaths on his government. He threatened to "swing into action against the group" who were planning to take two people to Uganda for guerrilla training.[11] The presidential accusation of treason was denied by Rubia

---

[10] *Daily Nation*, May 5, 1990. Muli was referring to the "change-the-constitution" group of 1977 that tried to prevent then Vice-President Moi from automatically becoming president. See chapter one.

[11] *Daily Nation*, May 12, 1990.

and Matiba, and Archbishop Manasses Kuria of the Church of the Province of Kenya. President Moi then followed up his "treason charges" by announcing that Kenyan trade unions were using "money to incite workers and cause chaos" on behalf of the multiparty advocates.[12] Accusations of treason were repeated by ministers in parliament, who said there were "not more than ten" working "for the downfall of the government," including Matiba, Rubia, Imanyara and several clergymen and lawyers.[13]

"NAKURU SCREAMS TREASON AT MATIBA: Charge Rubia and colleague" read the headline of the May 15 issue of the *Daily Nation*, reporting a move by Nakuru KANU sub-branch calling for the government to charge the two with treason for their call to dissolve parliament "which implied the government should be removed."

Thus the treason net had been thrown over the sections and institutions toward which the government felt a longstanding hostility. A warning was issued to the general public not to demonstrate support for multiparty politics by using the salute adopted by multiparty advocates, which was the raising of two fingers to signal pluralism.

President Moi made another speech, at Sixty-Four Stadium in Eldoret, charging that multiparty proponents were linked to a whole decade of "subversive activities." He said they began a campaign against his government in 1980. Subversive activities included the attempt to overthrow the government in August 1982, establishing the clandestine MwaKenya movement, and "engaging in other destructive and tribal activities." He said "subversives" had concentrated their efforts on criticizing the queue-voting exercise among other things, and were using calls for a multiparty system "as a cover-up." He said he knew "many other things about these people" which he would reveal "at an opportune time."[14]

---

[12] Ibid.

[13] *Daily Nation*, May 14, 1990.

[14] *Daily Nation*, May 18, 1990.

APPLYING FOR A LICENSE

Rubia and Matiba announced plans to apply for a license to hold an open, public rally to explain the merits of a multiparty system, and to reply to the allegations leveled against them. The chosen venue was Kamukunji grounds, used as a center for the nationalist preindependence struggle and described by President Moi as a place for "hot politics" when he announced plans for the recently released Nelson Mandela to address a public rally there the same month. The license was therefore refused before it was submitted. President Moi asked in a public rally: "They want licenses under what law? They know the law and if they meet without a license they will face the law."[15] Rubia and Matiba went ahead with a formal application to the Nairobi Provincial Commissioner, Fred Waiganjo, for a permit under the provisions of the Public Order Act. The title of the proposed meeting was "The Case for Multiparty," with Charles Rubia named as convener and both he and Matiba listed as the speakers.

Starting with a prayer, the meeting proposed promoting the case for a multiparty system, and finish with a closing prayer. Under Section 5 of the Public Order Act Cap (Chapter) 56 of the Laws of Kenya, the application was, in fact, wholly legal: "Any person wishing to hold, convene, organize or form a public meeting or public procession shall first make an application for a license to the District Commissioner of the district in which the meeting or procession is to take place."

"CHOPPING FINGERS" ORDER

Nakuru district KANU branch chair, Wilson Leitich, issued an order on June 12—the day after the application for the meeting had been submitted—that youthwingers should chop off the two fingers flashed by anyone to show multiparty support. Youthwingers were instructed to patrol in plainclothes carrying knives ready to cut off the fingers of anyone who showed a multiparty salute. The chopped fingers, he said, should be brought to the Nakuru KANU office. Leitich complained that the two-finger salute was being seen in market places and bus stops, and encouraged the youthwingers to "track down agitators." He also instructed

---

[15] *Daily Nation*, June 10, 1990.

them to take away trading licenses from multiparty advocates and bring
them to the KANU office.

Leitich was later forced to withdraw his instructions when the
Director of Legal and International affairs at KANU headquarters, Steve
Mwenesi, said it was an "incitement to criminality...KANU is not interested
in promoting illegal actions." Mwenesi issued a statement saying: "It is
contrary to the party's code of discipline as well as the laws of the land
for any citizen to chop off any of the two fingers the cowardly multiparty
propagandists have been raising."[16]

CALLS FOR DETENTION

After President Moi publicly announced that Rubia and Matiba
would not get a license for their meeting, two cabinet ministers called for
their detention for "allegedly plotting to destabilize the government."[17]
KANU rallies in Bungoma, Narok and Sega Market, Ukwala Division
repeated calls for detention and encouraged people to show support for
the one-party state with a show of one finger. Many M.P.s called for the
use of detention without trial. In parliament, assistant minister Abdi Noor
Ogle requested the government to detain multiparty proponents:
"Enough is enough! Things have gone too far and it is about time action
was taken against those opposing President Moi." Nicholas Biwott,
minister for energy and close confidant of President Moi, reassured
ministers that the government would respond to Ogle's remark. Burudi
Nabwera, in charge of internal security and provincial administration,
warned that the government would be taking action against Rubia and
Matiba.

Two days later Kenneth Matiba's wife, Edith and their daughter
Susan, were seriously injured when a group of men raided their house
around midnight and attacked them. During the attack, Edith Matiba
sustained a fractured skull and a deep wound on the back of her neck.
She was able to see the men, however, and described them as "looking
well-fed" and apparently following instructions from one member of the
gang. The orders were apparently conveyed in a "disciplined" rather than

---

[16] *Daily Nation*, June 13, 1990.

[17] Ibid.

"thug-like" style, and the men allegedly addressed each other as "corporal" and "captain." Edith and Susan Matiba and a maid were held in the bedroom while men armed with axes, machetes and guns searched through drawers and cupboards. They threatened to cut off the maid's ear, and hit Susan Matiba across the face with the blunt end of an axe. Kenneth Matiba, who was away during the attack, implied it was a politically motivated attempt to kill him: "It is no coincidence that they came here, well armed, looking for me at this time, and then tried to make it look like a petty robbery."[18]

While visiting Edith Matiba in the hospital, Rev. Timothy Njoya described the attack as political thuggery: "The trend has been that anybody who raises a voice [is] to be 'thuggerised.'" Two weeks later, the family of exiled writer Ngugi wa Thiongo was also attacked. His wife, Nyambura Thiongo, was seriously injured when a group of about thirty men armed with axes and metal bars attacked her in the bedroom around midnight. She was hit on the head with a metal bar when she was unable to produce one million shillings ($38,462), which they insisted Ngugi had recently sent her. It was also reported that one of the gangsters told her "we have been sent to kill you."[19]

President Moi was reported as sending his sympathies to Edith Matiba, saying the government "had launched a manhunt for the culprits."[20] Three months later, she was called to testify in court against two men accused of assaulting and robbing her, but discovered they bore no resemblance to those in the group she described as "well fed and disciplined." Edith Matiba had been taken to Kiambu police station and shown two men to identify; there was no lineup. She later described the men she saw as "well-known local vagabonds." A camera and binoculars were also shown to her, said to be hers and found in their possession. The camera, however, was the wrong make and the binoculars did not belong to her. Edith Matiba does not believe these two men were implicated in the attack.

---

[18] *Financial Times*, June 15, 1990.

[19] *Daily Nation*, June 29, 1990.

[20] *Daily Nation*, June 17, 1990.

THE PRESIDENT HALTS DEBATE

On June 16, President Moi announced that the "debate" on multiparty politics was over. Addressing rallies in a number of towns, he had previously ordered a massive recruitment drive to start on May 11. During his public speeches he called for figures on recruitment targets so that, he said, he could "announce the daily figures [and] prove the huge support KANU had throughout the country."[21]

On June 20, plans were announced by the KANU National Executive Committee to set up a 10-member KANU team to review the party's electoral process and the expulsion of members. Chaired by the vice-president, George Saitoti, there was also a recommendation to create a national vice-presidency to "harmonize party administration from the grassroots to the national level."[22] This was the genesis of what was to become the KANU Review Committee, which heard an unprecedented—and evidently unexpected—number of comprehensive complaints from the public on the political structure during a nationwide tour. Its initial formation at this stage was greeted, however, with more scepticism than enthusiasm. If it was proposing to examine some of the most unpopular aspects of KANU—like the queue-voting system, the 70 percent nomination rule and disciplinary methods—it simultaneously made recommendations strengthening some of the most repressive aspects. The KANU youthwingers were to become the KANU Youth League, "strengthened and revitalized" in order to "continue assisting the country's security and administration."[23]

---

[21] *Daily Nation*, June 17, 1990. Results included were: Baring 65,000, Elgeyo Marakwet 22,731, Kajiado 24,400, Kericho 110,000, Laikipia 25,000, Nakuru 93,299, Nandi 65,542, Narok 33,000, Samburu 21,000, Trans-Nzoia 22,000, Turkana 18,000, and West Pokot 24,000. There was some discrepancies between original targets set, and later targets announced, as in the Uasin Gishu branch that was given a target of 110,000 in a speech by Moi on May 17, but was reported a month later as an 80,000 person target. Mass recruitment drives are achieved primarily under duress and harassment, see chapter one.

[22] *Daily Nation*, June 21, 1990.

[23] Ibid.

There was a recommendation that all branch treasurers become members of the national Governing Council, which was an unwelcome emphasis on finance when corruption and forced *harambees* (public donations) were a point of major contention. Recommendations were made to extend the terms of office for KANU officials from three years to five to match the parliamentary office. The Executive Committee rejected any suggestion that the proposed Review Committee was a result of pressure by multiparty advocates, saying people had clearly demonstrated support for the one-party state in the numerous public rallies addressed by the president.

On the same day as the announcement of the proposal for a Review Committee, Special Branch officers attempted to seize Matiba and Rubia during a consultation with their lawyer, Paul Muite. Six plainclothes officers burst into Muite's office and declared that an illegal meeting was being held. Under the advice of Muite, Matiba and Rubia refused to accompany the officers, who failed to produce a warrant for their arrest, and demanded their offense be disclosed. Muite agreed to consult with Matiba alone and let Rubia accompany another lawyer, which was done, according to the *Daily Nation*, "to avoid a breakdown of law and order by the crowd gathered outside the office."

After the incident, fifty-four lawyers issued a statement condemning the storming of Muite's office, saying it "spells doom for the independence of the bar and the rule of law in this country." Muite said there should be a "common destiny" between lawyers and policemen, whether Special Branch or uniformed law-enforcement officers, to ensure law and order "in a society which enjoys stability and rule of law...." The following day, four policemen went to Muite's office but left after refusing to question him in the presence of his lawyer, Dr. John Khaminwa. Muite then called together about twenty lawyers and a number of journalists to make a statement that he feared for his life. The conference was broken up almost immediately by intelligence officers, who ripped up journalists' notebooks and confiscated film, calling Muite's office a "center of subversion."

Matiba, who also feared that his life was in danger, decided to take protective measures since his house was raided on June 14. His revolver had been impounded by the police some weeks earlier, and repeated requests by Matiba to have it returned were ignored by the authorities. He hired five personal bodyguards. On June 24, four days after Special Branch officers had attempted to arrest Matiba and Rubia, two of his bodyguards were arrested—one, at the Central Police Station, when he went with Matiba to find out what had happened to the other bodyguard. Security personnel again broke up a press conference called afterwards by Matiba, who complied but said their action "spoke louder than words."[24] Officers at the Central Police Station denied that the two guards, John Gichangi and Garston Ngotho, were being held there.

CHURCH SUPPORT VOICED

The statements issued by Protestant Archbishop Henry Okullu regarding limiting presidential tenure and questioning the 1982 amendment on the one-party state drew fire from KANU but support from other clerics. On June 22 the Catholic Church, traditionally the most conservative and reticent church body, lent support to government critics in a pastoral letter signed by four archbishops and fourteen bishops. In the letter, they complained that "the superiority of the party over the authority of parliament" had become "an accomplished fact, and that KANU had become government per se." Fears were also expressed that the "philosophy of national security" was leading Kenya to "political murders, unlawful home searches, arbitrary detentions, confessions under torture and death squad actions that escape the control of the public forces of order." Publication of the letter led to the arrest of the editor of the *Daily Nation* by Special Branch officers (see chapter twelve).

FACING THE MUSIC

Although events in Nairobi were restricted primarily to a small, wealthy, professional circle and dismissed by President Moi and KANU as a "Kikuyu plot," the harassment of the former cabinet ministers provoked a more broad-based restlessness. Popular dissatisfaction had found new bravado during the Ouko demonstrations. For many, life had become increasingly difficult because of unemployment, rising prices, lack of land, police harassment and a corrupt and aggressive administration. Symbols of defiance demanding change, like the two-finger salute, surfaced.

In Nairobi, music was used as one of the most effective means of reaching the poorest sections of the population. Cassettes satirizing

---

[24] *Daily Nation,* June 24, 1990.

government corruption and supporting multiparty politics included songs with such titles as "Problems that Befell the Poor People of Muoroto" (see chapter fourteen), "Matiba's Tribulations" and "Who Killed Dr. Robert Ouko?" and were played in shantytowns, bars, music stores and, eventually, on public transportation as well.

The songs, along with Kenyatta's speeches, were played in the *matatus*.[25] The attorney general announced a ban on subversive music, saying it was illegal to buy or be in possession of the tapes. In warning the public that it was "a serious offence to publish, circulate, or be in possession of seditious materials, be they in writing or audio-visual," he nevertheless failed to be specific about which songs the government considered seditious or subversive. The effective result was another blanket mandate to arrest, interrogate and harass the population, in an attempt to deter any mass-based resistance.

On July 3, police raided music shops in Nairobi, Nyeri and Nakuru during the early hours of the morning, confiscating thousands of cassettes, cassette recorders, dubbing machines, guitars and saxophones and arresting dozens of people. Police broke into stores and arrested groups of men and women, charging them with "listening to subversive music," and confiscating their tapes. Retailers said many thousands of tapes were taken from shops in an apparently arbitrary fashion; police were unable or unwilling to identify which tapes were illegal. A number of matatus were reportedly impounded. Street hawkers were arrested after police and youthwingers searched for the subversive music in Nakuru. Music dealers, street hawkers, musicians, shop employees and members of the public were taken by the police in both Nairobi and Nakuru—some held for a few hours only, others charged with sedition and remanded in custody when the state prosecution routinely denied bail. Only a very small number had legal representation (see appendix C).

None of the seditious music cases have yet to come to trial. It is believed that all those in remand were eventually released after the charges were withdrawn. Some, however, spent two or three months in remand at Kamiti Maximum Security Prison under degrading conditions before being released. Africa Watch interviewed an anonymous source from Kamiti who described their circumstances as wretched:

---

[25] Private mini-buses, the main form of public transportation in Kenya.

I met five cassette sellers who had been charged with
selling seditious material—meaning those songs. They
said they had been given bail of 50,000 shillings [$1,923]
which of course no street seller can hope to raise.
They're just hawkers selling a few things. When I saw
them, they had been in for weeks and there was still no
consent to prosecute. They lose hope—the case gets
mentioned every two weeks, but you're still there waiting
for consent. I'm not surprised they lose hope. In Kamiti
[prison] you meet people who have been waiting for two
and a half years with only a routine mention. You get
treated like a criminal anyway. There are many in the
cells, and its very unsanitary. Just one basin which gets
cleaned out every morning—that's very embarrassing; it's
humiliating.

Under Kenyan law, the attorney general's warning and the
subsequent action did not have any validity. Specific songs were not
banned under any law and, also by law, mere possession of material does
not mean the owner subscribes to the views it contains nor is the mere
adherence to certain views a crime (see chapter eight). By deliberately
imposing very high bail on members of the poorest sections of society,
the result was in effect a denial of bail. In some cases, bail was opposed
by the state prosecutor on the grounds that "investigations were still
underway" and the "full extent of the charge" had yet to be determined."
(See chapter five, "Holding Charges.") Those remanded in custody were
punished as "political prisoners" in a maximum security prison without
the state having to prove them guilty under untenable charges.

KAMUKUNJI: "HOT POLITICS"

Charles Rubia and Kenneth Matiba publicly conceded they were
unable to hold any meeting without a license. Throughout their
campaign, they had emphasized their wish for peaceful and legal methods
of political change, and took legal advice on their actions and intentions.
On June 29, however, an assistant minister, David Mwenje, accused the
two in parliament of secretly organizing Nairobi residents to rally at the
Kamukunji grounds on July 7. President Moi followed up the accusation
by announcing a "plot by anti-government people to have wananchi

[people] shot by the plotters at an illegal meeting at Kamukunji grounds, Nairobi, July 7...the group planned to shoot innocent wananchi if their unlicensed meeting was interrupted by the police so that they could blame the shooting on the police."[26] He also announced that matatu drivers were going to be used to take people to the illegal gathering. Matiba and Rubia emphatically rejected the allegations and publicly disassociated themselves from any person or group organizing or intending violent actions: "We have in the recent past criticized KANU and the government on very specific points and have called for change, but all the points that we raised seem to have been ignored...[but] we have not said anything that has not been said by others in the past and all our utterances have been made in extremely good faith." They emphasized the fact that all they had to say had been said publicly in order to avoid spurious accusations of organizing underground.

But President Moi's pronouncements were met with more calls by members of parliament for "anti-government elements" to be detained without trial. Moi captured the mood of the government on July 4 in a long speech about the security of the state; it was a prelude to a climax of events. State security was not, he said, "negotiable." Anyone who wished to "confuse the freedom to express their views with licence to undermine State security" would be dealt with "by the full might of the law." Lawyers, he said, should temper their criticism of the police: "The truth is that all freedoms, including those guaranteed in the Constitution, are qualified. There are no absolute freedoms and our Constitution carefully qualifies all its provisions to ensure that the main purpose of advancing the common good is maintained." The speech concluded the many recent references he had made about disposing of "anti-government elements."

President Moi's fear of opposition increased when the former cabinet ministers met with former Vice-President Oginga Odinga—a veteran critic, who had made previous attempts at forming an opposition party (see chapter one). President Moi excoriated Matiba and Rubia as "dictators, tribalists, anti-Nyayo, hyenas and traitors" who he would "deal with."

---

[26] *Daily Nation*, June 30, 1990.

DETAINED

Rubia and Matiba were arrested by Special Branch officers the day after President Moi's speech. About eighteen plainclothes policemen took Matiba from his Nairobi office at around 6:15 P.M. Rubia was taken shortly afterwards when about fifteen Special Branch officers stormed the Muthaiga Club where he was attending a committee meeting. The official newspaper notice of their detention on July 6 was followed by other detentions of high-profile critics. Ex-detainee Raila Odinga (son of Oginga Odinga) was taken from his Nairobi office by a large contingent of plainclothes policemen. Ex-detainee, lawyer Dr. John Khaminwa, was also taken after he went to the Criminal Investigation Department (CID) headquarters to inquire about his clients, Matiba and Rubia. Gitobu Imanyara, editor of the *Nairobi Law Monthly* was later taken from his house, and lawyer Mohamed Ibrahim taken from his office. Gibson Kamau Kuria went underground, as did Paul Muite, lawyer of Matiba and Rubia, when the chief of police announced there was a "manhunt" to arrest them. Kamau Kuria took refuge in the American embassy and fled into exile.

This use of preventive detention—which international law permits only during times of emergency that imminently threaten the nation and then only in circumstances when directly necessary to meet the exigencies of the emergency—was accompanied by KANU's commendation of the president for the peace and stability prevailing in the country, and a pledge to guard "peace and tranquillity" at all costs.

4
SABA SABA
THE JULY KILLINGS

In spite of government warnings not to attend a pro-democracy rally on July 7, 1990, thousands of people gathered at Kamukunji that Saturday, and were caught up in the worst violence in Kenya since the failed coup attempt in 1982.

The inspiration for the protest against the government emanated primarily from Kenneth Matiba and Charles Rubia's attempt to hold an open rally for a multiparty system. The day before the gathering, MwaKenya leaflets were also circulated in Nairobi encouraging people to attend. Eyewitness accounts tell of the growing curiosity of people just to see if there would be a gathering regardless of the warnings; a sort of passive defiance that gathered its own momentum. Many described the mood as "everybody knew something was going to happen—nobody really knew what."

People began gathering at Kamukunji[1] in the late morning, and by early afternoon there were thousands waving branches, shouting political demands, flashing the two-finger salute symbolizing multiparty politics, and calling for the release of Matiba and Rubia. Initially, the gathering was nonviolent, even though the atmosphere was highly charged. One participant described the feeling as dream-like:

> People just expected Matiba to appear from detention like an angel from heaven. They needed to know he was coming just to cool off their minds—they were full of excitement and hope. Trouble started when people saw the CID, and started pointing at them, getting angry and saying they had come as spies. They decided to drive them away. I don't know who called in the riot police and the GSU. But, you know, it was a compulsion. People just wanted to go there.

---

[1] Kamukunji is an open area east of Nairobi's shantytown, Muoroto, the scene of violent evictions in 1990.

Security forces were on high-profile standby, with trucks of
paramilitary forces positioned near the Kamukunji grounds and a police
helicopter flying over the area. Violence broke out when crowds turned
on two unmarked police cars and began stoning them. The police
escaped, but as they drove away, people surged out of the grounds
towards the city center and the suburbs. Security forces waiting in the
wings were quick to react. Two truck loads of General Service Unit
officers charged into the crowd firing tear gas canisters and beating
people with batons. Running for cover, people hurled stones and other
missiles in response to the attack. Subsequent running battles between
stone-throwers and police forces lasted for three days.

Once people moved out of the Kamukunji grounds, battles with
riot police and GSU spread into the poorer suburbs and shantytowns
where most of the worst violence took place. Demonstrators flashed the
two-finger salute and shouted "Release Rubia and Matiba" in Kiswahili.
Armed police encircled Nairobi with roadblocks as security forces pursued
the crowds, firing live ammunition and tear gas, beating and arresting
everyone in their path. Eyewitnesses describe seeing "a wall of uniforms
and gun-barrels" sectioning off parts of the crowd, and the desperate
attempts of people to drag the seriously injured away from the path of
the stampede. Other serious and fatal injuries were caused by multiple
car accidents as drivers tried to escape from stone-throwers and
roadblocks.

New roadblocks were erected by groups of young men who
stoned drivers if they refused to display the two-finger multiparty signal.
Matatu drivers went on strike, bringing the city to a virtual standstill, and
demanded that the government listen to political demands and release
Matiba and Rubia.

Truckloads of riot police and GSU were brought in to break up
the crowds, but they only fueled the battle as their brutal tactics provoked
more anger and violence. As the fracas spread, a full-scale riot broke out,
resulting in widespread looting and the burning of vehicles. One young
boy told Africa Watch that the security forces had appeared completely
unrestrained:

> The police were terrible. Maybe ten would suddenly
> manage to corner a group of young boys, shooting at
> them as they ran, and then they would beat them to the
> ground and continue beating them until they were
> useless. They had covered trucks where they threw in the

injured and dead. I saw a group of GSU corner some young boys who had been throwing rocks. One—I remember him because he had a white t-shirt on and his hair was all rough and he was covered in dirt—fell on the ground because I think he had a bullet in his leg. I remember him because four or five piled on to him, beating him with their sticks and guns while the others chased the rest of them. I remember them dragging him to the truck and I could see his t-shirt was red. But those boys got beaten so badly. Then picked up and thrown in the back of the police truck. Then the police beat them worse in the back of the truck. I think some of the injured must have died from the beating.

Looting and theft occurred in Nairobi, where some of the urban poor and young men used the demonstrations as an opportunity to steal from cars and shops. Looting was not a feature in demonstrations outside the capital. Kenyatta Hospital confirmed dozens injured by bullet wounds, as well as serious casualties from beatings and road accidents. An eyewitness provided Africa Watch with the following account:

At first, the strike by the matatu drivers was organized very well—they paralyzed public transport. They knew they had the power to paralyze the city and they did it because they wanted to force the release of the detainees, namely Matiba and Rubia. They were in the best position because security are not in any position to provide transport for the public. They can't provide an alternative, and they certainly can't force the matatu drivers to drive. We were very happy because pressure was brought to bear by people who can't be pinned down.

But then it fell into the hands of groups of youths, who mounted roadblocks and were asking for money, stoning the cars and threatening people. At first, the roadblocks were well organized and there wasn't a lot of property destroyed. It wasn't the matatu drivers who organized the planned roadblocks—they had been organized in an underground fashion. When the security forces and youth took over, that's when it got out of control.

Residents said a lot of people stayed at home, and were unable to get from one district to another. Cars whose drivers were going against the boycott were burned and destroyed. At the police roadblocks, most of the regular police were said to have shot in the air—and in some areas, it was said that the police actually expressed sympathy with the crowd. Residents recalled incidents of police persuading people to go home and even flashing a two-finger sign. In Wangiga, there were stories of an army truck passing through and soldiers flashing a two-finger sign. Town residents say that although the army was not officially brought out during the disturbances, they were in evidence.[2]

There were widespread reports of rape by GSU and riot police in some of the poor suburbs—particularly in Dandora and Ndenderu—although there are no reliable figures because, at the time, confirmation of such casualties was not sought from hospitals. President Moi, who was forced to return early from an Organization of African Unity meeting in Addis Ababa, instructed security forces to use "all necessary force" to restore order.[3] Heavy gunfire was reported in some parts of the city, including incidents where paramilitary units fired into crowds and shot at individuals. Reports that bodies were left lying in the street by security forces were confirmed in at least two cases.[4]

A news blackout by the Kenya Broadcasting Corporation (KBC) meant most towns and villages outside Nairobi were unaware of the demonstration and riots until the following day. Nevertheless, three days

---

[2] General Mahmoud Mohamed pledged the support of the military to President Moi when he was forced to return from the conference of the Organization for African Unity in Addis Ababa.

[3] A "Shoot-to-Kill" policy was not introduced for the occasion as was mistakenly reported, for such a policy was already in operation in parts of Kenya. See chapter seventeen.

[4] "Riots spread across Kenya," *The Guardian*, July 10, 1990. The article mentions a "victim's body lay sprawled across a road throughout the morning" in a Nairobi "low-income neighborhood." Another body was left for more than twelve hours in Kiambu town, near Nairobi.

after the initial demonstration at Kamukunji, open unrest had spread to at least six towns in central Kenya, including Kisumu, the provincial capital of Nyanza, and repercussions were being felt in a number of north western towns. In the central provinces, paramilitary forces put down demonstrations in Nyeri, Naivasha, Muranga, Limuru and Kiambu. There were also demonstrations in Nakuru, Rift Valley Province. Hundreds of people were arrested on charges of "disturbing the peace" and "rioting."

OVER 1,000 CHARGED

One thousand and fifty-six people were reported in the national press as having been charged with "riot-related" offenses. The majority did not have any recourse to legal representation, and a number of those charged appeared in court with "visible injuries."[5] Many were remanded in custody when the state prosecution objected to bail, others were granted bail of 10,000 shillings ($385). Sentences ranged between three months and two years' imprisonment. Umbrella charges of creating a disturbance included shouting and calling for the release of Matiba and Rubia; demanding a two-party political system in Kenya; driving matatus in convoy and flashing lights; stoning police and motorists; looting; and flashing the two-finger salute.

In Nairobi, offenses were said to have been carried out primarily in poor suburbs, specifically Juja Road, Mathare, Kawangware, Shauri Moyo, the Burma Market, Dandora, Kangemi, Pumwani, Eastleigh, Kariobangi North and Kamukunji. The following is a sampling of the total number of cases that appeared before the Kenyan courts.

Nairobi Courts
Five hundred and eleven defendants appeared before Chief Magistrate Omondi Tunya, on July 10. The majority pleaded guilty to charges of looting and were jailed for four months without the option of a fine. Very few, if any, had legal representation. Others who were found guilty were fined between 1,000 and 2,000 shillings ($38 and $76 respectively) or three months in jail in default.

Those who denied the charges were remanded in custody until October 3 and 4, and denied bail on the basis of objection by the

---

5 *Daily Nation*, July 11, 1990.

prosecution. Under the Kenyan system, to be remanded in custody for three months was a harsh option compared to pleading guilty. Once in custody, suspects can wait years for their cases to come up and, in the meantime, suffer notoriously dehumanizing conditions, with only a routine mention in court every two weeks.

Makadara Courts

Sixty-three people appeared on riot-related charges. Most denied charges that they participated in the weekend riots by throwing stones at motor vehicles and police and shouting for the release of detainees. They were charged with "creating a disturbance by singing and shouting in Nairobi streets to the effect that they wanted two parties and the release of Mr. Matiba and Mr. Rubia." All the prosecutors in the Makadara courts objected to bail "owing to the circumstances in which the accused were arrested and the present atmosphere within the city, it would be unsafe to release them."[6]

Kibera Court, Nairobi

Nine people were charged with riot-related offenses. They denied the charges and were released on 10,000 shillings ($385) bail with sureties.

Nyeri Court

Fifty people, described as workers, students, businessmen and "touts" were charged with throwing stones. All denied the charge and were remanded in custody.

DEATH COUNT

Officially, the government admitted to twenty deaths; in reality, there were certainly more. Journalists who went into the streets during the riots were intimidated by security forces in order to inhibit media coverage. The national press failed to report full details of the action taken against the public by the security forces because of fear of recrimination (see chapter twelve).

---

[6] Ibid.

The majority of foreign correspondents were absent, either attending the Organization of African Unity conference in Ethiopia, or having already retreated to areas of the city that stayed calm. The few who reported the riots were restricted by fear of attack and, in some cases, were physically abused by security forces. Members of the national and international press were manhandled, beaten and some had equipment, notebooks and cameras confiscated. Local journalists were severely beaten, and five international correspondents were held by police for a few hours; one was beaten on the head, and another detained for twenty-four hours.

As a result, there was no detailed information on the killings and abuse by the security forces, particularly in the poorest suburbs and outside the capital. There was, in fact, no coverage of events in other affected towns outside the Nairobi area apart from scant details in the national press about some of the main towns in Central Province. Journalists who kept a daily tally of deaths and serious injuries in the Nairobi area alone assert, however, that the government figure of twenty deaths is impossible by even the most conservative estimate.

The following killings occurred between July 8-10 as reported in the national and international press:

- Two people shot by GSU at Muthurwa canteen, Landhies Road.
- One man killed in Kawangware residential area by security forces when a bus was set on fire.
- One man died after being beaten on the head by riot police.
- One 7-year-old schoolboy was shot by security forces at Ndenderu, Kiambu.
- Two people shot by security forces in center of Kiambu town, near post office.
- Two people shot by police while "trying to hijack a petrol tanker" at Rungiri Trading Center, Kikuyu district. They were named as 20-year-old Stephen Ndungu and Cobbler Njoroge.
- One man found shot dead at Kawangware bus terminus.
- Three shot dead by police in Muranga while "trying to steal a car."
- One man shot dead in Nakuru.

On July 10, Hezekiah Oyugi, Permanent Secretary in Charge of Internal Security, Office of the President, announced that there were fifteen deaths and seventy-three seriously injured people, including six policemen. On the same day, two more deaths were confirmed in Kiambu, and Oyugi announced that three people in Muranga were killed when "trying to steal a car." There the official tally halted as the government denounced "hooligans and drug addicts" as responsible for the unrest, and directed KANU youthwingers to seek out those calling for multiparty politics. The commissioner of police was authorized to "use the force at his disposal" and called on members of the public to "fully co-operate."

In Nairobi, four days after the riots began, armed patrols toured the city as normal business slowly resumed. Heavily armed police continued to post roadblocks on the road to Kiambu, where some of the heaviest casualties had been reported, and new roadblocks were established on a number of roads on the outskirts of the capital.

KILLINGS IN KIAMBU

The town of Kiambu, about fifteen kilometers north of central Nairobi, suffered particularly brutal reprisals by the security forces. A central town in the troubled tea and coffee growing area and Kenyatta's former home district and power base, Kiambu is perceived by President Moi's government as a malcontented "Kikuyu stronghold." The Kiambu KANU office was burnt during the demonstrations. The most affected area in Kiambu District was Githunguri, home of former Vice-President Josephat Karanja, now represented in parliament by Arthur Magugu, minister of commerce. Before the demonstrations, Magugu demanded that all Kenyatta portraits be moved out of sight in homes and offices.

Kiambu residents said they felt the town had been singled out by security forces, who shot directly at groups of youths—including children—in the surrounding plantations and at crowds and individuals in the town itself. Africa Watch was told by independent sources on three separate occasions that thirty-seven people had been killed in Kiambu.

According to locals, shooting atrocities were committed by police and GSU who were brought in from other districts. Some residents also told Africa Watch that local personalities regarded as "corrupt and power-hungry" took part in the killings. They related, for example, how in Kamandora, on the main road in the Rift Valley going west, a CID officer was stopped at an impromptu roadblock. Money was taken from him. Armed with a gun, he pursued the young people who had demanded the money. Eyewitnesses described how he chased them and was "flashing his gun around." He went on to Kamandora where he was confronted with fresh demands for money, had his watch stolen and was forced to do a two-finger salute. As a result, he "went crazy" and shot dead one of the young men.

At Ndumberi also, there were reports of people shot dead by security forces. One man was apparently shot as he was leaving his home, and later died. The body of a Catholic man, shot in the forehead, was left in Ndumberi town until the next day: some of the residents said the police left the body as a warning. As the dead man's relatives lived outside the town, his body remained on the ground as no one dared move it for fear of reprisals. Friends and relatives of those shot in the streets said they were too scared to move the bodies, which were eventually taken away in the vehicles of the security forces.

People wounded by security forces were afraid to go to the hospital in case they were arrested—those who could, went to private hospitals. In Nairobi, one taxi driver described how he took a man with bullet wounds from Dandora suburb to Kenyatta hospital. At the hospital he was urged by the staff to leave quickly because police guarding the ward were "taking charge of the bodies."

Some of the injured refrained from seeking hospital attention for fear of arrest. Others who were taken to Kiambu hospital left as soon as possible, fearing they would be arrested by police. In the hospital, some patients were handcuffed to their beds or otherwise abused by the police. People who went to visit the wounded in hospital say there were as many as twenty who had been admitted to the men's ward. All were suffering from gunshot wounds; most had been shot in the legs, some in the shoulder and face, some in the stomach. One woman had half her face disfigured by a bullet wound, and was taken for treatment to Nairobi. In Kiambu, one woman member of the local KANU committee was shot in the thigh; in another case, a man was shot through the windpipe and was unable to speak. Apparently many people took their injured to Nairobi, or, if they had the resources, moved them from the government hospitals, fearing they may be arrested. A tradesman described how he decided to go home to Muranga once the riots started in Kiambu:

> I was going down the valley, across through the stream
> and found a lot of police in the coffee plantation. They

shot me in the leg without giving any warning or reason, without even stopping me or questioning me. It was the police who took me to the hospital because they wanted to charge me with rioting. I found a friend of mine there, a boy of about fourteen, who was shot in the shoulder and the boy told me that he actually had nothing to do with the rioting but was just shot by the police. He said he had come to visit his sister and got drawn into the crowd and he heard a shot—and he found out that he had been shot by them.

At Githiga school, Githunguri Division, three children, including the son of a clergyman, were reportedly killed. Later, only the death of the clergyman's son was confirmed.

Police guarded the hospital wards, and two armed officers stood outside the hospital entrance. Visitors and inmates of the hospital say pressure was put on the doctors by police to immediately discharge the patients so they could bring charges against them. Newspaper reports that appeared days later said that the wounded would not be charged so as to avert more trouble breaking out, but in Kiambu, police were eager to bring charges against the injured.

On Wednesday and Thursday following *Saba Saba*,[7] police and GSU patrolled the roads in vehicles described as "heavy, covered vans and trucks." Africa Watch sources reported that Kiambu village appeared deserted. "We were all in the houses. All that everyone was aware of were these police vehicles and GSU trucks patrolling up and down the road with the barrels of their guns pointing out of the windows." Though our sources say that there was a widespread conviction that excessive force had been used and innocent people killed in callous reprisals by the security forces, it was considered futile, if not dangerous, to complain to the government. When Africa Watch raised the possibility of a complaint with residents, they dismissed the idea as absurd. People said they believed that the recent events could easily happen again.

---

[7] Saba Saba is Swahili for seven and refers to the riots that began on July 7, 1990.

Testimony (1) of a man wounded in Kiambu

On July 9, I was walking home past the shops when I saw a mob of people running. I avoided this crowd and walked straight down a back lane near one of the town bars. I went behind the bar and got between the walls of two shops—to take cover. Then I heard shots, and a blast in my knee—I don't know who shot me.

I was alone there. I heard a lot of shooting and was very afraid for my life. I managed to walk about 100 meters to a friend's house. The town was very wild then with shooting, so my friend locked me in his workshop to protect me. When it calmed down after about half an hour, I was taken to hospital in a vehicle by my friend.

I was astonished to see dead bodies at the hospital, on the floor. There were many injuries—one shot in the head, one in the chest, one in the abdomen—all men. They were lying on the floor of Casualty with the injured. I helped the doctor check out the ones not dead—we counted twenty-eight dead. There were no police at that time. I stayed for about fifteen minutes selecting the live ones—some wounded in the legs, some in the chest and head. Most were men, but there were four children and two women as well. We know some later died of injuries and we know some got transferred to Nairobi.

The police came to the ward after four days. Then there were always three of four of them on shift, keeping guard as well as Special Branch. They handcuffed me by my left wrist to the bed. They told me they were handcuffing me so that we could be properly treated.

It was very, very bad. Having a bullet wound you must keep turning all the time, but handcuffed you can't move properly or sleep properly. It's like being in a jail.

I stayed in the hospital for one month. I was handcuffed for three weeks. The police were always there. One in particular got very harsh and violent, taking my cigarette by force from me. I abused him for it then, shouting "is it the hospital authorities doing this?" A surgical officer came and told the police not to interfere with the patients, and he went to the police station to ask that the police stop it. Those police were shifted. I know the doctors were getting worried because the police also refused to let us have any sort of exercise as part of our treatment.

When I was discharged, by the medical officers, the police took me from the hospital to the police station. We were cheated—we were told to wait for the OCS [Officer in charge of the Station]. We waited, and then we were made to sleep in the cells that night. The cell was really overcrowded, and I ate nothing and had no blanket. I was in a lot of pain.

In the morning I was taken to court after fingerprinting me. I was charged and remanded. In court I was given no chance to explain. I pleaded not guilty. Of course I had no lawyer—my income can't allow that. I was given bond of 5,000 shillings [$192] which my friends managed to raise.

When I went back for the hearing, the OCPD [Officer in Charge of the Police Division], the Senior Superintendant of police, and the OCS were there as witnesses. They told the court I was manning a roadblock, creating a disturbance, throwing stones and shooting. Then, in court, they changed their minds on the shooting charge, saying instead they shot at me when I started throwing stones. I asked them questions they couldn't answer, and the magistrate eventually dismissed the case.

Testimony (2) of man wounded in Kiambu

I was coming home from work—it was about 4:30 in the afternoon—and I called into the petrol station. There were a lot of AP [Administration Police] around. I saw a person on the ground who had been shot dead, and I bent down to look to see who it was. I just looked at him, and when I stood up I was shot, through my neck. I know it was an AP because they were the ones shooting. They made no attempt to assist me, but I was taken almost immediately to hospital by another person.

I only saw one dead person in the street, but in the hospital I saw others. The dead and injured were all lying together on the floor of Casualty.

The police came four days later and took the names of us, the ones who had been shot. They weren't really violent but their expression was not good. They threatened to charge us with creating a disturbance and rioting. I was in hospital from July 9 to the 20th. Some people were handcuffed to the bed for up to three weeks while they got treatment, but I wasn't—I had been shot badly and the doctors were very concerned. But they [police] guarded the beds and wards day and night. Even the entrance of the hospital.

On July 20, I was sent to Kenyatta by hospital transfer. I was brought back to hospital here on the same day, but I ran away when the other patients told me the police were bringing charges—I know what they're like. I've stayed with relatives since—outside the town. Sometimes I go to Kenyatta for treatment.

KIKUYU PLOT RHETORIC

The Kikuyu-dominated central provinces, which appeared to be a focus for discontent during July, have been one of the worst-hit areas economically, suffering acute land shortages, population growth and unemployment. Many tea and coffee farmers have suffered a loss of livelihood as a result of government corruption and mismanagement of the state-operated boards. Unrest is also attributed to Kikuyu bitterness over their progressive loss of political and economic power under

President Moi, who has increasingly used anti-Kikuyu rhetoric publicly and privately.

The details Africa Watch obtained on repression in the central provinces did not, however, differ significantly from accounts nationwide—apart from the peculiarity of the Kikuyu plot allegations made by the security apparatus. The following testimony is a typical reflection of police behavior during Saba Saba, but also illustrates how the security forces took advantage of the Kikuyu plot rhetoric. The following is from a woman who was an active member of KANU before July:

> I was at home on the 9th and I was going out to get the children back from outside because of the sounds of bullets, but about three steps from my door I was shot. I didn't see the ones who were shooting. The first bullet went into my leg and came out of my thigh, another in my other thigh remained. I fell on the ground. It was about 5:30 P.M. I was taken into my house by the children but I could not get anywhere because of the police officers patrolling. I wasn't taken to hospital until about 7:00 P.M. The children were crying—they didn't know what to do. The landlord was the one who helped us and took me to hospital. When the police stopped shooting, I sent one of the children to the landlord's house and he came with a vehicle.

> I met a lot of people who had been shot in the casualty ward. Some were dead. When I left the casualty ward there were about ten people on the ground who were dead. I was taken to the X-ray department and then transferred to a ward. In the ward there were three injured women, one girl nine years old shot on the 10th in the leg. Another woman had her jaw shot off.

> The police came the following day at 6:00 in the morning. They asked me why I was throwing stones, I said I never threw stones. They took our names and said they would bring charges. I was so angry because I was shot for nothing and now charged. I thought that I would just get treatment and then go home. I had to stay in

hospital for two weeks. The police were always near to the bed. They kept telling us that we could leave hospital and then we would be taken to court.

After two weeks I was dismissed from hospital at about 10:00 A.M. but then I refused to go home because I was frightened to go. I hung around until about 4:00 P.M. The police were so angry and became very harsh and they wanted me to go on my way. They were even following me to the toilet and they asked me why I didn't go home, but I made up a story and said my children had not come, they didn't have my things. They told me instead to go to the police station.

At 4:00 P.M. my son did come. He paid the bill and so we went to the police station together. I was taken to CID and there they started telling me that I was manning a roadblock and stoning police, and that I was a multiparty supporter. I said "no" and they started beating me. They were slapping my face and I fell down: they kicked my body and stomped on me. I was told to sign a statement that they had written. The statement included a confession that I wanted to overthrow the government but I refused. When I stood up and refused to sign, they said I wanted to overthrow the government so the Kikuyu could rule again.

One of the officers opened a drawer and took out a whip. He beat me on my back and shoulders, but I still refused to sign. At that time I was upstairs, then I was taken down into the cells. I stayed in the cells for about two hours.

After two hours I was removed to another CID office. There I was told to write a statement on how I was shot. The officer commanding CID said I should be locked up in the cells, but I demanded to see the OCPD [Officer in Charge of the Police Division]. When he came he asked me if I had 5,000 shillings [$192] but I said I had nothing. Then he said if I had 1,000 shillings [$38], I could go. I had 1,000 and I gave it to them. I was told to go and report to them on Monday morning. This was on Friday.

I didn't go on Monday morning because I told them that my legs were still not all right so they said all right, leave it for two weeks. After two weeks I went to the station, but the OCPD was not there so I went home. After about three weeks I returned and again asked for the OCPD. I was angry and told the OCPD that if I was not going to be taken to court I needed a refund of my money and I got it back. When I got the money I told them that I wasn't going to go back until I was called, and I have never been called back.

Now every time the party writes to ask me to attend meetings in my official position, I just don't attend and I don't answer.

One woman told Africa Watch she saw a group of girls brought to the hospital after they had been raped by GSU soldiers:[8]

During the time that I was in the hospital I know that there were women who had been raped. Several girls from Gitwe Secondary School were brought to be checked. There were six girls between the ages of 14 and 17. The doctor refused and said they should be taken elsewhere. He was frightened because they were brought by a government vehicle. The raping was done by the GSU but the girls were brought by the police. We knew their intention was not genuine. One girl was trying to tell her story to the sister in charge, but the others were all silent. When we heard on the ward that the girls had been brought, I went to see them. The sister-in-charge was talking to them and she was asking them what

---

[8] Despite many references to rape by the security forces, Africa Watch was unable to collect accounts from the victims themselves because of the shame and humiliation associated with rape.

happened. One girl said that the GSU had found the girls in the classroom. When they knew that the GSU were coming, most had run, but those who remained in the classrooms hiding under the desks were raped, while the others had run away.

The four police soon drove them off in their vehicle—we don't know what happened to them, we don't know where they went. We do know the president went to the school and said they were raped by hooligans and drug-addicts.

SABA SABA IN NAKURU

Three months after Saba Saba, Nakuru was still suffering the aftermath of a major security crackdown. After 7:00 or 8:00 P.M., the town was subdued, with many streets almost deserted apart from patrolling armed police with police dogs. Additional roadblocks erected during July remained and the atmosphere was one of suspicion and fear. Nakuru is considered politically volatile—which is most frequently attributed to the fact that it was the country home of Kenyatta and now of President Moi. During the Saba Saba period, President Moi's Nakuru residence was broken into by armed men. The town has also been directly or indirectly targeted by the government as a Kikuyu center of subversion—it was the home of many Kikuyu squatters, but has members of many other main ethnic groups, including the Kalenjin. The constituency has been contested by a number of politicians who subsequently became security prisoners or exiles,[9] and a disproportionate number of MwaKenya charges were levelled in the region.

Anonymous, reliable sources said "dozens" of people had been shot dead during the riots and demonstrations. At the hospital, there were reports of security personnel removing dead bodies from the wards and the streets in covered trucks late in the evening. However, Africa Watch has been unable to confirm or accurately estimate numbers shot dead by the security forces in Nakuru.

---

[9] Koige wa Wamwere, Mirugi Kariuki and Rumba Kinuthia.

After the riots, over 700 people were arrested—nearly all were teenagers. They included an 11-year-old schoolgirl from Standard Five who was remanded to Nakuru prison for three weeks before lawyers were allowed access. The girl was not released until her lawyers could produce a letter from the headmaster to show the court she was still in school. The magistrate's court granted her free bond, but did not drop the charge. Her case was still pending at the time this report was written.

During the weeks following the disturbances, many people were brought to court at around 8:00 P.M. According to the legal community, magistrates were called from their homes every evening and sat until midnight in sessions which were riddled with irregularities. Most of those charged had no legal advice or representation, and the effect of conducting business outside normal court hours meant, according to one lawyer, that "those people had absolutely no way out. Even if they had lawyers to act for them, they were unable to reach them during such hours." The majority were charged with "taking part in illegal demonstrations"; some pleaded guilty and were jailed for more than a year.

Of those who did get legal representation, a number were released on bond after two to three months in remand when their lawyers successfully argued that there was no consent of trial from the attorney general. In Kenya, consent from the attorney general is necessary before charges connected with political activities can proceed to trial, but no consent was ever received for those convicted immediately after the demonstrations and riots. Many teenage boys were thus illegally jailed on guilty pleas after they were tried at night without the necessary consent of the attorney general. According to one lawyer: "The legality of those convictions is very questionable. There should be no trial without consent; yet those people now already jailed—most are young teenagers."

According to testimonies given to Africa Watch, the security forces specifically targeted young adults. There were consistent reports of rape and abuse of women. Young men were pursued into their houses, beaten and arrested. One young student, who had just arrived home from the university, said he became a victim of the riots:

> I had arrived back in Nakuru on June 30 and on the day of the demonstrations I went into town to see what was happening because everyone was saying that the workers were demonstrating, they were marching in town. It is just unheard of, things like that, so many people went to

watch. I was with a group of bystanders—mainly
women—and we met the demonstrators coming. Then
the GSU fired gas canisters. Of course there was chaos,
complete chaos. Demonstrators and bystanders all mixed
up, and they were picking out anyone they could get
hold of. We fled back to our houses. I had been resting
for some hours before they came to the house. They had
followed people back to make sure no one was
meeting—that's how they diffuse it. They [GSU] were
going from house to house, pulling out the men. They
pulled me out of the house and we all had to sit on the
ground. Then they harass you—they slap you on the face
or kick you; if they have sticks they use them or rifle
butts—just to frighten you—and they asked us what we
were demonstrating for. I was beaten and slapped
around, then we went back to our houses.

According to another young man, the violence used by the
security forces has had a lasting effect in the town:

Since July the police have been really tough—especially
in State House area. Nobody in their right mind walks
that area at night. I have been stopped several times in
the early evening by police, and I've been beaten. A
friend of mine was beaten on the elbows with a
rifle—that's how the police do it, on your elbows and
knees.

Now the shops close at 6:30 P.M. and people are going
home by 7:00 P.M. By 8:00 P.M. you shouldn't be on the
streets. You know we have a sort of curfew now. And
everybody knows you shouldn't be around by about 8.30
so if the police catch you they say you are asking for
trouble and ask why you are not at home.

Women say they have suffered another sort of abuse by the
security forces:

I was with a friend when we got stopped. They asked us
what we were doing and my friend got angry, so they

said we were under arrest. We were told we must come
with them. This was about 9:00 P.M.—they made us walk
with them until after midnight. We just had to walk a few
steps behind them and we weren't allowed to say
anything. If we did, they hit you and abuse you. But I
found it very interesting because I found out what they
do all night—they look for women and try and make
them do what they want. We ended up five of us, three
women included, having to walk with them until after
midnight. Finally they told us all to go and kept one
woman with them. They told her she was a prostitute
and would end up in jail after she had been kept at the
station. That girl wasn't a prostitute.

The informal curfew in Nakuru was still evident some three
months after July. Attempts to identify the number of dead appeared to
be floundering in an atmosphere of intense fear and suspicion, despite
evident outrage that the government acknowledged only one death in
Nakuru. Testimony from residents makes it clear that it is widely believed
that many more died.

During the time of the riots it was terrible for the young
men because they were being picked out of the houses
and beaten badly. One young man died after his kidneys
were damaged by a rifle butt. Some people were shot
dead, but more died later from beatings.

The police and GSU were harassing everyone—even the
women. They made swoops on the estates. I was staying
in Lakeview estate and the GSU came and pulled out all
the students and beat them. For nearly a week you
couldn't walk on the streets. If you came out of your
house they could accuse you of being a demonstrator.
They would ask you why you were out, and not at home.

We don't know how many people died—I know one boy
on my estate was beaten very badly because we heard
him screaming, but I don't know what became of him.

KISUMU

There were demonstrations and riots in Kisumu and a number of injured people were admitted to the main hospital. A professional living in Kisumu said he believed the demonstrations there—which were smaller-scale than in Nairobi and Nakuru—were principally taken up because of the very large number of unemployed youths present in the town.

> ...in Kisumu the unemployed come in from the slum areas every day to town and try and make some money selling things. You couldn't strictly call them hawkers because many of them are students and young people looking for jobs. We call them "street youths"—there are so many these days and they have nothing to lose. These youths have no reason *not* to demonstrate. You could say they lost what little they had in July—most of them ended up in our jails for a few months.

NATIONWIDE INFORMATION BLACKOUT

Reports of a number of incidents in different parts of the country indicate there was an effective news blackout as the security forces used "whatever force necessary" to put down unrest. In Kapenguria prison, northern Kenya, prisoners rioted and briefly took over the criminal section. According to an eyewitness account, prisoners from the criminal section managed to physically overcome prison officers. Police were called in to contain the riot and assist prison officers while order was re-established. One of the police called in to the prison said extra security was needed for one week:

> The leaders of the riot were longterm criminals who took over. They said we should either release them or shoot them, because they have been there for so long without seeing even the light of day—they said they were being treated like animals. They said the prison officers didn't treat them like human beings and they would rather be dead than go on like that.

When the prison officers took control again, those prisoners were beaten terribly for rioting. They were beaten terribly on their knees so they could hardly move. They have had extra years put on their sentence now. Kapenguria [prison] is the worst place you can imagine; it makes Kamiti [maximum security prison, Nairobi] look like a hotel.

According to this person, there are also political prisoners held at Kapenguria in appalling conditions.

On around July 8 or 9 in Eldoret, north western Kenya, soldiers took keys for the armory in what was said to be an attempted mutiny. A number of soldiers and officers were arrested and, according to members of the legal community, will be court-martialed without any opportunity to get legal advice or representation. Members of the legal community say they are extremely concerned about the fate of these men as the incident was not reported, and has never been acknowledged by the government.

5
SECURITY FORCES

In Kenya, the fear and distrust inspired by the security forces is demonstrated by the regularity with which people assume that suspects are victims, evidence is fabricated and trials are showcases. Few Kenyans believe that either the legal machinery or the security apparatus function fairly or justly.

The police often refuse bail in an attempt to detain suspects without charge for prolonged periods. In sedition cases, for example, police frequently rely on the excuse that "prosecution documents are not yet ready from the attorney general's office." More often, the prosecution ask the court to allow them additional time to prepare their case on the grounds that investigations "are not yet complete" and "may lead to more serious charges."[1] Defendants held in these circumstances are regularly pressured to sign confessions; some have been tortured.

By relying on intimidation and violence, the various branches of the security forces have systematically abused the law and shown a cavalier disregard for the constitution. Physical and psychological abuse by the security forces are routine; beatings in police custody are the order of the day.

THE SPECIAL BRANCH

The Special Branch was formed by the British colonial government to deal with matters of intelligence. During the colonial period, it was commanded by active or retired British police officers and employed colonial officers from Commonwealth countries. It relied on an extensive network of informers. At independence, the new government did nothing to change the role of the Special Branch but enhanced its status from state security to presidential security.

The Special Branch is theoretically led by the Commissioner of Police, but, with its considerable growth of power and influence since

---

[1] Known as the "holding charge." It is illegal because it means the police do not have enough evidence to prosecute.

1985, is effectively autonomous and answers directly to the Office of the President.

The Special Branch is essentially a secret service of the state vested with the duty of keeping watch on potentially subversive or illegal movements; but its concept of state security matters has proved to encompass every aspect of normal social life. The constant weight of suspicion on the population is evident—sensitive conversations are frequently accompanied by glances over the shoulder and lowered voices. The most mundane topics are studiously avoided for fear they could be construed as politically critical. The Special Branch depends heavily on informers, some of whom regularly report to a local office, others who are given a nominal fee for specific information. This creates widespread insecurity and mistrust within the community, and effectively allows the Special Branch to police minds far beyond its real capacity or its real purpose. According to a member of the security forces who spoke anonymously to Africa Watch:

> Special branch and [Criminal Investigation Department] CID officers are paid to keep secret files or secret documents; information that can later be used to intimidate you, to harass you, is compiled on you. This started during the Njonjo tenure as attorney general—he became Kenya's J. Edgar Hoover. He, in fact, revolutionized the system of intelligence in Kenya. He made it more competitive, more aggressive, made it more corrupt. Njonjo institutionalized the act of corruption within the police force.

Plainclothes Special Branch officers infiltrate the community in a similar way to plainclothes CID officers, but are reputedly more treacherous in their desire to lure a person into demonstrating a critical stance. The Special Branch has used systematic torture to force guilty pleas from the individuals it targets, after detaining them for long periods incommunicado in cells at their Nairobi headquarters, Nyayo House. There is no legal provision for access to the Special Branch cells. The International Committee of the Red Cross (ICRC), which currently visits security detainees in forty-two countries around the world, has no access to detainees in Kenya. The Nyayo House basement, the 24th, 25th and 26th floors, are listed as protected areas.

Special Branch officers need not be appointed from the police force or have police training, but the majority are police officers. Special Branch officers are trained at a center in Nairobi South C, and many go for further training in Israel. Unlike CID, Special Branch officers are expected to be skilled academically as well as competent police officers and marksmen. Headed by a more senior person than any in the CID, the Special Branch assumes priority and superiority over all cases. According to detailed information provided Africa Watch, this has led to mounting tension between the two forces, with resentment in the CID over the fact that Special Branch frequently carries out operations without consulting them. The Special Branch has increasingly taken over cases which should normally be handled by CID. This testimony given to Africa Watch indicates how the command structure works:

> Most of the orders are verbal. Your boss gives you an order which he has received from the Office of the President. These orders are rarely written down and don't you dare ask for it to be written down. One day everybody wants to say he did not know anything about it.

> It's hard to trace exactly where the orders come from. All you know is that it came from the Kitchen Cabinet, consisting of Moi, Biwott, minister Professor Samson Ongeri, Joseph arap Letting [head of civil service], Hezekiah Oyugi [head of internal security and public administration] and Mulu Mutisuya [powerful, nominated M.P. from Machakos] and Kip'Ngeny arap Ngeny [managing director of Kenya Post and Telecommunications].[2] These people are the policymakers who rule Kenya. They are Moi's closest advisers and also some of the richest men in the country. They are the people who have the power to invoke the president's name to get people arrested and get whatever they want. That might be anything from government

---

[2] Telecommunications has important links with the security forces; for instance, telecommunications vans are used at night as security vehicles to collect detainees and suspects.

tenders, to ensuring that government projects are carried
out in their areas as a priority. Anything they want, they
get, not in 24 hours after they pick up the phone, but in
an hour. You have no choice but to do their bidding,
because if you hesitate, they interpret your reluctance as
anti-Nyayo and anti-president.

Special Branch activities outside Kenya are not, in most cases,
aimed at foreign nationals of the host country but at Kenyan residents
abroad. The Kenyan government made it a priority to monitor the
activities of Kenyan students abroad after MwaKenya was said to be
recruiting them as well as businessmen and women in Europe. Well-
placed sources have informed Africa Watch that as many as one out of
every ten Kenyans who goes abroad is either an active member of the
Special Branch or a paid informant who actively involves himself or
herself in the various activities that Kenyans may undertake abroad, from
social events to academic studies. These people gather information, which
is then relayed to the Kenyan embassy and the information is passed to
officers in Nairobi.

PASSPORT CONTROL AND IMMIGRATION

Immigration has become one of the most important means of
policing movement. This has been summed up for Africa Watch by a
member of the security network working with that department:

Immigration is one of the most powerful tools used to
subvert someone's liberties—and one of the most corrupt.
In immigration, files disappear, applications for travel
documents disappear, passports, visas, extensions of
passes [disappear]...immigration is the worst known
offender for accepting bribes. Sometimes a normal bribe
for a visitor's passport or visa is 10,000 shillings [$385],
sometimes 20,000 [$769] depending on what class, what
permit you are looking for.

According to information provided Africa Watch, members of the
Special Branch "on two payrolls—the government and influential
businessmen and politicians" use the senior assistant principal

immigration officer for revoking and denying permits, particularly those of competitors or, in the case of the government, of foreign journalists.

The confiscation and denial of passports for government critics is routine. Applications for passports undergo a process of government investigation before being issued. The applicant is investigated by the Special Branch and the CID to "determine loyalty to the government."[3] If the passport is cleared by both security departments, it may be issued. A passport is seen as a privilege and not a right.

CRIMINAL INVESTIGATION DEPARTMENT (CID)

The Criminal Investigation Department has its headquarters in Nyati House, Nairobi. Much of the work done by CID is similar to that of the Special Branch. Their standing orders are not publicly available.

The CID primarily investigates nonpolitical crimes, but they have a mandate to investigate political crimes as well. The latter crimes are now almost completely monopolized by the Special Branch, whose powers have superseded those of the CID in the last five or six years. Earlier, the CID was the more powerful and feared of the two, and merely backed up by Special Branch. The CID, however, now has the reputation of being the most corrupt section of the security forces. An anonymous member of the security forces provided Africa Watch with the following testimony:

> CID officers are the most corrupt. CID officers who come into contact regularly—every minute—with the public are the worst. They come into contact with everyone, from politicians, to businessmen, to church leaders, to lawyers, to court officers and criminal elements. People have been known to bribe CID officers to misplace particular files that are supposed to be appearing in court, or for investigation files to go missing. It was considered normal, for example, when the Kiambu resident magistrate ordered the officer commanding the police station to have his men empty a pit latrine which had been the dumping ground for files for over two years.

---

[3] Anonymous testimony from security official.

CID personnel are drawn from the regular police force and given special training at their school in Nairobi's South C area. It runs fingerprint bureaus at district, provincial and national levels, as well as a National Forensic Laboratory in Nairobi. Further training for CID officers is largely academic, in specialized fields such as forensic science and fingerprinting—unlike the Special Branch where advanced training is both academic and practical.

The size of the CID is unknown. It recruits many police officers, and, according to information passed to Africa Watch, its numbers have increased rapidly because of the growing political crisis in the country. It has been suggested that it at least doubled in size over the last three years. Plainclothes CID officers are stationed throughout the large towns, where they infiltrate clubs, bars, hotels and restaurants. They are also primarily responsible for the deaths in the towns and villages resulting from the shoot-to-kill policy (see chapter seventeen).

POLICE FORCE

The police force is one of the most formidable institutions in the hands of the government and the ruling party. Police brutality is commonplace; the number of incidents of torture reported indicates that it is frequently used against suspects held in police custody (see chapter six).

The activities and conduct of the police are regulated by the Police Act, Chapter 84 of the Laws of Kenya. Section 14 (1) of this Act states that:

> The police force shall be employed in Kenya for the maintenance of the law and order, the preservation of peace, the protection of life and property, the prevention and detection of crime, the apprehension of offenders, and the enforcement of all laws and regulations with which it is charged.

Recruits are sent to Kiganjo Police College, in Nyeri district. No qualifications are specified in the Police Act for recruits, and the size of the police force is at the sole discretion of the president. Training is physically gruelling. Recruits are given extensive lessons in physical combat, and receive assault and arms training. The commencement is usually officiated by the president, in his capacity as the commander in chief of the armed forces.

Competition is strong to join the police force as the pay is considered good in Kenya, and the opportunities for making money through corruption are excellent.[4] Corruption is endemic and as its reputation for corruption and violence grows, the police force has attracted an increasing number of recruits who aspire to profit from the corruption associated with the system. In an anonymous testimony given to Africa Watch by a member of the security forces, the extent of this corruption is detailed:

> Police officers are bribed by lawyers to get files out of court. Police have been bribed by lawyers in conjunction with court clerks in the high courts of Kenya, up to the district level, to manufacture evidence. The police prosecution branch has been known to collaborate with some lawyers in an unscrupulous way either to facilitate the sentencing of individuals or their release. It depends on the particular preference of the police prosecution boss involved, or the lawyer, and the amount of money changing hands.

There has been no real attempt by the government to discipline the force or take corrective action against known offenders, despite frequent complaints from all sections of society about corruption and violence in the police force. The police force is led by the police commissioner who is a personal appointee of the president.

THE POLICE RESERVE

The word "Force" in the Police Act refers to the Kenya Police Reserve as well as regular police officers. The Police Reserve "assist police

---

[4] However, Africa Watch spoke to one young officer who claimed he had been forced to join the police force by a relative who is a senior officer. He said he had made repeated attempts to leave, but was prevented because of threats from family members inside the police force. He claimed this was common in small, isolated villages.

officers in their duties," but there is no clear mandate as to what this assistance involves. According to well-placed sources, the Police Reserve are simply another section of the Special Branch.

Members of the Kenya Police Reserve are not required to be full-time police officers. Most are recruited from the civil service and are given special training at Karen School of Intelligence which is located in a wealthy suburb of Nairobi. They continue to work as civil servants. They are only employed during emergency periods, such as riots and demonstrations, national events and during political crackdowns. Until 1988, the Police Reserve was led by a British settler, Patrick Shaw, who was infamous for his ruthlessness and influence, and whose controversial death provoked rumors of assassination attempts and political conspiracies. His official workplace was the school in the Starehe Boys Center, a home for disadvantaged boys.

SPECIAL POLICE OFFICERS

Section 48 of the Police Act states that:

> The Commissioner may at any time, if it appears to him to be expedient in the interests of public order and safety so to do, appoint persons to be special police officers for such period and within such area as he may consider necessary, and every such officer shall, during the period of his service as a special police officer be deemed to be a police officer.

This provision allows the appointment of individuals for specific missions; otherwise, the same duties are covered by the Police Reserve. Information gathered by Africa Watch indicates that the role of a Special Police Officer is primarily one of agent provocateur, and of obtaining secret information in circumstances where members of the regular forces are unable to do so. These special officers are sometimes recruited from the civil service.

ADMINISTRATION POLICE (AP)

During the colonial period, the Administration Police were known as the Tribal Police (TP). Their role was to help the chiefs, who were set up to govern for the British colonial government. Tribal Police became Administration Police at independence, and developed a reputation for being the most brutal of the security forces. It is said that their excesses are worse than even those of the paramilitary GSU.

The AP are supposed to be distinguishable from the regular police force by their administrative role. They have become associated, however, with the most violent of duties, such as land evictions, riot and demonstration control, housing evictions and border patrols. The AP have been responsible for civilian deaths in a number of land and housing evictions (see chapter fourteen). They are also used at border posts, including for example, the Kenyan-Somali border which is usually policed by APs unless a crisis necessitates reinforcements from the armed forces. Border posts have provided APs with a lucrative source of money from refugees who are forced to pay to enter the country illegally.

Administration Police officers are also uniformed officers serving in government institutions as gatekeepers, reception watchers and house guards for government officials and members of parliament; they are usually armed with G3 rifles. At the district level, they guard administration figures: the provincial commissioners, the district commissioners and the district officers. They also serve the administration chiefs and have administrative posts in the villages.

The general powers and duties of the AP are identical to those of ordinary police officers in arrests. However, with the advent of the KANU youthwingers, who have taken on duties similar to those of the AP, the latter's role is becoming more and more obscure—especially in the remote rural areas. APs are increasingly associated with lawless duties connected with land disputes and the protection of local powerbrokers. The Administration Police Act vests authority in the president to determine the size of the force. Administration Police are led by a commandant.

THE GENERAL SERVICE UNIT (GSU)

The paramilitary wing of the police force, the GSU is well known for its violence and cruelty. Recently unleashed with devastating results on the pro-democracy demonstrations and riots in July 1990, the GSU is made up of rapid-deployment units mobilized whenever the government feels a situation is volatile or politically threatening. The GSU has frequently demonstrated its ruthlessness in riot and demonstration control. Its crowd control techniques rely principally on beating people to the ground with blows to the head and kidneys; frequently causing broken bones. Deaths have resulted from their firing directly into crowds. During the July 1990 demonstrations and riots, there were a number of reports of GSU officers raping women and schoolgirls.

During the colonial period, the GSU was called the Emergency Force. It continues its original colonial function as a section of the police force used in difficult areas and emergency situations. Provisions originally drawn up under the colonial government prevent the GSU from being deployed in the North Eastern Province, but this law is not respected in practice and the GSU is deployed everywhere.[5] During the riots following Ouko's death, GSU was flown to volatile areas. It was sent to Kisumu before the president arrived for the funeral, and later terrorized the town (see chapter two).

As an emergency force, the GSU is deployed to trouble spots such as the sites of border disputes, cattle raiding and local rivalries. They were used, for example, in the border disputes round the Elemi Triangle, on the Sudan border, where large numbers of cross-border communities are feared to have been killed as well as around Isiolo (see chapters fifteen and eighteen).

During former President Kenyatta's time, the GSU were the best trained and equipped force; they were given special training in Israel where they continue to receive instruction.

The GSU wears army camouflage uniforms, is equipped with weapons ranging from light machine guns to armored personnel carriers, and is headed by a commandant. Its headquarters are at Ruaraka. The training GSU officers receive is said to be modeled on the British Special Air Services SAS, commando-style for "anti-government and counterinsurgency operations." British training and assistance continues; currently one of the most senior GSU officer in Kenya is a British

---

[5] Emergency regulations provide that security forces can be mobilized to any part of the north eastern province and operate under the mandate of the emergency provisions. According to one former member of parliament in the north eastern province, this allows any security force "to act like the GSU."

expatriate. The GSU has provincial companies each comprising a platoon which is fully mobile and self-supporting.

STOCK THEFT UNIT

The Stock Theft Unit was formed specifically to deal with the problem of stock theft prevalent in northern Kenya, especially along the borders with Somalia, Ethiopia, Tanzania and Uganda. The unit was notorious during Kenyatta's rule for its violent commando-style methods in subduing rural and nomadic communities. Officers in the Stock Theft Unit are taken from the regular police force, and undergo training with the police.

The actions and role of the unit have been considerably modified since 1977, when the Ngoroko movement—formed from the Stock Theft Unit—terrorized the country. The Ngoroko acted as former President Kenyatta's personal mafia and reportedly were opposed to President Moi's succession. Moi's successful ascendancy was accompanied by a determination to contain the Ngoroko. What remains, though still forceful and violent in the more remote communities, is a substantial modification of the previous Stock Theft Unit.

Anti-Poaching Unit

The Anti-Poaching Unit is is a formation under the Stock Theft Unit. It comprises security personnel whose work is to protect the parks and the forests in Kenya from poaching, but, like the Stock Theft Unit, is associated more with violent and indiscriminate policing of nomadic and rural communities.

The Anti-Poaching Unit occupies an important role in a country which relies heavily on tourism for foreign currency earnings. Protection of game parks has received much international assistance, including arming the Anti-Poaching Unit with automatic weapons, helicopters and powerful spotlights. A shoot-to-kill policy has resulted in hundreds of suspected poachers being killed or injured, and with harsh penalties imposed on communities entering the parks for grazing purposes. With the shoot-to-kill policy, the Anti-Poaching Unit has been given a free hand in its brutal policing methods (see chapter seventeen). According to the security forces, however, many poachers, heavily armed with automatic weapons, are said to be shot in self-defense.

OTHER FORMATIONS IN THE POLICE FORCE

Prosecutions Branch is another section of the Police Force, which undertakes prosecutions in all subordinate courts. They undergo a course in criminal law, court practice and procedure at the CID training school in South C, Nairobi.

Traffic Branch is vested with the responsibility of traffic control and patrol, the investigation of accidents and traffic prosecutions. They are decentralized at district and provincial levels with their national headquarters at Nairobi. They are reputedly one of the most corrupt departments.

Dog Section comprises police officers with police sniffer dogs. This section is actually a branch of the CID and is vested with the responsibility of maintaining and training police dogs. The section has been decentralized to district level. In sensitive areas like Nakuru, dog patrols are used extensively at night.

Mounted Branch was originally formed in 1945 to patrol rural areas on mules and camels. Now, it is confined to Nairobi and uses horses in controlling crowds—and has been used in suppressing riots and demonstrations, particularly at the University.

ARMED FORCES

The president may determine the composition and size of the armed forces, with the advice of the Defense Council; the council is made up of the president's own appointees. Corruption in the armed forces is less frequent than in the other security forces, perhaps because salaries are high by the national average and frequently come up for review. Education for soldiers starts with those who left after second form. An officer cadet is required to have A levels or a university degree.

The present chief-of-general-staff, General Mahamoud Mohamed, was promoted after he played a vital role in preventing a coup in August 1982. General Mahamoud Mohamed led troops loyal to the president against soldiers of the Kenya Air Force who were attempting to overthrow the government. He was appointed chief-of-general-staff and his brother, Malim Mohamed, was given the Office of the President portfolio as a nominated minister. The Mohamed family, who are ethnic Somalis, has become one of the richest in Kenya. By virtue of their position, the two brothers have immense power over the rest of the Kenyan Somali community.

The army is on a permanent war footing in the North Eastern Province; it is also used for border disputes. In areas where the army is stationed, like the more volatile border posts, local people complain of harassment and rape of women, beatings and extortion.

Kenya is host to British army bases in Mau Navok and a U.S. Navy base in Mombasa. Territory in northern Kenya is used for exercises by the British army because of its desert-like climate and terrain. British and American soldiers have reportedly abused local residents with impunity on occasions, particularly women. In the early 1980's, a young girl in Mombasa was murdered by an American soldier who suffered no penalty other than a fifty dollar fine.

HOME GUARDS

Home guards are a colonial legacy and are used only in areas that have nomadic communities. Home guard units have been created in a number of towns and villages. In Isiolo, where there are constant disputes between groups within the community, the government armed about 150 men with sixty-three rifles who are answerable to the local administration and police chief. In northern Kenya, Lockichokio, on the Sudan border, the government has armed a large number from the Turkana community (see chapter eighteen).

The creation of home guard units often increases local resentments and rivalries, because although recruitment is voluntary, it is nearly always discriminatory. It typically excludes groups considered hostile or troublesome by the authorities.

Home guards get nominal payment, ammunition and a G3 rifle. Their "duties" are entirely at the discretion of the local police chief and District Officer.

CITY COMMISSION ASKARIS

Nairobi City Commission is the local government authority serving Nairobi. It is an arm of the Ministry of Local Government and is

led by a chair assisted by fifty-four commissioners. Until 1983, the City
Commission was known as Nairobi City Council and used to be led by a
mayor assisted by many elected councillors, but this council was dissolved
in 1983. The Department of City Inspectorate enforces the commission
by-laws with city commission *askaris* (soldiers). The number of askaris is
not regulated and they have been recruited from time to time as dictated
by the expansion and needs of the Commission

City Commission askaris' duties are deliberately vague; they are
said to be used for "purposes of security and the general welfare of the
city." One of their chief roles over the last few years has been clearing
hawkers and kiosk-owners from the city. Askaris undergo rigorous
military-like training at the City Inspectorate Training School at
Dagoretti Corner, Nairobi. They are not officially armed, except with
batons, although recent testimonies from hawkers and vendors suggest
some askaris carry firearms. The Assistant Director of the Commission,
Johnston Kunga, is a trained police officer, who relinquished a post as a
provincial police boss in Nyanza Province to join the city commission.
The commission suffers from poor organization and endemic corruption.
One chairman of the commission formed his own construction company
when appointed, and succeeded in taking over three-quarters of all the
tenders allocated within the Nairobi City Commission. All tenders for the
reconstruction of roads, bridges, painting and maintenance, and civic
construction work go to the Nairobi City Commission.

"City clean-up operations" are also directed at prostitutes and
beggars, particularly when Nairobi hosts an international conference. The
askaris patrol in open trucks, aided by contingents of regular police
officers, Administration Policemen, and KANU youthwingers. The
campaign against hawkers and vendors (see chapter fourteen) has
exposed the existence of an investigative team of plainclothes askaris,
who reportedly patrol the streets before a major operation.

CORRUPTION AND POWER IN THE SECURITY FORCES

All branches of the security forces have been used to undermine
and abuse human rights in Kenya. Power and policy are controlled by
those who control the files—especially those in the Office of the President,
Immigration and the Special Branch. According to Africa Watch sources,
corruption and lack of accountability is encouraged because:

You can only institutionalize loyalty and accountability if
there is accountability from the president's own cabinet
all the way down. The talk in Kenya is not what does the
president own; but what is he going to buy next? It is a
policeman's ambition to be spoken about in the same
manner. It is a quick way out of poverty. At the end of
the day, the answer is quite simple—so long as a
policeman gets paid such a minimum rate, so long as
there is inadequate education, and so long as there is
inadequate training of police recruits, there will be
corruption here. If their own bosses do not have respect
for the law, the policemen will not have respect for the
law. We have sold our soul to the shilling. But after all,
why should we expect a policeman to be an angel among
sinners?[6]

The willingness of the security forces to go on two payrolls to
intimidate political rivals and critics, means that an individual's liberties
and livelihood can be effectively devastated. The full weight of the
government machinery is brought to bear by involving as many relevant
departments as possible. The income tax department is used to attack
critics, by supplying the security forces with information; the licensing
board will find something wrong with that person's business license; the
central bank will refuse to provide foreign currency allocations; the
agricultural and financial state-owned corporations will call in loans; the
banks, the post office and any financial institution owned by the
government will refuse loans or foreclose on them. One member of the
security forces summed up the working environment:

In Kenya you have to be ruthless to make it, and
importantly, you have to be corrupt and sycophantic.
You have to do a lot of mindless clapping—in fact,
clowning, is probably the best way to put it. That has
become the normal state of affairs for one to get
somewhere. We facilitate everything by turning a blind
eye. We facilitate the passing of information, harassment,
corruption—and everything needs the approval of the

---

[6] Africa Watch interview with a member of the security forces.

officer, the senior commanding officer, all the way up. It is a network that is going on. Will they be exposed—will names be mentioned? No. The reprisals for breaking the code of silence that exists for any one of us are too much. We know the rules, the risks and the challenges. For Kenyan policemen, you play within the rules and don't break them—if you break them, your life is in jeopardy. It has become normal practice to have high friends, friends within the police and the armed forces. A mention of their names invokes terror and fear.

This is the machinery which steers the course of justice in Kenya and enforces law and order.

6
TORTURE

Secrecy and fear in Kenyan society, aided by an enfeebled judiciary and press censorship, have inhibited the flow of information about torture to the outside world; and the international community has apparently been eager to believe that what is not known, does not exist. According to a member of the security forces, the denial of torture is promoted internally:

> Most acts of torture are not sanctioned in writing or by higher authorities but are clearly understood to be part of normal police work. Let me put it this way, the government does not acknowledge that it is torture, it will deny that there is any form of torture going on; the police force will not acknowledge there is any form of torture going on; it will be denied officially everywhere. Unofficially it will also be denied. It does not exist, in other words. You see, who can you pinpoint these actions to directly? You can pinpoint them to a low-level officer who is doing it but, like the Nuremburg trials, he will say: I was following orders.[1]

Systematic torture in Kenya was said to have disappeared after all detainees whose names had appeared in newspapers and who had been accused of MwaKenya sympathies were released by President Moi in 1988 and 1989. These former detainees gave detailed accounts of torture, and three unsuccessfully attempted to sue the government for illegal torture and detention. Internationally, pressure from human rights organizations led to speculation that a special torture unit had been disbanded. After this period, information on torture effectively ceased because there were no high-profile accounts coming from the experiences of intellectuals and professionals in Nairobi. Public information on torture and ill-treatment of prisoners comes from very limited sources in

---

[1] Africa Watch interview.

Kenya and is, almost without exception, restricted to cases and personalities in Nairobi. By 1990, however, reports in the national press and details given in the affidavits of political prisoners made it clear that torture continued. According to these reports, the following torture methods are used:

- keeping suspects naked, in waterlogged cells, without toilet facilities;
- severe beatings with wooden sticks, iron bars and whips; throwing suspects against the cell walls, and knocking the head of suspects against the floor and walls of the cell;
- rape;
- inflicting injury to the genitals using excessive pressure, kicking and instruments like pliers—includes one documented case (see below) of inserting peppers into the vagina;
- pricking sensitive parts of the body with needles and inflicting cigarette burns;
- tying arms behind the back or over the head and suspending suspects from metal grills, iron hooks and trees for long periods of time;
- threatening to kill, torture, assault and harass family members—including one case where, according to his lawyers, the mother of a suspect was deliberately placed in an adjacent cell;
- depriving suspects of food and water for several days;
- threatening suspects with death at gun-point;
- confining suspects naked for several days;
- throwing icy cold water over suspects when they have become debilitated from lengthy confinement and lack of food, and leaving them in cold, damp cells;
- deliberately disorienting suspects by obscuring patterns of night and day, and withdrawing all forms of communication;
- keeping suspects confined for long periods of time in handcuffs or leg irons;
- interrogating suspects naked and depriving them of washing facilities;
- denying access to lawyers, family and friends.

TREASON TRIAL

At a court hearing on November 2, 1990, lawyers for Koigi wa Wamwere, Mirugi Kariuki and Rumba Kinuthia said their clients alleged they had been "subjected to severe torture and extremely inhuman and degrading treatment."

The court was told that Koigi wa Wamwere had been kept for long periods without food, exercise, washing facilities or sanitation, and at times was naked and in leg irons. In his affidavit, Wamwere said he finally signed a confession when he was told that the coughing and moaning of a woman in the cell next to him was that of his mother, who would be subjected to torture if he refused to confess. Requests for access to private doctors by the accused's lawyers have been unsuccessful.

Africa Watch has recieved information from people who have been forced to sign false confessions in order to incriminate those held on charges of treason. According to the information we recieved in 1991, the security forces have tortured people into confessing they belong to the Kenyan Patriotic Front, and have been interrogated on international contacts, particularly in Scandinavian countries.

SEDITION TRIAL

Torture was alleged by all the defendants in Kenya's longest running sedition trial. George Anyona, Augustine Kathangu, Edward Oyugi and Ngotho Kariuki, arrested July 11, 1990, were found guilty one year later on July 11, 1991, of holding a seditious meeting. They said they had been tortured and ill-treated in police custody and in remand at Kamiti Maximum Security Prison, Nairobi. During the trial, which began on January 11, 1991, Augustine Kathangu told the court that he was confined naked to a waterlogged cell for several days without food or toilet facilities. He said he was slapped, beaten, knocked against the wall and his genitals were assaulted causing severe pain. He was interrogated while naked and forced to sign a confession at gun-point.

George Anyona said he had been tortured and described the conditions under which he was held in remand:

> At Kamiti Prison, we have been placed in a block consisting not of remand prisoners but of convicted prisoners, the majority of whom are lunatics...I do not

know whether remand prisoners are supposed to be kept together. We are being kept incommunicado and are kept in cells throughout and only allowed out for a few minutes daily to empty our bowels...we have to wipe ourselves with our hands.

We are kept in rooms with dim lights and like now, in this courtroom, my eyes are hurting. We sleep on a concrete floor which is very cold and are only provided with two old blankets...we have no soap, no towels or water, we have no time to wash as we are locked in cells throughout. We are made to wade through urine and human faeces while queuing for the toilet in our bare feet which have sores. We have been provided with prison uniforms which we have been wearing permanently and I have seen prisoners walking naked in there.

Ours looks like a political case and not a criminal one otherwise we should be treated like other prisoners facing criminal charges.[2]

Anyona was not allowed to give specific details of torture in court. He was told by the magistrate that prison was "not expected to be a hotel."

CASES OF TORTURE IN 1990

Other allegations of torture, reported in the *Daily Nation* in 1990, included:

Ali Omar Hamisi, one of four men accused of robbing a British teacher, said on July 2 that he had been tortured by police officers before being forced to sign a statement he had neither written nor read. He said two police officers consistently beat him on the head with pieces of wood.

---

[2] Printed in *Society* magazine, Nairobi, October 1990, no. 14, as heard in court.

William Kipkosgei Mibei charged with murdering a former Uasin Gishu councillor in 1988 said in court on July 6, that police had threatened him with death if he did not admit to the murder. He said he was severely beaten by detectives investigating the murder.

Grace Chumba, on the same charge as above, told Eldoret High Court on July 9 that she had been kicked in her genitals for 30 minutes to force a confession from her.

A 14-year-old boy died on July 27, following alleged beatings whilst being held in police custody. He had been arrested by four plainclothes police on July 26 for "possession of *bhang* [marijuana]."

Joseph Kimani Gitau, charged with the murder of a Kiambu chief, said that police officers had tortured him by pricking his fingertips with needles and had threatened to cripple him through beating. He told the court that police officers had ordered his hands be tied up on a ventilation grill, with only his toes touching the floor. He said that while in that position an officer poured cold water on him and left him in that position overnight. He was then marched to another police station without shoes and was ordered to put his signature on papers which he was not allowed to read: "I requested the officer read the contents to me, but he refused. He told me he was going to do that after I had signed it. The officer got furious and together with other officers in the room, they started beating me up. Some used their fists, others kicked me, while others used whips." He said two of the officers held his arms tightly, and one of them pricked his finger tips: "The pain was unbearable. I saw they meant what they said and I agreed to sign the statement." The *Daily Nation* report dated September 20, did not state how long Gitau had been held in police custody.

Eight businessmen and women from Kiriainini market, Kangema, said in court on October 4 that they were arrested and "illegally confined" at the Kiriainini police station for five days where they were tortured. They said they were beaten and tortured by the CID.

There are other cases where torture has been alleged, but no affidavits are available. Charles Wamwere, brother of Koigi Wamwere, pleaded guilty to belonging to a clandestine movement the Kenyan Patriotic Front in September 1990, after being held thirteen days incommunicado. Wamwere had no lawyer representing him and said nothing in mitigation. He was reported as "sweating profusely" during a brief trial that was brought to court late in the afternoon. It is also feared that torture was used in the case of Sheik Abdulaziz Rimo, convicted of sedition in March 1990 after being held for a lengthy period incommunicado in police custody (see chapter eight).

A TESTIMONY OF TORTURE

An anonymous testimony given to Africa Watch in June 1991 clearly demonstrates the willingness of the security forces to use torture to obtain false confessions. The circumstances leading to the detention of this woman in 1990 cannot be disclosed because of the need to protect her anonymity.

> They accused me and threatened me, but would not allow me to explain anything. I was slapped very hard on my face. I was taken to Nyayo House and put in solitary confinment for some days. I was interrogated and threatened and accused of lying. They told me I would not see my children again which made me very frightened. I was not allowed to see anyone. I agreed to get them information so that they would let me go. They wanted information on some of my friends and family. They let me go but said they had not finished with me.

> After a few days they came to my home in the evening and searched thoroughly, scattering my belongings everywhere. They took me back to Nyayo House and interrogated me again for some days. This time I was beaten very seriously—they kicked me and hit me. I was put into a cell with water up to my knees. I was left there without any toilet facilities. I was threatened with death and told I would never see my children again.

> I was given a blank sheet of paper and they told me to write what they told me. I did as they said and wrote a "confession" saying my friends and my family and myself are against the government. I wrote that my family and friends are holding seditious meetings and are conspiring to overthrow the government. I was then released; but they told me they were not through with me yet.

Several weeks later I was detained by them while I was working. I was taken away in a white car. They blindfolded me and put me in the back of the car. They accused me and my family of being members of an underground movement and having foreign contacts.

I was driven to an isolated wooded area, where they removed the blindfold and forced me out of the car. They told me they were going to tell my husband what was going to happen to me, and he would never want to see me again. I was thrown on the ground and raped violently by one of the men. I did not put up much resistance because they were so violent I was afraid of getting hurt more. They told me they would entertain my husband with the details in prison, and insulted me. Then a second man raped me while the other laughed and abused me. I was terrified, in a lot of pain, and bleeding. They left me in the wood.

I was very weak from the attack and the bleeding, but I managed to crawl to a dirt road. I couldn't walk. Someone found me and drove me home. I needed medical attention but was afraid to go to hospital in case the CID found out. A neighbor of mine, a nurse, checked me and I treated myself with pain killers.

REVEREND LAWFORD NDEGE IMUNDE
TORTURED TO CONFESS AGAINST THE CHURCH

Many cases of torture, like the one above, add to an invisible catalogue of abuses by the security forces. In March 1990, however, one case attracted national and international attention.

Rev. Lawford Ndege Imunde was convicted of sedition on March 30, 1990. After being sentenced, he revealed to his lawyers that he was subjected to torture during the two weeks he was held incommunicado in police custody. Imunde recounted in a detailed affidavit how two plain clothes policemen searching him outside a Nairobi hotel, kicked, punched and abused him, kicked his genitals and threw him to the concrete road with sufficient force to cause severe backache. The police provided him with drugs when he found he was unable to sit up because of the damage to his back.

In Kileleshwa police station,[3] Imunde was kept naked in a cell and given no food for two days before being blindfolded and made to lie prostrate on the floor of a landrover, and transferred to "a very dark cell." The details of his interrogation before a panel of eight men indicate that Imunde had been transferred to the Special Branch underground cells in Nyayo House, Nairobi.

Between interrogations Imunde was returned naked to his cell, continually abused and taunted, and kicked in the buttocks. He was taunted about having a "Marxist" beard. At one point he was examined to see if he was circumcized, after being asked if he could prove he was Kenyan. He was given no washing or sanitation facilities and was told he "smelt like a wild animal." Officers in charge of the cells threw freezing cold water over him causing pneumonia, which was not treated until after he was convicted.

During the second week of interrogation, Imunde was tied with his hands behind his back, blindfolded and driven to a place he believes was a forest. Still blindfolded, he was made to touch the barrel of a pistol, and told to "cooperate." A metal container was put over his head and security officers shot at the container. At this point, Imunde says he was so terrified and disoriented, he was convinced they were going to kill him, but he was again thrown into the landrover and returned to the cells for further interrogation.

Imunde eventually signed a statement that had been prepared for him, incriminating church groups and the Law Society of Kenya. He was promised his freedom if he agreed to sign; and simultaneously threatened with death at gun-point if he refused.

NYAYO HOUSE: THE TORTURE CHAMBERS

Systematic torture is carried out by the Special Branch force, who interrogate political prisoners on the 24th floor of Nyayo House. A multistory civic building in central Nairobi, Nyayo House has at least

---

[3] Suspects arrested for political purposes are taken to police stations in the wealthy Nairobi suburbs, like Kileleshwa and Parklands, because the stations are inactive and the cells empty compared with the central and slum areas.

eight underground cells known as "torture dungeons" specially constructed for holding political suspects. Lawyers believe that political prisoners taken in other provinces—with the probable exception of the North Eastern Province—are transferred to Nairobi for interrogation.

Political prisoners are typically kidnapped by plainclothes officers without any opportunity to contact lawyers, friends or relatives so that psychological vulnerability is immediately established. The person is often incarcerated without even the reassurance that people are aware of their arrest. Prisoners are kept blindfolded and transported to Nyayo House on the floor of a vehicle, or tied up in the trunk. Many have said the journey is made deliberately long and rough to cause disorientation. The underground cells in Nyayo House are described as extremely small and are painted black or red. Prisoners say the cells are usually kept dark, and the lack of ventilation causes great discomfort. Prisoners have also complained of continuous noise, like banging machinery.

Cells in Nyayo House are constructed to allow waterlogging. This method of torture is called the "swimming pool" treatment, and has been used as recently as 1990. The cell door is raised a couple of feet from the ground so that the floor may be flooded with water. Prisoners are stripped naked and kept in the dark, water-filled cell for days. More water is thrown into the cell periodically with buckets or aimed at a prisoner through a high pressure hose. Prolonged exposure to water causes breakdown of the skin, resulting in peeling and sores. Prisoners must either stand in the water, causing intense pain and swelling in the feet and ankles, or sit, causing damage to the buttocks and genitals, as well as inducing infections in the bladder and kidneys. Being hosed at great pressure is described as "like being punched with a sharp object" and usually causes the person to collapse as the water is aimed at the face, stomach and genitals. Prisoners are deprived of food and water and are given no sanitation facilities. Prisoners have described how they are eventually forced to drink the water in the cell, mixed with their own urine and feces, in order to survive. Some have resorted to eating skin peelings from their own limbs.

During the water treatment, the prisoner is taken for long interrogation sessions before panels of eight to twelve Special Branch officers. Interrogations may take place intermittently to take the prisoner by surprise, but others say these take place daily so that the prisoner feels great stress and fear in anticipation of the next session. Prisoners are put on an elevator blindfolded and taken to the 24th floor of Nyayo House. Under interrogation, they are often beaten with sticks, chair legs and whips made from rubber tires, and made to do humiliating exercises naked or semi-naked, like push-ups, touching toes and running in a circle with one finger on the ground. One man who was interrogated naked in 1986 described his ordeal:

> I was ordered to start doing exercises by about ten security men. The order is given to do press-ups up to say one hundred times. About ten security men armed with canes, whips, batons, broken furniture—mainly the legs of chairs and tables—beat me up to make me reach the number of counts. The count is usually 1, 2, 3, 4, 5, 6, 7, 8, 9, 10 when the leader announces that the "dissident" touched the ground with the stomach and that all the counts are to be withdrawn. The security men beat my ankles, feet-soles, buttocks, back, head, and fingers.

> Another exercise is then ordered, for instance, lying on the back, putting the hands outstretched at 180 degrees and raising both feet at 45 degrees. Then the officers put their boots on my face and hands and others beat my ankles, feet, toes and knees...If you do not pass out, an order is given to "DO THE SPINS." You place one finger on the floor and have to spin round the finger at great speed while being beaten, chased and having abuse shouted at you.

Beatings are sometimes severe enough to cause internal damage, as in the case of ex-detainee Mirugi Kariuki who is presently held on a charge of treason. Mirugi Kariuki suffers from permanent kidney damage after Special Branch officers beat and kicked him. Others have to live with permanent disabilities, like stiffness of joints and badly healed broken joints. Intense migraines are common, as are stomach ulcers and damaged eyesight.

One young man who was severely tortured during the political crackdown said to be aimed at MwaKenya, told Africa Watch that he was subjected to humiliating sexual abuse:

> They do anything to your body to try to get you to sign a confession. I can never recover properly...they pushed

metal rods into my anus, and I still bleed from the
damage. They make you stay naked and mock you, and
make you bend down naked so they can open up your
anus. They damage your testicles by kicking and beating
you there until you just pass out. All the time you can go
crazy...I think many people do what they want
quickly...they want to know who you know. They kept
asking me if I knew N'gugi wa Thiongo and other exiles,
and told me they had a list of names of people who knew
my activities.

Other methods of torture associated with the MwaKenya political
crackdown were cigarette burns, razor slashing, starvation, death threats
and being suspended upside down for long periods from the feet and
hands tied behind the back.[4]

GOVERNMENT FAILURE TO PROSECUTE

Torture and inhuman and degrading punishment or other
treatment is expressly prohibited by the Kenyan constitution,[5] but
allegations made in court that defendants have been tortured are not
investigated. Complaints are dismissed, and many are silenced before
their allegations have been put to the court. When torture was alleged by
Koigi wa Wamwere's lawyer, the court made no attempt to investigate
the complaint, but simply ruled that Wamwere was being lawfully held in
custody.[6]

---

[4] Although this was known as the MwaKenya crackdown, it is important to
recognize that there have been similar political crackdowns by the government
where torture has been used in the same manner to incriminate and incarcerate
those who are considered critical of the government and are therefore perceived
as a threat.

[5] Article 74 (1) of the Constitution of Kenya, states that "No person shall be
subject to torture or to inhuman or degrading or other punishment."

[6] *The Standard* (Nairobi), January 10, 1991.

There has been no attempt by the government to bring the guilty to justice, even when use of torture on political prisoners during the MwaKenya crackdown was well documented by international human rights organizations. President Moi has consistently denied torture is used.

ATTEMPTS TO SUE THE STATE FOR ILLEGAL TORTURE

Three former detainees who attempted to sue the government for illegal torture and detention were held for a substantially longer period after other detainees were released by the president in February 1988. It is assumed that this was in reprisal for filing suits against the state. Detainees are pressured not to obtain legal representation as, they are told, it will complicate their case and reduce their chances of release. Filing suits for illegal torture was greeted with hostility by the state. Wanyiri Kihoru (detained in July 1986), lawyer and land economist; Mukaru Ng'ang'a (detained in April 1986) history lecturer and political scientist; and Mirugi Kariuki (detained in December 1986), a lawyer, all submitted notices to sue for illegal detention and torture in February 1987. They were not released until June 1989.

None of the applications against the state was successful, and harassment by the security forces and threats have culminated in exile or re-arrest for all three ex-detainees:

Mukaru Ng'ang'a fled into exile in April 1990 after being constantly harassed by the Special Branch. He had been unable to find employment and was in constant fear of being arrested and tortured again. In March 1990, about forty Administration Police, armed with automatic guns, riot equipment and tear gas, came to his home to take him away. He was given no reason for the attempted arrest. He spent a week underground and then unsuccessfully attempted to secure reassurance in court that he would be afforded protection from any further illegal detentions and torture. Despite his repeated protestations that he would not be forced to leave Kenya, he felt compelled to seek sanctuary abroad in April 1990.

Wanyiri Kihoro fled into exile in March 1991. He issued a statement saying he had been warned of a threat to his life.

Mirugi Kariuki, who returned to his legal practice in Nakuru after his release, was arrested by the Special Branch in October 1990. He was held in custody for two weeks and charged with treason, which carries a mandatory death sentence. There are fears that Kariuki has been tortured again. The torture he was subjected to during his detention after his arrest in December 1986 is detailed in the affidavit that was prepared by his lawyer, Gibson Kamau Kuria.

> During the eleven days of unlawful imprisonment police officers, in gross contravention of the Plaintiff's fundamental rights under section 74(1) of the Constitution, and in blatant abuse of their powers, savagely tortured, assaulted and beat him and subject him to great humiliation, insults and indignity.

> On 11th December he was blindfolded and taken before a panel of eleven plain clothes interrogators who savagely beat him with whips, pieces of rubber tyres and timber, until he fainted, thereby occasioning him various wounds. One of the interrogators stepped on his private parts and on his kidney causing him to urinate blood for five days and his urinary system is damaged.

> Mirugi Kariuki is an asthma patient [who] was also denied any form of medical treatment and suffered at least five bouts of asthma and the wounds caused by torture until after he was detained. From 10th December 1986 [he] was kept stark naked in a cell flooded with cold water; he was sprayed with water coming out of a hose pipe at very great pressure thereby causing intense pain to him, and he was not given any food.

> Mirugi Kariuki was taunted, jeered at and humiliated by police officers; he was not given any opportunity to sleep, and he was subjected to great pain and suffering, mental and physical distress.

> ...[He] was informed orally of detention and asked to wait for the detention order but [it] was not served upon him until 4.7.86 after he had been crippled and made to suffer; being threatened that unless he confessed to a false charge, the interrogators would use any means to get him convicted of some offence; being taken to the

Nairobi law courts one day; being denied an opportunity to talk to anybody or communicate with any relatives; being sprayed with water coming out of a pipe at great pressure every day at 4 A.M., at 7 A.M., at about 1 P.M., about 7 P.M. and at midnight—that water making him feel as though he was being punched with sharp objects; being hit with two buckets of water every morning after he refused to make a confession at the request of the interrogators; being subjected to sessions of interrogations at which he was beaten by more than 8 officers and ridiculed; being made to suffer the indignity of drinking the water in his cell which was mixed with his urine and excreta; have bright lights shone on his eyes; being denied the opportunity of sleeping; being denied medical care even when he was so sick that he had to be taken to and from the interrogation chambers by police officers.

Mirugi Kariuki's application was unsuccessful. In September 1987, the state denied torture or unlawful arrest, saying:

...[his] arrest, search and detention in police custody was done in accordance with the Police Act and Criminal Procedure Code in that the [state] had reasonable grounds to suspect and investigate [Mirugi Kariuki] of the MwaKenya group and possessing seditious literature.

Torture has in some cases been modified. Individuals interrogated by the Special Branch in Nyayo House during the so-called multiparty crackdown in 1990, say torture was constantly referred to, but not implemented. In some cases, the Special Branch counts on its reputation to be effective without actually having to inflict physical torture.

"HAVE WE TORTURED YOU?"

In an interview with Africa Watch, a person held in Nyayo House in 1990 as a result of the multiparty debate described how he was picked up unexpectedly by the Special Branch and then left in a Nairobi police cell. Special Branch officers returned after midnight, unbooked him and told him to "cooperate." They put him in the trunk of a car—"which is very uncomfortable. You feel so frightened; you have no control over anything any more." He said they chose "the roughest roads—so I didn't know which direction they were taking me."

He arrived at what he realized was Nyayo House:

> The car went down as if it was going underground. I heard the door lift up—like a garage door—and then drop down behind us. They took me out of the car without saying anything to me. They marched me still blindfolded to an office. I saw a toilet and a bathroom opposite the office and a corridor leading to cells. There are no doors on the bathroom or toilet so that they can watch you. The blindfold was removed and I was taken down the corridor to a cell, about 6' by 7'. Those cells are small and pitch black, because they are painted all over in black. And the floor is sunken. I think there are about eight cells. I was given a mattress and two blankets, and in the morning they brought me a cup of tea. They told me to prepare myself because I was going somewhere soon. They blindfolded me again and walked me along the corridor, up some stairs and into a lift. I felt it going high up, not stopping. I was moved out of the lift and walked quite a long way, then given a chair and told to sit down. The blindfold was taken off and I was in a room with a panel of about seven people seated and a table looking at me. There was no introduction, they just started asking me lots of details about myself—where I was born, where I went to school, my entire life history. They wanted to know my relationship with certain people and anything I knew about their alliances and who visited them. If I said I didn't know they would persist and press me continuously for details.
>
> ...[The] interrogation was very tiring. We would do about four hours in the morning and maybe three in the afternoon—I had about seventeen hours of interrogation. During those days I would be asked every morning "and have you been tortured? Have you been badly

treated—because people always go out of here and complain they are tortured." I was not tortured, they didn't do anything like that—but when they asked me, I always replied "not yet, you haven't tortured me yet." You don't know what might happen to you in there.

Another victim of the multiparty crackdown was a school teacher who was tortured by the Special Branch in a forest. He was tied with his hands behind his back, suspended over a river, beaten and threatened with death. He was repeatedly dropped into the river and held under water as Special Branch officers told him to sign a confession.

TORTURE AND ILL-TREATMENT IN POLICE CUSTODY

Deliberate brutalization by the security forces has been encouraged by the failure of the authorities to prosecute and punish the torturers. Torture appears to be prevalent when the police become fixated on the wrong person who refuses to confess, or when a spurious charge is used to justify the incarceration of a targeted individual.

Some cases of police torture have been reported in the national and international press—most notably, the case of Peter Njenga Karanja, who died in police custody after being tortured in February 1987. Karanja died from internal injuries to the stomach and bowel, and the tissue that holds the upper and lower intestine in position was torn. The feet, lower legs, thighs and arms were covered in septic wounds, and there was blood in the fluid found in his lungs. Although the inquest concluded that the injuries appeared to be a result of torture, the Attorney general did not make any effort to investigate, as ordered by the chief magistrate. President Moi, former Attorney General Matthew Muli and Police Commissioner Philip Kilonzo have all publicly asserted there has never been any incident of torture in Kenya, and that if there were, action would be taken immediately against the culprits.

In March 1990, allegations of police torture were made in court by a Tanzanian woman, Jane Betty Mwaiseje, accused of murdering her husband, a marine scientist working for UNESCO who vanished in Nairobi in 1986. In November 1986, his partially burned body had been discovered in Nairobi. She made repeated visits to Kenya to appeal for police assistance, and reported that she was detained by the CID on

March 28, 1988. She was brought to court March 5, 1990, and charged with murder.

During police interrogation, Jane Mwaiseje said she was "severely tortured" by officers who stripped her naked and injured her genitals with pliers. She said she was constantly threatened by policemen who made her sign a statement from an inspector, listed as Isaac Onyango from Kilimani police station. After CID officers failed to identify her positively in a lineup, she said the inspector told other officers to tear up the relevant documentation: "I was then placed in the police cells with some policemen who started beating me up." A pistol was put to her head and a policeman threatened to "blow my head off, saying, you Tanzanians are bringing a lot of trouble." She was stripped naked, her legs were forced open and she was tortured with pliers. Her head was covered by a tin filled with hot peppers and she was told she must sign the statement. When she refused, peppers were inserted into her injured genitals. She told the court—two years later—that she was still in a lot of pain and had difficulty urinating as a result of the torture; she added that although CID officers had taken her to see a doctor, a woman police officer pulled her head back and threatened her when she attempted to tell the doctor of the torture.[7]

A man who was subsequently charged with the murder of Jane Mwaiseje's husband also said he had been tortured during police interrogation. He said the police beat him severely on the buttocks, thighs and soles of his feet. He said he was then tied in a sack and taken to a forest where they continued to torture him and threaten death. He appeared in court on March 9, 1990; his so-called confession had been made on October 14, 1987.

In June 1988, Crispine Odhiambo Yonga, a sixth form student, was doused in petrol and set alight by Administration Police during interrogation over the alleged theft of a radio. The policeman concerned was identified as Corporal Michael Hassan, who was remanded in custody, but no action was taken after he denied burning Yonga.[8]

More recently, incidents of police brutality were reported during the government screening imposed on all ethnic Somalis from November 1989 to March 1990. One elderly man, known as Musa, approximately

---

[7] Accounts from *Kenya Times, Daily Nation, The Standard*, March 6, 1990.

[8] BBC African Service, June 16, 1988.

70 years old, was arrested in Busia at the beginning of the exercise. He was kept in police custody for two months when the police inspector refused to believe he was a legitimate Kenyan citizen. During interrogation, Musa says the police inspector ordered officers to break both his legs. Africa Watch received a photograph of Musa with both his legs in plaster casts. After his legs had been broken, Musa was transferred to Nakuru Hospital where he was handcuffed to the bed for over a month. While he was in the hospital, relatives took his case to Provincial Commissioner Yusuf Haji in Nakuru, who discovered he was a Kenyan citizen and intervened. Musa was released from the hospital and, with encouragement from his relatives, took the case to court. The police then charged Musa again with being an illegal alien and confiscated his documents, saying they were falsified. Members of the family went to Isiolo and obtained copies of the original documents. Africa Watch is unaware of any further developments in the case.

Police also separated many women from their children. There were numerous accounts of breast-feeding women incarcerated in police cells without their babies, denied any opportunity by the police to relieve their accumulating milk supply. Severe pain was at times compounded by medical complications, like abscesses and mastitis.

POLICE BRUTALITY

The notorious reputation of the police means that civilians not only fear the conditions of arrest, but also the consequences of any routine contact with the police. One man told Africa Watch how he was arrested in a Nairobi police station when he went to report the theft of his radio:

> I was seized and thrown in the cell. They kicked me and punched me and beat my knees and elbows with a stick. They called me a thief and a liar and told me I could stay overnight. In the morning they wouldn't let me leave. Then one policeman said I could go if I paid money. I didn't have any. It wasn't until late that day my sister came to look for me. She gave them fifty shillings [$1.92] and they let me out.

Beatings with batons and rifle butts are typical and routine forms of abuse in police custody. The police also have batons with leather thongs attached, which are used like whips, and a hinged two-part stick used in crowds as well as on individuals in police cells. When Africa Watch spoke to people who had experienced physical abuse in police custody, most said blows were deliberately aimed at knee and elbow joints. Some described how they were forced to sit on the floor, their legs outstretched and tied together at the ankles, while their knee-caps were beaten. Some also described beatings on the back, kidneys and neck.

In the North Eastern Province where emergency legislation allows the security forces full powers, Africa Watch sources say beatings are commonplace. Men complain of injuries inflicted on the testicles, saying it is a "favorite" method of torture by the police. The security forces routinely pick up young men in North Eastern Province and subject them to humiliation and racial insults as well as physical beatings. Women also suffer harassment and abuse, and say they are sexually taunted and accused of prostitution.

In one example of police brutality, a man named Abdi described to Africa Watch how he was arrested in Garissa and accused of sympathizing with the Somali Patriotic Movement, a Somali movement operating across the border. He spent one week in Garissa police station. He says he was not told of a charge, but knows he was listed as a poacher in the Occurrence Book. He said no one was allowed to bring him food and he only received a cup of tea and some *chapattis*[9] every day. He was beaten and interrogated:

> They sometimes beat you on your body generally, or just on your knees and elbows. They made me place my finger on the floor and run round and round it in a circle until I passed out.

> The conditions in the cell are really terrible—more than twenty people in that small cell.[10] Some people were accused of poaching, some of hiding firearms—and lots of them were there with no real reason. Every one is afraid

---

[9] A form of unleavened bread.

[10] The cells in Garissa Police Station are about 10' by 10'.

even to look at the police in case they call you out and beat you again. When they make you come out for a roll call they make you all cower down on the floor behind the police desk—and they kick and punch at any excuse. They abuse you all the time, calling us "dirty *shiftas*" and "poachers"—they treat you like an animal, and make you sit in your own dirt. People get hopeless and think they will never get out. They have a small, dirty place at the back of the station where they interrogate you.

In another case, Paul (not his real name), a Ugandan refugee who had worked as a gardener in a Nairobi suburb, South C, for more than ten years, was picked up by a police patrol in August 1988. When the police found he had no identity card, they arrested him and he disappeared. The family he worked for began searching for him in the local police stations when he failed to return home; but they gave up when they found his name was not registered in any of the Occurrence Books. More than a month later, a man just released from South C police station came to the family and told them he had been in a cell with Paul, who had sent him to get assistance. When the family went to South C police station they demanded to see Paul, and found him in a shocking physical state with serious injuries to his head and stomach. He spent over a month in Kenyatta Hospital recovering. Africa Watch was told by the family how he had severe bruising on his limbs and stomach, "a rupture in his stomach" and cuts and bruises on his head. The family said he was in a confused mental state, but did not know whether this was directly due to head injuries. Paul recovered and continued to work for the family. His fear of the police was so great that the family said he rarely left the house and began to drink heavily. The sad ending to Paul's case is that his worst fears were realized; in June 1989, he was picked up again, just outside the house, in a police swoop on "illegal aliens." The family again searched for him in the local police stations but have not seen him since that time.

CONFESSIONS THROUGH TORTURE

The Kenyan Evidence Act states that:

A confession or any admission of a fact tending to the proof of guilt made by an accused person is not admissible in a criminal proceeding if the making of the confession or admission appears to the court to have been caused by any inducement, threat or promise...a confession is not admissible in court if obtained by a person in authority through threat or violence or promise for gain...of some advantage or avoidance of temporal evil.[11]

Under the provisions of the Evidence Act, any confession is directed to be treated with extreme caution, in an attempt to stop abuse of "the proper administration of justice," but this has become a dead letter in Kenya. The security forces routinely rely on obtaining self-incriminating, confessional evidence to convict. Many of those convicted complain in private—and sometimes in court—that they have been harassed, intimidated and tortured in police custody to force them to confess or sign prepared statements. Some say they are promised freedom, or their family is threatened—some are threatened with additional charges and physical violence. The absence of an independent judiciary has encouraged disregard of these regulations, as magistrates are all too willing to accept, without question, confessions offered by the prosecution.

Courts frequently cooperate with the prosecution and security forces by refusing bail and allowing the prisoner to be returned on a holding charge. A holding charge—which has gained currency in Kenyan courts—is used to hold someone on the grounds that the police are still carrying out their investigations. Typically, the arrested person has been brought to court on a specific charge, the plea is taken, and the prosecution then opposes bail claiming that further investigations are needed because more serious charges may be brought. In effect, the prosecution is admitting that there is not enough evidence to convict. Under such circumstances, evidence obtained in police custody should be inadmissible as it will be obtained under duress or coercion. This has been done in many cases.

---

[11] Section 26 of the Kenyan Evidence Act (Cap 80).

TORTURE CONTINUES

Despite evidence of torture, consistent denials by the government have seemingly been effective in muting condemnation from the international community. The use of torture is persistent enough, however, to provoke immediate and widespread fears for the safety and well-being of any detainee or prisoner currently held in Kenya.

7
DETENTION WITHOUT TRIAL

Detention without trial is used to silence critics. It is commonly practiced in Kenya by disguising political charges with criminal ones, and holding critics for lengthy periods without bail or trial. Provisions for preventive detention, where a person can be held without charge, exist under emergency legislation when war or disaster threaten the security of the nation. However, preventive detention is now used as part of the standard law at times when the country is described by the government as stable and peaceful.

The KANU manifesto described preventive detention as inhuman and pledged to abolish "these undemocratic, unjust and arbitrary practices." This was not to be, however, as President Kenyatta retained emergency laws—but changed their name—in order to suppress opposition and make Kenya a de facto one-party state. The retention of the emergency laws was justified by Kenyatta on the basis of the on-going war of secession in the Northern Frontier District (now North Eastern Province). According to one study of the emergency laws:

> Powers ideally meant to preserve the life of the nation
> were used as a weapon in intra-party war to preserve the
> narrow interests of a ruling faction, camouflaged as the
> interests of the State.[1]

Moi made identical provisions for detention without trial when he became president in 1978, but increased the scope of his powers. Upon taking office, President Moi released all twelve political detainees held under the Preventive Detention Act, but warned there would be no hesitation in taking "immediate and firm action" if he believed it

---

[1] Kathurima Inoti, "Emergency Powers in Kenya," unpublished MA these with the University of Nairobi (date n/a).

necessary.[2] In 1982, he demonstrated his willingness to use detention as a means of suppressing any hint of political opposition (see chapter one).

DETENTION UNDER THE CONSTITUTION

The constitutional basis for detention without trial reads:

The President may *at any time* [emphasis added] by order published in the "Kenya Gazette"[3] bring into operation generally or in any part of Kenya, Part III of the Preservation of Public Security Act or any of the provisions of that part of that Act.

This gives the president unlimited discretion in bringing emergency laws and detention without trial into operation—in other words, he may detain at will. There is no requirement for either parliament or the president to be satisfied with the existence of any particular or peculiar circumstances. An emergency or threat need only exist in the mind of the president himself.[4] The only legal requirement is that a detention order be published in the Kenya Gazette, although there is no time limit specified. Such unlimited discretion means there is no effective check on abuse of detention without trial in Kenya, and makes legal challenge of a detention order very difficult. In fact, no legal challenge of a detention has been successful in the Kenyan courts because the detaining powers are not required to establish their reasoning.

Detention of a person is prepared by order by the Minister in Charge of Internal Security under Part III of the Preservation of Public Security (Detained and Restricted Persons) Regulations. Under this legislation, there are no gazetted detainees at this writing. All three political detainees arrested in July 1990 were released by June 21 1991.

---

[2] *Daily Nation*, December 13, 1978.

[3] The "Kenya Gazette" is the official log in which the names of detainees have been listed.

[4] Kiraitu Mirungi, "Legal Basis for Detention without Trial in Kenya," unpublished MA thesis with University of Nairobi, 1982).

DETENTION IN SPITE OF THE CONSTITUTION

Detention without trial is also practiced without reference to the specific provisions in the constitution. Under the emergency legislation, the government is obliged to gazette and therefore enumerate political prisoners being held without charge; but by using criminal charges for political reasons and deliberately denying bail and postponing trial dates, the government may effectively detain without having to admit to it. For the purposes of eliciting aid and support from Western governments, the Kenyan government eagerly resorts to camouflaging political prisoners with bogus criminal charges and convictions. Human rights organizations believe there are thousands of such prisoners in Kenya.

UNACKNOWLEDGED DETENTIONS

Detainees are sometimes missing in Kenya, at least temporarily. The cases that reach public attention are those that—eventually—are brought to court because of the efforts of relatives and lawyers. One such person was detained by the Special Branch in Nyayo House for almost a month before she had an opportunity to contact a lawyer:

> I was picked up from home by the Special Branch three days after arriving back in Kenya. They took me straight to the Nyayo House dungeons and interrogated me. I only had the clothes I was standing in. They put me in a small cell painted black. They would come without warning and take me up to one of the highest floors in the building, always with a blindfold on. I was interrogated by a panel of plainclothesmen sitting at a table in front of me. Most of the time they asked questions about who I had seen abroad, who my friends were abroad, what their addresses are, their occupation and political beliefs—that sort of thing.
>
> They accused me of being anti-government. I didn't know what they could do to me, but they kept on calling me anti-government and threatening me. It was

humiliating and terrible—I thought the worst would happen.

They kept me for almost a month—but you lose track of time. Sometimes they interrogated me; sometimes I was just in that small black cell. I asked for my family and my lawyer but they just dismissed anything like that.

Frances (not her real name) was eventually taken to court on spurious charges relating to foreign currency. She was remanded and transferred to a women's prison.

I was lucky there because I recognized one of the prison guards from home. We talked and I convinced him what had happened, and begged him to make contact with my lawyer. My lawyer came and arranged bail for me.

When I got back to my home, I found that everything I had arrived with had been taken—I literally only had the clothes I was standing in. They had confiscated every single piece of personal property. My lawyer told me we could get it back but that I should keep quiet about my experience. I did. I consider myself lucky. Many of the people I left behind will rot in prison.

LEGAL REPRESENTATION AND RIGHTS OF THE DETAINEE HELD UNDER THE PREVENTIVE DETENTION ACT

Persons detained under the Preservation of Public Security Act (also referred the Public Security Act or Preventive Detention Act) are typically abducted by the security officers—who usually do not identify themselves—and are given no opportunity to consult members of their family, or lawyers, unless by circumstantial chance. Once detained, only a police officer or a religious minister have access to the detainee, unless the commissioner of prisons or the officer in charge has given written authorization to someone else. However, detainees are rarely given the opportunity to see the people they are entitled to.

Detainees have complained that they are prevented from exercising their rights under the law. They may occasionally be granted certain privileges at the discretion of the authorities. Lawyers find they have to battle hard to secure the minimum, most basic amenities for their clients.

The legal rights of detainees are clearly stated in the public security legislation. These basic rights—such as legal representation and consultation, visiting rights and conditions of imprisonment—are legally enforceable, and are not negotiable privileges. They are listed in the Public Security (Detained and Restricted Persons) Regulations 1978:

- The detainee must be issued with a statement he or she understands giving details of the grounds for detention. This must be provided no more than five days after detention begins.
- The detention must be published in the Kenya Gazette not more than fourteen days after the detention begins, giving particulars of the regulations under which the detention is authorized.
- The case must be reviewed by an "independent and impartial tribunal" not more than a month after detention begins, and then at intervals of not more than every six months.
- The detainee will be given reasonable facilities to consult a legal representative of their own choice, who is then permitted to make representations to the review tribunal.
- At the Review Tribunal, the detainee will be permitted to appear in person or be represented by a legal representative.

According to the testimonies of detainees, these rights are constantly abused by the authorities. There are also detailed rules concerning the conditions under which detainees are kept that are more typically disregarded than adhered to. Kenneth Matiba complained he was kept confined in his cell without any communication with the detention officers, although it is specifically stated in the Public Security (Detained and Restricted Persons) Rules 1978 (part 111 20 [p]) that:

> no cell shall be used for cellular confinement unless it is
> provided with a means whereby the detained person may
> at any time communicate with a detention officer.

He was denied appointments to see his lawyer and a minister, and was given no reading material—all without explanation. According to the regulations, denial of visits, reading material or letters must be explained in writing when they are imposed as a punishment.

REVIEW TRIBUNAL

Technically, the Review Tribunal is supposed to prevent unlawful detention by acting as a check on the power given to the president to detain at will. It is supposed to examine the case of a detainee at regular intervals to ensure that correct procedure is followed and that continued incarceration is justifiable. But according to ex-detainees, the empty ritual of the Review Tribunal does nothing to engender hope, but rather completes the feeling of despair. The members of the tribunal are appointed by the president and are neither impartial nor independent. Detainees say they feel no faith when arguing their case, and many have been afraid to discuss complaints. Significantly, the tribunal is not bound by the normal law of procedure and evidence, and its sessions are a closely guarded secret. The result is that, although the tribunal is technically a detainee's only opportunity for legal representation, the lawyer representing the detainee is unlikely to be present. Rights of consultation are not observed, and even if a lawyer represents a detainee, he or she will not necessarily be told of the date or venue of the hearing.

Getting representation is usually a significant achievement rather than a right—in spite of the fact that there are legal provisions for representation. Detainees get little opportunity to communicate with a lawyer of their choice. They are pressured—sometimes under torture—not to accept or seek legal representation, and are told it will reduce their chances of release. There is no provision that guarantees detainees legal representation under a legal aid scheme.

Letters are sent and received entirely at the discretion of the officer in charge and have been frequently withheld from detainees without any acknowledgment or explanation, or deliberately delayed for lengthy periods. Medical attention is often inadequate or withheld, rather than made instantly available as required in the Public Security Rules.

HARASSMENT OF FAMILIES OF DETAINEES

The families of detainees suffer harassment by the security forces who deliberately obstruct them in their efforts to pursue the case of the detained person. Wives of detainees are frequently treated dismissively, abusively or deceptively. The security forces also encourage isolation—the wife of one former detainee told Africa Watch:

> At the time you most need help and support, you are least likely to get it. Your friends—even your family members—will cross the road from you. You can only follow up on your husband through stubborness. I went to the police every day and refused to leave. It's a full time job, finding out where they are and what is happening and listening to all the lies they tell you.

Access to the detainee's bank account is often denied, unless precautionary arrangements have been made prior to the arrest. Wives and children frequently suffer harsh economic penalties wielded by the authorities when debts are called in and mortgages closed.

During Raila Odinga's detention in the mid-1980s, his wife, Ida Odinga, was harassed and threatened by security forces for taking action on behalf of her husband. She filed a habeas corpus and was told her husband was being held under the Public Security Regulations. Almost immediately she received a letter from the Teachers Service Commission demanding that she vacate the house she had been living in at Kenya High School, making her both homeless and jobless at once. In fact, she was required to move out of the house on the same day she recieved the letter, which had been written only the day after she learnt of her husband's detention.

In July 1990, when lawyers Mohamed Ibrahim, Gitobu Imanyara and John Khaminwa were detained along with former cabinet ministers Kenneth Matiba and Charles Rubia, the wives of the detainees wrote a letter to Nelson Mandela appealing to him to intervene personally during a visit he made to Nairobi.

TABLE 1
GAZETTED DETAINEES
Political Detainees held under
Preventive Detention Legislation 1982-91
(No detainees in 1984, 1985 or 1989)

1982 Detained
George Anyona
Al-Amin Mazrui
Edward Oyugi
Kamoji Wachira
Mukaru N'ganga
Willy Mutunga
Koigi wa Wamwere
John Khaminwa

1982 Restriction Order
Jaramogi Oginga Odinga

1983 Detained
Raila Odinga
Otieno Mak'Onyango
Alfred Otieno
Geoffrey Muriiithi

1986 Detained
Gacheche wa Miano
Wanyiri Kihoro
Mirugi Kariuki
Kariuki Gathitu
Patrick Onyango
Mukaru N'ganga
Katama Mkangi
Ngotho Kariuki

1987 Detained
Gibson Kamau Kuria
Paul Amina
Raila Odinga

1988 Detained
Israel Otieno Agina

1990 Detained
Kenneth Matiba
Charles Rubia
John Khaminwa
Mohamed Ibrahim
Gitobu Imanyara
Raila Odinga

8
SEDITION
DEALING WITH INVISIBLE EVIDENCE

The Kenyan government has come to rely extensively on criminalizing opposition through charges of sedition, subversion, breach of the peace and treason. The number of people charged with sedition increases dramatically whenever the government feels particularly vulnerable—as demonstrated in the 1982 attempted coup; in the 1986-87 MwaKenya crackdown; after the murder of the Foreign Minister Robert Ouko; and following the calls for multiparty democracy. This use of the Criminal Code to legitimize repression is a colonial legacy

In February 1990, Sheikh Abdulaziz Rimo was sentenced in Malindi (Coastal Province) to six years' imprisonment for "uttering seditious words." This effectively marked the beginning of the most recent spate of political trials. The case received almost no publicity, but was typical of sedition trials. Sheikh Abdulaziz Rimo was brought to court on February 14 after criticizing the government in a sermon in August 1989. He had been held incommunicado in police custody for an unknown length of time, was unrepresented and pleaded guilty to the charges. One month later, Rev. Lawford Ndege Imunde was sentenced to six years for having a "seditious desk diary." Imunde's case was held in Nairobi, journalists and human rights lawyers were alerted to his disappearance and there was considerable press coverage. In January 1991, Kenya's longest sedition trial began. After a six month trial, George Anyona, former member of parliament, Edward Oyugi, university professor, Ngotho Kariuki, former academic and Augustine Kathangu, a party official, were sentenced to seven years for "holding a seditious meeting."

The pattern of sedition trials demonstrates a calculated disregard for the legal process, and a cynical interpretation of the legislation. There have been frequent allegations that police officers plant supposedly seditious publications on individuals, and use physical and psychological torture to obtain guilty pleas. The manner in which the trials are conducted indicates that the charge is used to impose political conformity. Human rights lawyer, Kiraitu Murungi, said in April 1990 that sedition cases carry all the hallmarks of a manipulated trial:

There have been a series of cases of sedition in this country in which, without exception, the accused persons have been brought to court after long periods in security police custody and have invariably pleaded guilty. They are brought to court in odd hours and are not given adequate facilities to consult their lawyers and prepare their defense. In the past I've taken instructions from clients who have undergone both physical and psychological torture to extract confessions and pleas of guilt.[1]

Persons brought to court under charges of sedition normally plead guilty, and are therefore found guilty on their own admission. There has been no documented attempt by the court to question abuse of procedure by the arresting officers—the guilty plea is automatically accepted.

HOW THE LEGISLATION IS USED

Sedition is defined in the Penal Code (Cap. 63 56[1]) as an intention:

(a) to overthrow by unlawful means the Government of Kenya by law established; or

(b) to bring into hatred or contempt or to excite disaffection against the person of the President or the Government of Kenya by law established; or

(c) to excite the inhabitants of Kenya to attempt to procure the alteration otherwise than by lawful means of any matter or thing in Kenya by law established; or

(d) to bring into hatred or contempt or to excite disaffection against the administration of justice in Kenya;

---

[1] Press interview, April 1990.

(e) to raise discontent or disaffection amongst the inhabitants of Kenya; or

(f) to promote feelings of ill-will or hostility between different sections of classes of the population of Kenya.

These intentions can take the form of a publication defined as "containing any word, sign or visible presentation expressive of a seditious intention," or can be uttered, printed, sold, offered, distributed, reproduced or owned. Proprietors, publishers, printers and editors who are convicted of publishing a seditious publication may have their newspapers or magazines prohibited for one year by the court. Printing equipment, including a wide range of typesetting machines, photocopiers and duplicating machines, can be confiscated and the operators charged.

Theoretically, intention must be conclusively proved before a person can be convicted of sedition. This includes consideration of the tendency or the ability of the words to incite disaffection or raise discontent. In other words, the court must consider for which audience the seditious act was intended, before it can decide whether the words or acts could be seditious.

CRITICISM: LEGITIMATE OR SEDITIOUS?

A proviso to Section 56 is intended to qualify the definition of seditious intention and prevent the legislation from being used to suppress valid criticism. Under the proviso, "intention shall not be taken to be seditious...[if]...it intends":

(1) to show that the government have been misled or mistaken in any of their measures; or

(2) to point out errors or defects in the Government of Kenya as by law established or in any written law or in the administration of justice, with a view to the remedying of such errors or defects; or

(3) to persuade the inhabitants of Kenya to attempt to procure by lawful means the alteration of any matter in Kenya as by law established; or

(4) to point out, with a view to their removal, any matters which are producing or have tendency to produce feelings of ill-will or hostility between different sections or classes of the population of Kenya.

However, the proviso has not been used to acquit a person charged with sedition. When the court was challenged to consider this in 1982, in the case of a student charged with writing a seditious essay, there was no willingness to use the relevant legislation. In this case, David Onyango Oloo of the University of Nairobi, was charged for writing an incomplete essay titled "A plea to comrades." The handwritten essay was found when security officers searched his suitcase in a train. His lawyer advised him to plead guilty. When Oloo refused, the lawyer stopped representing him. Conducting his own defense in court, Oloo argued that as a student he was within the law to write a critique of various aspects of Kenya's national life, and challenged the court to show where fair criticism ended and sedition began. The court did not take up the challenge, but found him guilty and jailed him.

AN INDEFENSIBLE LAW

In Kenyan law, even truth is not an acceptable defense in sedition charges. If, for example, a person states that employment is allocated on tribal considerations rather than on ability, and can prove it, he or she can be convicted of sedition if the court thinks the statement has caused disaffection or raised discomfort. In other words, the legislation ensures that a person can be convicted of sedition on the basis of the effect, even if the assertion or publication is correct.

Section 57(2) also stipulates that:

...in determining whether the intention with which any act was done, any words were spoken or any document was published was or was not seditious, every person shall be deemed to intend the consequences which would naturally follow from his conduct at the time and in the circumstances in which he so conducted himself.

This means that a person can be convicted of sedition even if they do not intend it. Thus, if discontent or disaffection is the unexpected result of a person's words or actions, a conviction of sedition can still be sought on the basis of the effect rather than the intention. In sum, this legislation allows a person to be convicted of sedition even if the intention was not seditious, even if the publication or assertion was not seditious (providing a guilty plea is obtained), and even if the statement made was true. Calls to repeal the sedition laws have focused on the diffuse and vague nature of the legislation and its contradiction with the constitutionally guaranteed freedom of expression.

ABDUCTION AND DETENTION

Defendants are typically abducted by the Special Branch and kept incommunicado for long periods without access to lawyers. They are frequently held without charge for periods exceeding the legal requirements. Many have testified that they were subjected to torture by the police. A man held in July 1990 for "possessing a seditious publication" was taken to a forest and suspended face-down above a river with his hands and ankles tied; he was repeatedly swung into the river and threatened with death. During the 1986-87 MwaKenya trials many of the defendants were kept without food, naked, in waterlogged cells and beaten in order to get them to confess. The use of torture was also alleged during the 1991 trial of George Anyona and his codefendants.

DENIAL OF BAIL

In Kenyan law, bail should not be denied without good reason. In practice, it is routine to refuse bail in sedition cases when the prosecution objects. Paul Muite called this denial of bail a "dangerous trend" in August 1990. He said the charge of sedition was an attempt to "clothe with judicial respectability what is otherwise political persecution in blatant breach of the fundamental rights guaranteed in the constitution." He observed that bail:

> ...is a constitutional right. That constitutional right has been reduced almost to a dead letter in the Law in Kenya today because it has become extremely rare for

the court to grant bail in politically sensitive cases in the
face of objection to bail by the prosecution.[2]

Denial of bail punishes the individual without guilt having to be
established. It was used for this purpose in the cases of George Anyona
and his codefendants arrested in July 1990, who served six months in
remand before the trial started.[3] Gitobu Imanyara, arrested March 1991
on charges of sedition, was kept in solitary confinement, even when
seriously ill, and was repeatedly denied bail before the charges were
eventually dropped in May.

UNFAIR TRIALS

Sedition trials are frequently held outside normal court hours to
minimize the likelihood of relatives and lawyers being present. The
defendants are brought to court through a side entrance at the end of the
day—often as late as 5:00 P.M. They are heavily guarded by Special
Branch officers instead of regular prison guards.

The trial itself disregards all due process. The seditious
publication is not available for inspection because the contents are
deemed to be "prejudicial to state security." It is, therefore, invisible
evidence and uncontestable. There is usually no other evidence other
than self-incriminating admissions obtained in police custody. These cases
are commonly brought before the chief magistrate, led by Deputy Public
Prosecutor Bernard Chunga.[4] There is no jury system in Kenya.

BREACH OF THE PEACE: THE LAYMAN'S SEDITION

Breach of the peace charges are widely used to stifle political
expression. They are used in much the same way as charges of sedition,

---

[2] Application for bail for George Gachoka, by Paul Muite, as heard in court.

[3] They were kept as if they were political prisoners. See chapter six.

[4] Bernard Chunga led the prosecution for the MwaKenya trials in 1986-87.

which are brought mainly against intellectuals and professionals. Section 95(1) of the Penal Code defines "breach of the peace" as anyone who:

> a) uses obscene, abusive or insulting language, to his employer or to any person placed in authority over him by his employer, in such a manner as is likely to cause a breach of the peace; or

> b) brawls or in any other manner creates a disturbance in such a manner as is likely to cause a breach of the peace is guilty of a misdemeanour and is liable to imprisonment for six months.

Breach of the peace is used, in this context, to inhibit oral communication—a strategy used primarily against the poorer and illiterate sections of the community (see appendix C). Fear of the potency of oral communication among the poorer sections of society was evident in the Saba Saba period, when charges of sedition and breach of the peace were brought against people playing seditious songs, wearing seditious t-shirts with the two-finger sign, remarking thatKANU was stupid, or saying that the government would not last for more than a year, or shouting "down with Moi." The cases, although verging on the farcical in content, elicited disproportionately harsh sentences. Most people were remanded in custody for lengthy periods of time before being released on bail.

RUMORMONGERING

In 1990, hundreds of people were interrogated by the Special Branch for rumongering—that is, verbal speculation as to whether the death of Dr. Ouko was politically motivated. By announcing that rumongering should be stopped immediately, President Moi gave security forces the authority to pick up any person perceived to be critical of the president or of the party. Hundreds were subsequently picked up throughout the country. In the Nyanza and central provinces, residents said many people were held in police cells overnight and others were held for two or three days before being release without charge.

The crackdown on rumors provided an opportunity to harass well-known personalities considered critical of the government. This appeared to be an attempt to discredit and isolate critics and also to use high-profile examples to intimidate the rest of the population.

Professor Wangari Maathai, leader of the environmental Green Belt movement, was among those interrogated in April 1990 over rumormongering (see chapter three). Professor Maathai saw it as a frightening experience designed to intimidate her:

> I wouldn't pay any attention to the threats if I knew they wouldn't do anything to me unless they took me in a court of law and proved beyond all reasonable doubt that I was involved in anti-government activities. But I do know we do live in a situation where accusations can be made against you. If the security police decided to pick you up and try you in camera nobody would ever know what you were charged with....[5]

Ex-detainees and political prisoners are particularly vulnerable. An ex-prisoner convicted on a false charge of sedition in 1986 described his experience to Africa Watch:

> I was arrested again in early September 1990. My residence was searched. I was taken to a number of police stations in Nairobi before eventually being transferred to Nyayo House for interrogation. I stayed there for about one week. During that time I was questioned about my connection with the detained former cabinet ministers, a number of lawyers championing the cause of human rights, the press releases they issued, and many other issues. As there was no evidence for them to charge me I was released. But not without being given a stern warning about my political attitude... I was told that as long as I maintain my own political attitude I can forget that I will be allowed to hold a job in this country....

---

[5] Press interview, April 1990.

SETTING THE SCENE: SYMBOLS OF SEDITION

When the security apparatus has become fixated on charging a person, the scene is often set by placing the person in a context which the government considers incriminating. Typically, the police will confiscate books and literature described as "left wing" and "socialist." These publications are entirely legal, have never been prohibited, and are never used as evidence, but are referred to in court in a manner designed to discredit.

Beards are treated as incriminating by the authorities because they are seen as a symbol of radicalism and dissent. In some of his public addresses and speeches, President Moi has referred to "certain bearded individuals" when voicing condemnation or suspicion. In April 1990, a school teacher at Ruiru, Kiambu, was forcibly shaved in public by the District Commissioner who—illegally—insisted that it was not acceptable in school. One defendant said in mitigation during a sedition trial that he did not advocate communism despite being taunted during interrogation for having a "Marxist beard": "I am saying that because wearing beards has nothing to do with ideological conscience."[6]

PLANTING EVIDENCE

There have been a number of accounts from those who refused to sign self-incriminating statements on how they are set up with planted evidence. Planting banned or seditious publications is considered a routine practice of the police force. Where the Special Branch has no concrete charge, a search of the suspect's house or office will result in the discovery of a banned or seditious publication. Typically, this search will be additional to one initially carried out when the suspect is arrested or abducted by police officers. Marijuana is also frequently used by the police to victimize individuals they view as troublesome among the poorest urban sectors of the population.

---

[6] Rev. Imunde, March 1990. See chapter six.

STITCHING UP THE SABA SABA

Accounts given to Africa Watch indicate that planting was used extensively during the July 1990 Saba Saba period, including cases where people were arrested for possession of publications not listed as banned. One person interviewed was arrested, interrogated about his associates, and then charged with possessing a seditious publication which he says was planted:

> I was taken from the police station back to my office. They told me to watch while they searched; they told me to watch them very, very carefully. About seven Special Branch officers started to search, taking everything with names on it—like wedding cards, company cards, notes, that sort of thing. They went through all the drawers, but there was something insincere about the way it was done. There was a box file on my desk. An officer opened it and said "Oh, MwaKenya. I've found it." They showed it to me—it was a leaflet calling for the overthrow of the government, or something like that. Then a copy of *Financial Review* was taken from the drawer of the desk. I had never seen the copies before and I knew they had been planted. It doesn't even make sense, does it? Would anybody keep such things in a file on their desk? Then they took me home and did a search there, but it was very brief—even though you would have thought they would search thoroughly if they suspected me of something.

In another case, Peter (not his real name), who was arrested during the multiparty debate because of his close association with an ex-detainee, told fellow inmates in Kamiti Maximum Security Prison how he had been framed by the Special Branch. When he refused to incriminate his friend and cooperate as a prosecution witness, he was taken to Karua Forest, physically abused and threatened with death by drowning. He continued to refuse. After two weeks in Nyayo House, he was released and told to go home. Within days of being released, Special Branch officers came to his home early in the morning and told him to come to the police station for a routine interview. They insisted he bring his coat, but he refused because he was reassured he would return home the same day. Police officers insisted on collecting it from his house and carried it to the police station. Peter said he did not appreciate its significance until a MwaKenya leaflet was "found" in his coat pocket at the police station. The Special Branch left him at the police station and he was remanded to Kaimiti Maximum Security Prison on charges of sedition.

WINNING SOME, LOSING SOME
THE CASE OF REV. LAWFORD NDEGE IMUNDE

Rev. Imunde, a minister of the Presbyterian Church of East Africa (PCEA), was picked up by two police officers as he was leaving his hotel in Nairobi, who searched his bag and confiscated his diary and letters. Imunde disappeared until he managed to get a note smuggled out of Kilileshwa police station begging his lawyers for help. Imunde's wife was notified and she filed a habeas corpus writ, but the priest thereafter was brought to court late in the afternoon in an attempt to avoid publicity and legal representation.

Imunde's lawyer, Kiraitu Murungi, informed the court he was the lawyer of the accused and asked to consult his client. It was Imunde, however, who then rejected the legal counsel he had gone to such lengths to seek. He pleaded guilty and received a six-year prison sentence.

The evidence for the conviction were two entries in Imunde's desk diary, which were not revealed in court as they were deemed "prejudicial to state security."

> In my diary I had a note on the Ouko death. I noted this has some implications on the stability of the regime. I had another note or comment on the government statement on the death of Ouko. I wrote, "I do not like the implication that he shot himself."

> There was also another entry [in] which I said, "the President admits that the government has a problem with unemployment, especially the youth. Could this be the beginning or the end of the system with which most of us are fed up?..."

I had also an entry [about] the big fund raising[7]. The only comment I had made was, "how much of this will be used for the purposes for which it was intended?" Then I added "The opinion of the ordinary wananchi [citizen] is that only those at the fount will benefit..."

There was an entry when the President said he had not started with vindictiveness, then said henceforth whoever engaged in rumor will be dealt with. Then I wrote: "the President turns vindictive. Will his enemies do something before he starts killing and detaining them?" There is nothing else in the diary.

Rev. Imunde said he was forced to add more to the diary, including the comment: "Can't someone or a group of people do something while he [President Moi] is away...to change our situation for prosperity?" These entries were used by the prosecution to support the charges of sedition. He was told to plead guilty and forced to sign a prepared statement defaming the Church (see chapter thirteen):

> I was locked up in the cell...I heard them say "write the statement quickly because we have been asked by his friends to produce him in court." They mentioned Kamau Kuria and Kiraitu Murungi.

> I was taken before them [the police]. I found a written statement....They told me that although they were hoping to release me my wife had spoilt everything by rushing to court...I was asked to accept [plead guilty]. I said I could not do so before I knew the charge. They told me that they had instructions from their seniors to release me if I pleaded guilty to the charge which they would suggest. I was given a charge of sedition based on Cap. 63. I told them that I would consider it...I was asked to

---

[7] President Moi presided over a huge public *harambee* where the public donated money intended to support an educational charity for the children of needy families.

sign. I hesitated. One of them pulled out a pistol and threatened me. I signed the statement.

He was warned not to take legal counsel, and that a guilty plea would ensure his freedom:

> I was handcuffed and we went to the CID headquarters. The charge was read to me. I was charged with possessing seditious documents. I asked what I would say. I was given a pen and I wrote, I shall reply to the charge in court. I signed. They said they were in a hurry, they said Chunga was waiting for them...that they had instructions from above, so that if I did not allow Kamau and Kiraitu to insult the government, they would release me and show me how to plead guilty. I was told I should not appear to be fighting the government. I told them that I did not want to implicate anybody and whatever decision I made was in the best interests of my family. I was told to copy the points which I later read in court. They took away a copy which they brought the next day. They told me that I should not worry whatever the court decided as they would help me. I was given the statement just a few minutes before we got to court. That is why I said I should read the statement...I told Mr. Kiraitu not to represent me (when he stood up in court) because I did not want to implicate him or to give the impression that we were fighting the government.

> I was shocked when I was sentenced to six years because it was a betrayal of trust. They had told me that they would release me. I pleaded guilty because I had been induced.

Rev. Imunde was released on March 19, 1991, when Justice Porter ruled that although he was guilty by his own confession, the sentence was too harsh for the offense. This did not in fact rule in favor of the appeal put forward by Kathurima M'Inoti, Imunde's lawyer, who argued that he should be acquitted because comments in a private diary could not be seditious as they were not intended for an audience:

The law of sedition does not punish the intention per se. It punishes when and only when it is exhibited or manifested in a manner tending to bring about the disorders contemplated by Section 56 (1). The mischief the law tries to stop is where the publication is manifested to others with that intention.[8]

Justice Porter ruled that even if the document was not a publication by legal definition, it was by Imunde's own admission. Justice Porter did not accept that the guilty plea was obtained under duress.

THE MWAKENYA TRIALS

The government's eagerness to use charges of sedition to jail critics was demonstrated in the 1986-88 crackdown, when many people were arrested and convicted on charges relating to the MwaKenya underground movement. In over one hundred political trials at that time, every defendant pled guilty except three, and none of those charged was allowed to consult a lawyer while in custody or during the trial. Of the three who pleaded not guilty, two changed their plea after being returned to custody (see chapter six). The most common charges were "possession of a seditious publication" carrying a maximum seven year jail sentence; "distribution of a seditious publication" carrying a maximum ten year prison sentence; and "taking an unlawful oath"(Article 61), also carrying a maximum jail sentence of ten years. Apart from three, who received fines, all were convicted and given between four and six year prison sentences; no appeals to the High Court were successful.

One of those convicted in a 1986 sedition trial told Africa Watch. how his house was searched for several hours before he was told he was under arrest. Describing how he was tortured and held incommunicado in Nyayo House for twenty-one days, he said he was often unconscious by the end of interrogation sessions.

I resisted and refused to accept the false allegations against me, and there was no evidence against me...I was

---

[8] Argued by Kathurima M'Inoti, and included in the judgment of Justices Porter and Mbaluto, March 19, 1991.

nevertheless told I would not, like it or not, be released. I was told I faced three alternatives. First, and the worst of all, I would be tortured to death—some people were later tortured to death by the same Special Branch officers. Second, they would, after torturing me, take me to detention where I would rot for years. Third, I would be jailed under a false charge which I had no choice but to accept if I wished to save my life. Being released was not an alternative despite lack of evidence against me.

I was all this time held incommunicado. I was not allowed to see or talk to any member of my family or friend. My attempt to obtain a lawyer was bluntly refused. I had no choice but to accept the false charge if I wanted to escape further torture.

I was in the end, when the torture became excessive and unbearable, forced to accept the false charge. I was therefore forced to accept I was found in possession of a seditious document entitled *Mpatanishi and the Draft Programme* even though this was completely false.

After being charged under Section 57 (2) being found in possession of a seditious publication, the defendant was tried in what he called a Kangaroo Court:

I was arraigned before a chief magistrate at around 7:00 P.M. The whole trial, which lasted less than five minutes, was a complete farce. Everything had been arranged in advance and all that I was required to do was to plead guilty. The only members in court besides myself and the magistrate was the government prosecutor and a dozen Special Branch police officers. These were the same men who had been torturing me all along. Their presence was aimed at intimidating me and therefore accept the charge. I had no desire to go back to the torture chambers and I accepted the charge.

I was jailed for five years. Five years for nothing! I however served the five years, since my appeal was

summarily rejected by a high court too eager to uphold
the illegal conviction... I was released in August 1989
after completing five years, less the necessary remission.

Where defendants refuse to plead guilty, despite torture, they are
found guilty on invisible and spurious evidence. No tangible evidence was
produced during the trial in 1991 of George Anyona and his
codefendants, who denied charges of holding a seditious meeting in a
Nairobi bar. No plot to overthrow the government was revealed, there
were major discrepancies in the prosecution evidence, no other witnesses
other than the police were called and the court heard allegations of
torture from all the accused. Despite this, all received the maximum
sentence of seven years on July 11.

9
THE JUDICIARY
A SYSTEM OF INJUSTICE

At the heart of the human rights crisis in Kenya is the lack of an independent judiciary. Courts are used to dispose of political opponents and critics. On a broader basis, the courts have also become a weapon for the powerful and wealthy to settle personal vendettas and local disputes. The court system is three-tiered:

a)   the Magistrate's Court, which deals with all criminal cases except for treason and murder, and has one magistrate sitting;

b)   the High Court, which has a criminal side, and is presided over by one or two judges;

c)   a Court of Appeal, which has three judges sitting.

The most significant players in this system are Chief Justice Hancox, Chief Magistrate Omondi Tunya, Criminal Duty Judge Porter, Civil Duty Judge Dugdale, and Attorney General Amos Wako.

THE ADMINISTRATIVE METHOD OF CONTROLLING
THE OUTCOME OF JUSTICE

The system is controlled through a mechanism that operates like a funnel. All political criminal cases are filtered through the chief magistrate who takes the plea, controls the terms for bail, sets the hearing date, allocates the case to the judge of his choice, and deals with any complaints arising from either the prosecution or the defendant (for example about health, treatment and access to lawyers). The chief magistrate is therefore in a position to determine the case if so directed by the government.

In almost all the recorded human rights cases, the defendant has been without representation and brought to court at the end of the day when few lawyers remain in the building; in the Nairobi courts, the defendant is usually heavily guarded, and brought in between 4:30 and 5:30 P.M.

It is a hallmark of the cases brought before the chief magistrate that there is no further inquiry into complaints of torture, lack of reasonable access to counsel, ill-treatment, or excessive periods in police custody. The chief magistrate is not known to have sought—or given—an explanation regarding periods in police custody that exceed the stated time limits.[1]

Cases that have gone directly to the chief magistrate include the application for a preliminary inquiry into the treason charges against Koigi wa Wamwere and all applications concerning the editor of the *Nairobi Law Monthly*, Gitobu Imanyara, and his codefendant, Joseph Watoro.

Criminal cases heard in the high court come before the duty criminal judge, Justice Porter, who receives all appeals and allocates them to a judge for hearing. He may allocate to another judge, or to himself, or he can sit together with another judge. Judge Porter hears all bail applications in criminal cases and complaints in the same manner the chief magistrate does in the magistrate's court.

The same mechanism operates in the civil wing of the high court, processed through the civil duty judge, Justice Dugdale. It is in this court that challenges to human rights violations take the form of a constitutional challenge or a judicial review. For a judicial review—that is questioning the way in which the law was used—the civil duty judge must first "give leave" to allow the case to proceed. All such cases must, therefore, first come before Justice Dugdale in the high court. Justice Dugdale has consistently refused leave in sensitive cases (as in the application to hold a public inquiry into Bishop Muge's death); but did not hesitate to give leave to an application to cite the Law Society Council for contempt, even though it was a matter concerning allegations regarding himself (see below). Once leave has been refused, an application may not proceed. Thus a case can be killed before it is heard. Applications for habeas corpus have never been known to be successful in the high court.

---

[1] In 1990, the court of appeal said in a judgment that it was "unhappy" about detention in police custody that exceeded the stated time limits.

PERMANENT DUTY

Normally, the duty judges must rotate every three to four months; but Justices Dugdale and Porter have remained in their respective positions for an extended period of time. Justice Dugdale has remained as civil duty judge for nearly two years. It is routine for these judges to allocate all the sensitive and political cases to themselves, and then proceed with pro-government rulings.

The court system thus acts as a funnel allowing the government to control the outcome of a case by determining the players and the direction. Presiding over this apparatus is the Chief Justice Hancox, who has great influence quite apart from his judicial position. According to one Kenyan lawyer:

> Justice Hancox has fully utilized the system—he is not the architect, but the exploiter. There can be no independence of the judiciary, no spirit of independence, when one person is imposing on it like this.

The chief justice normally sits in the court of appeal, but is empowered to sit anywhere. From their powerful strategic positions, therefore, Justices Hancox, Dugdale and Porter and Chief Magistrate Omondi Tunya can impose immediate control on a case and prevent it reaching any other part of the system. The dependency of the government on expatriate judges to facilitate the abuse of the system and to perpetuate Kenya's human rights crisis has attracted national and international criticism.

THE ROLE OF BRITISH EXPATRIATE JUDGES

British judges have been in Kenya since independence, but were slowly phased out with the Africanization of the judiciary. As part of British aid to Kenya, the Overseas Development Administration supplements the local salary of judges. Initially, British judges were considered necessary when there were insufficient senior lawyers from Kenya to take up judgeships. They were also installed in the belief that they were incorruptible compared with their Kenyan counterparts. The present chief justice, Justice Hancox, continues to assert this as a crucial reason to retain the expatriate judges, although the evidence suggests they are just as susceptible to pressure as their Kenyan counterparts. The expatriate judges are on renewable contracts and must carry out their duties favorably if they wish to stay. According to a former expatriate judge,[2] these contracted judges feel no patriotic allegiance to the country, but are motivated by a desire to safeguard their position, status and security in the country.

The Kenyan government does not offer sufficient financial incentives to attract the necessary candidates for the judiciary from its own lawyers, who do not get the financial supplements the British government pays to expatriates. According to members of the legal community, senior lawyers are also increasingly reluctant to take up judgeships because there is too much interference from the executive. The "funnel" prevents independently-minded professionals from interfering with its government established mission, because the key players do not allocate sensitive cases to those judges. Cases are also moved from one judge to another to get the required outcome.

Lawyers also point out that the way in which magistrates and judges are appointed facilitates government interference. Magistrates are appointed immediately after graduation and become professional magistrates—they have never practiced independently. Judges are picked from the magistrates. The weakness of the judiciary grows, as promotion depends on compliance and approval by the government. The process is described by one member of the profession as:

> depending on pleasing the person who promotes you—and you know he hasn't got there by showing an independent initiative. The fact that none of these people have practised before becoming magistrates or judges means they don't show any independence of spirit. Having to show compliance to get promotion skews the common law system in favor of the government.

British Expatriate Judges and Human Rights: An International Scandal?

The role of British expatriate judges in facilitating censorship and human rights abuses by consistently ruling in favor of the state was discussed in a letter in the July 14, 1990, issue of *The Guardian*, published soon after Justices Dugdale and Porter had dismissed appeals against

---

[2] See *New Law Journal* (Butterworths, London), June, 28, 1991.

preventive detention orders in July 1990. The letter said that the paper's criticism of "the state of justice and the use of preventive detention in Kenya neglects the question of which judges are sanctioning detention orders":

> In fact, Chief Justice Robin Hancox refers most lawyers' appeals against preventive detention orders to Justices Dugdale or Porter. These British judges have presided while the government has insured it need give no specific reason for detaining leading political figures such as Ken Matiba, or their lawyers such as Mohamed Ibrahim, beyond that of state security.

> ...Justice Porter refused to admit defense counsel James O'Kwade to the hearing of an application for habeas corpus which he had filed for his detained client, Mohamed Ibrahim.

> Far from assisting Kenya to sustain and develop the tradition of the common law these judges are nurturing the authoritarian state...

> It is an abject scandal that the British taxpayer subsidises a part of these men's salaries...Cannot the British government, so quick to support the "rights of men" in Eastern Europe, move to axe these judges...?

In April 1990, a British publication, the *New Law Journal*, carried an article "Kenyan Injustice" which also focused on the role of the expatriate judges:

> ...two British judges in Kenya, Justices Dugdale and Porter, have played a major role in facilitating censorship and human rights abuses. Dugdale, in particular, will always be remembered by Kenyan human rights lawyers for audaciously ruling in July 1989 that the courts in Kenya have no power to enforce the Kenyan Bill of Rights.

On May 13, 1991, the Law Society of Kenya issued a unanimous statement objecting to the pro-government rulings of the same judges:

> There has been a line of decisions and rulings by the Hon Mr Justice Dugdale, the juridical basis of which is extremely difficult to discern.[3] The Hon Chief Justice Hancox has, since his appointment in 1987, retained Mr Justice Dugdale as the "permanent" duty judge....Council has similar difficulties in following the juridical basis of some of the rulings and judgments of the Hon Mr Justice Porter.
>
> Council is of the view that a Tribunal ought to be set up in terms of Section 62 of the Kenya Constitution to inquire into the ability of his Lordship the Chief Justice and the Honourable Mr Justice Dugdale to perform the duties of their office with a view to removing them should the Tribunal so recommend. Council would argue in detail before such a Tribunal for the removal of the two judges.

After this statement was released, there was no public response from the state or the judges, but action was taken by proxy. Four lawyers brought an action of contempt against the Law Society Council, saying that the statement was political, and therefore breached an injunction that had earlier been placed on Chair Paul Muite. Mr. Muite had been instructed to refrain from making any political statements in his capacity as chair (see chapter eleven). To bring such an action for contempt of court, the applicant has to apply for leave (to allow the case to go forward) from the duty judge. In this case, leave was given by Justice Dugdale, who allocated the case to himself—despite the fact it is a principle of common law that a judge does not adjudicate on matters concerning himself or herself.

----

[3] Cases thereafter listed: the Kihoru Constitutional Reference, *Maina Mbacha v. Attorney-General*, Misc. Appl. No. 356 of 1989; *Professor Wangari Maathai v. the Attorney-General* HCCC No. 5404 of 1989; the late Bishop Muge's case Civil Application No. 177/90, the KPCU case No. HCCC 1316/91, and Election Petition Number 13 of 1988—*John Rotich v. Nicholas Mberia & Another.*

On June 17, 1991, Justice Dugdale was asked to disqualify himself in court from hearing a constitutional case, as he was "likely to be biased." James Orengo, acting for Jaramogi Oginga Odinga, sought to register the new National Democratic Party under the provision for "freedom of association and assembly" in the constitution. He argued that an expatriate judge did not have security of tenure and was therefore likely to be biased:

> In view of cases that have come before you affecting Constitutional matters, most of which touch on rights and freedoms of individuals as stipulated in Sections 70 and 80 of the Constitution, and which you have always ruled in favour of the State, the applicants in this matter feel you should disqualify yourself from this case.[4]

Justice Dugdale called this submission "ridiculous propaganda" and warned the lawyer that he was "heading for trouble...say any more, and you've had it." Orengo was found in contempt of court and Justice Dugdale called in the police.

The following week, the British publication, the *New Law Journal* carried an interview with a former expatriate judge, Eugene Cotran, who said he believed the selection process was wrong, and that expatriate judges were "more susceptible" to influence by the executive than local judges:

> I think they are more susceptible...because of the way the system operates—because ODA [Overseas Development Administration] will only extend supplementation if the local government ask for it. If an expatriate judge has to go, he has, with few exceptions, no job to go back to. That is a very big pressure.

He also described how pressure was put on the judiciary:

> It's exerted by taking [a] case away from judge A so that it is heard by judge B. It is exerted by telephone calls, by being told that government would like a certain result in

---

[4] *The Standard*, June 18, 1991.

a particular cases. It is exercised by shifting people from one area to another...

Certainly you had direct pressure, direct communication while you were doing a case, which is to be deprecated in any system.

Cotran emphasized that Kenya was "unique" in having expatriate judges when there was "no shortage locally":

I don't think it is the function of the British government to keep supplementing the situation where the locals resent these judges....What the British government don't realise is that although it looks good to have expatriate judges upholding the law, so to speak, the population don't see it this way. They see these judges as doing the reverse and not serving or upholding the law. If judges manipulate the law in order to achieve the wish of the central government then they are not doing their job properly. It doesn't happen every day—but it happens invariably in the politically sensitive cases. If it happens time and time again when the judge presiding is an expatriate judge, it is inevitable the local lawyers and the local judges perceive this as a plot between the executive in Kenya and the British government to achieve ends judicially with results which are not in conformity with their ideas of an independent judiciary.

Two expatriate judges have resigned because of this pressure, Justices Dereck Schofield and Patrick O'Connor. In late 1987, Justice Schofield of the high court refused to renew his contract of service after the chief justice at the time took him off a case in which he had ordered the police to bring to court a detainee they had arrested, following a habeas corpus suit filed by the detainee's wife.[5] In an interview with the *Nairobi Law Monthly*, Judge Schofield explained his reasons for not seeking a renewal of contract:

---

[5] The suspect died in police custody. See chapter seventeen for details about the case of Stephen Karanja.

I cannot operate in a system where the law is so blatantly contravened by those who are supposed to be its supreme guardians.

DEPARTURES FROM THE COMMON LAW

It is a fundamental principle of common law that the activities of judges must be open to scrutiny, the aim being to prevent abuse of the system. Published law reports are essential to open justice so that all judgments can be obtained for examination by the public (who are affected directly by these judgments and may wish to take action on them), by professionals, academics and the international community. In Kenya, however, regular law reports stopped appearing after the 1980 reports were published (see chapter twelve). Consequently, obtaining a judgment has become extremely difficult, and is often obstructed by bureaucracy and unwillingness to operate publicly.

This absence of official information contributes significantly to the failure of the judiciary to develop or maintain its independence. The manipulation of judges not only affects those who succumb to it, but collectively undermines the judiciary as a whole. According to one member of the legal profession:

> The failure of spirit, the lack of independence, affects the whole system. It's not just the one or two judges who are acting for the government—which is a failure anyway— but it is the fact that the whole judiciary gets a bad name. Even those who are independent suffer in morale and professional respect. It can be seen very clearly with the amendments in 1988. Not a single judge resigned or made a public statement when tenure was removed. What does that imply about the spirit of independence?

Kiraitu Murungi, interviewed by a member of the international press corps in Nairobi after Rev. Lawford Ndege Imunde was convicted of sedition, said his attitude to the judiciary was extremely negative:

> The judiciary was given a key role in safeguarding the freedom of the Kenyans which they had won at independence. The Bill of Rights, which was written in

the constitution, was to be enforced by the judiciary. But
the judiciary has been unable to play this key role which
it was given. Firstly because in the initial stages of our
independence the judiciary was manned by expatriates
who did not feel it was their business to involve
themselves in the political aspirations of the Kenyan
people. But after that, the judiciary has to a large extent
been Africanized but because of lack of security of
tenure, the judiciary has taken the role of suppressing
the human rights it was supposed to enhance. And it's a
big tragedy because only last year one of our judges gave
a judgment without hearing arguments of either counsel
to the effect that Section 84 of the Constitution is not
enforceable; which means that the Kenyan Bill of Rights
is all a sham which cannot be enforced by our courts.

PAPERWORK

Much of the manipulation of cases goes on behind the scenes
through the administration network before the case is even heard in
court. Corruption taints the court system as thoroughly as any
government department, particularly among court clerks who are bribed
to lose and transfer files. Many case files are transferred if the
government wishes to have a particular case dealt with in Nairobi, where
they have greater control over the outcome. Case files are frequently lost
because interested parties have paid the clerks to remove the files and the
judge is often told a few minutes before a trial starts that the files cannot
be found. In this way, many cases fail to be heard.

Manipulation of election petitions is, according to sources within
the judiciary, routine. When a petition is brought to court, the
government tells the judge who they want. The chief justice either
presides over the case, or tells the presiding judge what the outcome
should be. Judges who have not conceded to instructions have
subsequently been asked to change the judgment.

SECURITY OF TENURE

There was much criticism of the government when it removed the security of tenure of high court and court of appeal judges in August 1988. It was seen as manifest interference with the ability of the judiciary to operate independently.

Security of tenure for judges was restored in 1990 on the recommendations of the KANU Review Committee, after the lack of independence of the judiciary featured in the complaints submitted by various representations of the public. While the move was welcomed by Western governments and diplomats, legal critics described it as cosmetic.

A CHANGE OF SPIRIT?

Amos Wako was appointed attorney general in May 1991, after the former attorney general, Matthew Muli, had come under much public criticism.

Matthew Muli played a central—and increasingly controversial role—as attorney general from 1983 to 1991. An editorial in the *Weekly Review* called Muli a "confused man" and quoted a number of instances where his decisions appeared unprofessional and contradictory. Pointing to Muli as a "liability," it advised him to resign, and reviewed some of the most disturbing events of his eight-year term:

> ...he has exceeded all previous Attorney-Generals in contributing to the erosion of public confidence in that critical office... In fact, a great deal of the criticism levelled against the government about its human rights record has emanated from court prosecutions. The government has suffered a great deal as a result of Muli's ineptitude in leading major prosecutions, particularly those involving government critics. Many such prosecutions have appeared unnecessary from the point of view of law and order and even security, raising suspicions of witch-hunting on the part of the government. On Muli's instructions, state prosecutors have tended to deny such accused persons bail, even when the denials serve no purpose. Muli's unnecessary delays in giving consent to prosecute have also earned

him criticism, even from the judiciary. And there have
been occasions where he has personally taken up cases in
court, only to end up exposing his inadequate
interpretation of the law and in the process, ruining the
prosecution's case.[6]

Earlier an editorial in the *Nairobi Law Monthly* pointed out that
Muli had made decisions which the court of appeal said were "not
sanctioned by any Constitutional or Statutory provision in the laws of
Kenya." The appointment of a new attorney general came at a time when
the government was under concerted international pressure over the
continued detention of Gitobu Imanyara, Kenneth Matiba and Raila
Odinga. Concern for Kenya's human rights record had taken its toll on
pledges of aid from Western governments. The government has
emphasized Mr. Wako's experience and his participation in international
human rights conferences and membership of United Nations committees
dealing with the protection of human rights. Kenyan diplomats and
government officials gave reassurances at the time of the appointment
that it should be taken as showing a "new spirit." Shortly afterwards,
Imanyara, Matiba and Odinga were released unconditionally.

TAKING UP THE REINS

The ability of the current government to manipulate the legal
system relates very much to the system it inherited. Using criminal and
political charges to silence opponents was intrinsic to the nature of the
colonial government, which introduced the present legal system. The
British tendency to use the legal machinery to legitimize repression was
adopted by both Presidents Kenyatta and Moi, and identical use is now
made of the Criminal Code to criminalize opposition through charges of
sedition, subversion, breach of the peace and treason. Other criminal
charges used for purposes of harassment and restriction of movement are
drunk and disorderly conduct, prostitution and vagrancy. The legal
machinery that the British took pride in exporting to the colonies was
very much a refined one, and did not incorporate the same democratic
content operating back home in London.

---

[6] *Weekly Review*, April 12, 1991.

Both President Moi and the late President Kenyatta have exploited their inheritance. Under Kenyatta, the malleability of the legal apparatus was used through his powerful attorney general, Charles Njonjo, who held the post of attorney general from 1964 to 1981 and is considered the chief architect of the "funnel" system. He maximized power through the court system. President Moi has taken up the reins by enfeebling the judiciary, co-opting and corrupting the legal community, and attacking independent and human rights lawyers. The extent of his success has been to effectively politicize and criminalize the legal profession itself: judges, magistrates and lawyers are perceived as either loyal to the party and the president, or opposed to them. Consequently, the vital notion of independence and professionalism has all but been destroyed. Lawyers are perceived as sharing the views of their clients, not just representing them. Independent and human rights lawyers are undermined by subjudicial public attacks by the president.

It has in many ways proved a successful tactic as the political motives are, in the eyes of the general public, clothed in legal obscurities. Although a group of predominantly Nairobi-based lawyers publicly tackle the abuse of the legal system through the courts, the significance of the action is generally recognized by only a small and elite community. Public ignorance of the law is encouraged through lack of information and absence of legal aid, and, as a result, battles over legal technicalities in court are often widely perceived in the way they are deliberately projected by the government as anti-establishment harassment.[7] Controversial human rights cases draw more sympathetic attention, but it is only relatively recently, and only among a very small section of urban-based communities, that a new willingness and bravado has surfaced in taking complaints to court.

Africa Watch does not have detailed information on how the legal system functions outside Nairobi, which, according to members of the legal profession and provincial communities, is very prone to the dictates of the powerful provincial administration and the local fiefdoms of politicians. Pressure on the judiciary has increased since 1987-88. Previously, if a judge received instructions on how to rule, the justification given used to be the security of the state, or "the wishes of

---

[7] There is a legal advice center in Nairobi, Kituo Cha Sheria, which provides legal aid in a limited number of cases. There are no legal advice centers or legal aid provisions in the provinces.

the President." This was extended to other powerful figures close to the president. Since the late 1980s, however, pressure has been exerted from more quarters and with less subtlety. The result, according to one lawyer, is that "everyone uses it; the ministers, the assistant ministers, the Provincial Administration, the District Administration—anyone who can exercise some power wants to exercise it through the courts." Thus although the tenure of judges has been restored, it is likely to prove an empty gesture.

HIJACKING THE LEGAL MACHINERY

Kenya prides itself on a sophisticated legal machinery and a determination, in principle, to pursue legal solutions to social and political problems. It is probably for this reason that the government prefers to manipulate legal structures rather than abandon them. The international climate has made the government more reluctant to detain without trial and openly harry its critics, yet in facing a serious political crisis, its desire to dispose of opponents has become more urgent. The result is that the government has come to rely heavily on a legal system skewed in its favor. Therefore, many human rights abuses in Kenya are facilitated within the court system as opposed to being pursued extra-judicially.

10
PRISON CONDITIONS

Prisons in Kenya have become extremely overcrowded. In 1986, the former commissioner of police, Philip Kirui, admitted that although Kenya's seventy-five prisons were meant to hold a maximum of 14,000 inmates, they already held at least 30,000.[1] Recent government statistics on prison population have not been made available, but evidence suggests that the number of inmates has since doubled to around 60,000.[2]

There have been few—but telling—reports in the national press on the prison crisis. In February 1987, a high court judge, Justice Togbor, expressed horror at the overcrowding he witnessed in Kingongo prison, Nyeri, Central Province. According to his reports, he saw 1,000 prisoners confined in a prison designed to hold a maximum of 400 prisoners.[3] In February 1987, an inmate in Kamiti Maximum Security Prison, Nairobi, described his prison ordeal in the national press as:

> the cells for holding five people had eight or nine squeezed in each. While sleeping at night, one could not turn unless the whole lot in the cell turned.[4]

Overcrowding has caused severe shortages of the most basic necessities for prisoners. Exceptionally poor sanitation, shortages of prison clothing and blankets, lack of medicine and medical equipment,

---

[1] *Daily Nation*, November 18, 1986.

[2] Africa Watch was given the figure of 60,000 by a number of people in the legal community who have first-hand knowledge of the prison system. It is also based on prisoners' testimonies and in information published in the national press.

[3] *Weekly Review*, February 6, 1987.

[4] *Weekly Review*, February 1, 1987.

and insufficient access to medical attention result in chronic illnesses and disease. Professionals working with the prison system say that death from diseases such as cholera and meningitis are common, with annual epidemics in many prisons, which are rarely reported. In 1986, five prisoners were reported as having died in Kodiaga Prison, Kisumu, after an epidemic of cholera. Four inmates of the Slikuse Borstal Institution in Kakamega reportedly died at the same time, but no details were given as to the cause of death. Prisoners also express increasing concern about the spread of AIDS among inmates, facilitated by the homosexual practices of long-term prisoners[5] and the re-using of disposable syringes and razor-blades.

As recently as June 1989, Commissioner of Prisons James Mareka, appealed to courts to consider releasing minor offenders on bail or bond to reduce the number of people awaiting trial. At the time, he estimated some 9,000 petty offenders were in remand. The inefficiency of the system means it is routine for remand prisoners to wait more than a year before being tried. In October 1990, a man held on murder charges was found not guilty and released after being in remand for nine years. According to the commissioner of prisons, chronic overcrowding could be relieved by making petty offenders serve sentences at home—although at that time he claimed the prison population was only 20,000 above the maximum intake.

Others who have gone on record about their concern over prison conditions are a Kakemega magistrate, Mr. J. M. Khamoni, who urged the government to expand existing prisons in 1989; and Nakuru judge Justice P. K. Tanui who, in the same year, urged courts to minimize the number of remand cases to avoid increasing congestion. A councillor with Trans-Nzoia County Council, David Wekesa, was reprimanded by the area KANU branch for saying that prisoners at Kitale prison walked half naked for lack of uniforms.[6]

In June 1990, journalists from the *Sunday Standard* newspaper reported allegations that twenty prisoners in Eldoret were found semi-naked in four rows next to the perimeter fence, guarded by three prison

---

[5] The fact that homosexual practices become institutionalized in prisons is not peculiar to Kenya. There have been a number of studies about the way these practices evolve as a system of power for long-term prisoners.

[6] *Sunday Standard*, June 3, 1990.

wardens. They reported similar allegations of semi-naked prisoners in Kitale, Kodiaga, Kericho and Nairobi's Industrial Area prison.[7] Women prisoners not only lack adequate uniforms but are usually also devoid of any sanitary protection.

Kenya's prison system is a colonial legacy, with most structures built by the British. Small cells, 10' by 10', or 5' by 6', were designed to isolate and demoralize political prisoners during colonial times and were constructed under emergency conditions for a considerably smaller population. The current crisis, caused by overcrowding, reflects a massive population explosion,[8] and increasing political crackdowns. As the system becomes heavily overburdened, it becomes increasingly inefficient, compounding overcrowding and shortages.

The majority of prisons are considered exclusively criminal prisons, without any designated section for political prisoners. Political prisoners are known to be kept at Nairobi's Kamiti Maximum Security Prison, Mombasa's Shimo-La-Tewa, Naivasha and, according to recent reports, also at Kapenguria and Kisumu. These prisons have a political wing distinct from the criminal sections. However, as most political prisoners are charged with criminal offenses—breach of the peace, banditry, drunk and disorderly behavior, causing a disturbance—the definition of what constitutes "political" and "criminal" is deliberately misleading. According to one previous inmate:

> It is misleading to judge political prisoners on those held under the Public Security Act—we have very few of those. But we have a lot of people who have been sent to prison on national security grounds, and have not been afforded a fair trial. They all plead guilty to the charges. Attempts by lawyers to see them, even in court, have not been successful and their convictions are not supported. So there has been no real improvement regarding political prisoners—I would say the opposite was true.[9]

---

[7] Ibid.

[8] Kenya has an estimated population of 24 million people.

[9] Africa Watch interview, March 1991.

Some prisons, like Kamiti, are known to have what is commonly called the "lunatic" wing where the criminally insane are kept. These are deliberately used to house political prisoners, whose cells alternate with the mentally unbalanced.

In Kenya, mentally sick people are treated like criminals, beaten and incarcerated in prisons. The laws regarding mental illness and insanity are archaic—only the police can admit mentally ill patients to psychiatric hospitals. Some become institutionalized in prisons and their condition deteriorates rapidly, living in the cells without any personal hygiene or care and subjected to frequent beatings from the guards. Many are restrained with chains and handcuffs, and are continually re-sentenced on the basis that they are violently insane.

SURVIVING THE SYSTEM: A TESTIMONY

Bedan Mbugua, former editor of the banned magazine, *Beyond*, described his experience in prison before he was cleared of the charges brought against him.

> First of all I was in Nairobi's Industrial Area prison, which is used like a clearing house for those on remand. But I wasn't there long. I heard the warden in charge in Industrial Area prison saying "I don't think I can handle this case—it has too much attention." At the time there had been a lot of coverage about my case in the papers and a lot of people visiting me. So then I was moved to Kamiti Maximum Security. Many prisoners there had no clothing, but I was given some by sympathetic wardens who said "we must give this editor some clothes—he's not a criminal."

Mbugua was told he must arrange for his relatives to bribe the prison guard if he was to survive the system. Corruption in the prisons is as institutionalized as the violence, and is seized on by most prisoners as a means of survival. Bribing a prison guard is often the only way a prisoner can ensure that he or she gets a blanket, a mat and regular food. For 1,000 shillings ($38), a prisoner can get reasonable work—like a job in the kitchen, the dispensary or the pharmacy. Prison guards are long term prisoners who have been promoted in the system for cooperative behavior:

> The warden was a Kalenjin, he started asking me—"why are you fighting Moi's government?" and talked about love, peace and unity and all the Nyayo talk. I got very angry and said, "If it is a government of peace, love and unity, I want to see it working inside here." He pointed at me with his stick and told me, "You are going to see."

> Then I was taken to a very small cell, with about six others inside. I had only one blanket, which I know was an order which came from the warden. I was with some young Maasai guys who had been jailed for one month, some for three to six months. They were illiterate, and seemed to have no idea why they were inside. They were given nothing—no blanket, just the bucket. The cell is about seven by five. Another prisoner gave me a blanket, so I had two, so we shared these two blankets among the six of us. The wardens are very harsh. Prisoners say the wardens take marijuana. When you are first put in, they search you. They tell you to strip off all your clothes, and you are made to jump to prove you have nothing. For work we were breaking stones for the road. You break from a big pile of stones with a heavy hammer. The day begins at 5:00 A.M., when you are woken up and counted.

> Between the cells there is a wide corridor—they make you go out on the corridor and count you, all squatting. You all come out and squat as quickly as you can where they want you and make sure you try and do everything right because they don't need any excuse to start beating you.

In male prisons, the bribery system is extended to sexual power and privileges. Homosexuality is, according to one former prisoner, simply another means of surviving—although fear that AIDS is now rapidly spreading within the prisons makes this particular survival tactic one with deadly consequences. Severe shortage of food has been a major incentive for young convicts to become sexual partners of older inmates, who, by virtue of their seniority, are able to secure regular food rations. Young prisoners are particularly vulnerable, as described in this anonymous testimony given to Africa Watch.

Many of the older, long-term prisoners have turned homosexual. There's a big homosexual problem there. I saw two young boys suffer, who were put in about the same time as me. They were only about 16-years-old and were actually too young to be there; but they had cheated to get ID so they could get a job. You could see they were much younger than the ID, even by their looks. When they were brought to the cell, you could see the older prisoners looking at the boys, they were watching them everywhere.

The boys were immediately singled out by those in charge and given good blankets and good food by the senior prisoners. One of the boys, Otieno, came to me soon and told me he couldn't sleep because the other prisoners kept on removing his trousers and he was fighting and struggling all the time. He asked me what should he do. He was frightened. I told him he must speak out, it was the only way—I know the only way to fight is to expose it. So, that evening, when the one in charge asked as he always did if there was anything we wanted or needed to say, Otieno did just that. He said it just as he had told me. It was like a nuclear bomb—the reaction was incredible. We knew that the one in charge was a close ally of one of the ones Otieno named. But the one in charge pretended to be very shocked and serious and transferred the offending fellow. He was brought back after a few days of course, although he was eventually transferred to another place through one of the prison authorities. Those older prisoners have a lot of power; they are given power by the prison authorities and then try and prove they are more strict than the authorities themselves.

In the big cells, you see it happening all the time. The
older prisoners tell the boys to go to the corner where
the toilet is. Homosexuality is unbelievably taboo in
Kenya—you could be killed by the public, you would be
killed in your own village if anyone suspected you of
that. But it is part of the system in the prison. The ones
in charge try to be more repressive even than the
wardens. I identified five homosexual prisoners in the
cell when I was there. The authorities encourage all
forms of intimidation by the senior prisoners.

MEDICAL FACILITIES AND PROVISIONS

Prisoners are dependent on the medical services provided by the
prison and have no alternatives if they prove inadequate or unsuitable.
The widespread sickness and disease is due to the insanitary conditions,
poor diet, lack of exercise and lack of sunlight. Conditions of solitary
confinement include deprivation of food, sunlight, exercise, personal
hygiene and sanitation facilities. Prisoners in solitary confinement are
allowed two periods of 30 minutes daily out of their small 6' by 6' cells.
Sometimes these exercise periods are also denied as a punishment.

Medical treatment is generally regarded by the prison authorities
as a privilege, not a right. When the prison medical officer does prescribe
a drug, prisoners are often deliberately under-administered so as to leave
the medical personnel with private stocks of the drugs for black
marketeering. Drugs are also sold for drug abuse. Disposable syringes are
re-used many times.

Former prisoners have told Africa Watch that complaints of ill-
health are generally considered by the authorities as deliberate
exaggerations to secure privileges and leniency. If a guard believes a
prisoner is malingering, that prisoner will be punished with a beating.
Transfers to hospitals can take inordinate time—sometimes
months—resulting in a serious deterioration of health which at times,
according to our information, has proved fatal. Prisoners transferred to
a hospital are normally kept chained to the bed, and may often only
remain in the hospital for long enough to suppress symptoms and carry
out tests; there is no follow-up care once a prisoner is returned to the
cell. One remand prisoner in May 1991 was repeatedly refused bail and
returned to solitary confinement despite recommendations by senior

consultant surgeons that he be immediately hospitalized for a brain scan (see chapter twelve). A prisoner released in December 1988 wrote:

> The worst that can befall a prisoner is to get sick. Medical services are virtually non-existent and the medical officer in Kamiti, Dr Owino, was known to order guards to beat patients because of "malingering." It was particularly painful for me to watch John Mungai Waruiru progressively waste away for about eight months without treatment until he died on May 5, 1988. Waruiru was serving a seven-year term for sedition. In another case, Titus Adungosi Oloo was transferred from Naivasha Maximum Security Prison to Kamiti in a hopeless situation. By the time of his transfer to Kamiti, he could not even eat. In spite of this, the prison authorities simply left him to die. He finally died on December 27, 1988. Adungosi was a former chairman of the Student Organisation of Nairobi University (SONU).

USE OF FORCE

The Prison Act states, Cap. 90 Section 12 (1):

> Any prison officer may use such force against a prisoner as is reasonably required to make him obey lawful orders which he refuses to obey or in order to maintain discipline in a prison.

Excessive force, according to former inmates, is routine in Kenyan prisons. Strip searches, anal searches, beatings, psychological humiliation, and gruelling physical exercises are an integral part of a system designed to break people down rather than to rehabilitate them. This contravenes the Prison Act, which states that a prison officer "must have reasonable cause to believe that the prisoner is about to disobey or to cause grave danger on the officer" before force can be resorted to. The violence, according to prisoners, depends very much on the officers in charge—some of whom reportedly participate in beating and humiliating the prisoners. Each prison is administered on a provincial basis by a provincial prisons command, headed by an assistant commissioner. The commissioner of prisons and the service's headquarters in Nairobi have overall responsibility for the prison system. One former inmate described how the new convicts are broken in by the guards.

> When we first got in there, we were told to take all our clothes off. They make you jump up and down to prove there is nothing being carried on your body. Then you are made to bend over naked and they search your anus with a cane. They do it like a torture. Then they make you sit squatting—still naked—for long hours at a time, and tell you they will "initiate" you. They told us "you people are going to see." You are left squatting naked in the cell, in the dark, and suddenly they burst in and beat you thoroughly with sticks and batons. They attack you particularly on the joints, on your shoulders, head, knees and elbows. You will be beaten like that for some time—over a period of days. After three days, our names were then read out for what kind of work we would be doing and our "initiation" ceremony had finished.

The extent to which prisoners are subjected to such violence is difficult to ascertain because prisoners fear reprisals. Prisoners are afraid that if they complain officially, they will be victimized further. One former prisoner described abuses by prison guards, just after he was released from a maximum security prison in February 1989:

> Prison beatings normally go beyond what can be considered "reasonably necessary." Take for example a case where a prisoner is found with half a cigarette; when he is taken to the duty officer all the prison guards in the office will be hitting the prisoner with their batons. The most horrifying aspect of this beating is that the guards normally have as their target some of the most sensitive parts of the body, mainly the knee and hand joints, and at the end of it the prisoner can hardly walk. At times, after such a beating, the prisoner is taken into the cell naked and cold water is poured into the cell and he can be made to stay like that for even two days. At times the guards seem to derive a lot of pleasure in beating the prisoners so that even where a prisoner readily admits

the charges against him, he will not be spared. Such beatings are normally justified on the dubious argument that "you must know what kind of place this is."[10]

Although the Prison Act provides that "if a prison officer strikes or uses force against a prisoner, they shall have the prisoner as soon as possible examined by a medical officer and shall immediately report the incident to the officer in charge," this provision is rarely respected. This former prisoner goes on to describe the routine humiliation in the system:

> One of the most humiliating and degrading aspects of prison life is the so-called search—or in prison vocabulary "terror." In a great number of cases...every morning prisoners are required to take off all their clothes, come out of their cells or wards and squat, naked, facing the wall. On many occasions the guards carrying out the search are more interested in the nakedness of the prisoners than in the search. Disparaging remarks are made regarding the naked prisoners. At times the naked prisoners are ordered to jump up and down, sometimes to hold both ears as he squats. Its sole purpose is to humiliate and degrade the prisoners as human beings.
>
> There are times when a prisoner is required to open up his anus wide on suspicion that he might have stuffed in some money or cigarettes...the fact that a number of guards derive a lot of amusement and delight from this sort of mistreatment makes the whole thing more despicable. The constant abuse hurled by the guards is also inhuman and degrading. It is not uncommon to hear guards call [a prisoner] "ape." To complain about such insults is to invite being beaten, so a number of prisoners are inclined to adopt a flattering attitude towards the guards. The point is that prisoners are supposed not to talk unless talked to by the *affande* [master]. The colonial mentality amongst the prison guards is overpowering.

---

[10] *Nairobi Law Monthly*, February 1989.

The treatment described by prisoners not only contravenes the Prison Act, but also the constitution, which provides that "no person shall be subjected to torture or to inhuman or degrading punishment or other treatment."

DEATHS IN PRISON

Statistics on prison deaths are not publicly available, but prisoners' testimonies and press reports give some indication of the circumstances in which prison deaths occur. There have been, for example, some cases where relatives have been informed of a prisoner's death without any prior indication of serious illness, and without being given satisfactory details about the circumstances in which the person died. This has led to suspicion that prisoners are at times killed by the authorities through deliberate violence or negligence. Sometimes the prison authorities fail in their legal duty to inform the relatives immediately of the death of a prisoner. In October 1990, for example, lawyer Mohamed K. Ibrahim filed an application for a woman whose son died in prison after being convicted on a petty criminal charge. The young man was said to be in his twenties, and though he reportedly died from illness in May 1990, the mother was not informed of the death until two months later. His mother discovered his body had been buried in an unmarked city commission grave. This alone caused great distress for the relatives who strongly believed it was vital for religious and cultural reasons to perform a funeral rite.

SHOT "WHILST TRYING TO ESCAPE"

A large but unknown number of prisoners have been shot "whilst trying to escape"—a description that some prisoners say is used to cover up prison murders by over-zealous prison authorities. The Prison Act states that:

Any prison officer may use any weapons...including firearms against a prisoner if:

a) he is escaping or attempting to escape, and refuses, when called back;

b) he is engaged with other persons in breaking out or
attempting to break out of prison and continues to break
after called to desist.

Accounts from those familiar with the prison system say that a
shoot-to-kill policy is routine for escaping prisoners—even when they
could be easily restrained by other methods, such as maiming (see chapter
seventeen). In October 1990, for example, a prisoner was shot dead by
prison guards while prostrate on the ground outside the Nairobi Law
Courts. The man, described as "in his mid-twenties," was facing a charge
for possession of cannabis. He made his unsuccessful dash for freedom as
he was taken from the court to the prison van. Many shots were fired, but
the fatal shots were witnessed by the public as delivered after the man fell
on the ground in a fenced-in parking lot.[11] According to one lawyer
who was in the court when the shooting took place:

> His case is like so many other cases. That young man was
> probably made desperate after being in custody for
> months and months—if not years—just with a routine
> mention in court every couple of weeks. We've all seen
> it before—it's not the first time.

In another incident reported in June 1990, three prisoners were
shot dead in Bungoma by police and six other prisoners were wounded.
They were allegedly trying to escape.[12] Concern that the phrase "shot
whilst trying to escape" is a justification for the murder of prisoners is
illustrated by the account of former prisoner Oduor Ong'wen, jailed from
1986 to 1988. He describes the circumstances in which prisoner James
Marite was shot dead on July 31, 1988, after he had argued with a guard.

> On July 31, 1988, prison sirens went off at about 3:30
> P.M. as we were just about to have our lunch. We were
> immediately locked inside our cells, the food destroyed
> and within 10 minutes guards had come with truncheons
> and were battering us. In total, about 400 prisoners at

---

[11] *Standard*, October 23, 1990.

[12] *Daily Nation*, June 12, 1990.

Kamiti Maximum Security Prison were maimed, some presumably for life as some had broken spines. What is worse, we had no idea of what had offended the "good order" of prison administration. One prisoner, James Marite, had argued with a guard and was shot dead. Another prisoner, M Githinji, died during the beatings. The shooting of Marite was later explained away—"he was trying to escape."

WOMEN PRISONERS

Prison conditions for women are generally the same as for men, but they suffer particular vulnerability and abuse. Women are not allowed to wear underwear, and are not allowed to use any sort of sanitary protection during menstruation. Lawyers working with women prisoners say complaints of rape are not uncommon, but legal action against police and prison guards is almost unheard of. In 1985, magistrates heard a case of a 26-year-old woman who was beaten severely on the inside of her thighs after she had been detained overnight for a petty offence. The police officer covered his head with a cloth and entered the cell at night to assault her.

Most women are arrested for petty economic offenses, brewing alcohol, trading *magendo* (illegally obtained) goods and prostitution. Prostitution sweeps are common in Nairobi and the main towns. Women out late at night, in the bars or walking on the streets, are targeted in these sweeps; they are immediately taken to the local hospital and forced to submit to examination for venereal diseases. Women found to be suffering from venereal diseases are then charged with prostitution, imprisoned or fined. This approach is a colonial legacy—when prostitution was encouraged and sometimes institutionalized but controlled by subjecting the women to regular medical examination and treatment. Charges of prostitution are used to harass women. The real threat of being arrested and charged with prostitution restricts a woman's freedom of movement at night.

The national newspapers often carry reports of sweeps that have netted more than one hundred women in an evening. Reports of prostitution police sweeps increase—or are given more prominence—during times of heightened political tension and police crackdowns.

In prison, beating is the most common form of abuse suffered by women. There have also been reports of minors beaten or raped in police detention while waiting transfer to juvenile centers. Minors, who usually have no legal representation, are known to have been sent to prisons on remand. In Nakuru, an 11-year-old schoolgirl was in remand for three weeks before lawyers were given access to her during the July demonstrations (see chapter four). Many children, including very young babies, suffer appalling conditions of detention in police cells and prisons while they stay with their imprisoned mothers. One woman who was detained for 48 hours in police custody with four young children, including an eighteen-month-old child, told Africa Watch she and her children were denied any water or food. She said her eighteen-month-old child became hysterical because of confinement in the poorly ventilated cell, but the police officers refused to respond to her pleas for water.

11
LAWYERS
CHALLENGING LEGITIMACY

Lawyers who are independent, critical or active on human rights cases have repeatedly been harassed and detained as anti-government subversives. The government authorities sees such lawyers as a threat to their influence over the legal system, which is critical to the power structure. There is a determination by the authorities to encourage ignorance of fundamental rights and limit access to legal advice and representation. The determination of the government to silence its critics in the legal profession is explained by the impact the lawyers have had internationally. Continued support from the West depends on presenting at least an illusion of legitimacy, which can be most effectively dismantled by these independent and critical lawyers.

THE LAW SOCIETY OF KENYA: DISPOSING OF THE BODY

The Law Society of Kenya (LSK) has come under increasing attack since 1982, and is known as the unofficial opposition party along with the various churches. The attacks culminated in a threat to destroy the body completely in June 1991, after the society elected candidate Paul Muite as chair. Muite's election was accompanied by speculation in the national press that the LSK was headed on a collision course with the government now that the radical faction was in control. Lawyers opposed to Muite's appointment and sympathetic to the government took action against the new chair immediately and protested that his maiden speech was political and therefore outside his mandate as chair of the society. In his speech, Muite called for respect for human rights, democratic reforms and a sound judiciary. The application made to cite Muite and seven elected members of the LSK Council for alleged contempt of court, is seen as an attempt by the government to dispose of the independent faction through technical manipulation.

An injunction was placed on Muite on March 19, preventing him as chair from making any political statements. The council issued a statement interpreting the injunctions as restraining them from making statements on behalf of other members, but not from making statements as the council, and so continued business. The contempt of court charges were brought when Muite and the council called for a tribunal to be set up to inquire into the ability of the chief justice and Justice Dugdale to perform their duties (see chapter nine).

The Law Society remains an independent but threatened body. In 1989, the former director of international and legal affairs at KANU proposed that LSK be affiliated to the party. President Moi publicly opposed the suggestion on the grounds that KANU should not be affiliated with an organization that was a "foreign identity." There followed a catalogue of attacks on the society by the government. Government interference in the Law Society elections in 1990 resulted in allegations of electoral malpractice. This included complaints from many members of the society that they had not received ballot papers and that pressure was being exerted on them to support the incumbent, pro-government chair, Fred Ojiambo. Members who were known to support the independent candidate, Muite, said they were deliberately being deprived of ballot papers, and made allegations of an instance where a ballot paper returned to the Law Society had been opened and destroyed because the vote had been placed for the "wrong" candidate. Advocates supporting Muite made a public statement criticizing the increasingly enfeebled role of the Law Society, and listed complaints that included:

- ...decline in standards, rampant corruption, constant vilification of lawyers, the tarnishing of lawyers' public image, and the weakening of institutions for the maintenance of rule of law and the administration of justice.
- ...the Law Society's remoteness from advocates in rural areas, the Law Society's failure to lobby against legislation adversely affecting advocates, the Law Society's indifference to lack of law reports and legal literature.. [and its] failure to uphold the noble ideals of the profession.

The election results in his favor were announced by incumbent Chair Fred Ojiambo. There was major resistance to his re-election by members who declared the results unacceptable. President Moi directly intervened and announced that Ojiambo's election was valid.

The attempts by the government to impose conformity on the LSK did not stop critics speaking out independently, especially regarding human rights abuses and political reform. Attempts were made to reduce their forum. In March 1990, the Law Society Seminar—which was to include papers given on considerations for political pluralism, human rights issues and the Rule of Law—was cancelled.

CANCELLATION OF THE
INTERNATIONAL BAR ASSOCIATION CONFERENCE

The extent to which the independent lawyers had become an Achilles' heel for the government became clear at the height of pro-democracy agitation in 1990. The prestigious 23rd International Bar Association (IBA) Biennial Conference in Nairobi was cancelled by the government, four months before it opened. Preparations for the conference had begun as early as 1980. The event, which would have hosted some 3,000 lawyers and delegates, was expected to bring vital foreign exchange into the country. Almost as soon as the attorney general had announced the cancellation, however, the president reversed his decision and called for preparations to continue. The greatest blow came when the IBA decided that Nairobi was an unsuitable place to hold the conference. According to the press release, the IBA said the conference had been cancelled because:

> Safety of delegates is paramount and following three days of serious unrest in Nairobi and other central areas from 7-9 July 1990, which left some 25 dead and many more injured...[means]...such safety cannot be guaranteed.

> Another matter of great concern to us is the state of human rights and the rule of Law in Kenya. A number of persons are detained without being charged, including four lawyers, at least one whom was arrested when he went to a police station to interview his client. Many hold the view that by proceeding with our conference the IBA would be lending support to a regime that has suppressed those attempting peacefully to express their

political views and exercise their international recognized human rights.

HARASSMENT OF LAWYERS

Harassment and verbal attacks on lawyers increased when they came to the fore of the pro-democracy movement. The incidents of harassment and intimidation in 1990 are numerous. The government attempted to prevent lawyers from giving legal advice to those leading the calls for political pluralism, like Kenneth Matiba and Charles Rubia (see chapter seven) and Jaramogi Oginga Odinga.[1] As previously described, when Paul Muite attempted to consult with his clients, Matiba and Rubia, plainclothes officers forced their way into Muite's office and arrested them. Muite held a press conference to say he felt intimidated and threatened. At the press conference other lawyers complained of the harassment meted out to advocates in the course of their duty. Policemen stormed the office, declared the meeting illegal and denounced the law office as a center of subversion. Police confiscated notebooks, films and cassette recorders from the journalists attending.

Security personnel maintained constant and visible surveillance on the offices of Paul Muite, Gibson Kamau Kuria and Kiraitu Murungi, John Khaminwa and Gitobu Imanyara in the month leading up to the Saba Saba demonstrations. Kamau Kuria and Kiraitu Murungi had experienced increased pressure and harassment begininging in April 1990, during the crackdown on rumormongering, including surveillance and threats that the partners would be "dealt with" (see chapter three). Kiraitu Murungi received instructions from the president's office that he should go to State House in April, presenting him with the dilemma that a refusal was tantamount to an insult and cooperation was tantamount to collaboration. He avoided visits from the president's staff, sent to the office to pick him up, and spent at least one evening driving round

---

[1] James Orengo, lawyer for Oginga Odinga, was charged with contempt of court by Justice Dugdale in June 1991 during the attempt to get Odinga's National Democratic Party registered (see chapter nine). Orengo's passport was impounded in July 1991 after he had attended a conference on human rights and democracy in London.

Nairobi late into the night in order to avoid the anticipated phone calls and visits to his home.

Kiraitu Murungi is now in exile in the United States. He was attending a meeting outside the country during the July crackdown, and received urgent messages that it was unsafe for him to return to Kenya while the security forces were looking for both him and his partner, Kamau Kuria. An announcement by Chief of Police Philip Kilonzo, that Paul Muite was also being sought forced Muite into hiding. He was instructed to apologize to the president, to which he responded by resurfacing and going to State House to explain his actions to the president. This was reported in the press as an apology.

On June 25, 1990, John Khaminwa, Kiraitu Murungi, Mohamed Ibrahim and Gibson Kamau Kuria were meeting in the offices of Kamau Kuria and Kiraitu Advocates when six Special Branch officers forced their way into the office and ordered the lawyers to disperse their illegal meeting. They refused to accept that the lawyers were holding a legal consultation.

The pressure on independent lawyers continued after the three lawyers detained in July were released, which encouraged an unprecedented camaraderie in the critical section of the legal community—known as the "informal opposition party." When Imanyara was released from detention but charged with sedition, over forty lawyers stood up in court to represent him.

One of those lawyers, Pheroze Nowrojee, well-respected for his work on controversial human rights cases, was charged with contempt of court. Noworojee had written a letter to Justice Dugdale about the delay in ruling on the public inquiry requested by the widow of Bishop Alexander Muge into the circumstances of her husband's death (see chapter thirteen). In the letter, Noworojee said that it is "most unusual for the date of the ruling of an urgent matter not to be fixed," pointing out that the imminent procedure of another related case would have the effect of destroying his own application if the ruling continued to be delayed.

> Such delay amounts in law to a refusal to adjudicate..
> These departures from the usual, the indefinite delay,
> despite reminders, and the unwillingness to specify a
> fixed date, may create an impression that the ruling date
> is being tailored to the completion of the...case in
> Eldoret....It means that the Court's inaction to date will

have defeated the possible remedy given by our law to
the applicant.

I still await a reply to my earlier letter. I convey my
anxiety at the unusual treatment of this, or any,
applicant to our courts, and in the belief that trust in our
judges is a major contributory to the security of our
nation. The events taking place in this case could tend
to the erosion of that trust.

The contempt charges, brought by Justice Dugdale, were
dismissed in the high court by Justices Bosire, Msagha and Mango.

PRODUCING THE ENEMY

The arrest of lawyers Mirugi Kariuki, in Nakuru, and Rumba
Kinuthia, in Nairobi, under charges of treason, shook the legal
community in October. Kariuki had worked in his Nakuru law firm since
being released from detention in June 1989, and had maintained a low
profile, except for issuing a statement in support of multiparty
democracy. Kinuthia, also from Nakuru but maintaining offices in
Nairobi, was known for his critical stance: he had publicly resigned his
membership of the party, advocated multiparty democracy, and assisted
in editing the critical legal magazine, *The Nairobi Law Monthly*. Lawyers
representing those charged with treason have been harassed with
surveillance, obstruction and petty criminal charges. Dominic Kimatta,
was subjected to searches of his office by Special Branch immediately
after the arrest of his partner, Mirugi Kariuki, and arrested on charges
of possessing a seditious document: a banned magazine which he denied
owning. Martha Njoka and her partner, Beatrice Nduta, who represent
two of the accused in the treason trial, have come under increasing
pressure—Beatrice Nduta was arrested and brought to court in February
1991, charged with "malicious damage to a Kaunda suit." The damaged
suit, which Nduta allegedly spilt beer on at a nightclub, belonged to
Philip Murgor, the state counsel in the treason case, and the son-in-law
of former attorney general, Matthew Muli. Twenty-nine lawyers appeared
in court to represent her. These charges were dropped when new
Attorney General Amos Wako, took office.

DETENTION

The first lawyer detained by President Moi was Dr. John Khaminwa in 1982 when he acted as counsel for former Vice-President Jaramogi Oginga Odinga. His willingness to take on sensitive cases attracted government wrath at a time when Moi's accumulation of power was in its early stages. In 1981, he represented a former deputy director of intelligence who was suing the government for what he claimed was wrongful retirement from the civil service—unprecedented in that it challenged the power of the president to hire and fire at will. Khaminwa also acted on behalf of George Anyona, a known government critic, and filed a habeas corpus after Anyona was taken into police custody. Anyona was then charged in court with sedition, but later detained in May 1982. In addition, he represented Maina wa Kinyatti, a historian arrested in June 1982 and detained for six years, charged with possessing a seditious publication. Khaminwa was also arrested and detained when he was held without trial before being released unconditionally. Khaminwa was again briefly detained in 1990 when calls for multiparty democracy culminated in demonstrations and riots; Khaminwa had publicly committed himself to the principles of multiparty democracy and was acting for pro-democracy advocates who were later detained. He was released after three weeks in detention.

In 1985 and 1986, G. B. M. Kariuki, a former chair of the Law Society, was threatened with criminal prosecution when he opposed the introduction of queue-voting to replace the secret bailot.

In 1986, two lawyers were tortured and detained without trial. Mirugi Kariuki was detained during a government crackdown on the underground movement MwaKenya. Soon after his detention, a local councillor charged with sedition claimed he had been introduced to the movement by Kariuki. He was never given an opportunity to answer the allegations, which had been extracted from a man held incommunicado in police custody for a prolonged period of time. Kariuki was so seriously tortured that he suffered permanent damage to his kidneys (see chapter six). He filed an application of illegal torture against the state, and was held until June 1989 along with two other detainees who filed similar applications. Kariuki was arrested again in October 1990 and is now being held on treason charges. Allegations of torture have been made public through his lawyers.

Wanyiri Kihoro, a lawyer working in Mombasa, was arrested in July 1986 and held incommunicado for nearly two months before his detention was publicized. At the time of his arrest he was working for a commercial law firm and was involved in a research project on "Law and Human Rights in Kenya," supported by the Africa Center in London, where he had worked as program and education officer. He suffers permanent health problems as a result of the torture inflicted on him (see chapter six). Kihoro went into exile in March 1991 saying he feared for his life.

Gibson Kamau Kuria was detained without trial for ten months in 1987. Kamau Kuria is Kenya's best-known human rights lawyer. Among other high-profile cases, he took up the cases of a number of students charged with sedition in 1982, following the August coup attempt. He became well-known after filing a case on behalf of four detainees in March 1984, saying that their detention was illegal and demanding their immediate release.[2] This was the first time detained persons made an application on the legality of their confinement. The case was heard by former Chief Justice A. H. Simpson and former attorney general, Justice Matthew Muli, appeared for the state. Kamau Kuria argued that the detainees had not been served with detention orders and statements of the grounds of their detentions as required, and that the detention orders were not publicized within the required fourteen days. He also argued that the rules and regulations of the detention had not been laid before parliament for the stipulated twenty days as required by law, which must therefore render the detentions null and void. The chief justice dismissed the case, ruling that there was nothing illegal or irregular with the detentions.

Kamau Kuria attracted attention again in 1987 when he filed an application in the high court on behalf of another detainee, Raila Odinga—who had been in detention since 1982 (see chapter six). In the application, he said that Mr. Odinga's right to have his case reviewed by an independent and impartial tribunal had been contravened. He also sought a court declaration that the applicant be told the grounds on which he had been detained. Kamau Kuria said in the application that Odinga had been subjected to inhuman treatment. The case was dismissed by former Chief Justice C. B. Madan.

---

[2] George Anyona, Koigi wa Wamwere, Edward Oyugi and Kamonji Wachira.

Kamau Kuria was detained in 1987 after accepting applications by three detainees to sue the state for illegal torture and detention.[3] According to Kamau Kuria, it was clear during the interrogation what the purpose of his detention was: to prevent details and exposure of the torture cases; to stop him and other lawyers from acting for perceived government opponents; to instil fear into him and other independent lawyers; to collect intelligence on other lawyers and their clients; to economically ruin his practice so as to prevent him from continuing with his controversial work; and to prevent him having contact with the outside world. He won the 1988 Robert F. Kennedy Human Rights Award but was unable to collect the award personally after his passport was confiscated. The award was collected by his lawyer, Paul Muite, whose own passport was confiscated when he returned. During his detention, Kamau Kuria said he was ill-treated and humiliated. Kamau Kuria sought refuge in the American embassy during the crackdown on the pro-democracy movement in July 1990 and is now in exile in the United States. He is still subject to public attacks by President Moi.

In June 1990, three lawyers were detained without trial after actively participating in the move for multiparty politics, and presented with detention orders issued on the grounds that they had been "associating, meeting and plotting with ..well-known anti-government characters. Two of the lawyers, Dr. John Khaminwa and Mohamed Ibrahim, were acting for former cabinet ministers, Charles Rubia and Kenneth Matiba, who were detained as the leaders of the pro-democracy movement. Mohamed Ibrahim originally attracted the wrath of the government when he rejected the screening of all ethnic Somalis, refusing to participate and denouncing the exercise as unconstitutional. The other detained lawyer, Gitobu Imanyara, had published articles favoring a multiparty system and criticizing the government in the magazine he edits, the *Nairobi Law Monthly*. Ibrahim and Khaminwa were released unconditionally after three weeks, and Imanyara was charged with sedition.

---

[3] Mirugi Kariuki, Wanyiri Kihoro and Mukaru Ng'ang'a.

SANCTIONS AND SURVEILLANCE

Control of the Bar and the judiciary is carried out through economic leverage as well as intimidation and harassment. In 1988, legislation under the Trade Licensing Act required practicing lawyers to obtain annual licenses from the minister of commerce. The legislation was challenged, but despite government promises to repeal all the relevant legislation, it remains in place at the time of publishing this report. Individual practices of independent and human rights lawyers are undermined economically by the government by directly influencing and intimidating the clients. After Dr. John Khaminwa (see above, Harassment of Lawyers) was released from detention in 1982, the government sought to cripple his legal practice by withdrawing all its contracts for work with his firm.

Gibson Kamau Kuria, who was detained for nearly ten months in 1987, eventually had all government contracts withdrawn from his practice and some individual clients were pressured to leave. Kamau Kuria's third partner, Gitonga Ringera, was pressured by the government into leaving the firm in December 1989—by which time all government-contract work, cooperative unions and other major clients had been withdrawn.

Constant surveillance by Special Branch officers of targeted lawyers is another major contribution to economic pressures. In 1990, Paul Muite and other lawyers issued a statement complaining of harassment. Describing the intrusive presence of the Special Branch officers in Muite's firm, the statement said:

> ...Special Branch Police Officers have stationed themselves at two vantage points on both floors of the offices of Waruhiu and Muite Advocates, while others keep surveillance on the ground floor and in the basement. They only leave as the last man in the said firm leaves at night. Though they have not stopped any clients or visitors going to or leaving the said offices, their presence is quite obvious and ominous. The 80-strong staff of the firm have been shaken by the events... and can hardly concentrate on their work. This is more so with the knowledge of the Special Branch Officer sentries outside. Many of the firm's clients have kept away for the last three days and the business of the said

firm has been affected adversely. It is to be expected that
any new clients who might otherwise have consulted the
firm will opt for other firms. The actions of the Police
are deliberate and calculated to intimidate the members
of the said firm and their clients and to bring the
business of the firm to a standstill...

This type of surveillance by the Special Branch includes direct
interrogation of clients—visitors to the officers under surveillance must
give their name and purpose of visit, which is recorded by the Special
Branch officers.

Economic persuasion and reward is an equally powerful weapon
used by the government. In March 1990, Fred Ojiambo, incumbent chair
of the Law Society, was appointed the director of a government bank at
a time when every effort was being made to exclude the independent
candidate from being elected to office. In another incident, in April
1991, Minister of State Burudi Nabwera announced that the government
was looking for ways of rewarding patriotic lawyers. A few days later
Mutula Kilonzo and Amos Wako, two prominent pro-government lawyers
who have rebuked the stance of their independent colleagues, were
appointed directors of the government-owned Kenya Airways.

According to members of the legal community, the government
has used the state-owned companies increasingly over the last few years
to offer directorships and legal work to compliant lawyers. It has also
created posts within the judiciary itself as a means of inviting allegiance
and loyalty: for example, there are now four chief magistrates (since
1990) and a new post of principal deputy registrar. The government also
pressures lawyers on an individual basis: for example, human rights
lawyer Kiraitu Murungi was informed by a senior party official in April
1990 that it was the wish of the president that he stop human rights work
and leave his partnership with Kamau Kuria. He was offered substantial
status and material rewards, and an appointment to see President Moi,
which he rejected.

A lawyer practicing in western Kenya described most lawyers as
opting for the "easiest and most profitable" workload, because there is no
motivation to take on cases which attract unwanted attention from the
authorities. In his testimony, he illuminated the demoralizing affect of
this work environment:

Everybody is looking over their shoulder. I think it is
tight all over the country now. You don't know if your
secretary or clerk is a police informer so you have to
take precautions all the time. It's normal for lawyers to
get pressure from officials and the Special Branch—when
I covered a case involving debts and the local
administration, I received calls from the Special Branch
and from the District Officer. I had a meeting in the
office with them all and they tried to threaten me—you
know, if you don't do it this way then you'll find yourself
in trouble. But it's necessary to stay firm and not to try
and befriend them, otherwise you'll find them in your
office all the time.

We haven't filed any habeas corpus here that I'm aware
of—that tends to happen only in Nairobi. Political
prisoners are transferred to Nairobi or are picked up
initially in Nairobi anyway. In towns like this you get the
occasional police swoops on prostitution or breach of the
peace. There is no legal aid at all here, which makes
things very simple—people who can't afford a lawyer go
to jail. Everything I do, I do for money. Every file I
open costs me VAT [Value Added Tax] so if they don't
have money, I tell them not to waste my time. I'm not
aware of any lawyer who takes on legal aid type cases
here, but there is legal aid for murder cases. That
doesn't work very well, though, it's a problem because
the case can go to anyone appointed by the Attorney-
General. So it could go to an inexperienced newly-
qualified person, which it often does, in which case you
will probably hang anyway. It's quite normal for murder
cases to remain in remand for up to two or three years.
The newspapers recently covered the story of a man who
was released after spending nine years in remand for a
murder he was found not guilty of. Well, at least he was
found not guilty.

But I think as far as I'm concerned the worst thing you
deal with in this profession is the police cells—cells
measuring about 6' by 4' and always extremely

overcrowded with standing space only. The people who
come to court from the cells are stinking. They get two
meals a day, in the morning, a mug of tea and some
bread—if its available—and later *ugali* [maize meal]. For
sanitation, prisoners only have a pail. They are allowed
out once a day, they frequently spend about a week in
prison cells before coming to court—and the 24 hour law
is so commonly abused that nobody takes any notice of
it any more. They can easily abuse the 24 hour law by
transferring to different police stations. We have to deal
with corruption and abuse in the police force all the
time, though it's the junior officers who are most likely
to abuse their powers. So, you see, we don't get much job
satisfaction unless we go for safe play—in fact, that way,
you can get very rich.

A FEAR OF JUSTICE

The general public is very often fearful of using the court system,
as it is seen as an anti-establishment action. For the vast majority, the
concept of a right to representation and a right to justice has never
existed. It did not exist under the colonial system, and has not been
allowed to develop—on the contrary, it has been deliberately exploited.
According to testimonies taken by Africa Watch in a number of different
regions, there is a widespread belief that the hiring of a lawyer—however
obvious the abuse of justice is—would cause displeasure to the authorities
and thus reduce the chances of an acquittal, not increase them. There are
a number of documented cases where the investigating officer has warned
against using lawyers (see chapters eight and sixteen).

SEEKING JUSTICE

In spite of all the attacks on lawyers and the legal system,
Kenyans are fortunate that a sense of solidarity and professionalism has
gained momentum recently within the legal profession. The willingness
to elect a lawyer under direct atttack from the government as chair of the
Law Society reflects the refusal of many lawyers to be cowed. Even more
significant has been the willingness of some lawyers to take on human

rights cases at great risk to themselves and of scores of lawyers to stand up in court when one of their number is subjected to harassment for doing his or her professional duty.

Unfortunately, the independence and courage that has been demonstrated by some lawyers has not often been matched by the judiciary. With honorable exceptions, judges have allowed themselves to be used by the government to nullify the legal protections contained in the constitution and laws of Kenya.

12
THE MEDIA AND SELF-CENSORSHIP

Many consider Kenya to have a relatively free and lively press compared to other African countries. However, Kenyan journalists consider themselves to be working within dangerous limitations. Since 1988, four magazines have received banning orders; the largest selling daily newspaper has been subjected to unprecedented reporting restrictions; editors have been arrested, jailed, detained and harassed; and journalists were arrested, beaten and assaulted.

Moves to circumscribe press freedom have increased since July 1990, after pro-democracy demonstrations and riots shook the confidence of the government. When sections of the local press decided, despite the threat of harassment, to cover the launching of Jaramogi Oginga Odinga's new National Democratic Party in 1991, a campaign of intimidation resulted in an editor and a journalist being arrested and detained on charges of sedition, and another editor going into hiding. Magazines were seized from street vendors by Special Branch officers, and editors, printers and journalists were questioned and threatened.

PUSHING THE LIMITS

In spite of intimidation, the press has proved more willing to carry statements and interviews by government critics since the calls for political pluralism. This can be attributed to a new boldness in challenging illegal actions against publications, encouraged by the first successful repeal of a ban in court in July 1991 and the persistent demands for political reform. According to one journalist who has worked on a number of publications since the 1970s:

> The morale has been high, much higher, among the press since the multiparty debate in August [1990]. You can see in the dailies that whereas before they wouldn't carry statements about the new party, they have taken it up now. That's because the monthlies carried it. When politicians began criticizing the magazines, the dailies

picked it up and gathered courage. So I believe we have,
in a sense, more freedom now. The press have been so
suppressed for so long and now they are coming out.
Courage is gathering.

Challenging the boundaries has made the limitations clearer.
Journalists and editors say the greatest inhibition for the press is not
knowing where the boundaries are. Editors of the daily papers receive
instructions about what should be printed as a matter of course, but do
not know which of these instructions are sanctioned by the president's
office, and which emanate from powerful individuals capitalizing on an
established system of intimidation. Most editors have considered the
consequences too great to risk finding out, or, as this editor explains,
have become too preoccupied with safeguarding their own interests:

> The authorities have got used to bulldozing the editors
> around and no one stands up to it. The tendency in
> Kenya is for senior politicians to call and say that story
> is not required. When they do that, you take it that it
> comes from the President's Office—but we can never
> check. Some editors avoid the phone calls when they
> know they are coming, they make themselves scarce until
> the story is printed. Then, sometimes, when the story is
> printed, nothing happens—absolutely nothing! So you see
> everyone uses the system, it's a way of using the old
> man's name [President Moi], but it's not necessarily from
> him.

> The problem with the daily papers is their big business
> interests. The editors are employees and have been there
> for a long time, and over the years, the editors acquire
> their own interests. The editors form personal
> friendships to protect their interests—it's not a case of
> being made a director on a parastatal [state-owned
> company] or that sort of thing; often it is just a beer and
> roast meat and maybe an envelope with some money in
> it for publishing "good stories." I think some editors have
> been given a plot of land. But more often it's done to
> protect yourself and look out for your family. So, if a
> reporter does a hitting story, they kill it. The powerful

people have got used to this now and have taken to using the telephone a lot.

THE DAILY NEWSPAPERS AND LEADING MAGAZINES

The daily papers are controlled primarily through the business interests of their owners.

- The Nation Group of Newspapers publishes the leading daily newspaper, the *Daily Nation*, and several local publications. The *Daily Nation* has a circulation of about 165,000. Owned by the Agha Khan, almost half of the Nation Group shares have been sold to the public. Buyers of the shares have never been disclosed, however, and there is suspicion that they were bought up by a small group of rich and powerful politicians and businessmen.
- The second leading daily paper, the *Standard*, has a circulation of 64,000. It is owned by the London-based Lonhro Group, The Standard Limited.
- The *Kenya Times* has a circulation of 36,000. It is the newspaper of the ruling party and is published by the Kenya Times Media Trust Ltd., owned by British publisher Robert Maxwell in conjunction with KANU.[1]

The editorial policy of the *Daily Nation* and the *Standard* is independent, but tied to safeguarding business interests. Economic motivation for self-censorship, according to one senior editor, is the most effective weapon the government holds over the so-called independents:

They are not free because first and foremost they must make profits, they must satisfy their shareholders that there is dividend, and one way of ensuring that in Kenya is to be seen to be on the "right side." You do not want to take courses that may lead to closure or temporary

---

[1] Committee to Protect Journalists (CPJ), "Press Conditions in Kenya," April 15, 1991 (New York: CPJ, 1991).

interference with advertisement revenue. So they exercise a high degree of self-censorship, they kill stories that are on the face of it really harmless. In Kenya, people have learnt to tune to foreign stations and rely on foreign institutions, the BBC, the Voice of America, Radio Deutsche Welle—even Radio Moscow to find out what they should be finding out in the Kenyan press.

Even the *Weekly Review*, which is the oldest magazine we have here, started as a very, very bold weekly news magazine that had a real grasp of what was happening in the country. But they themselves have not been free from the kind of pressure that the others meet. They are printed by the Kenya Times media, the people who print the party-owned newspaper. They cannot afford from an economic point of view to lose that printer...and they would lose everything if they took a critical stance against the government.

Self-censorship has not, however, protected journalists and editors on an individual basis. Editorial staff and reporters are vulnerable to the arbitrary attentions of the government, ministers, district and provincial administrators, and security personnel. Reporters have been attacked by police and paramilitary forces during riots, demonstrations, evictions, identity raids, press conferences and public addresses by senior politicians. Editors have been arrested and interrogated for reporting facts which the government wishes to deny.

On June 21, 1990, the editor of the *Daily Nation*, George Mbugguss, was arrested after attending a press conference given by Paul Muite on behalf of Kenneth Matiba and Charles Rubia. The press conference was broken up by police, who stormed the building where it was being held, confiscated notebooks, film and cassettes and ordered journalists to leave. Plainclothes officers told Mbugguss that he was being detained for security reasons, as they arrested him in his office. Police also threatened the deputy editor of the *Standard*, Mitch Odero, with arrest.

Seven days later, police arrested Odero along with three colleagues: Francis M'Thaiya, managing editor of the *Sunday Standard*, Francis Githui Muhindi, managing editor-designate, and production editor, James Kimondo. They were held overnight and later charged in court for publishing reports "likely to cause fear, alarm and despondency." The charges related to the *Standard*'s coverage of the violent evictions from Muoroto shantytown, in which it had been alleged that a number of people died, including a city employee. Articles published by the *Standard* alleged that the body of the employee was buried and then secretly exhumed to be buried in a rural area. The Nairobi City Commission denied the man had died during the evictions; they said he had died from cirrhosis of the liver. The court ordered the editors to surrender their passports and they were released on bail.

Ground Rules

The daily papers are regularly called upon to be patriotic and responsible: critical and investigative reporting is regarded as an act of political disloyalty. At the regional level, journalists are very vulnerable to attacks from local politicians and government ministers. In March 1990, Minister for Labor Peter Okondo, "slapped an indefinite ban on newspapers from reporting any of his functions in Busia District because they had become 'malicious.'"[2] The action he boasted of taking against them is not untypical: "I have already talked to the top management of the Kenya Times Media Trust about their stringer and I am happy they have promised stern action against him."[3]

This atmosphere, say Kenyan journalists, has encouraged poor standards of journalism, and professional apathy. In June 1989, the *Daily Nation* was accused in parliament of being disrespectful to Kenya's political leadership when it criticized the lack of debate in parliament (it had also carried recent reports on corruption in the Customs and Ports Authorities and in the awarding and administration of public tenders). Accusing the paper of frustrating the work of politicians, and practicing tribalism in its employment policies, the government took the unprecedented step of banning the paper and its sister publications from covering parliamentary proceedings.

During the ban, which lasted four months, the Kenyan Union of Journalists defended the paper and refuted the allegations from parliament that the paper had "persistently misreported proceedings in the house or refused to make appropriate corrections when requested to

---

[2] *Kenya Times*, March 12, 1990.

[3] Ibid.

do so." President Moi, however, made his disapproval of the paper clear. Barely a month before the ban, he accused the paper of promoting subversive activities against his government and setting itself up as an "unofficial opposition party." When the ban came into effect, the government-owned Kenya Broadcasting Corporation (then Voice of Kenya) was instructed to drop the *Daily Nation* from its press reviews in the early morning program.

This attack on the *Daily Nation* was seen by many journalists as an attempt to cripple its circulation and undermine it economically. The government has tried, unsuccessfully, to counter the influence of the newspapers published by the *Nation* and *Standard* groups by setting up its own party daily, the *Kenya Times*, but circulation figures for the *Daily Nation* have remained more than double those of both its competitors combined. Occasionally the *Kenya Times* produces stories which the other papers have no access to, on account of its relationship with the government; but the paper, which has the lowest circulation figures, is seen and bought as a party mouthpiece. Likewise, the Voice of Kenya and Kenya Television News are government-owned and highly selective in news and analysis. During anti-government demonstrations in February and July 1990, people pointed to the glaring failure of both Kenya Broadcasting Corporation and Kenya Television News to cover events adequately.

Kenya Times Editor-in-Chief Philip Ochieng, described how he perceived the role of the local media at a press conference held by the Minister for Foreign Affairs, Ndolo Ayah, in May 1990:

> I would like to affirm that our fundamental aim is to propagate the policies of the party and the government—this is true whether it is a newspaper associated with the party, like mine, or is the *Nation* or the *Standard*, or the electronic media. Our fundamental aim is to propagate the broad tenets of the ruling party and its government. This is most manifest usually in our editorial columns because that is where we come out with our explicit statements of opinion, where we affirm that the tenets of the party and the government are good. This does not oblige us all the time to cover up the failings of individuals, members or leaders of the party or government—if we think that a leader is failing and doing bad things we think so precisely because we feel he is

flouting the good tenets and policies of the government
and party.

Pulling Economic Strings

The government cannot rely on business interests to guide the
editorial stance of the independent monthly magazines in the same way
it can with the daily newspapers. However, the government is able to
wield power by taking advantage of the economic vulnerability of the
small publication businesses. One of the simplest controls the authorities
exert on the more outspoken independent monthlies is the manipulation
of registration requirements and the submission of annual returns.

How it Works

Under the Newspapers Act,[4] all publications must register a
security fee—referred to as a bond—of 10,000 shillings ($385), which is
payable for any legal damages incurred during the life of the publication.
This must be signed by the Minister for Land and Settlement. Copies of
each issue must be registered with the Registrar of Books and
Newspapers. Printers also have to register by completing a similar form
and signing a bond. If, at any time, the magazine is taken to a different
printer, then the printer must be re-registered. Once formalities are
completed, the Registrar General issues a certificate for the magazine. In
most cases, this is a procedure which takes up to a month to complete,
and the magazine can proceed while the bureaucracy is in motion.

Every magazine is also obliged to register its annual returns,
indicating the average number of issues sold in a year. It is a simple
requirement in theory—a matter of paying 20 shillings (77 cents) and
filling in a form for the Registrar General to inspect.

The First Stage

A magazine that has been targeted as anti-government initially
comes under economic pressure through the unwillingness of printers to
print at an acceptable charge and the withdrawal of advertising. The loss
of advertising revenue quickly hurts a small publication. Fear of
harassment, or direct pressure by the government, persuades printers to
either stop printing the magazine completely, or raise the charges to

---

[4] Introduced in the 1950s under the British colonial government.

reflect a high risk assignment. Kenya's most outspoken publication, the *Nairobi Law Monthly*, has had continual problems finding printers willing to print at reasonable cost. *Society* magazine, a relatively new publication that has also covered sensitive issues, had problems after it attracted criticism from the government. *Society* moved to another printer, who refused to sign the registration and bond forms, but proceeded to print the issue. *Society* discovered the printers had removed their name from the magazine masthead during the printing, which made the magazine vulnerable to charges of failing to register correctly. The magazine was forced to move again.

The Second Stage

A so-called failure to submit annual returns is commonly used by the authorities to undermine magazines considered critical of the government. By simply refusing to accept the annual returns, a magazine is left open to criminal charges of failing to submit the necessary papers. Some editors have confronted this tactically by sending their annual returns by registered mail in order to record the submission if a prosecution is brought.

The editor of the *Nairobi Law Monthly*, Gitobu Imanyara, explained how he was charged with a criminal offence:

I published an issue with Mr Kamau Kuria on the cover after he had been released from detention—and in the interview he spoke fairly freely and candidly. In the letters-to-the-editor page, there was one person asking the Commissioner of Police to step down and accept the blame for the many incidents of police brutality and the cases of people dying in custody. Shortly after this issue came out, I was arrested and it was alleged I was spreading alarm and despondency. When I pointed out that the same letter had been published in an abridged form in the *Standard*, they went—and instead of charging me with that particular application, they took me to court for not filing returns with the Attorney-General's office—although the fact of the matter is we filed our returns. The matter is still in court.[5]

---

[5] Africa Watch interview with Gitobu Imanyara, April 1990.

Imanyara has been charged with at least four such criminal offenses since 1988.

The Third Stage

In 1990 and 1991, the authorities seized magazines from vendors when they failed to stop them from publishing critical reports. In October 1990, police implemented a clean-up campaign in central Nairobi, aimed at street sellers. According to the *Sunday Nation*, news vendors were injured and arrested by security forces who "damaged and confiscated thousands of books and magazines belonging to news vendors and booksellers."[6] The sweep followed the first successful repeal of a ban in the high court, when the editor of the *Nairobi Law Monthly* disputed a ban imposed on his publication by the attorney general as unconstitutional.

In the following week, plainclothes policemen confiscated copies from vendors, who were told the publication was illegal despite the high court ruling. Vendors were informed they were banned from selling magazines, which included other monthlies, *Society, Finance* and some international magazines, like *Newsweek*. According to the publishers of one of the monthly magazines:

> If they don't have success with the editors, they'll go for the vendors. Most of the vendors are prepared to risk a lot to sell, but we notice that when they're harassed they just come for, say, five issues at a time. So they get five, sell them, then come for a few more. The only way they can be punished is through confiscation of their goods. By taking a few at a time, they only lose five magazines and not a whole livelihood. In February, some vendors lost 50-100 magazines, which is equal to about 2,000 Kenyan shillings [$77]. That grounds a vendor completely, so they take their precautions. We found after February, many Asians felt too vulnerable to continue stocking the magazines—they are vulnerable through their business interests because they own the newsagents. So we're having to rely more on the vendors.

---

[6] *Sunday Nation*, October 14, 1990.

The vendors are the least protected in the chain and the most easily harassed. The harassment of editors and journalists and the banning of publications attract international attention and protest by Western governments and human rights organizations, but the arrest, beating and jailing of vendors are invisible statistics. Vendors are unable to get legal representation. After hundreds of copies of the *Nairobi Law Monthly* were seized from the streets in February 1991, the editor of the publication collected the signatures of seventy-four vendors who had had their goods confiscated illegally; but no action was taken on their behalf after the editor himself was jailed.

The Final Killing

Section 52 of the Penal Code provides for the banning of "all past and future issues" of a publication in the interests of "public safety and public order."

Three monthly magazines have been banned since 1988, and a fourth one has received a banning order which was later overturned. Banning orders have typically followed a campaign against a publication, including condemnation by politicians in parliament of the magazine and its editor. Announcement of a ban goes to the press first, not to the owner or the editor of the publication, and is issued without explanation. The editors of *Beyond, Financial Review* and *Nairobi Law Monthly* all learned of the ban issued against their publications after journalists from the daily papers telephoned their offices to ask for comment. Banning is the greatest threat that hangs over a critical publication.

Banned Publications

Beyond was a monthly magazine published by the National Council of Churches of Kenya. It was banned in March 1988 after publishing detailed accounts of election-rigging. When *Beyond* was originally launched under editor Bedan Mbugua, it concentrated on issues relevant to social morality and family life. It was perceived as politicized when it supported the church in its opposition to the new queue-voting system, introduced in 1986. The magazine began to carry long articles by some of the most critical clergymen and ran campaigns of its own against all forms of public maladministration. Circulation rose from 15,000 to 60,000 in a month. After publication of the March issue, when it released its own findings alongside the official election returns of a number of sensitive constituencies, circulation figures reached 90,000. Accompanying the exclusive election reports collected by correspondents—many of them clergy who counted the numbers queuing behind candidates—*Beyond* published an editorial condemning the excesses which had been witnessed.

Two weeks after publication of the March issue, *Beyond* was banned. All past issues were proscribed, with an order for their destruction; one editor has likened this to a death sentence. The ban followed attacks by politicians, who called the reports it carried "malicious" and "unprofessional." The *Kenya Times* said the contents were an insult to KANU and to the population: "The government cannot entertain destructive and irresponsible journalism bordering on subversion."

Bedan Mbugua was arrested and charged with the technical offense of failing to submit annual sales returns to the Registrar of Books and Newspapers. The criminal charge, which was clearly being used for political reasons, was rejected by Mbugua's lawyers on the basis that he was an employee, not the publisher, and was not therefore responsible for submitting the returns. He was sentenced to six months in prison and spent two and a half weeks there before he was released on bail, pending appeal. Mbugua was acquitted by the Court of Appeal in August 1989 after numerous court appearances and international pressure.

No reason has been given for the ban, but the government has refused to reinstate the magazine. The ban was not challenged in court because, according to Mbugua, the publishers did not think it was possible to overturn a ban issued by the government.

Financial Review was a weekly economics magazine, previously sister publication to the *Weekly Review*, and was bought by its new editor-publisher, Peter Kareithi, in March 1987. Kareithi had previously been a senior writer at the *Weekly Review*. The magazine was attacked by President Moi in November 1987 for publishing a critical article about the quality of education, calling it subversive. *Financial Review* also criticized the new electoral system which was followed by a high court injunction on publishing material of a "purely political" nature. The high court ruling was brought through an application submitted by the editor of the *Weekly Review*, which is primarily a political magazine. The *Weekly Review* editor, Hilary Ng'weno, ordered Kareithi to settle up under the sale agreement and repay outstanding monies. Kareithi was forced to borrow from local finance houses to repay its previous owner. The magazine continued to carry articles exposing corruption and maladministration, which it called "serious flaws in the management of the national economy." In December 1988, Kareithi was arrested and charged with failing to submit financial returns. He said in an interview that producing the magazine had become a nightmare for him and the staff and he has since left the country:[7]

> When we met to discuss a cover story, most of our discussions were not how to get information but rather how to report it objectively and honestly without getting into trouble.

The *Financial Review* was finally banned in April 1989. The April issue featured a story about new regulations that empowered the National Cereals and Produce Board to commandeer private grain storage facilities "at such times as the board may direct and at such remuneration as the board may decide." It carried quotes from millers saying the new rules were tantamount to nationalization of their private investment. Attorney General Matthew Muli, wrote to Kareithi calling the quotations "mischievous" and demanded an unconditional retraction and apology. Kareithi refused, but asked the attorney general for the government's own interpretation of the rules, which he undertook to publish in the next issue. The magazine was then banned. Its editor believes that the millers' story was an excuse to get rid of the magazine after a campaign against it, and points also to the cover story of that issue. On the cover, a dejected Kenyan worker is pictured eating a mixture of grain and beans from a bowl, accompanied by the headline "Life Under Price Hikes." The feature said there was a widening gap between rich and poor in the country. Government ministers attacked this article the day before the banning order was issued. Sharif Nassir, then Assistant Minister for National Guidance and Political Affairs, urged the government, along with several other ministers, to ban the magazine "before it commits another outrage against the government."[8]

Development Agenda, a monthly social and political magazine, was banned in August 1989. The magazine had only published two issues before it was banned, and had not published anything which was considered controversial—in fact, it was hardly known to the public. With no official explanation given, speculation is that the banning was

---

[7] *Washington Post*, April 29, 1989.

[8] *Daily Nation*, April 25, 1989.

implemented to harass one of its backers, Charles Nyachae, a lawyer and son of a prominent former civil servant. Nyachae announced he would contest a parliamentary seat in the 1988 elections, but the party refused clearance. He proceeded to buy full-page advertising space in all the national newspapers and claimed he had become victim to a vicious political campaign to ostracize and bankrupt him. Since then, he has had to close down many of his businesses, and many people believed the banning of *Development Agenda* was part of that campaign.[9]

Section 53 of the Penal Code stipulates that individuals accused of printing, reading, distributing or possessing a banned publication can be imprisoned for up to seven years. Government critics are frequently charged with allegedly possessing issues of banned magazines.

ATTACKS ON JOURNALISTS

Freedom of the press is also undermined through individual attacks on reporters during the course of their work. There have been many attacks on individual press members, most of which have gone unreported. Some of the more serious cases reported are listed below:

- On March 3, 1991, two *Weekly Review* reporters, Gacharia Gaitho and Julius Bargorett, were whipped and beaten with sticks by plainclothes police after they attempted to attend a public meeting held between Nicholas Biwott, Minister for Energy, and the villagers in Kerio Valley. The meeting was embarrassing for the Minister of Energy because it concerned a land dispute, in which the villagers were seeking compensation for land taken by the Kenya Fluorospar Company. Plainclothes police, believed to include members of Biwott's own security team, ordered the journalists to leave and confiscated their notebooks and film. Their car was searched and they were ordered to leave the district. Before they were able to leave, however, one of the four security men took them into a room and beat them with sticks. They were told they were being

---

[9] For a complete discussion of the *Nairobi Law Monthly*, see below.

punished for interfering. Biwott has disassociated himself from the incident. The case is reportedly under investigation by the CID.

- March 2, 1991, J. N. Nganga, Pauline Njuki and Caroline Mburu, staff members of *Nairobi Law Monthly* were taken to CID headquarters and interrogated after the arrest of Imanyara.

- March 1, 1991, Gitobu Imanyara was arrested by armed police at his Nairobi office. On March 4, he was charged with sedition and remanded to Kamiti Maximum Security Prison. He was released unconditionally on May 5, 1991.

- February 27, 1991, Gitobu Imanyara, editor *Nairobi Law Monthly*, was attacked by three youths with stones, who shouted "now kill him." Special Branch officers keeping surveillance on the editor failed to intervene, and police officers at the central police station denied knowledge of the attack despite the fact that the editor had reported it to them.

- October 13, 1990, reporters from the *Sunday Nation* were harassed and beaten by police after witnessing a police sweep in central Nairobi aimed at hawkers and street vendors. Two reporters, Ardwings Odera and Opala Kennethy, said they were "roughed up" and "accosted by five askaris carrying whips" in their subsequent report.

- July 9, 1990, Mohamed Amin, Visnews bureau chief, and a Visnews cameraman, were stopped by police and roughly handled. Mohamed Amin was slapped over the head by an officer, and the journalists were forced into a police truck with detainees taken from the scene of the July demonstrations and riots. They were taken to separate police stations and later released without charge.

- July 5, 1990, Gitobu Imanyara, editor of the *Nairobi Law Monthly* arrested and detained under Public Security Regulations. He was released from Preventive Detention on July 26, but transferred to Kamiti Maximum Security Prison on charges of sedition. He was released on bail on July 30.

- June 28, 1990, Mitch Odero, deputy editor of the *Standard*, Francis M'Thaiya, managing editor of *Sunday Standard*, Francis Githui Muhindi, managing editor-designate, and production editor, James Kimondo, were arrested and charged with publishing reports "likely to cause fear and despondency." They were released on bail and charges were dropped.
- June 21, 1990, George Mbugguss, editor of the *Daily Nation* was arrested after attending a press conference by multiparty advocates.
- June 21, 1990, Mitch Odero, deputy editor of the *Standard*, was threatened with arrest.
- August 17, 1988, editor of banned publication *Beyond*, Bedan Mbugua, was sentenced to nine months' imprisonment for "failing to file annual returns of sale and accounts." See above for details.
- August 4, 1987, Paul Amina, freelance journalist and stringer for Reuters is arrested outside the high court after following the court inquest into a death in police custody. He was held incommunicado in police custody for two weeks before his detention under the Public Security Regulations was carried in the Kenya Gazette. He was detained until February 1988. Paul Amina, together with other detainees released at the same time, complained of police beatings, confinement to dark cells partially filled with water, and other methods of physical and psychological torture.
- January 1987, Mitch Odero, working with the *Kenya Times*, was suspended after participating in a BBC radio program in London titled "Talk About Africa." While on suspension, he left for a job at the *Standard*.
- November 14, 1986, Njuguna Mutahi and Wahome Mutahi, two journalists who are brothers, were each sentenced to 15 months' imprisonment after pleading guilty to neglecting to report the existence of an anti-government organization (MwaKenya), and publishing a seditious publication. Njuguna Mutahi, assistant information officer for the official Kenya News Agency, was arrested in Marsabit on October 15, 1986, and was held in police custody incommunicado. Wahome

Mutahi, staff member of the *Sunday Nation* newspaper, was arrested in Nairobi on October 16, 1986, and held in police custody incommunicado. Neither brother was legally represented in court.

- November 7, 1986, Mugo Theuri Wanderi, correspondent for the *Standard*, was sentenced to four years' imprisonment after pleading guilty to "taking an unlawful oath" and to "failing to report the publication of a seditious pamphlet." He was arrested in Nakuru in mid-October and held incommunicado in police custody.

- July 23, 1986, Salim Lone, journalist and Deputy Chief of Information, UN Office for Emergency Operations in Africa, UNICEF, New York, and editor of *Africa Emergency Report*, was arrested in Kitale and detained for 48 hours while on holiday in Kenya. He was interrogated about alleged connections with MwaKenya, and was released on July 24 after UN diplomatic efforts. His passport was revoked, he was deported from Kenya, and on September 2, 1986, he was deprived of his citizenship.

- May 9, 1986, David Njuguna Mutonya, journalist and civil servant, was sentenced to four years' imprisonment for the possession of seditious literature.

- November 13, 1985, William Onyango, reporter for *Kenya Times* and a candidate for the 1986 Kenya Press Club Journalist of the Year Award, was arrested and held for interrogation in connection with reports he had filed on the importation of second-hand clothing and used cars into Kenya.

- August 17, 1982, Otieno Makonyango, assistant managing editor of the *Sunday Standard* was charged with treason in connection with the coup attempt. In March 1983, the treason charge was dropped but he continued to be detained without charge until December 12, 1986. He was released unconditionally under a presidential amnesty. It is widely held that Makonyango was mistakenly arrested for a journalist in whose house he had expressed interest: the house was said to have been used by the coup plotters.

Makonyango also attributes his lengthy detention to political interests at the *Sunday Standard,* which were dominated at the time by followers of Charles Njonjo. During his detention, Makonyango said that he was beaten and harassed, and on one occasion was kicked and beaten by former Police Commissioner Ben Gethi, who was exasperated by the journalist's refusal to confess to involvement in the coup plot. In addition, Makonyango said that he was subjected to psychological intimidation and had several manuscripts confiscated by the government.

THE FOREIGN PRESS

The Kenyan government also inhibits comprehensive coverage by the foreign press. More than one hundred foreign correspondents are based in Nairobi. Foreign journalists have taken advantage of the relatively well-developed communications network and good living conditions to use Nairobi as a base for regional coverage, but are comparatively restrained in their reporting of events in Kenya.

Like local journalists, the foreign correspondents have been forced to exercise self-censorship because of the fear of eliciting displeasure and recriminations from the authorities. Often this has proved to be an exaggerated fear—though deliberately encouraged by the authorities—compared to the situation of their local counterparts. The reticence of many Nairobi-based correspondents in their coverage of Kenya has been criticized by human rights organizations, and by the editorial staff of some British and United States publications and institutions. The complaint, however, is reciprocated: correspondents in Nairobi find reports on Kenya generally get low priority in international news coverage.

Self-censorship by foreign journalists diminished in 1990, after most members of the Nairobi press corps found themselves covering events unfavorable to Kenya's international image. By Kenyan standards, most of these articles were considered critical, but none of the permanently-based foreign correspondents were expelled. There were, however, a number of scathing attacks against the foreign press, particularly the BBC, and a visiting British correspondent from *The Times* (London), Christopher Walker, was deported, ostensibly for not having a work permit. Walker had written some of the most critical pieces on

Kenya during the 1990 July riots, and made an unfavorable comparison to the Romanian dictatorship.

The Kenyan government is able to exert control over the composition of the foreign press corps through the granting or withholding of work permits. All journalists are required to apply for a work permit to the Ministry of Information and the Kenya Union of Journalists with a supporting letter from the journalist's employer or organization, and a letter from the journalist's home embassy. Many journalists have to work for long periods without a permit because of bureaucratic delays; delaying tactics have also been used to jeopardize the position of a journalist. Work permits have been blocked on spurious grounds by the Minister for Internal Security and Minister of State in the Office of the President, Hezekiah Ouygi, to prevent critical and investigative journalists working on Kenya. The authorities failed to renew the work permit of two correspondents who had consistently reported on human rights cases—Blaine Harden of the *Washington Post* in June 1987, and Lindsey Hilsum of the *Guardian* and BBC in November 1988—although the work permits were renewed after pressure was exerted on the Kenyan government.

Apart from fear of deportation, or loss of employment, foreign journalists are also discouraged from reporting on Kenya by the hostility and lack of cooperation typically displayed by government ministers and officials. Foreign correspondents are constantly harangued by the authorities for not getting it "right," but are rarely given official comment on even the most harmless of stories. Hostility to the foreign press is manifest in the government, the party and the security forces; fear of talking to foreign journalists is widespread among the general public. The consequences of talking to the press are tantamount to a criminal charge for the average Kenyan citizen. Talking to members of the press was stated as a reason for detention on orders issued in 1990.

Since the multiparty debate of the 1990s, the foreign press has received an unprecedented number of critical statements issued by multiparty advocates, and has found a new willingness from the government and its critics to respond to the press when approached. President Moi gave his first press conference to foreign journalists in May 1991, but refused to answer questions about Kenya other than those relevant to the presence of refugees. Despite this greater willingness on the part of the government to develop better relations with the international press, however, restrictions on work permits have become very strict.

Harassment of Foreign Journalists

Many foreign correspondents have received complaints, and occasionally direct threats, from ministers, government officials and security personnel, but few of these have been recorded. Some of the reported cases of harassment include the following:

- October 1990, Sulaiman Salim Sulaiman, a BBC reporter from Tanzania was detained for three nights at Nairobi Central Police Station and charged with working illegally in Kenya. He was arrested soon after arriving in Nairobi. A report, broadcast in Kiswahili, in which he detailed the summary deportation of Ugandan refugees, attracted condemnation from the government. Sulaiman Salim Sulaiman had been assured by the Kenyan embassy in the U.K. that he could legitimately work while his application for a work permit was being processed. The charges were eventually dropped in early 1991, but his work permit was not issued in the spring of 1991.

- July 9, 1990, Colin Blaine, BBC East African correspondent, Julian Ozanne, *Financial Times* correspondent, and Aidan Hartley, freelance journalist reporting for the *Daily Telegraph*, were stopped by police while driving to cover demonstrations and riots in a Nairobi suburb. They were threatened by the police, and Aidan Hartley was hit over the head with a baton. After being detained for a short period without explanation, the journalists were released.

- October 1989, Lucy Hannan, freelance journalist working for the BBC, was detained and searched by the military while interviewing Somali refugees in Liboi, North Eastern Province. She was transferred by armed guard to Garissa police station where she was held without charge for sixteen hours by the Special Branch. Her requests to contact the BBC or a lawyer were ignored. Her passport, notebook, films and personal possessions were confiscated. These were returned six weeks later.

- November 1987, Lindsey Hilsum, freelance journalist working for the BBC and the *Guardian*, was beaten by police while covering demonstrations at the University of Nairobi. Despite her injuries, she was held without charge for three hours before being released. She was severely bruised and needed treatment for a cracked bone in her upper spine.

- November 1987, Didrikke Schanche of *Associated Press*, Peer Meinert of West Germany's *Deutsche Presse-Agentur*, and Patrick Moser of *United Press International*, were arrested and Moser was beaten by police during the same university demonstrations. They were held for three hours without charge before being released.

- June 1987, Blaine Harden of the *Washington Post* was ordered to leave the country. The order came after he had written a number of articles critical of Kenya's human rights record. Pressure on the government succeeded in reversing the decision at the last minute. He was subsequently awarded the only interview President Moi has given to a foreign journalist prior to a recent interview with the Swahili Service of the BBC concerning the death of Rajiv Gandhi.

HOT FROM THE PRESS

Despite intimidation, the monthly publications *Nairobi Law Monthly*, *Finance*, and *Society* have continued to show a willingness to confront critical issues. The February 1991 issues of all three publications were confiscated by security police in a city sweep at the end of February. The editor of *Nairobi Law Monthly* and a freelance journalist were detained on charges of sedition, and *Finance* editor Njehu Gatabaki went into hiding after being threatened with arrest. Five Special Branch officers went to the offices of *Society* looking for the editor, Pius Nyamora, who was not on the premises. The Special Branch interrogated the director of the magazine, Loyce Nyamora. In a public speech, President Moi denounced Gatabaki as a "tribalist," and in late March the editor's home was searched by police. After pressure on the Kenyan government, the editor of the *Nairobi Law Monthly* and his codefendant were released. Publication of the three monthlies has continued.

Pressure on the press, however, has intensified: one journalist said that other events since July 1990 have distracted attention from an unprecedented campaign against the press. By looking back over the pattern of the decade, he said, it was clear that the government was responding to a new, more critical environment:

> Many of the editors were changed in 1988. The editors from the *Daily Nation* and the *Standard* were sacked because of conflict with the powerful politicians. They culled the editors because of political pressure, and appointed people right for the political climate. So we lost the independent-minded ones. After that, things did not go at all well—by 1989 the system of reporting had changed. The papers became like party papers. For example, we were told instead of writing "President Moi," which we always had done, we had to write "His Excellency President Moi." Many reporters didn't like that! Many continued to refuse to do that, and just wrote "President."

> You could see the editors were a scared lot. They were not brave enough to publish and were always telling the reporters that stories were "sensitive"—and of course the reporters had no idea on whose terms the stories were considered "sensitive." Then the politicians knew they could get away with telling the editors what to do—they just directed the editors what to print. It got to a point eventually where we couldn't even report things said in parliament, or in court, which was very strange. We've always been able to do that before, however bad. But things had really changed; if, for example a minister was accused of rape in court, it could not be used. I remember there was a case of a minister said to be connected with MwaKenya; that couldn't be reported. There were ministers being disciplined by the KANU Disciplinary Committee—those too were often not reported. It was not clear to the reporters where the pressure was coming from.

> If the authorities resort to that sort of behavior, then you should resort to court—but if you don't get justice in court, whose fault is that? Police beat the journalists but

we don't know on whose orders, if anybody's. We
complain, but we never know if any action is taken. But
even if no action is taken we don't necessarily take it that
the whole government is resorting to oppressing the
press because some individuals are so powerful. So you
have to work out how to do things. Now, if I know I'm
within the constitution and I can find a way of putting it,
I go ahead. We can say things in a way which is not head
on—you don't head straight into it, you avoid it a bit. You
just find a way of putting it forward.

THE CASE OF THE NAIROBI LAW MONTHLY
"SUBVERSIVE, SEDITIOUS AND CONTEMPTUOUS"

Gitobu Imanyara has come under frequent attack for the
publication he edits, the *Nairobi Law Monthly*. Launched in 1987, the
magazine focuses on constitutional liberties, human rights issues and the
maintenance of the rule of law in Kenya. Imanyara has been charged
twice with printing a seditious publication, once with contempt of court,
and five times with petty criminal charges relating to the registration and
administration of the magazine. He has also been charged—and re-
charged—with stealing money from clients. In 1990, he spent three weeks
in preventive detention before being remanded on sedition charges and
then released on bail. In 1991, he was detained in Kamiti Maximum
Security Prison for two months on another charge of printing a seditious
publication, during which time he became seriously ill. In May 1991, he
was released unconditionally and all charges against him were dropped,
except for two charges of theft.

SUBVERSIVE

In March 1990, the *Nairobi Law Monthly* was denounced by a
group of MPs after an assistant minister, Noor Abdi Ogle, called the
magazine "anti-Kenyan, anti-government, anti-progress and subversive."
Ogle called on the security forces to take action against it and said its

contributors were "sworn enemies of Kenya and the government."[10] The offending issue had carried articles debating the merits of a multiparty system.

Imanyara made a public statement condemning Ogle for making the accusations in parliament "where he enjoys immunities and privileges." According to the editor, the accusations were part of a campaign to silence him and the magazine. In a press interview, he described what effect the comments of the MP had had:

> It is a very dangerous accusation—people don't want to be seen with me; we've lost a lot of advertisement revenue; our printers will not print our magazine except at a high cost that we would not normally pay. A member of parliament has stood up and said the magazine is subversive—yet it is a magazine readily available in the streets and people buy it. We get letters from government departments saying we are doing a good service, and lawyers write to say that in the absence of any other legal publication in this country, we are doing a good job. If there is something that we've published that they think is subversive, they should tell us they have objections to a particular story instead of branding us subversives. So, the way I see it is that it was an attempt to kill us economically, and then the government does not have to say they banned us but that we went bankrupt.

> If they have evidence that we are subversive, I think the best thing to do is just to charge us in court and call up evidence. I am a trained lawyer and I am the last to publish anything subversive. I'm very particular about what we publish. I don't think it's right for an MP to call someone anti-government in parliament when that somebody has never been tried in a court of law and found guilty. They are making life very difficult for people when they brand them anti-government or

---

[10] *The Standard*, March 22, 1990.

subversive—because their families are shunned and they
must live in constant fear.

During the height of the multiparty crisis in June and July 1990,
the editor was under surveillance by the Special Branch. He was being
watched 24 hours a day just before he was detained under preventive
detention regulations. He was detained for three weeks, and then charged
with publishing a seditious publication. The so-called seditious edition was
entitled "The Historic Debate—Law, Democracy and Multiparty Politics
in Kenya," and included articles for and against a multiparty system. The
Nairobi Law Monthly was the only magazine to print articles in favor of
multiparty politics, in spite of the fact that the government referred to
the political crisis as a national debate. By condemning the magazine as
seditious, the government confirmed what was evident—there was no
debate, and criticism of the president or the party was considered
criminal.

SEDITIOUS

After his detention in Naivasha in July 1990, Imanyara was
transferred to Kamiti Maximum Security Prison in Nairobi where he was
treated as a political prisoner. He was kept with prisoners found to be
insane in homicide cases, under conditions Imanyara called "extremely
cruel." There were no washing or sanitation facilities and one small
bucket was provided to serve as both a wash basin and a toilet. Imanyara
was held incommunicado in a windowless, filthy cell and suffered from
the constant noise of mentally ill inmates in adjoining cells.

He was released on bail after five days, on condition he reported
to the security police every Friday. His passport was confiscated, and he
faced a new criminal charge for allegedly failing to submit two copies of
the "Historic Debate" issue to the authorities before publication. On a
third count, he was charged for failing to submit financial returns for the
magazine in 1989. These charges were in addition to a previous charge
in April 1988 of failing to register the magazine and not filing official
returns.

Imanyara continued to publish the magazine with an independent
editorial stance. Further charges were put forward on September 4, 1990,
alleging that the editor had stolen money from a client—this was related
to a charge for which he served a two year sentence in 1984-85. In 1984,

Attorney General Matthew Muli, had insisted on bringing Imanyara to court over a matter of an uncleared cheque—after the case had been already dismissed by the Law Society and the money in question repaid. The attorney general took the unusual step of conducting the case personally. Imanyara believes the attorney general took the matter to court for political reasons and says he was treated as a political prisoner throughout his two years in prison. He attributes this to sensitive cases he took on as a practicing lawyer. One such case was the defense of a young boy who was tortured, according to Imanyara, to confess to murdering internationally-renowned wildlife conservationist, Joy Adamson. In another case, Imanyara was the first lawyer to step forward to defend one of the soldiers charged with treason in the August 1982 attempted coup. After his two-year prison term he said he was shocked to see people treated "like animals"—Imanyara was barred from practicing law and so established the *Nairobi Law Monthly*.

In October 1990, the former attorney general, Matthew Muli, issued an order banning all "past, present and future" issues of the magazine. No reason was given, but it followed publication of an issue that catalogued submissions to the KANU Review Committee. In it, Imanyara documented critical submissions on a number of themes—like the queuing system, the single party, corruption and land grabbing—including a speculative article by two human rights lawyers in exile on how the government would manage to implement minimum change with maximum credibility. The issue was entitled "Kenyans Want Change: KANU Review Committee Told." In his editorial column, Imanyara published the submission he had been unable to make to the committee at the time of his detention and imprisonment. He called for restoration of the supremacy of the constitution, a return to democracy and the rule of law, an independent judiciary, multiparty democracy and accountability of the occupant of the office of the president. He concluded:

> The current Parliament is the biggest single threat to our national security. It must be dissolved as soon as possible and a new government of national unity and reconciliation formed for the sole purpose of leading the country during the interim period within which free and fair elections would be held. These elections must cover every facet of public life. They must cover the Presidency, the National Assembly, Local Authorities, co-

operative societies and all public organizations including
the Law Society of Kenya. The new Parliament must
then constitute itself into a constituent Assembly to draw
and draft a new Constitution for this Republic. A general
amnesty ought to be promulgated to enable all Kenyans
in external and internal exile to participate fully in the
affairs of their motherland. This means that all detainees
must be released and allowed to participate in the
management of the affairs of the country. Sedition and
other politically motivated cases ought also to be
withdrawn.

Imanyara called the ban issued by the attorney general
"outrightly unconstitutional" and said he would challenge it in court. On
October 8, his lawyers won the first successful legal challenge to a
banning order in Kenya. Holding it unconstitutional, the order was
suspended by Justice Frank Shields pending review by a higher court. It
is significant that the case was brought in front of Justice Shields rather
than Justice Dugdale, who has routinely ruled in favor of the government
on constitutional issues. It appeared to have slipped through the system
(see chapter nine). The CID immediately launched an investigation into
how the case was mistakenly placed before Justice Shields instead of
Justice Dugdale. Six court clerks were detained for questioning overnight.
    In the week following suspension of the ban, some thirty
plainclothes police officers seized sidewalk news vendors and confiscated
copies of the *Nairobi Law Monthly*. Vendors and hawkers selling the
magazine were told it was still an "illegal publication" despite the High
Court judgment, and a blanket ban was temporarily enforced on all
magazines and periodicals sold on the street.[11] The informal ban was
revoked by the City Commissioner within a week, but plans were
announced to restrict the sale of magazines to shops and centers only.
    Inadvertently, the government helped to popularize the
specialized and scholarly periodical by linking its fate with the livelihood
of some of the poorest sectors of society. The editor issued press
statements condemning the government's harassment of the hawkers and
vendors. Vendors continued to display the magazine in the streets. The
magazine increased its circulation far beyond the small legal and

---

[11] *The Standard*, October 10, 1990.

academic community, because it became a symbol of defiance. One taxi driver told Africa Watch that he preferred *The Law* above anything else because of the editor's resilience: "Now this is more popular than any other magazine, because we think the editor is a very brave man." Since June 1990, the magazine has carried more political analysis on current events and on relevant international issues, but its increased popularity in Kenya is related to its symbolic role as a determined independent voice.

CONTEMPTUOUS

A charge of contempt of court was lodged against Imanyara following his publication of an interview with Paul Muite. In the interview, Muite commented on allegations made by the government in July 1990 that a "shadow cabinet list" existed. His comments included references to George Anyona, then on trial for alleged sedition. The charge was later dropped by the newly appointed attorney general, Amos Wako.

In January 1991, Imanyara contributed to the multiparty debate by filing an application in the High Court seeking an order that the 1982 constitutional amendment, which made Kenya a de jure one-party state, should itself be declared unconstitutional. Although the calls for a multiparty system had, to a certain extent, been stifled by the government, they had not been entirely suppressed. Renewed support for multiparty politics in the New Year showed that the debate was by no means over, with Jaramogi Oginga Odinga, former vice-president, launching a new political party in February.

Imanyara argued the 1982 amendment violated section 80 of the constitution which provides for freedom of association. He also declared he was not a member of KANU by choice and that millions of other Kenyans, he believed, felt the same way. Citing his detention in July 1990, Imanyara said the grounds given were illegal, and nothing in the constitution prevented him from associating with people whose intention was to set up a new political party.

> I verily believe that it is necessary for the said constitutional amendment to be struck out of the laws of Kenya to prevent its misuse, and also to enable me and

millions of other Kenyans to enjoy their fundamental
right to belong to a political party of their own choice.

This application was rejected in May 1991.

In February 1991, the *Nairobi Law Monthly* featured the formation
of Odinga's National Democratic Party and printed its political
manifesto—despite a blackout in the daily papers. Two other monthlies,
Society and *Finance* also covered the launch of the new party. Imanyara's
accompanying editorial said that one of the greatest problems facing the
country was favoritism on a tribal basis in public offices and state-owned
and operated organizations, and listed positions held by the president's
own minority tribe, the Kalenjin.

An official response to the editorial in the *Kenya Times* refuted the
allegations of tribalism. The editorial said that although the list was
accurate, Imanyara had deliberately omitted organizations and state-
owned and operated organizations dominated by other communities. In
particular, argued the *Kenya Times*, Imanyara had failed to show that the
Kikuyus from Rift Valley hold prominent positions.[12]

On February 27, 1991, plainclothes police confiscated thousands
of copies of the *Nairobi Law Monthly* from news vendors. In a sweep of the
city, confiscation of the *Nairobi Law Monthly*, *Society* and *Finance* magazines
was carried out without any regard to legality; the officers did not identify
themselves or cite authorization. The security officers threatened vendors
and warned them not to sell the *Nairobi Law Monthly*. In fact, copies were
reportedly replaced almost as fast as they were confiscated.

During the same evening, Imanyara was threatened by a group
of young men who surrounded him outside his office, menacing him.
Rocks were hurled at the editor and his general manager, Mr. Nganga.
Imanyara sustained a minor injury on his arm. During the attack, a
number of Special Branch officers were present for surveillance purposes
but did not intervene. The editor filed a report on the incident at a
nearby police station, though this was denied by police the following day.

---

[12] The Kikuyus are the largest single ethnic group in Kenya, and are
concentrated in the central provinces and Nairobi. President Kenyatta used
tribalist policies to elevate members of his own Kikuyu community, and there is
lasting concern among other ethnic groups that the Kikuyu may again dominate
Kenyan politics. President Moi has capitalized on this fear. See chapter one.

This denial had to be retracted later because the report had been routinely entered in the station logbook.

Two days later, Imanyara was seized by eight plainclothes officers as he entered his office early in the morning, March 1. He was taken to his home, which was searched. He was then brought back to the office, but was prevented from speaking to lawyers and the press, who had gathered. His office was searched, but no warrant produced. Several files were taken by the police before they left with the editor through a back door. One lawyer, Martha Njoka, managed to follow the officers to Kileleshwa police station. At the station she was surrounded by police officers who seized her car keys and roughly handled her—they refused to accept her efforts to file a complaint. Over the next two days, J. N. Nganga, Pauline Njuki and Caroline Mburu of the *Nairobi Law Monthly* staff were interrogated by the Special Branch and surveillance of the office continued.

Arrested on Friday, Imanyara did not appear in court until Monday, when he was charged with publishing a seditious document with intent to incite tribal hatred. Bail was routinely refused at the objection of the prosecution and the editor was remanded in custody at Kamiti Maximum Security Prison.

On April 10, 1991, Imanyara was discovered unconscious in his cell by a prison guard at 6:00 A.M. He had been kept in solitary confinement with only 30 minutes exercise and sunlight a day since being remanded in March. Visitors who saw the editor regularly said Imanyara had been suffering from increasingly severe migraine headaches, for which he was receiving medication, during his confinement.

On April 18, his lawyer, Dr. John Khaminwa, asked the court to release a seriously ill Imanyara on bail so he could receive proper medical treatment. In a medical report presented to the court, a consulting surgeon and traumatologist said he found Imanyara to be suffering from severe bouts of left-sided headaches, leading to loss of consciousness, possible epilepsy, blood-clotting, high blood pressure, pus in the nasal passage and occasional severe pain in the left upper face.

During the court hearing, Khaminwa asked for Imanyara to lie down as he was unfit to proceed. Friends of the editor said he soon collapsed and was taken, with a prison doctor, back to Kamiti Maximum Security Prison. He was returned to solitary confinement while the court studied the doctor's report in connection with a renewed bail application.

On April 22, a representative of the Paris-based International Federation of Newspaper Publishers persuaded prison guards to let him see Imanyara. After talking to the editor, the representative said: "One does not have to be a doctor to see that Imanyara is a very sick man." He said Imanyara was obviously aware he was seriously ill, but had difficulty remembering dates, times and details given by medical staff. At this stage, there was concern that the editor had possible brain damage. The following day he was taken to Kenyatta government hospital for tests, and all medication was withdrawn—he was then returned to solitary confinement. The bail application was adjourned for a second time.

On April 24, the court ordered that the editor be transferred immediately to a government hospital. An application for bail was adjourned for a third time. Three days later, the court adjourned the application for bail again so as to be able to examine the consulting traumatologist. On April 30, bail was refused, but the ruling order said that he should remain in hospital. During his time in hospital, Imanyara was handcuffed to the bed and guarded by seven warders.

RELEASED AND UN-BANNED

On May 5, 1991, the new attorney general, Amos Wako, dropped all eight criminal charges against the editor and ordered his release. Two charges of theft, relating to the charges for which he was jailed in 1984, remained.

On July 4, Wako revoked the ban issued by the former attorney general, Matthew Muli. In a statement to the press, Imanyara said the removal of the ban was a cause for "jubilation," and that the new attorney general had "affirmed his commitment to the rule of law":

> Ideas are to be met with better ideas, not with might.
> Those who meet ideas with a show of might only serve to
> vindicate the very ideas they wish to suppress.

13
CHURCH AND STATE

The church, as in many nations worldwide, has always regarded itself a legitimate watchdog of the state. Along with critical lawyers, it is also known as the unofficial opposition party, and as a truly popular body, its power to influence and organize presents a formidable threat to the government.

Of the main churches, the Church of the Province of Kenya (CPK) has twelve dioceses with the same number of bishops and about 1,500 priests, and the Catholic Church has eighteen bishops, with seventeen regional dioceses and one military diocese. Just over half the population belongs to Protestant churches and under a quarter are Catholic. Apart from the main churches, there are a plethora of small evangelical sects, each with their own small constituency.

The church has a unique status and mandate in Kenyan society which allows it to criticize the government on moral rather than political grounds. According to the church, active monitoring of the government is an intrinsic duty in preaching the bible. Rev. Bernard Njoroge Kariuki of CPK states:

> Since human rights are God given, their promotion and protection are essential for freedom, justice and peace. The proclamation of human rights is not an auxiliary function of the church. This proclamation is the very substance in the proper sense of the gospel. It is the authentic proclamation of the kingdom of God. We need to feel the pain of those who are mistreated as if [we] ourselves are suffering.

> The church has three important responsibilities in its relationship with the state. (1) The church must make sure that the state acts responsibly. (2) The church has a duty towards those who suffer from the actions of the state, since it is the duty of the church to be on the side of the victim. (3) The church has a duty beyond the rescue of victims of oppression. It must try to destroy the

cause of oppression. The church would have to enter the political arena to do this.[1]

The willingness of some church leaders to speak out on sensitive political and social issues has brought the church into direct confrontation with President Moi's government. Along with some critical lawyers, it is known as the unofficial opposition party. Compared to other critical groups, the church has often had greater impact on the government because it is not confined to the elite and the literate; its constituency is nationwide. Over 70 percent of the population describe themselves as Christian, and the president himself regularly attends church, making frequent references to Christian morality and standards in his public addresses.

Since the church is a popular body, the threat it presents to the government is considerable. One of the most important of which is its ability to educate their constituencies about their rights. In the words of one churchman "[raising] consciousness and education...is the back of our work. This is very important because if you don't create awareness of rights and obligations, and empower people, you will have little effect on the larger society." In a state where legislation bans meetings of three people or more, the church is the only remaining popular forum. Congregations are the only legitimate gathering of the public outside party rallies, and sermons are the only regular, legitimate forum for addressing large groups of people. This, and the unrivalled knowledge of social problems through intimate acquaintance with the poorest sections of society, makes its critical observations hard for the government to dismiss. The government is inhibited in criminalizing opposition by the church, in the way it has done with other critics, because of its national stature and international clout (see chapter eight). Nonetheless, the government is engaged in a relentless campaign to undermine the effectiveness of the church and to discredit its outspoken leaders. According to one churchman, the effect is that "because of fear, many people have left the work up to the bishops, so that has meant that only some bishops are active, and some clergy."

---

[1] Reverend Bernard Njoroge Kariuki, *Role of the Church in the Promotion of Social Justice in Africa* (publisher unknown, September 1990).

WORKING WHERE IT COUNTS

Vital community services and resources were provided by missionaries and the church long before an independent government had been established. In fact, the church educated the leaders of the nationalist movements and remains a central administrator and provider (see chapter one). In the more remote communities, the church has been able to offer services that the government has failed to provide, such as water bore-holes, petrol stations, schools, agricultural projects and health clinics. Although the present government has significantly developed some areas, the church has consolidated more influence by virtue of its consistency.   For example, there is normally a high turnover of government personnel within the provincial and district administration compared to the permanent presence of the church.

Local church-based development groups significantly expanded in the late 1970s. In the Catholic church, donor agencies funded a variety of income generating projects, agricultural projects, small business ventures, women's projects and advisory services through what was known as the "Delta Scheme." Skilled workers, trained by the diocese development teams, went back into the community to train at a local level and set up an administration and established workshops aimed at social and economic improvements. As the Delta trainees and workers became more economically independent, they were increasingly perceived by the government as a competing administration with valuable resources and influence.

Apart from introducing important new community projects, the scheme also pushed for change within the church. There was a demand for greater accountability from the priests, especially the expatriate priests. One expatriate worker told Africa Watch:

> The expatriate priests had large amounts of money and a lot of local power and influence, but were not accountable to the bishops. They could build schools, health clinics, bore holes, start agricultural projects and community services whenever they liked, and were not accountable to the Catholic Church, to the administration

or to the Christian community.   They became little
barons in their own right.[2]

This pressure on the church hierarchy—many of whom believed
the Delta scheme had become overly political—created a deep division in
the church. The government was able to exploit these divisions by co-
opting the conservative faction.

The grass roots organizations established by the church came
under concerted government attack after the 1982 coup attempt.
Hundreds of people involved in the Catholic Delta scheme and other
development projects were harassed, interrogated and detained. In areas
like Kitui, Machakos and Turkana where Delta organizations were strong,
personnel were targeted in a nationwide political crackdown. A number
of skilled personnel and trainees were subjected to surveillance by the
Special Branch before being detained without charge for up to two to
three weeks in police cells. Priests and church leaders were also followed
and intimidated. The church effectively purged their own ranks for fear
of government reprisals. The conservative factions of the church were in
any case eager to close down a scheme they considered too politicized.
The government exerted pressure on the church by studiously building
up intelligence and surveillance and compiling Special Branch files on the
personal lives of many of the bishops and church leaders. Many of the
community workshops were closed down unceremoniously.

CHURCH SERVICES

As problems with land, electoral malpractices, unemployment and
police harassment increase, the church has been pushed—sometimes
reluctantly—more to the forefront of the political arena. One church
representative explained to Africa Watch how the church gets brought
into disputes by the congregation:

> A group of coffee farmers came to the church for help
> because they found they were powerless under the heavy
> bureaucracy of a body like the Kenyan Coffee Planters
> Union (KCPU). They used to identify with the KCPU—it

---

[2] There are still expatriate bishops in Kenya.

was very important—but then it came under attack by President Moi. These farmers lined up behind KCPU, but they had to come to the church as the only supportive mediating body. Then church representatives went to see the president. They could carry the complaints all the way to the top as the guardian of the people. The church can put it all forward in a way no-one else can.

The church plays a key role in the land crisis in Kenya. Africa Watch was told by one church representative that the church has become a vital intermediary between the landless and the landowners:

The relationship between the church and the state is in many ways ambivalent, but on the land issue, the church has been compelled to take a more radical position. Each parish, each diocese, each constituency of the church has documented thousands of cases of evictions and disputes. No one has more damning evidence on "land-grabbing" than the church. The growth of documented landlessness is incredible. The church is bringing up the cases when they can.

Land issues featured in the deteriorating relations between church and government in 1990, when Rev. Peter Njenga and Bishop Alexander Muge took a public stand on incidents of violent evictions and land-grabbing.

REV. PETER NJENGA AND MUOROTO

After the violent Muoroto evictions in Nairobi, Rev. Peter Njenga, Provost of All Saints Cathedral in Nairobi, was brought to the scene of the eviction by many members of his church who begged him to take action (see chapter fourteen). He held a press conference and gave details of eight people who died during the evictions. Despite harassment from the government, he refused to withdraw his allegations. President Moi called Njenga's claims "shameful." In a public rally held in Kisumu,

President Moi refered to "Church leaders who propagate lies and falsehhoods..."[3]

Pressure on Njenga increased when full-time Special Branch surveillance was assigned. In July, the former attorney general, Matthew Muli, ordered an inquest into the death of Peninah Nduta Njenga, the bishop's wife.[4] Through his lawyer, Dr. John Khaminwa, Njenga applied to stop the inquest on the grounds it had been prompted by his allegations on the Muoroto deaths. Muli ordered the inquest to begin on October 12, 1990, then later moved the date up to September 20, 1990. During the proceedings, Khaminwa argued that the state had instituted an inquest into the cause of death of Njenga's wife as a means of embarrassing and harassing him. To show the pressure Njenga had been put under to withdraw his allegations concerning Muoroto, Khaminwa produced a letter addressed to the churchman from the CID. It read in part: "...[I]f you do not apologise to the Kenyan public on receipt of this letter, my intention is to take you to a court of law to be charged accordingly".[5] Khaminwa also challenged the power of the attorney general to appoint a judicial commission of inquiry in this case.

In areas where land-grabbing is endemic, and violent evictions frequent, access to information is only possible through church records— since mid-1980's, the Land Registry is only available to the public with direct clearance from the president's office. One of the most diligent and systematic compilations of land problems was overseen by Rev. Alexander Muge, bishop of Eldoret (see chapter fourteen).

BISHOP ALEXANDER MUGE: A THREAT

Bishop Alexander Muge had an ambivalent relationship with the government. He became a well-known critic during his opposition to queue-voting, but was also known for his scathing attacks on other

---

[3] *The Weekly Review,* June 8, 1990.

[4] Peninah Njenga's body was found hanging in the kitchen of the family residence in October 1989, and a government pathologist, Dr. Jason Kaviti, determined the cause of death as suicide.

[5] *The Weekly Review,* September 28, 1990.

outspoken church leaders. Muge did not support calls for a multiparty system, but called for political reform within the one-party state. He publicly campaigned against corruption in the government, focusing on illegal land acquisitions by senior government ministers. Most of the complaints brought to him by his congregation concerned land-grabbing and evictions. As well as compiling detailed records of these cases, Muge collected photographic evidence of killings by Administration Police during illegal evictions of squatters. In 1990, Muge was tenacious in his calls for a full investigation into the murder of Foreign Minister Robert Ouko.

In the memorandum he presented to the KANU Review Committee he called for major changes in the political system, and denounced corruption and political murders. He also called for a declaration of wealth by leaders and the resignation of those who were returned to Parliament through rigging. The allegations put forward, based on submissions made by the people of his diocese, were substantiated with details of the alleged involvement of Minister Nicholas Biwott and a civil servant in a land scandal. Biwott and Muge operated in the same province.[6]

Muge was threatened with death by then Minister for Labor, Peter Okondo. Three M.P.'s, Pancras Otwani, Moody Awori and Philip Masinde, warned at a public rally that Muge and Bishop Henry Okullu should keep away from Busia. Peter Okondo said that if Muge and Okullu went to Busia, "they will see fire and may not leave alive...because they want to poison the minds of Busia people against the government."[7] Muge took this threat seriously, but insisted on travelling to Busia two days after the warning. Before he went he told family and colleagues that he was aware of a plot to assassinate him, and issued a press statement responding to the ministers' death threat.

Muge was killed on August 14, 1990, the day after issuing the statement when his car was hit by a truck, about 65 kilometers from Eldoret. He was travelling back from Busia where he had been received enthusiastically. Two other passengers in the car, secretaries Rodah Chebor and Clare Kerubo, were critically injured with head and body

---

[6] Memorandum submitted to KANU Review Committee, August 1990. For details, see chapter fourteen.

[7] *Daily Nation*, August 13, 1990.

wounds. The truck, whose driver was later convicted for dangerous driving, belonged to Western Carriers of Luanda, Western Province

Few believed that Muge's death had been accidental. Archbishop Kuria appeared on Kenyan television to appeal for public calm. Herma Muge, the bishop's widow, called for a public inquiry. Members of the public who were amongst the first to arrive on the scene of the accident expressed suspicion. The attorney general issued a statement ordering a public inquiry into the death of Muge on August 18, which was later withdrawn on the grounds it was not within his jurisdiction. When Herma Muge's lawyer complained about the delay of her application to institute a public inquiry, he was threatened with contempt of court (see chapter eleven). Police were given orders to contain demonstrations over Muge's death.[8]

On August 19, a local priest and three other church officials were arrested in Eldoret when they attempted to hold an open air service to commemorate Muge's death. They were detained for six hours in police custody. In a memorial service held for the bishop, Nicholas Biwott was forced to leave. On August 20, after the bishop's funeral in Nairobi, peaceful protests in Nairobi were led by university students who demanded the resignation of several ministers. Peter Okondo announced he had offered to resign over statements he was reported to have made about Muge.[9]

DIVIDE AND RULE: SILENCING THE CHURCH

Public attacks on the church have increased significantly under President Moi. Senior politicians have threatened to curtail the constitutionally guaranteed freedom of worship and issued calls to detain church leaders. The strategy of the government has been to try and temper the criticism of outspoken clergy by intimidating and publicly ridiculing them, and by encouraging division within the church and the different sects. Between Lodwar and Kitale in northern Kenya, for example, there are twenty-two different religious sects, many of whom are rivals, competing for influence and resources. The extent to which

---

[8] Reuters, August 19, 1990.

[9] Peter Okondo was reinstated in 1991.

religious-based development projects and church organizations own and control resources in their individual constituencies led one nongovernmental organization (NGO) representative to describe them as being "like little colonies."[10] Fanning rivalry, the government has attempted to cultivate a loyal core within the church hierarchy, and encouraged the alienation of those perceived as critical. Its success in doing this has resulted in a very ambivalent church-state relationship. According to one church official, the government routinely influences and manipulates church appointments:

> The persecution of the church moved to another level in the mid-1980's when Moi began to manipulate, through the security intelligence system, the election of church officers, or use already elected officials through bribery and appointment to various positions in state-run corporations. One glaring example is the appointment of Elind Mahihu as the chairman of the tea corporation. He was also nominated to parliament. Mahihu played a major role in setting the Presbyterian church of East Africa against Rev. Timothy Njoya.[11] Mahihu was an elder from the Coast Province, which is one of the smaller areas of support for the PCEA [Presbyterian Church of East Africa], and used this position to become the head of the Business Committee of the PCEA. This committee succeeded in usurping a lot of power from the General Assembly of the PCEA. From his position in the Business Committee, Mahihu saw to it that he was appointed as the Chairman of the Special Committee to investigate Rev. Njoya. Partly as a result of this, Njoya was suspended from his church ministry for a whole year. Also, under Mahihu this committee issued a statement warning clergy and lay leaders against speaking to the

---

[10] Africa Watch interview, June 1991.

[11] Rev. Njoya has long been a critic of the government's human rights record. In order to deprive him of a platform, he was transferred in 1987 out of St. Andrews Church in Nairobi and sent to a small church in the provinces. He is now back in Nairobi working at the headquarters of the PCEA.

press on social or political issues. It is in this way that the
government and persons close to the government have
been able to influence the church. But there have been
psychological approaches too. President Moi's agents use
friends of outspoken and progressive clergy or lay
leaders to warn their friends. He may use relatives.
President Moi's government may also put pressure on
employers to fire outspoken lay leaders or deny
employment to wives of critical churchmen.

One churchman interviewed by Africa Watch explained the
government's divisive tactics:

> Bishop Gitari [of CPK, Mount Kenya East] has been
> running a polytechnic which has some teachers who were
> supported by the government, and were suddenly let go.
> So the church can not manage the school; it does not
> have funds for the entire school, and so the people will
> say that the church is not supporting them. Those are the
> things that have been contributed by the government.

The churches depend on donations for their work; they hold
harambees to raise funds.[12] Normally, churches do not require a license
to hold harambees; in recent years, however, the withholding of licenses
has been used in an effort to rein in critical churchmen. In 1989, Bishop
Gitari was told to obtain a license in order to organize a fund raising
event after it was decided that he had made political statements.

The government has more typically been preoccupied with
monitoring the main church bodies than with small sects and the growing
number of breakaway churches, whose divisions have aided a divide and
rule strategy employed by the government as it focuses on personal and
regional disputes. The CPK and the PCEA have attracted much of the
criticism levelled by the government on account of well-known critics like
Rev. David Gitari of Mount Kenya East (CPK), Rev. Timothy Njoya
(PCEA) of Tumu Tumu, the late Rev. Alexander Kipsang Muge of Eldoret

---

12 A *harambee* is a licensed fund raising event, often featuring an address
given by a well-known politician, where the public make contributions for
charities or civic purposes.

(CPK), and, more recently, Rev. Henry Okullu of Maseno South (CPK). As demands for a multiparty system increased in 1990 and 1991, more conservative leaders like Archbishop Manasses Kuria joined in the call for political reform.

However, small sects considered to be a threat—either by way of their message or their constituency—are ultimately more vulnerable to government attack than the larger institutions. Without the international support the main churches enjoy, small sects can be harassed more easily. In February 1990, the Tent of the Living God was banned. According to *The Weekly Review*, the Tent of the Living God began to be perceived as "sinister and perhaps militant" because of its devotion to Kikuyu traditional religion and ancestor worship.[13] The leader of the group, Gitahi Ngaruro, wore dreadlocks which were likened to the style of the Mau Mau. He reportedly called leaders of the Mau Mau, Dedan Kimathi and Stanley Mathenge, heroes.[14]

On February 3, 1990, policemen broke up a meeting of the Tent of the Living God on the Kamukunji grounds. Police officers then forcefully dispersed the crowds after producing a banning order signed by the registrar-general, J. N. King'arui. The group had been removed from the registration list without their knowledge on the previous day by notice 571 in the *Kenya Gazette* "in the interests of peace and order".[15] The scene turned violent when the crowd turned on the police with stones, and several members of the group were arrested and charged with causing a "breach of the peace." Ngaruro, the leader, was also arrested. Before the arrests, President Moi had repeatedly publicly condemned the group. The week before the group was banned, he said in a rally at Kiambu that they deliberately exploited the constitution in order to create chaos, and implied that disgruntled politicians were behind its activities.[16]

---

[13] *The Weekly Review*, February 2, 1990.

[14] The Mau Mau fought for independence as a secret organization (see chapter one). Ironically, the Mau Mau which was based in the Kikuyu lands, is now seen by the government as representing dissent, secrecy and opposition.

[15] *Kenya Gazette*, February 2, 1990.

[16] *The Weekly Review*, February 16, 1990.

Attempts to create divisiveness among the main churches reached a peak in March 1990 with the arrest of Rev. Lawford Ndege Imunde of the PCEA (see chapter eight). Held incommunicado for two weeks before being charged with sedition, the church was a central feature of his interrogation by the Special Branch. Special Branch officers focused on the role being played by the church in calls for a multiparty system; in particular, PCEA's Rev. Timothy Njoya who began the debate in his new year sermon. In his affidavit, Imunde described the interrogation:

> They told me they were holding me because I belong to the PCEA...They said that if the church had people like me, they would have nothing to do with religion...They asked me about bad sermons and Rev. Njoya...I was told the church was talking against the government and they have a lot of evidence. I was told the church was just a political party. I said I was not aware. They asked me where we got the money from...They asked me the number of foreigners we had in my church...[Then] they asked me about the sermons which have been delivered by Rev. Njoya...[saying] that the minister would write a mild sermon for public consumption, then he would write another scathing version attacking the government and it was the scathing sermon which was distributed to the people. I denied knowledge of this. They asked me whether the church leaders ever condemned the sermons after the government had indicated that they were offensive. I said I did not know...I had [also] been asked whether I knew that the NCCK[17] had started an organisation to continue the work of the banned magazine *Beyond*. I was asked [about] the Kikuyu M.P.s and businessmen who funded the church to criticize the government. They said Njoya did not speak without support.

---

[17] The NCCK is the National Council of Churches of Kenya which is the umbrella organization for all the Protestant churches in Kenya.

Imunde was forced to sign a prepared statement implicating the church as a "main political opposition group...sabotaging the government." In court, the state prosecutor said:

> The Rev. Imunde had said that as a church minister he was aware of some churches and individuals based abroad who were channelling money to some churches in Kenya solely to destabilise the Government.

Critics have suggested that the government picked on Imunde because there was controversy about his appointment within his own church, the PCEA. At the time of his arrest, Imunde was working on a part-time basis for the All Africa Conference of Churches and was responsible for coordinating the training of church lay leaders. He ran unsuccessfully for parliament in the last general elections in 1988, and his involvement with politics created tension with his church hierarchy. Disciplinary proceedings had been brought against him with a view to his being defrocked. Imunde wrote "My arrest was not a case of mistaken identity. They [the Special Branch] had been tipped."[18]

After Imunde's conviction, the PCEA issued a statement disassociating itself from his case and the NCCK denied his allegations. The absence of a unanimous church condemnation of the illegal way in which Imunde had been held, indicated the success with which the government could exploit divisions within and between the churches. Ochola Mak'Anyengo, M.P., called for an investigation into the churches. Peter Ejore, assistant minister for cooperative development said the government should "de-register" the NCCK.

The attack on the church through Imunde did, however, encourage some of the most conservative church leaders to join their more outspoken colleagues to call for political reform. Archbishop Kuria responded with "Enough is enough. Stop dragging the CPK into disagreements."[19]

Calls for political reform from church leaders became bolder in 1990-91, although much of the criticism on political reform had been put

---

[18] Quotes appearing in this and the following paragraph are from an affidavit submitted by Imunde through his lawyers.

[19] Interpress Service, Nairobi, April 2, 1990.

forward by the church in the mid-1980s. The church had earned its reputation as the unofficial opposition party when it vigorously opposed the introduction of new electoral procedures in 1985. Church leaders closely monitored rigging during the general elections of 1988 in the parishes and diocese. These procedures, which the church called "un-Christian and un-democratic," were eventually scrapped on the recommendations of the KANU Review Committee.

Action against the church was urged in parliament in 1989 when Minister for State in the Office of the President Burudi Nabwera said that churchmen in Kenya delighted in "feeding lies" to foreigners to get money.[20] Other M.P.'s urged the government to open an investigation into the NCCK. The church was accused by government ministers of being funded by "foreign masters" who were influencing it on social and political issues. Vice-President George Saitoti challenged churchmen to form an opposition party, saying:

> We reject allegations made by ill-informed and ill-intentioned elements who pray for disunity in the country behind disgraceful organisations that brazenly expose internal matters of our country to foreigners.[21]

Other prominent politicians, like Nicholas Biwott, accused the church of a "colonial hangover" and an allegiance to foreign masters and called on church leaders to make plain their political intentions. An assistant minister for regional development, John Okwara, challenged leading critics Bishop Muge, Bishop Henry Okullu and Bishop Gitari of the Church of the Province of Kenya (CPK) to give up religion and enter politics:

> Let them resign and seek parliamentary or KANU seats if they want to prove that they are popular instead of hiding behind the church.[22]

---

[20] *The Weekly Review*, December 15, 1989.

[21] Ibid.

[22] Ibid.

PRAYING FOR CHANGE

Having started the multiparty debate in January 1990, the church effectively stood back for four months before taking the argument a significant step forward. In May, Rev. Henry Okullu issued a press statement calling for the removal of the constitutional clause that makes Kenya a one-party state, and for limiting the presidential term to two terms. In the statement, he said "power corrupts even a person with the best will in the world." Following the announcement by KANU that it would hold a conference called "The Kenya We Want," he expressed doubt that the party would in fact tolerate a genuinely open debate.

Okullu's statement instantly drew angry reactions from politicians, but criticism was reined-in by Nicholas Biwott, who advised the party that the best response was to ignore the bishop.[23] One week later, President Moi accused the CPK of being involved in an assassination plot. In his speech at Kerugoya Stadium, he said of the church:

> Churches should avoid politics because they do not know what the politicians want. These same groups introduced politics into the church. Now they are introducing thuggery—even murders in their plans for the future. Others have said: Start parties in Scandinavia, then import them into Kenya when they are ready. They also planned...to enter Kenya through Uganda to kill Kenyan officials and churchmen so as to make it look as if the government was involved in the killings.

> They also say they will cooperate with the NCCK to exploit that part of the constitution which guarantees freedom of assembly or association. Then, if the government arrests them and takes them to court, they will bribe the judge with a lot of money to acquit them, so that he will be sacked and lose his benefit...I will have to swing into action now. They rely on human rights. We shall have no mercy....The CPK is doing a great disservice to its followers.

---

[23] *The Weekly Review*, May 4, 1990.

Archbishop Manasses Kuria challenged the government to name the alleged plotters, saying: "People are known by names...let them be called by their names and not by that of the church."[24]

ATTACKS CONTINUE

The church remained in the forefront of the demands for political reform, with calls by Archbishop Kuria to overhaul KANU[25] and a statement by Rev. Henry Okullu calling for the government to resign after its declaration of war on the people.[26] Calls for political reform now included the Catholic Church which had been considered the most conservative and reticent of the main denominations. On June 21, 1990, eighteen Catholic bishops issued a pastoral letter marking the closing of the centennial of the Catholic Church in Kenya. After congratulating the government on its role in leading Kenya toward peace and stability, the letter commented on what the bishops regarded as the source of Kenya's current social and political problems:

> The close identification between the government and KANU, those who criticize particular acts by the party are seen as attacking the government.

> Superiority of the party over the parliament seems to be an accomplished fact. This has led to a confusion of the three main arms of the government: the Executive, the Legislative and the Judiciary with prejudice to their legitimate autonomy. The most affected seem to be the judicial.

> The unlimited authority of the party leads to abuses of power. Any sign of dissent in the face of any particular

---

[24] *Daily Nation*, May 14, 1990.

[25] *The Weekly Review*, July 6, 1990.

[26] *Daily Nation*, July 9, 1990. Statement made in response to July 7 demonstrations.

decision of the party is often interpreted as subversive and as endangering the security of the State. There is concern as to the possibility of future political murders, arbitrary arrests and confessions obtained under torture.

No social group, for example a political party, has the right to usurp the role of sole leader, since this brings about the destruction of the true subjectivity of society and of individual citizens, as happens in every form of totalitarianism.

The use of queue-voting and the 70 percent rule.

The increased cost of living in Kenya, which is surpassing increases in the minimum wage. This is creating corruption of alarming proportions. Corruption is destroying the moral fibre of the nation especially when it takes place among government officials, parastatal [government-owned] bodies, and even the forces of public order.

Forced harambees.

The existing and widening gap between the rich and poor.

The bishops welcomed the government's proposal to hold a national conference to address the issues, but urged that such a forum should be organized with "some form of guarantee acceptable to all that no one will be victimized later as a result of opinions expressed or ideas proposed during the conference." The conference, however, never took place, and President Moi increased public attacks on the church, accusing church leaders of preaching ideas which "could bring chaos and bloodshed" and "trying to create a situation where people could think church leaders were being persecuted."[27]

Threats included physical attacks on critical church leaders. On July 22, 1990, about forty youthwingers, armed with whips and sticks,

[27] Reuters, July 17, 1990.

mobbed Bishop Okullu and threatened to arrest him in Rae, Kisumu
District.[28] Other critics from the church reported harassment by
youthwingers and officials. Bishop Gitari said in April 1989 that he had
only avoided assault by hiding in the roof of his house when a large gang
attacked the family at night. In April 1991, policemen violently broke up
the Giagatika Evangelical Crusade in Nyeri, organized by Rev. Timothy
Njoya. Worshippers and journalists were beaten when riot police charged
a dispersing crowd. There had been a dispute between Njoya and the
local administration about the legality of the function. A number of
worshippers were admitted to hospital with injuries from the beatings,
including broken bones. Churchmen who spoke to Africa Watch said that
fears for the safety of their families inevitably had an effect on their
work. One churchman commented that "my only worry is if they send
some people to my house at night. Because then they can say it was a
robbery. And it is very difficult to disprove that. My family—that's the
only thing that I worry about."

THE NONGOVERNMENTAL ORGANIZATION BILL
CONTROLLING COMMUNITY WORK

Kenya has the largest NGO community in Africa, more than half
of which is religious-based. As international confidence in the government
falters, both because of political developments and the rampant
corruption, donor funding for development work has increasingly been
channelled through religious-based nongovernmental organizations. This
has caused consternation to the government, and provoked attacks on the
church for being paid by foreign "masters" and used as puppets to
destabilize the regime. Church leaders believe a desire on the part of the
government to exercise greater control over the church led to the
introduction of a new bill in parliament in 1990, *The Nongovernmental
Organization Bill.*

Although the new bill does not specify the church as an NGO, its
functional definition of one is anticipated to include church associations
carrying out social welfare work and development projects. According to
one legal analysis of the bill, "the loose, seamless definition given to an
NGO seems to be specifically and deliberately enacted to engulf all

---

[28] *Daily Nation*, July 23, 1990.

activities in which the church and other voluntary associations are involved and over which the government presently has no control. The specific inclusion of the word 'charity' seems tailored to catch church organisations and associations."

The bill proposes to register all NGO's with precise details of their sectors, affiliations and locations of activities. A board, known as the NGO Coordination Board, will examine the annual reports of the NGO's and advise the government on their activities and role in Kenya. Government appointees dominate the board which proposes to carry decisions by a simple majority. The bill gives the government access to the internal affairs of NGO's and effectively divests them of autonomy. The bill also makes it an offense to operate an NGO for welfare, research, health relief, agriculture, education, industry, the supply of amenities or any other similar purposes without registration under the Act. Penalties are severe—eighteen months imprisonment, 50,000 shillings ($1,923) fine or both, and the subsequent disqualification of the person from holding NGO appointments for ten years. According to legal analysts in Kenya:

> Given the very loose definition of an NGO in the Act one who runs an association providing any of the matters listed above will not know whether they are running an NGO or not. The idea of imposing criminal sanctions on non-registration of an NGO seems to shift the burden of identifying an association as an NGO from the government to those running it...many associations will be forced to register themselves as NGO's with the consequences.

NGOs are threatened with even harsher administrative controls. The guidelines give the minister wide powers to control importation of assets by NGOs, prescribe training of staff and specify information to be supplied by each NGO in its application for registration. False statements in relation to exemption from registration carry severe penalties—a 200,000 shilling ($7,692) fine or a three year imprisonment term, or both, and disqualification from NGO employment for ten years. Criminalizing the activities of NGO officials will inevitably cause hesitation in the discharging of voluntary work, while the lack of clarity will facilitate breaches of the law.

When the bill was debated in parliament, it was with implicit threat. Minister of State Burudi Nabwera said that "even the Green Belt movement would not evade the axe if it did not plant trees as it professed in its articles of registration...Once the board is established no NGO will be allowed to operate outside the system. If an NGO engages in activities inimical to the interests of the Country it will be deregistered".[29]

According to one churchman who spoke to Africa Watch, the bill is an attempt by the government to "get at the churches and prevent them from working on social issues." He added that "In Kenya, we have a saying that "if you want to see how deep the ocean is, you use a stick to try to touch the bottom. That is what the government is doing; it is trying to see how far it can go." He attributed the government's antipathy towards the church in part to its authority, and in part to the fear that it might use its power to play the same active role as some of the liberation theology churches in certain Latin American countries and the Philippines.

---

[29] *Daily Nation*, December 14, 1990.

14
KENYA'S LAND CRISIS

Loss of land and the worsening plight of landless squatters were the primary catalyst for the fight for independence. It is, therefore, painfully ironic to Kenyans that the government is now waging war against peasants and squatters in its bid to hold on to power.

When President Moi came to power in 1978, the Kenyan economy was characterized by two major crises: unemployment and landlessness. A lack of good arable land for a rapidly growing population forced an increasing number of people into the urban centers, and government policies exacerbated the existing land crisis. Nomadic and seminomadic communities were progressively deprived of traditional grazing lands for political and economic reasons and pressured to settle in areas that were already overpopulated. Unemployment rose rapidly because of increasingly poor economic performance and unsuitable educational policies. Shantytowns and slums mushroomed, and a rising number of people were forced to rely on the informal sector to eke out a living.

In spite of the rapid growth of urban centers, however, over 90 percent of Kenya's population, estimated at 24 million, still live on the land. Not more than a quarter of the land is arable, much of which remains idle or underused. The large-scale farms established by the European settlers have not always been fully used by a wealthy African elite. The rest of the country has vast, untapped regions of dry bush and semiarid land suitable only for sustaining nomadic pastoralism.[1] Half of the good, arable land is controlled by a small number of large-scale farmers and foreign companies. The rest is increasingly divided into smaller and smaller units for subsistence and smallholder farming.[2]

---

[1] After Kenya officially resumed diplomatic relations with Israel in 1988, the the Kenya News Agency reported that Israeli experts had been consulted on irrigation projects for the North Eastern Province.

[2] Institute of Race Relations, *Race and Class*, vol. 31, no. 4 (London: 1990).

As discussed in chapter one, vast tracts of land were apportioned to white settler farmers, and a new and entirely alien concept of individual land ownership imposed on communities that previously inherited land by virtue of being a member of the clan or family. Indigenous small-scale farmers evolved within the new capitalist economy, but were unable to match the successes of the settlers and their cash crops. With few exceptions, such cash crops as coffee, tea and dairy farming, had been made illegal for Africans until after the 1950s. Colonial legislation prevented equal participation. So-called native farmers were unable, for example, to use pesticides and had no comparable access to credit facilities. Moreover, control of movement, control of labor, creation of boundaries and white acquisition of land created a huge landless peasantry. These people, mainly Kikuyus concentrated in the central and Rift Valley provinces, were known as squatters; they worked for the capitalist farmers in return for a small subsistence farm. Under the colonial administration, the squatters had no legal rights to their land. If land changed hands, there was no obligation for landowners to ensure that squatters retained their plots or were given alternative sites.

Between 1960-63, a three-part strategy was undertaken to meet the problem of landlessness. There were justified fears that unless this was addressed, political upheaval was inevitable. First, land reform was intensified. Customary land law was replaced with the British (or Western) type of land law. Also, productivity of land was increased through modernized farming practices whereby land could be bought and sold and used to secure loans. The objective was to maintain the structure of the colonial economy by protecting the interests of the landowners—who were primarily European—but to also ensure a livelihood for the local people.

The second strategy was to neutralize the power base of KANU by taking away from it all or most of its landless supporters. Known as the settlement schemes, this was done by acquiring unused land or buying from departing Europeans, then subsidizing the farms and redistributing them to the landless. Assistance was provided by the British government and the World Bank in purchasing the land and developing it.

The third strategy was the transfer of ownership from Europeans to Africans on a "willing buyer, willing seller" basis. Agricultural banks were established to assist. The primary transfer was of agricultural land, but included some residential land. Cooperative societies were formed and companies incorporated to raise funds to purchase land from Europeans. The rationale for these strategies was economic continuation.

Independence, therefore, did little to rectify or alleviate the deep-seated land problem, and the balance is still tipped overwhelmingly in favor of a handful of wealthy large-scale farmers and foreign companies. Only the significance of the racial component has been reduced by independence and the policy of "Kenyanization." Land laws were not revised to provide security for the squatters, many of whom believed they had rights to land from which they have subsequently been violently evicted. On the contrary, the untidy legal situation concerning the issue of landlessness was ultimately exploited by successive independent governments that capitalized on the opportunity for land-grabbing.

LAND-GRABBING

In the desire to hold on to power, President Moi's government has portioned out valuable acreage of good, arable land to a small circle of politicians and officials, and, through a corrupt administration, has misused its powers to dispossess the poor. One of the most contentious issues is the flagrant violation by the government of Kenya's Companies Act. President Moi's government has dispossessed shareholders of land owning companies and re-allocated the land. This reallocation includes rural and urban sites. Cooperative societies formed by squatters have been treated similarly, with shares handed out to individuals.

Large tracts of Kenyan land have also been taken for internationally-sponsored game reserves and flora and fauna research, as well as for international companies, plantations and exotic commercial crops for export. For example, the creation of Kora National Park in the 1970s was sponsored by England's Cambridge University for the purposes of flora and fauna research and became famous through internationally-acclaimed conservationist, George Adamson. Its creation dramatically reduced the availability of important traditional grazing lands for the seminomadic Somali and Borana, who, as a result, have been increasingly persecuted for illegal movement (see chapter seventeen). In interviews with Africa Watch, local residents said that "an animal's life is worth more than a human's" now that unauthorized people caught in the park are vulnerable to the government's shoot-to-kill policy.

"Conserving the environment and boosting forest industry" justified the eviction of thousands of squatters from forest areas, according to Rift Valley Provincial Commissioner, Mohamed Yusuf Haji, who said the province had managed to plant eight million indigenous trees and fifteen million exotic trees in 1989. He also said the government was concerned about squatters who had started cultivating in forests and "interfering with water catchment areas."[3] Since the 1940s, these squatters had been allowed to occupy certain areas where they worked for the forest department cutting and harvesting mature trees. In return for their labor, they would then be allowed to plant their crops on land interplanted with saplings. When the newly-planted trees grew tall enough to prevent any further cultivation of crops, the squatters would move their labor and their crops to another area. However, many thousands of squatters occupying forest areas suddenly found themselves evicted, destitute and homeless as the government stepped up its campaign against squatters in the late 1980s. This harassment was seen by some as government fear that squatters would be involved in the MwaKenya opposition movement as they had been involved in the Mau Mau movement.

Tourism, which has top priority as a vital source of foreign exchange, has also been a central player in the land issue. In the Coastal Province, local and international environmentalists have expressed concern about the ecological effects of specially constructed diving reserves—areas of the reef that are artificially dug out to promote tourist facilities—and the effects of tourism on the lifestyle of the local communities. The needs of the tourist industry have, in places, almost completely destroyed the traditional livelihood of small fishing communities. Squatter communities located on the large sisal plantations since independence have been bulldozed and their inhabitants evicted to facilitate the interests of big landowners. Their homes and smallholdings are destroyed and their crops confiscated. Peasants attempting to salvage crops of coconut, pineapple and vegetables are arrested and charged with "wilful damage of property." As a result, many have tried to seek an alternative livelihood from the sea, which, according to information provided by an environmental consultant to Africa Watch, is having an adverse effect on the ecological balance and is unlikely to be sustainable.

---

[3] *Kenya Times*, April 3, 1990.

COSMETIC SOLUTIONS

The government's response to the land crisis has been a policy of repression. Recently, in urban centers, entire shantytowns have been bulldozed to clean up areas of the city characterized by poverty and unemployment. At the time this report was written, many of Nairobi's major shantytowns had been flattened by bulldozers. In a matter of hours, targeted slum townships were reduced to empty, featureless wasteland in a two month "clean up the city" campaign.

In the rural areas, many hundreds of thousands of squatters and small peasant farmers have been violently ejected from land they have lived on since independence. Evictions by security forces are characterized by wanton destruction. A disregard for human life has resulted in a number of deaths, including point-blank shootings.

The construction of military buildings and training grounds have likewise caused massive displacement. Forty-five thousand squatters were evicted from state land near Nanyuki in January 1990 to make way for the expansion of a military barracks.

TRANS-NZOIA: DYING FOR LAND

Before his controversial death, Bishop Alexander Muge from Trans-Nzoia, submitted a memorandum to the KANU Review Committee detailing accusations that land in his diocese had been "grabbed" from the poor by "a clique of Ministers," including the influential Minister for Energy, Nicholas Biwott, one of President Moi's closest advisers:[4]

> ...Hon Nicholas Biwott is accused by members of the public for using his position to grab land. A case in point is "The Growel Farm" in Uasin Gishu, where agents of the minister harrowed a five acre maize belonging to the Sitienei family who have been squatters in the said farm since 1962. The harrowing was supervised by the

---

[4] Muge was killed in a road accident on August 14, 1990, after his life had been threatened by former Minister of Labor Peter Okondo.

Memorandum to the KANU Electoral Review Committee from the Christians of the Diocese of Eldoret (CPK).

Administration Police from outside the district. Biwott's agents have now planted wheat in the said farm. The poor family reported to the relevant authorities, the chief, area councillor, the DO [District Officer] and the police and no action was taken despite the fact that destruction of crops is a criminal offence. Is this justice in our independent Kenya?[5]

Muge, as Bishop of Eldoret, had enjoyed an unusually high degree of confidence from people who otherwise felt they had no one to go to for advice and protection—leading many to believe his death was a political killing. According to his wife, Herma Muge, the Bishop spent the last few years of his life compiling numerous complaints concerning cases of corruption, abuse of administrative powers and police harassment. He had, in particular, taken an active interest in land cases because of the many violent evictions in the district and had documented cases of unlawful eviction, dispossession and corrupt acquisition in his diocese.

The Bishop publicly denounced government officials and Ministers for "unashamedly grabbing public resources" and "us[ing] their positions to kick out the poor peasant using the Administration Police." The evictions, he said, were "brutal and lawless."[6]

According to Muge's associates, Trans-Nzoia District has been particularly vulnerable to land-grabbing as it was one of the last areas vacated by white farmers. Large areas of good arable land became available in the late 1970s for government disposal in contrast to other districts in the country where much of the high-quality farmland had already been portioned out under President Kenyatta's government. Full advantage was therefore taken of the comparative abundance of land around Eldoret and Kitale.

Africa Watch obtained the following firsthand, eyewitness accounts of an eviction in Trans-Nzoia where Administration Police shot and killed a squatter in 1990.

---

[5] Press Release on Accusations before His Excellency the President: Bishop Alexander Muge.

[6] Memorandum to KANU Electoral Review Committee: Bishop A. Muge.

Case of Nicholas Akatu Shosho

A small community of squatters that had been living on a farm near Kitale since 1960 was told in 1977 that the land was to be divided and they should transfer to new plots. By 1983, a group of forty-eight people had moved elsewhere to establish and cultivate new *shambas* or small plots of land. In 1990, they were ordered to leave by the landowner, a shopkeeper in Kitale. When they refused to go, the landowner complained to the police and District Officer that property had been damaged. A ringleader was identified, and the landowner enlisted the police for eviction. No eviction order had been served on the community when the police came. A member of the community described what happened:

> They came through the maize, hiding in the maize—four APs in uniform and two plainclothes policemen. They all had guns. One of them asked me where the brothers were. I said I didn't know but they could see Nicholas making his home and the askaris [soldier] said "that's the one." They landed on his house and started taking things from inside. The two plainclothes police said that is Rotus, the one they wanted.

> The plainclothes had come with a landrover and started breaking up the house with anything they could lay their hands on—*pangas* [machetes], sticks and knives—putting his property in the landrover. Nicholas, Rotus's brother, complained and wanted to stop them. He said they weren't doing it properly. They had come without identifying themselves, not explaining their job or intention and not even asking any proper questions. Nicholas said they should not abuse the property and that they should leave it alone. But they continued.

> I told them to stop bothering him because he was not the right one anyway—for in fact they said they had come for his brother Rotus. Two of the askaris agreed with me and said he was the wrong one—but the other two insisted. When Nicholas kept complaining and telling them to stop, one said to the other "what are you waiting for? Why can't you shoot?." And then they did. One shot him

straight, they shot him in the head. They left the body on the ground and drove off in a landrover with the property taken from the house.

By this time the neighbors had gathered. We were all women, about ten of us altogether. We just left the body where he had been shot. A man came and went to the police station to report the matter. When he got to the police station, he found that the askaris had not reported that they had shot the man. The police sent two landrovers [with] about twenty-five men—AP and police. They met a whole crowd of people around the body and tried to disperse the crowd. Then they collected the body and took his mother, two sisters, sister-in-law and his wife to make a statement.

Nicholas's brother pursued the case. He related what happened to him when he tried to bring the police to justice:

The police station in Kitale did report the shooting but denied it was the way it happened. They said it was another person who had slashed at them with a panga and the police defended themselves. But I insisted and said I would go to the CID boss. Nothing was done. They just took the guns to Nakuru police station but there was no action on the askaris.

In September I left here on the 6th for Nairobi to follow up the case. I was told the file for my brother's case had not yet arrived, and I was told to go to Nakuru to check whether it was there or in Kitale.

On the 13th I left to Nakuru. I met the CID officer who told me the file was in Kitale. I was sent to Kitale and told to get hold of the CID officer there who would tell me the time the case would be heard.

When I arrived in Kitale police station I was immediately jailed. There were two of us, me and a relative, Peter Nakoje, and we were taken and put straight into the police cell. We stayed there for four days. The conditions are bad—food is the greatest problem, and it is so overcrowded you sit up when you sleep.

After four days they put us in a police landrover and told us we were thieves. They brought us to our farm, where Nicholas was shot, and took six maize stalks and a wire post using pangas. That is what we are supposed to have stolen. They slapped me around on the head and said if we made a noise they would shoot. They had guns. Then we were taken back to the police station and put inside for two more days.

On September 17 we were taken to court and charged with theft and damage. Our neighbors managed to raise 60,000 shillings [$2,308] for us, each, for bond. We are not optimistic. When we were in the cells the police told me they knew I had taken my brothers case to the bishop, but that now that Muge is dead they said they would be sure to get me.

Bishop Muge acted immediately when told about the shooting of Nicholas. He managed to get into the mortuary and take photographs of the body, which were later passed to Africa Watch. The charge sheet of Rotus Shosho and Peter Shosho said they had, on June 22, 1990, "jointly wilfully and unlawfully damaged fencing wire valued at Ksh1,600 [$62] the property of Mrs. Ruth Wanjira Mureu [the landowner]...jointly stole[n] 180 fencing post valued at Ksh3,600 [$138] the property of Mrs. Ruth Wanjira Mureu" and that Rotus Shosho had on September 9, 1990 "stole[n] 25 green maize cobs valued at Ksh50 [$1.92]" from the same landowners.

Destroying Lives

At the time Africa Watch was following the case of Nicholas Shosho, reports emerged of another man shot dead by Administration Police in the same district. The victim—identified only as "a young man" by the national press—was shot and killed on September 14, 1990, at a farm in Saboti Division during what was described as a "confrontation" between villagers and security men. Kitale Police Chief Supt Kiplagat arap Soi said villagers had "defied policemen and attacked them with

pangas damaging two G3 rifles in the scuffle. Administration policemen
then opened fire on the panga-wielding mob, killing the young man in
self-defence."[7]

This was the third reported victim shot dead by Administration
Police in the district in less than eight months, for allegedly "attacking
policemen" during land disputes. The MP for Saboti division, Wafula
Wabuge, called on the government to investigate the shooting of innocent
people, rejecting police claims that shooting is used by Administration
Police as a last resort in evicting squatters or dealing with land disputes:
"Why kill them? If they have committed offenses the culprits involved
should be arrested but not shot," he said.[8]

Detailed information gathered by Africa Watch shows that many
squatter and peasant communities in Trans-Nzoia district have been
forced off land which they have occupied for decades. These evictions
have taken place without legal proceedings and without legal
representation. One account discusses the illegal eviction of a group of
eight squatters by a well-known government minister:

> We repeat again—we *were* [emphasis in original] evicted
> using APs from outside the district, who are still in patrol,
> even today. We are prepared to lead a delegation to the
> minister's house as a reaction to show him our bitterness.
> Maybe the minister should tell us where we should get
> another *shamba* in replacement?

Another victim described to Africa Watch how a group of peasant
farmers bought land with a local women's group under the Settlement
Fund Trustee program,[9] with an initial down payment of 10 percent.
The land, however, was "re-bought twice" by an influential Assistant
Minister who offered the land as security when applying for loans. The
original buyers faithfully reported the matter to the provincial
administration who wrote to the bank concerned to explain in detail

---

[7] *Kenya Times*, September 17, 1990.

[8] Ibid.

[9] Settlement Fund Trustees were established by the British at independence
to help settle landless squatters on farms of departing white settlers.

about the loan. No reply came from the bank, and the land was subsequently divided up under pressure from the Minister.

> The MP threatened the District Commissioner and subsequently influenced his transfer. The minute book was taken from the secretary at gun-point, and we did not get our rightful share of 1,615 acres for over 70 people, but got about 400 acres.
>
> [Then]...the location chief brought Administration Police and one of his bogus one-man surveys to sub-divide the said 400 acres for 70 people. The action of the chief defeated the cause of justice and the laid down machinery...[because]...the Settlement Fund Trustee office in Nairobi shows that the farm is still one and not what these people claim.
>
> And what has the former county council chairman...done? As if the 800 acres he owns...is not enough, and having grabbed over 100 acres from us, he then swindles Ksh75,000 [$2,885] harambee money which was for construction of a school in the farm, claiming to be selling land to the school. Where is the school now? It is nowhere. The squatters' land is what [he] claims to have sold to us. He did not sell us his land.
>
> The most hit by these events are some 21 widows we have in the farm, and because they have no say, no power nor the means, they were swindled of their rights and livelihood. Their hope is that someone, somehow should stand up and uncover these brutal injustices of our Kenya times which seems to be the practice of those who are the able, crushing the weak.

According to others interviewed by Africa Watch, corrupt local administrators use the threat of eviction to compel individuals to participate in corrupt deals. They show no hesitation in evicting the uncooperative. Victims have no recourse to justice when they discover corruption infects the entire administrative and legal machinery. Many lawyers reportedly operate floating accounts to bribe officials at the land registries to facilitate land transfers and other legal paperwork.[10] Members of the public frequently make complaints in the national press that land-buying companies register members to purchase nonexistent land.

At the root of the problem is the lack of any satisfactory land policy. Land reform has followed the model of replacing communal family tenure with individual tenure but was implemented in a manner that allowed the wealthy, the influential and the educated to capitalize greatly on post-independence land inheritance. Many families who are forcibly dispossessed now, failed originally to register their names as owners because they believed it sufficient for one family member to be given a registered title.

Two distinct areas have given rise to problems of landownership and land-grabbing. In the former African reserves where clan and communal landownership were replaced by individual ownership, the rich have gradually increased their share of land. Secondly, in the former whites only farming areas, like Trans-Nzoia, some land was subdivided for squatter settlement. Wealthy and powerful individuals have acquired large estates on these areas of land and are attempting to force many farmers out.

Where the courts should be determining whether a person is a rightful owner or not, the government has encouraged disputes to be settled outside formal institutions. According to human rights lawyer, Gibson Kamau Kuria, this has proved to be the basis for the denial of fundamental human rights. In an interview with Africa Watch, he commented that:

> One of the fundamental rights of our constitution is the right to life. We don't have a legal aid system in Kenya—but individuals making a claim to land ought to get legal aid because failure to enforce his right to land is really a defeat of his right to life, because opportunities for employment are very few indeed. The government has tried to say land disputes should be settled by traditional elders along with provincial administration. This flies in the face of the doctrine of separation of powers which is supposed to curb abuse of power—such

---

[10] *Kenya Times*, September 24, 1990.

a doctrine requires that this should be adjudicated by the courts. In fact there have been claims that there is a lot of bribery and corruption when these informal institutions are used.

WAGING WAR ON SQUATTERS
ZEROING IN ON THE INFORMAL SECTOR

Towards the end of 1989 there was a noticeable increase in the number of mass evictions reported in the national press. Although land disputes and land acquisition had been recurrent problems in independent Kenya, it seemed there was an invigorated campaign against the poor and the landless—both in the rural areas and the urban centers. Nairobi and Mombasa became noticeably pitted with demolished kiosk sites, bulldozed at dawn without warning; and in the rural areas, thousands of squatters were being systematically evicted by armed police, who appeared to have been given license to kill as well as to brutalize.

Nyeri District

Armed Administration Police set fire to about one hundred houses belonging to squatters living in the forest area on the slopes of Mount Kenya, Kabaru Location, on January 13, 1990. Police, armed with guns and whips, descended on Ndathi Village at 3:00 A.M. and set fire to the huts while the occupants were still asleep; "As the police set on the houses, the squatters were woken up by the screams of the first victims," reported the *Daily Nation* the following day. Property belonging to more than 400 squatters was burned to ashes. The villagers lost all their household goods and property in their desperation to save their lives. One of the squatters told reporters that he had been employed by the Forest Department in 1924 and retired in 1963 and was given a plot of land in the village where he had lived ever since. "The squatters have constructed makeshift structures for their children. Most of the children were half-naked as old men who have lived in the village for as long as twenty years sat on half-burnt pieces of wood...Transporters were busy ferrying families of the squatters from Ndathi village to various destinations at exorbitant fares," according to the *Daily Nation*.

Toward the end of March in the same district, thirty families were violently evicted from Mount Kenya Forest Reserve by armed APs who arrived in the morning without warning. They used the same tactics, and set fire to the grass-thatched homes without giving the occupants time to remove their goods. Corrugated iron sheet-roofed houses were pulled down, and household goods found inside were burned to ashes. Squatters told reporters from the national press that they had been promised land in 1971 in the forest reserve by the Kirinyaga County Council, following new forestation projects in the area. These claims were "lies" according to the council chair. The District Commissioner said the families were aware that they occupied the land illegally "having been served with eviction notices four months previously." He said the exercise was not unique to Kirinyaga District as the campaign to evict squatters from government land was being carried out "countrywide."[11]

Laikipia District

On January 4, 1990, the *Standard* reported that 5,400 families[12] were evicted by armed police officers in Kwambuzi Village. The police used guns, batons and winches to destroy the village and threaten the occupants over the course of two days. Administration Police and regular police used landrovers to pull down homes. Left homeless and destitute, the squatters said it was the second time they had been evicted. Most had been evicted from Gathiuru and Kahurura forest in Laikipia district in 1989. They had bought plots from the original Kwambuzi squatters but had been evicted from their new land within weeks. According to Gibson Kamau Kuria, this war against the squatters had its counterpart in the urban centers:

> Not only have squatters been chased from the farms they have been living on for decades, and others been chased from working in the forest—but it is being accompanied by action against people who are earning their livelihood out of owning small kiosks. They have been forced to close. There's really a kind of zeroing policy on people

---

[11] *Kenya Times*, March 21, 1990.

[12] A conservative estimate where each family consisted of five people would bring the total number to about 27,000 people.

who find it difficult to earn a livelihood. It would appear
that it's being made a crime to be poor.

His fears were confirmed by reports in the national press in
January 1990 that the Nairobi City Commission had vowed to evict
10,000 to 15,000 so-called defaulting tenants daily.[13]
On December 21, 1989, a 16-year-old schoolboy, Hilary Sakwa
Manyasa, was rushed to the hospital with serious head and body injuries
after some fifty City Commission askaris beat him up during an eviction
from Madaraka, a residential area where houses are owned by the City
Commission (see chapter five). The askaris descended on the family early
in the morning with two trucks, destroying or confiscating the contents
of the house and attacking the residents. In this case, a complaint was
successfully filed against the commission and the high court delivered
judgment in favor of the Manyasa family, ordering the commission to
meet the costs. The case, however, did nothing to curb the violence of the
askaris who continued evictions in the same estate using the same violent
tactics. KANU youthwingers worked in cooperation with askaris during
the evictions and massive demolition of Bul Bul, in Ngong township in
Rift Valley Province.[14] Bul Bul had a large number of Sudanese
residents who had lived in the township since the 1940s, when they were
given rights by the British to stay in Kenya in return for their role in the
Second World War. Some believed that the action in this case was partly
motivated by government xenophobia, which regularly targets so-called
alien communities (see chapter nineteen).

Black Friday: The Muoroto Killings
        "Scores injured in eviction fracas" reported the *Standard* on May
26, 1990, following a day of one of the most violent scenes of eviction
and demolition witnessed in Nairobi. Hundreds of City Commission
askaris, backed up by riot police and KANU youthwingers, attacked kiosk
owners and shanty dwellers at one of Nairobi's *Jua Kali* sites, Kiswahili
for "in the sun," a term for kiosk owners and traders in the informal
sector. Bulldozers moved in without warning in the early hours of the
morning to flatten Muoroto, a sprawling, densely-populated shantytown

---

[13] *Kenya Times*, January 9, 1990.

[14] About fifteen miles west of Nairobi.

about three miles from the center of the city. For more than seven hours, traders were chased and severely beaten by askaris as their stalls and dwellings were demolished. The *Standard* carried reports of people pursued and cornered by the askaris, inflicting serious injuries with batons. When the kiosk owners retaliated by stoning the askaris, reinforcements stormed in armed with stones, sticks, whips and iron bars. A number of people were hospitalized with severe head injuries. Eyewitnesses said the askaris pursued and beat people mercilessly, cornering them in shops, ditches and against walls while two or three askaris at a time rained heavy blows aimed particularly at the head. A photographer from the *Standard*, Jacob Waweru, was beaten on his hands, back and head as he tried to record the event.

As the bulldozers moved in, an Assistant Minister for Public Works, Ngumbu Njururi, tried to temper the violence by pleading with the riot police, youthwingers and askaris to stop. He expressed horror at the method with which the evictions were carried out. Tear gas canisters were fired as kiosk owners from the area began stoning cars and pelting the security forces with stones. According to the reports in the *Standard*, the askaris "appeared to be enjoying whipping people...askaris charged at the residents of nearby Muthurwa, pulling some residents out of their houses and those who were drawing water and hitting them with heavy sticks and whips."[15]

The degree of violence used appeared to shake even the normally passive and uncritical MPs, and five Nairobi members of parliament were critical of the city commission for beating the owners of the kiosks and shanty dwellers, calling the operation "savage." Most of the kiosks, it was pointed out, had actually been licensed and the owners had lost hundreds of shillings' worth of property and goods as well as suffering injury and shock.

There were no reports of the savage Muoroto demolition until Sunday, two days after the operation. According to information given to Africa Watch, the press had apparently received instructions not to cover the incident. Reports in the *Sunday Standard*, however, said two people died and eleven children remained missing after the bulldozers ploughed through peoples' homes. Askaris, youthwingers and police seized and beat people in their homes, including small children; families desperately searched for their missing children not knowing if they had run in fear,

---

[15] *The Standard*, May 26, 1990.

been taken by the security forces or been killed by the bulldozers. With their homes and livelihoods destroyed, people remained in the area, sleeping without shelter in the cold, many suffering from physical injuries and trauma. The number of dead remained unconfirmed, and Kenyatta Hospital said it was difficult to establish the number of people needing medical attention as many were treated in the casualty ward and discharged. At least twelve required hospitalization.

Condemnation of the bloody demolition came from many quarters, starting a bitter dispute between politicians, government officials and churchmen over responsibility for the action and the number dead. The head of the Anglican Church of the Province of Kenya, Archbishop Manasses Kuria, asked "who in their right minds in this country can stand and watch such vicious destruction of poor peoples' lives....How can the nation stand by and watch children being battered by the City Commission askaris and hundreds of people sleeping outside in the cold because their houses have been demolished?."[16] An estimated 2,000 people had lost their homes.

By far the most damning condemnation came from Reverend Peter Njenga, Provost of All Saints Cathedral, Nairobi, whose parish included a part of Muoroto. Rev Njenga had been brought to the scene almost immediately by distraught parishioners and had witnessed the destruction of life and property firsthand. In a press release, he wrote:

> It was publicly known by Friday evening that some people had been killed. Yet, there was no word about this in the Saturday papers—only injury. It is not two people who have been killed. At least seven people were killed. Even more shattering is the possibility of the missing children or some of them having been killed by the bulldozer in their parents' houses, or trampled to their deaths by grown ups running for their lives...the savage beatings inflicted on helpless people including children, women and old men is an occurrence which must raise the question—is this the Kenya we want? Is this the

---

[16] *The Standard*, May 28, 1990.

independence we fought for and for which we shall in a
few days time on June 1 be celebrating?[17]

His statement was challenged by the government, which began
a campaign to intimidate the Reverend. President Moi said in a public
rally on June 2 that Rev. Njenga—whom he called "a friend"—should
personally apologize to him for spreading "falsehoods" and admit he was
"misinformed." On this occasion, President Moi insisted no one had died.
The president had issued directives to the Ministry of Local Government
on May 28 to take action against the Nairobi City Commission officers
responsible for the eviction, and said he deplored the "manhandling" by
the askaris.

Blame was later laid at the feet of Johnson Wahome, assistant
director of City Inspectorate, by the government who said he deliberately
forewarned Muoroto dwellers the night before the eviction that the
askaris were coming, and thus incited them to resist. Wahome
subsequently retired, and the acting Town Hall clerk and commission
secretary, S. K. Kariuki, and the director of the City Inspectorate, Hassan
Kaittany, were indicted. A seven-man committee was set up, headed by
Fred Gumo, the chair of the city commission, to examine the role of
Kariuki and Kaittany and give recommendations on action to be taken.
The committee was generally perceived as a cover-up, intended to
provide the government with convenient scapegoats. Rev. Njenga refused
to apologize and maintained that at least seven people had been killed.

The Cabinet Minister for Agriculture, Maina Wanjigi, also came
under fire for his emotional condemnation of the eviction. Wanjigi had
arrived back from Europe the same day and driven straight to the site of
the destruction. Comparing it to a colonial incident called Operation
Anvil,[18] he described it as "hooliganistic" and called for the immediate
resignation of City Commission Chair Fred Gumo and Hassan Kaittany,
and all the askaris who took part. Visibly shaken by the scene of

---

[17] This is a reference to the anniversary of Madaraka Day, June 1, 1963,
when Kenya was granted "self-government" as a prelude to full independence
which came six months later, on December 12, 1963.

[18] During operation Anvil, April 1954, the British Army detained thousands
of Africans at the height of the Mau Mau. Excessive force was used to evict
people from homes and work places.

destruction and despair, he characterized the action by the askaris as "inhuman." As a result, Wanjigi came under great pressure from other politicians, who said his condemnation was motivated by tribalism, on the basis that as a Kikuyu, he was supporting the victims only because most were Kikuyu.

Fred Gumo dismissed Wanjigi's call for his resignation saying Wanjigi was a tribalist; the MP for Makadara, Fred Omido, said Wanjigi had "abdicated responsibility to which Cabinet ministers are bound." Wanjigi dismissed the charge, saying there was no collective responsibility when it came to an issue in one's own constituency, and decried the fact that the brutal incident had been "turned into a cat-rat race with personality clashes and vendettas being waged." The Minister for Local Government and Physical Planning, William Ole Ntimama, said on June 1 that Wanjigi's tribalist sentiments were designed to incite the villagers to revolt against the government. Wanjigi was fired from the cabinet and suspended from KANU for one year on June 7 "for preaching tribalism in Nairobi, and making press statements that contradicted the President's."

He remained a target of government hostility, and was interrogated by the Special Branch after the arrest of Koigi Wa Wamwere in October 1990, ostensibly in connection with his supposed relationship with the hawkers (see chapter six).

The representatives of Kamukunji, a sub-branch of KANU, however, defended Maina Wanjigi refuting that his concern demonstrated any tribalistic intentions. They referred to a resident of Muoroto who was still missing, and said that a Peter Njau was still at Kenyatta Hospital suffering serious head injuries. They also noted other details that substantiated Njenga's findings and that Hassan Kaittany had admitted in a memorandum that six of his askaris were injured, but pointed out that many more innocent people were injured at Muoroto and adjacent Muthurwa Estate. The branch also issued a statement saying Nairobi Provincial Commissioner, Fred Waiganjo, had approved the eviction and demolition, proved by a memorandum produced by Hassan Kaitany which informed the Provincial Commissioner of the intended action.[19]

The Minister for Local Government, William Ole Ntimama, was uncompromising in his support for the demolition, and warned that similar operations would continue. Reiterating that it was government

---

[19] *Sunday Standard*, June 3, 1990.

policy to protect private property, he said: "A little more force was used than was necessary...[but]...as you know, and as President Moi has said, the Muoroto people were forewarned about the impending eviction. But they did not heed the notice but instead acted in a manner that was not right."[20] He said the eviction was not a special operation but *an ongoing and routine* exercise (emphasis added), and that Muoroto was full of thieves and criminals. He warned against "living under the illusion that unplanned kiosks will be allowed...Nairobi will be turned into a carton city and this has very many things at stake as they could pose health hazards, security risks and could scare away tourists."[21]

HARASSMENT OF REVEREND PETER NJENGA

Despite great pressure from the government, Rev. Njenga eventually released details of those killed in Muoroto. On June 9, 1990, he wrote that:

> It is a matter of grave and weighty concern to me that the Government can continue to deny that any people died. Equally, I find it difficult to accept that the newspapers which have been calling on me to give details do not themselves have the information: What has happened to this nation's collective morality?

He then listed the people who he knew had died in the Muoroto demolition.

> 1) Muriithi, a young boy about eight years old. When I arrived at Muoroto on that fateful Friday, 25th May 1990 at about 11:50 A.M. people were still wailing around young Muriithi's body. I saw the body with my own eyes.
>
> 2) Mugambi, another young boy about the same age as Muriithi. Mugambi had been shovelled by a bulldozer

---

[20] *Daily Nation*, June 2, 1990.

[21] Ibid.

and his body (which I also saw with my own eyes) had been mangled almost beyond recognition.

3) An adult male whose body I again saw with my own eyes. I gathered then from the Muoroto residents that this was the body of the driver of the bulldozer who had apparently been shot down with an arrow. This was after he had shovelled the boy Mugambi with his bulldozer.

4) A City Commission askari killed by the mob near Sandak Sign Post towards Machakos Bus Station.

5) A City Commission askari beaten at Muoroto during the operation and who died in a Commission vehicle on his way to hospital.

6) Eunice Mbulwa beaten up during the operation and died on her way to hospital.

7) Simon Kimenju, beaten up and knocked down by the City Commission askaris. He managed to run away but died later on May 29, 1990 in his brother's house in Eastleigh from the injuries sustained.

8) A child whose body was discovered on Monday, May 28. The group which visited Muoroto with the Nairobi Provincial Commissioner ordered the body to be taken away.

He added:

In the afternoon of the same Friday, I visited the city mortuary where I again saw the three bodies of two children and one adult which I had earlier seen at Muoroto. I have since been informed that these three bodies and in addition a fourth body of another Muoroto victim were subsequently removed from the city mortuary in a blue van as were the relative register and records of dead bodies.

On Saturday morning, May 26, some of the affected people came to the Cathedral. They were in a pathetic state. Some had slept out in the cold. I handed out nearly Ksh6,000 [$231] from the Cathedral funds towards their immediate needs. When being called upon to give particulars, it appears that it is overlooked that even before I gave my press release on 28 May, the *Standard* newspaper had in its Sunday edition of May 27 carried a banner headline that *two* people had died in the Muoroto incident.

It was against this background that on Sunday May 27, I asked the Cathedral congregation in the morning family service to stand up in silence in memory of the people who had died at Muoroto.

As I said in my earlier press release, human life is a gift of God. It is sacred. I am dismayed with the emphasis being shifted from the sanctity of lives which were lost to Peter Njenga being called names and being asked to give particulars. The similarity with the manner in which the sanctity of the late Dr Ouko's life has been treated is all too obvious—the *sanctity* of life is relegated to second fiddle—public denials that the Government was involved taking prominence. Yet the identity of who killed Ouko and why remain unanswered.

There has been great erosion of credibility of even senior Government officials. Kenyans are no longer able to assume the truthfulness of public statements by Government officials. On May 30, 1990, the Commissioner of Police is quoted (see the *Daily Nation*) as having said only one person had been treated for minor injuries and immediately discharged. Yet in the *Standard* of June 4, there is a photograph of Peter Njau Mukera on crutches leaving hospital! In fact, a total of 36 people were injured, some of them seriously.

Public statements have been made denying prior knowledge of the demolitions and in which suggestions were made that it was not known who had authorized the demolitions. Yet, in Mr Kaittany's memo of 28 May, he says and I quote:

The clearance of these kiosks and other structures had been discussed by Provincial Security, Nairobi Area, and recommended that all structures along Presidential route be removed. This information was conveyed to me by the Commissioner of Police when I visited him in his office in April 1990.

This is why in my earlier statement I called for a public inquiry to establish the truth and the circumstances surrounding this disgraceful incident. I repeat this call. I do not believe that an enquiry under the Chairmanship of the City Commission Chairman (who should himself resign) is in a position to unearth the truth. No one can investigate himself. I also repeat my call on the Kenyan Government to accept moral responsibility and compensate these unfortunate victims.

Africa Watch has learned that in fact thirteen people are known to have died, including the eight described by Rev. Njenga. The government went to considerable lengths to cover up the deaths. Bodies were removed from the mortuaries and relatives were persuaded by intimidation and bribery to deny the deaths; they were given stern warnings by government officials and security personnel not to reveal any evidence of the dead and were given money to conduct funerals outside the Nairobi area. Well-informed sources told Africa Watch that the City Commission took the bodies to Thompson Falls, about 100 kilometers northwest of Nairobi, and that certain relatives were given land titles to keep them quiet.

Rev. Njenga was subjected to continual harassment which culminated in a public inquest, ostensibly to examine the circumstances in which his wife, Peninah Nduta Njenga, died in October 1989. The police had threatened to prosecute Njenga for his failure to apologize to President Moi for his statements concerning the Muoroto demolition. Accusing him of having killed his wife (or driving her to suicide), they threatened to use Cap 63 of the Penal Code Section 61 (1), which reads:

...any person who administers, or is present and consents
to the administering of any oath or in the engagement of
an oath, purporting it to bind the person who takes it to
act in any of the ways following, that is to say, to engage
in any mutinous or seditious enterprise is guilty of a
felony and is liable to imprisonment for ten years.

Clearly, the charge would never have stood up in court and was
used as a means of intimidation. It did not, however, have the desired
effect and Njenga held his ground. The inquest on his wife's death, which
began in September 1990, gave the government an opportunity to
slander the churchman, claiming his wife's death was the result of cruel
treatment. Njenga's lawyer, Dr. John Khaminwa, asked "whether it would
be an abuse of the due process of law and the constitution for the
Attorney-General...to hold an inquest where the cause of death is well-
known," and attempted to prove that the inquest was an act of
vindictiveness. Among the papers submitted to the court were newspaper
cuttings in which Fred Gumo urged Njenga to accept his explanation that
nobody had died at Muoroto just as Gumo had accepted the clergyman's
explanation that his wife had committed suicide.

During the inquest, Njenga was kept under constant surveillance
by the Special Branch at the Cathedral, including during the services, and
pressure was exerted economically through his bank and personal
finances. The effect was to isolate him. Njenga believed the outcome of
the inquest could be "the worst"—that he would be jailed on a charge of
causing his wife's death—but saw the primary objective as giving the
authorities a platform to discredit him thoroughly in the eyes of the
public.

HAWKING DISSENT: THE CULTURE OF DEFIANCE

The scale of the Muoroto demolition proved to be a mere prelude
to a campaign that progressed into an unprecedented flattening of large
slum areas in Nairobi. The fall-out from Muoroto—which brought
international criticism—initially created a lull and residents and hawkers
came back to the area under assurances they could reconstruct their
demolished shanties. Muoroto slowly reassembled itself as the controversy
over the killings continued. At the same time, however, the city
commission reasserted its intention to rid the city of so-called illegal

traders and dwellers, but dismissed as exaggeration reports that 7,500 kiosks would be demolished in the city.[22]

In the first two weeks of October 1990, askaris, GSU, youthwingers and Administration Police descended on the city hawkers with as much brutality as before. One of their first targets was Muoroto. Bulldozers once again ploughed through the reconstructed village in the early hours of the morning. This time, they met no resistance. According to residents, a warning to the people was leaked from a senior government source. Anticipated resistance, they were told, would be put down ruthlessly, and would be used by the government as evidence that the Kikuyu community were actively anti-government.

The operation was initiated at dawn, but the GSU were brought in during the night and kept vigil until the bulldozers arrived. Residents said they were given a choice: "if you want to pick up your things and go do it now." As the people moved out, the bulldozers moved in. Within a day, the entire village was flattened. What had once been a vital center for *Jua Kali* (informal sector) trade, packed with dilapidated tin-box dwellings and teeming with the resourcefulness of the poor, was completely wiped out, leaving only sticks and metal sheets strewn on a flattened wasteland. For some days, people from Muoroto remained near the site in a state of shock and hopelessness. Others gradually drifted off to other slum areas, only to meet the same fate ultimately, as the bulldozers and removal trucks cleaned out the city. In an interview with Africa Watch, one of the Muoroto victims commented that he felt too shocked to know what to do or where to go after this second eviction:

> I came to Muoroto in February 1985. Before that I was just moving up and down with no place. I set up a restaurant kiosk.
>
> The harassment started in May, when they came in the morning. I was up early in the morning, as it was light, preparing for business then—the bulldozers just started driving through. We were shocked and began fighting them—stoning them with bricks and bottles, but the askaris and APs beat us badly. Some people were admitted to hospital with serious injuries. Some people

---

[22] *Daily Nation*, June 1, 1990.

were killed, but they tried to deny it. Everybody knows people died in Muoroto. I knew three people who were admitted to hospital with serious injuries, one with his skull cracked and deep cuts on his head, but many more were there with minor injuries.

They took us so abruptly, charging like mad people from all directions and people were struggling to gather their possessions. I know of one man who was taken to Kenyatta hospital with skull injuries from the askaris. He was taken by the askaris, and when his injury got worse they moved him to Nairobi hospital and paid the bill. But no one got any compensation.

This time they came at 4:00 A.M. How could we resist? You wake up with a gun next to you, with those City Commission askaris and APs everywhere with their guns. The place was full of them—askaris, APs, GSU and KANU youthwingers. I think they outnumbered the residents, even though we have at least 3000 residents here now. So it was impossible to even think of resisting. When I saw all the guns and those people standing around with their camouflage uniforms I knew there could be real bloodshed. I just moved out. They had lorries which they loaded with our possessions, I saw them taking everything they could find.

Now we are harassed every day by security—the askaris and the police tell us disperse and move on. We know we are being watched by Special Branch all the time; they are probably even among us. What are we supposed to do? No money, our property lost, we are too confused to know what to do.

The intensity of the attacks on the informal, marginalized sectors of the population demonstrated a focused and relentless campaign by the government, despite the adverse publicity and controversy caused by the Muoroto operation five months earlier. As the national press carried daily reports of pitched battles between the hawkers and the security forces, the campaign became overtly political, with the arrest of dissident Koigi wa

Wamwere. According to the official statement, Wamwere was arrested attempting to "organize illegal hawkers and matatu drivers to participate in acts of violence and lawlessness, and generally to promote the defiance culture." Hawkers, the government argued, were subversive; slums and shantytowns were hot-beds of anti-government sentiment; and the defiance of those hounded and evicted by the security forces could now be attributed to organized anti-government activities. In his speech on Moi Day (October 10, 1990), the president said that "bad elements" had infiltrated the hawking community. He said they gathered stones, ostensibly to protect goods from being blown away by the wind but with the intention of using them "against my officers."[23]

President Moi continued by saying that hawkers who were "only selling one or two potatoes" were merely "posing," and did little more than demonstrate how out of touch he is with the economic reality in the slums of Nairobi. His evident fear of discontent among the poorest sections was well grounded, but for the wrong reasons. Bitterness among the poor came not only from the callousness of the evictions, but also from the popularly held belief that land in the city was being acquired by President Moi to give to loyal political supporters or for personal gain. The persistent refusal of officials to identify the owner of Muoroto land, despite the insistence that it was private property, reinforced this suspicion.

Former Cabinet minister and Kamukunji MP, Maina Wanjigi, was among those picked up and interrogated by the Special Branch soon after Wamwere's arrest. He told the press that the Special Branch was particularly interested in his relationship with hawkers and his reaction to the Muoroto evictions in May. His reply, he said, was that he was of necessity "passionately attuned" to the special problems of hawkers as he represented the largest population of hawkers in the city, and that the city authorities had created the problem themselves by inciting such bitterness.

For the people brutally evicted from Muoroto for the second time, the new blanket charge of subversion was met with great anger. One man told Africa Watch:

> I don't know why they've done it like this. How can a
> hawker overthrow the government?—with their potatoes

---

[23] *Daily Nation*, October 11, 1990.

and tomatoes? It really is a mockery. I have heard these allegations that Koigi knows the hawkers and is using them. But we don't know him—not even physically, to look at—we just trade and try and get a little money. Why does this government direct everything at one particular tribe? That's what we wonder. Most businessmen are Kikuyu—it's a way of destroying us.

What the government achieved was to destroy the livelihood of thousands of people and then to condemn it as subversion. The result was to provoke open speculation among the poorest sectors about the real intentions of the government. Africa Watch gathered a number of testimonies from hawkers who had been forced out of the city to areas where they were unable to find customers. One named Paul, who is well-educated but unemployed, says he was forced to turn to work in the informal sector because there is no hope of employment:

They don't want the poor people in the city. They are looking for a way to push us; but we don't cause trouble really. It's an excuse. Just an excuse to beat us and harass us—even trying to associate us with Koigi. We don't know him or what he's up to, or even what he looks like. When the dissidents try to defend us and talk about us, that's when they use the excuse to harass us.

We are not all hawkers—some of us are kiosk owners and mechanics—but they put us all together here without custom. Some have land and licenses as kiosk owners but now they have bulldozed down the place, they have broken the place.

I know four people who have been sentenced to prison. The way they arrest you—if you just talk, or tell them to leave you alone they arrest you.

We are expecting more people to come—they are moving more every day. This government, they are ready to surrender it to the Asians—it's only them who get the good treatment. This country is for the rich only not the

poor—when the government gets aid, where does it go?
It's better just to stop it.

Some of the men here are well-educated but have no
jobs—some are educated up to form six and some are
even degree holders, but they have no job. Well, we don't
want any help from the government now. It's too late.

Wanjiku depends on hawking to support her children and has no
other income. She says that the motive for the attack on the hawkers was
tribal:

I was on the street and many police arrived—about fifty
came in a lorry, with submachine guns. They pushed me
to move my properties [clothes] and they grabbed my
two-year-old child. Everybody was beaten up. They
forced us to walk here with our goods. Then they moved
in with the bulldozers and flattened our markets and
kiosks, beat us and made us move.

They say we are causing problems, because the majority
of us are Kikuyu and they say we are trouble. If you lose
your kiosk you lose your license anyway—it's no longer
valid—so my life is really destroyed now. More people are
coming everyday, this place is overcrowded and there's
no chance of me selling anything. The harassment
started about three months ago, when they would come
and collect our things, spill them on the ground, arrest
some of us. Some got taken to court and charged with
being unlicensed. Some do have a license but they treat
you all in the same manner.

Maina tried to trace a missing friend until he was threatened with
arrest if he continued to come to the police station:

They came at about 6:00 A.M. in the morning, so many
of them. I would say about 400 police and City
Commission askaris. It started in the town center. They
told us to pack, but most of us were just pushed and
beaten. Some resisted and they were arrested and

charged with causing a disturbance—some were released
on bond, or just kept in the cells or fined. We lost track
of all those people, there were so many picked.

All this is created by a few rich people who want to build.
We sell wares a bit cheaper so that we can maximize
profit. The big people bribe to make the City
Commission move us—and we get thrown out.

The askaris, the police—they were all together in this.
They threatened us and shot in the air; there were a lot
of guns about. Since it began, they come and bother us
nearly every day. Now, here, there are no customers and
we are suffering without any shade.

Four hundred and thirty hawkers appeared in court on October
12, 1990, charged with "creating a disturbance in a manner likely to cause
a breach of the peace."[24] All the hawkers were unrepresented; almost
all pleaded guilty and begged leniency as custodial sentences would
destroy their livelihood and leave dependents destitute. The magistrates,
however, said the offense was serious: "although the offence was a
misdemeanour it was serious in that you stoned police officers on
duty."[25] They were either fined 3,000 shillings ($115) or, alternatively,
imposed sentences of three months in prison. Some of those appearing
in court were juveniles, and some protested that they had been no more
than passers-by when police began seizing people and loading them
forcefully into vehicles. One woman said her child went missing after she
had to spend a night in jail:

The askaris from the City Commission are worst. At first
they would just come and harass us and confiscate our
property—now, if they catch you, they really beat you.
They have killed people. Also the KANU youthwingers.
They work with the askaris and take our property. They
just stormed us last week, beat us and picked so many of

---

[24] *Standard*, October 13, 1990.

[25] Ibid.

us up and threw us in the lorries—I was fined 400 shillings [$15]. On that day, I had put out my wares and was just waiting for customers. Throughout the day it was quiet then they just came and picked me at 5:00 P.M. Three askaris and Administration Police came and they threw me in the truck. Some had club sticks, some with guns—they beat with the stick, on my back and on my elbows. I slept in the cell overnight—so many people in one cell, and just a little food. I was charged with hawking without a license and fined 400 shillings.

Resentment among the hawkers was matched by concern for their immediate future. Many had been attacked and evicted from two or three different places and had no faith in promises from the officials that alternative sites would be found for them. Many also complained that they were not illegal hawkers, but fully licensed traders working on the outskirts of Nairobi where the security forces were concentrating the attacks.

Solomon said he felt angry at what had happened to him, and believed the government had carried out the operation as a security measure against the growing number of young Kikuyu men in Nairobi:

We were full mechanics, qualified mechanics—Jua Kali in River Road and now we have nothing to work on. So we must sell cabbages. Or what? Steal? The police took everything—our spanners, our tools—everything—but I can't go and collect them because if I go there I'll be grabbed and charged. So now I'm selling cabbage to get daily bread. They are still harassing us here—telling us to go back to the rural areas, but we can't. There's nothing to be done there. We got customers in town because all the town people are eating and buying in kiosks, it's cheaper. Now they've destroyed the kiosks, and people can't come here because it's too far. We don't even have a guarantee we can stay here. They just want us all together like sheep. It's not for trading. It's not for what they say it is—all this clean up the city thing—it's a security thing. Look at how they attack us.

Throughout October and November 1990, bulldozers continued to flatten most of the city slums. Vast areas of empty waste ground replaced what had been populous shantytowns. Askaris, Administration Police, riot police, youthwingers and GSU were constantly seen driving people out of their homes and stalls, throwing property and persons into the back of trucks while wielding whips, batons and rifles. The demolitions reached a peak in November when city commission bulldozers flattened Kangemi, Kibagare, one of the largest slums in the city, leaving an estimated 30,000 homeless. At no time was reasonable notice given for eviction, and no compensation offered to the injured and the destitute.[26]

Roman Catholic priests and pastors from the Church of the Province of Kenya called for an immediate end to the demolitions, describing it as inhuman. Father Vincent Kamere, St. Peter Clavers Church, Nairobi, said he was "shocked...to see with my own eyes some of the over 30,000 residents of Kibagare starving and sleeping out in the cold because all they ever owned in this world was razed to the ground by the askaris and APs."[27] International and local agencies provided medical assistance and food aid worth 25,000 shillings ($962) for the homeless from Kibagare, and church leaders warned of the consequences of such a brutal policy. Canon Gideon Ireri of the Anglican Church of the Province of Kenya warned that a "rootless" section of society was being created that was "nervous, angry and confused." But with no positive response from the government and the implementing officials, it can only be assumed that the violent and lawless evictions will continue, furthering what Gibson Kamau Kuria identified as the "criminalization" of poverty which is leading to a denial of the most basic human right—the right to life.

---

[26] In February 1991, officials made claims to Africa Watch saying that the victims had been given warning, but would cite no specifics. One official acknowledged that destroying the homes of 30,000 people to get at twenty troublemakers might have been extreme.

[27] *Daily Nation*, November 26, 1990.

15
EMERGENCY POWERS
AND THE NORTH EASTERN PROVINCE

Compared to the green and fertile lands of central and western Kenya, the desert-like semi-arid scrub of the North Eastern Province (NEP) is the most inhospitable region in the country. It was formerly known as the Northern Frontier District (NFD), when it included most of the pastoralist groups: primarily the Somali, Boran, Rendilles and Turkana. The British colonial administration kept this vast, relatively sparsely populated, nomadic area a closed district. As such the NFD was isolated administratively—no person could enter the area without a special license. Development has remained virtually frozen since its days of colonial isolation.

The area became almost exclusively Somali when it was redrawn as the North Eastern Province in 1963 and is now a community which has been separated from the Somali nation by a falsely imposed colonial border. Wajir and Mandera, two of the three main towns, have entirely Kenyan-Somali populations apart from non-Somali government officials and administration personnel, but Garissa, the capital of the North Eastern Province, includes communities of other minorities. Government policies hostile to nomadic communities have resulted in increased settlement although much of the Kenyan-Somali population remains nomadic or seminomadic. Apart from their dependency on livestock, Kenyan-Somalis are typically entrepreneurs and traders. Many trade in goods brought in from neighboring Somalia (in turn, brought from the Arab States) or set up wholesale and retail businesses in the towns.

At independence, the Kenyan government chose to retain the territory although the overwhelming majority of the Somalis wished to secede because of their cultural, political and economic attachment to Somalia. The newly independent Kenyan government justified its claims in the face of strong opposition by promising full integration of the territory into the new nation.

This promise of integration, however, has not been achieved; it has barely been attempted. The area has remained isolated and underdeveloped, and ethnic Somalis are treated as an alien community in their own country. The independent Kenyan government instead used

extraordinary powers to contain the secessionists and subdue what was
perceived as a hostile and essentially proscribed community. The
government's response to the demands of the secessionists was a special
regime of emergency powers introduced in the new constitution
applicable only in Kenya's newly-named North Eastern Province.

Insecurity in the North Eastern Province has been used by both
Presidents Kenyatta and Moi to impose repressive emergency legislation,
while simultaneously claiming peace and stability in the country. Kenya
has, in fact, technically been under emergency legislation since
independence, although the terminology has been changed because it was
considered to have "distasteful associations"[1] with the colonial era.

At independence, KANU pledged itself to remove the
"undemocratic, unjust and arbitrary practices" of the colonial legacy and
introduced new emergency legislation ensuring that emergency powers
could only be invoked as a drastic measure under certain circumstances:
Kenya either had to be at war, or emergency powers had to be formally
declared with the approval of parliament. The new emergency legislation
was specifically intended to be temporary and was strictly limited to
abnormal situations. In a spirit of "new justice," a list of rights was drawn
up to provide a safeguard for those whose liberties would be curtailed as
a result of such measures.

Parliamentary control of emergency powers, however, has
decisively failed. The courts, also, have proven incapable of policing abuse
of the legislation. The result is that emergency powers—renamed "Public
Security Measures"—are used as part of normal law in Kenya. Instead of
being used during a formally declared state of emergency, these laws are
used by the government as a routine means of silencing opposition and
policing the country.

DECLARING A STATE OF EMERGENCY

The first formal declaration of a state of emergency after
independence was in December 1963 while parliament was adjourned for
Christmas recess. A state of emergency was declared necessary in the
North Eastern Province because of the ongoing secessionist war—the so-

---

[1] Attorney General Charles Njonjo, 1966.

called *shifta* war.[2] Parliament was recalled to approve the state of emergency but contested it on the grounds that the government already possessed abnormal powers in the region. Only 60 percent of parliament approved it as opposed to the required 65 percent. Nevertheless, a state of emergency was passed. This permanent state of emergency in the NEP is somehow perceived as unconnected with Kenya as a nation. That it is not normally associated with Kenya indicates how minimal the efforts have been to integrate the ethnic Somali community into the rest of the country since independence.

Emergency powers in the North Eastern Province remain fully operational and are wide-ranging. Their enforcement has been responsible for massive and persistent human rights abuses. Immediately instituted at independence, the emergency powers gave the governor-general power to impose any regulation he considered necessary to control and govern the region. These regulations, however repressive and extreme, were deemed valid even when inconsistent with the constitution and its laws, and had an indefinite lease of life. They have never been removed, and include the following:

- Within the North Eastern Province, the Minister is empowered to detain or control residence and movement of any person if he believes it is "in the interests of public security."
- Members of the administration and the armed forces have enhanced powers of entry, search without warrant, arrest and detention.
- Security forces may detain a person for up to fifty-six days without trial.
- Unlawful possession of firearms, explosives and ammunition within the area carries a death sentence. The burden of proving lawful authority is upon the person possessing the arms.
- Consorting with a person possessing arms is also punishable by death if that person is deemed "of dangerous intent."

---

[2] As noted previously, shifta means bandit. It was deliberately used by the government to reduce the political significance of the secessionist war, and is still used in a derogatory and racist manner against the Kenyan-Somali population.

- Special courts, lacking the normal procedural safeguards in criminal trials, are provided.
- A prohibited zone created along the Kenyan-Somali border carries the sentence of life imprisonment if an "unauthorized" person enters it.
- Livestock found in the prohibited zone may be forfeited or destroyed.
- Special powers allow for forced labor.
- No meeting or gathering of ten or more people is allowed unless with the permission of the District Commissioner.
- The president can make laws by decree on detention, compulsory movement, censorship and prohibition of communications, banning processions and meetings; and the modification of any law as he requires.

The extraordinary powers given to the administration and the security forces to act at will in arresting, detaining and harassing the population have led to routine excesses. The armed forces are fully aware of the virtually unlimited powers they have in the region and have not hesitated to use them.

MASSACRES IN THE NORTH EASTERN PROVINCE

There have been two publicized massacres in the North Eastern Province, widely condemned as gross violations of human rights by international organizations. The government has either denied outright the massacres or attempted to minimize them by attributing them to "inter-tribal" conflict.

Bulla Karatasi
In November 1980, security forces burned down Bulla Karatasi, an entire village in the capital of the North Eastern Province, Garissa, after six government officials had been killed. Security forces swept through the village in arbitrary and gruesome retaliation. Hundreds of people died and many were wounded as they tried to flee. Bodies of those killed in what the government called "a necessary security measure" were buried early in the morning in a mass grave; other bodies were said to have been thrown in the river. The massacre reportedly began following

revenge killings by a local Kenyan-Somali nicknamed "Madhobe." He killed six government officials before being arrested and was then castrated by members of the Anti-Poaching Unit (see chapter five).

After the massacre, the local population was rounded up and interrogated. Thousands of Kenyan-Somalis were beaten by the security forces and accused by the acting District Commissioner of harboring anti-government elements—generally referred to as shifta. They were deprived of food, water and sleep for thirty-two hours. Provincial Commissioner Benson Kaaria said "a thousand Somalis will die" for every government official killed, and threatened to "eliminate" all Somali-speaking Kenyans. A dusk-to-dawn curfew was announced, with orders that anyone caught breaching the curfew would be shot on sight. Security villages were established to confine the Kenyan-Somali population, and all development committees were disbanded as a punishment.

In connection with the security operation in Garissa, Kenyan-Somalis throughout the North Eastern Province were rounded up. Reports surfaced of rape, beatings, stock seizure, forced relocation, arrests and detentions, house burning, and armed attacks on nomads. Three MPs from the North Eastern Province called for an emergency debate in parliament, which was dismissed on the pretext of a parliamentary technicality requiring a statutory fifteen MPs. There was otherwise no sign of alarm or sympathy in parliament; MPs continued to call for "strict measures" against shifta, and the Minister of Internal Security, G. G. Kariuki, was reported in the daily press to have said "the only good Somali is a dead one."

The Wajir Massacre

The Wajir Massacre of 1984 is the most publicized atrocity in the history of Kenya. In February 1984, the security forces mounted a major security operation said to be aimed at disarming competing local groups, particularly the Degodiya. At the beginning of February, the army closed all the water points—with the exception of Wajir town—to the Degodiya. Many of the nomadic groups with big camel herds moved out of the district into Ethiopia. The semisedentary people could not do this and made long journeys in search of water; many of their animals died.

On February 10, there was a roundup of Degodiya men who were given an ultimatum to surrender their weapons. Africa Watch has been given information from a local councillor, who says some 5,000 men were interned nine kilometers outside Wajir town at Wagala airstrip. According to the councillor, who was present:

Ordinary people [wananchi], businessmen, prominent religious leaders and civil servants were stripped naked and forced to lie on their bellies. Those who resisted to go nude were shot on the spot as the rest were denied water and food by the security personnel who [forced]...the people to continue laying down on their bellies under severe...hot sun. They were subjected to torture by the security personnel who continued to beat them. As days continued...atrocities by the security personnel inflicted on the people included clubbing some of the people to death and some were burnt alive.

He says this treatment continued for five days. Security forces doused people in petrol and burned them on the airstrip; many were beaten and shot. Survivors were prevented from receiving any treatment by the security forces, who, according to witnesses, moved the injured and dying into remote areas. According to the councillor:

As we searched for the survivors we also realized that most of the people who died in the camp were being transported and dumped far away, in the countryside, apparently for coverup. We managed to get some of the survivors and brought them to Wajir township for medical care. The authorities in Wajir have, however, persistently denied relatives [the opportunity] to retrieve their dead from the countryside for burial.

An estimated 2,000 dead has been widely accepted as the final toll; but an accurate compilation of identities from the massacre was prevented. All 5,000 rounded up at Wagala airstrip had their identity papers seized and destroyed, and many hundreds of people went missing for their bodies were never identified or recovered. The names of 363 people have been identified, who are known to have been killed on the airstrip. An additional 7,000 people, including children, women and old people were left destitute.

There were urgent appeals from Wajir to the Ministry of Health for large quantities of medical supplies to cope with the influx of casualties to the hospital, but the requests were turned down and nongovernmental organizations were refused permission to begin a relief program. Large numbers of wounded were admitted to Wajir hospital, but the administration was ordered to discharge all Degodiya and stop admissions. People who had taken the wounded and destitute into their compounds were ordered to eject them, and a police cordon was placed around the hospital. Many of the wounded are believed to have subsequently died in the bush.

Joint action was taken by development agencies OXFAM, AMREF and the Kenya Red Cross to regain access to the area. The agencies made direct representations to the Kenyan government and gave interviews to the press, and on one occasion attempted to drive to Wajir despite refusals from the Kenyan government. A demarche was organized by the diplomatic community. An AMREF doctor resigned after being refused clearance from AMREF to go to Wajir and investigate, on the grounds that it would cause difficulties with the Kenyan government. The doctor went to Wajir independently and was able to submit a detailed report to the aid agencies (having been persuaded to rejoin) which provided the basis of a plan of action. However, nongovernmental organizations were not allowed back into the area until May 9, when relief programs were set-up for the widows and a food distribution program established for 18,000 people. Sister Annalena Tonelli, a missionary in Wajir who publicized the atrocities, was frequently threatened by the authorities. Her program to feed and re-house destitute women and provide medical care recieved support when the aid agencies returned to Wajir in May; but the following year she was forced to leave Kenya when the government refused to renew her work permit.

Under pressure, the government admitted to fifty-seven dead and attributed it to "necessary action" taken against "inter-tribal fighting." An article appeared in the press referring to a "secret organization" in the North Eastern Province which had been the target of a military operation. On March 27, former Minister of State in the Office of the President in charge of Internal Security, Ole Tipis made a long statement in the National Assembly claiming only fifty-seven had been killed in the security operation. He said "firm action" had been taken but added that "this does not condone excessive force that might have been meted out." The minister agreed to set up a committee of inquiry into "causes of tension" in the area after strong lobbying from MPs in Wajir and Garissa.

According to the official version, hostilities between the Degodiya and Ajuran clans led to an ultimatum by the security forces for surrender of all weapons. The ensuing security operation was launched, according to the government, when the Degodiya failed to surrender their weapons. Other harsh measures followed the massacre, with 587 Degodiya children expelled from schools in Wajir district two months later, and aid agencies prevented from distributing aid to families affected by the massacre. Tight security was widespread. A dusk-to-dawn curfew and a ban on meetings of three or more people was imposed. Thousands of families were made homeless as the security forces burned homes and terrorized the district. The government did not hold a public inquiry, and has never compensated the families of the fifty-seven it acknowledged were killed.

New Evidence

Recently, a former security official provided information according to which the operation was carefully calculated and executed with the intention of punishing the community for supposedly harboring anti-government elements. The crackdown began at the end of 1983, supposedly after dissatisfaction over regional elections increased local hostility and discontent. According to the source, the government believed the local population was hiding rebel groups of so-called shifta and devised scare tactics, centered on Wajir but designed to alert the populations of Garissa and Mandera as well.

A late-night meeting was reportedly held in a Nairobi hotel, chaired by former Minister in the Office of the President Ole Tipis. Crucial participants in the decision were identified as: Philip Kilonzo, Nairobi Police Chief (now Police Commissioner); Amos Bore, Provincial Commissioner; Benson Kaaria, Provincial Commissioner (see massacre at Bulla Karatasi above); Mr. Yagan, District Commissioner; Mr. Barngetuny, nominated member of parliament; and Mr. Kanyotu, then director of Special Branch.

According to the former security official, Kanyotu produced a list of 211 individuals wanted by the Special Branch. These people were said to be acting against the state as armed shiftas, destabilizing the region and associating with local rebel groups. Pursuit by the Special Branch had proved fruitless because, he claimed, those wanted were being hidden by the local population. Ole Tipis apparently asked Kilonzo if a "village sweep" would "embarrass" the security forces. Kilonzo responded with the plan to plant firearms and then issue an ultimatum to surrender all weapons. This was apparently supported by Salaat and Bore. It was agreed that the government armory in the office of the Makadara District Officers would issue forty guns to Yagan, who, with the assistance of the Special Branch, would hide them in Wajir District.

According to Africa Watch's source, Amos Bore left Nairobi toward the end of January with four agents named as Mutemi, Omangi,

Njeru and Mwango, to organize the planting of the weapons. The plan was sanctioned by the president's office through Ole Tipis, then Minister of State in the Office of the President, in charge of national internal security. Two hundred and fifty thousand Kenyan shillings ($9,615) were supplied to buy gifts for troop leaders and cover entertainment costs for soldiers and security personnel.

The massacre was carried out by the paramilitary General Service Unit (GSU), reportedly with the help of thirty-six criminals who were completing sentences for murder and robbery. They helped execute the plan, dressed in GSU uniform, in exchange for freedom. This unit was apparently trained at the GSU center at Embakasi, Nairobi, and was known as Group 83/1. The creation of Group 83/1 was also said to include some of President Moi's personal agents, who trained separately at the Administration Police Center, but who met frequently with the GSU officers during the training. According to the detailed information provided, President Moi visited the camp when training had been completed, presented a cow for slaughtering, and called for loyalty, hard work and dedication. The former security official says the operation was seen by the GSU as an opportunity to practice some of their most brutal techniques (see chapter five).

After the massacre had taken place, a confidential report was allegedly filed at Special Branch headquarters commending the action as highly successful. Five leaders of the troops were awarded with large tracts of land in Kitale and Molo, an action which, according to the source, was personally endorsed by Nicholas Biwott. According to the account by the former security official, 2,169 residents were killed by the security forces, of whom 316 were children.

Africa Watch calls on the Kenyan government to conduct a public inquiry to examine the evidence about the killings at Wajir. To our knowledge, this was the bloodiest episode of human rights violations since Kenya became independent. It requires a full public accounting.

Other Killings Reported in the North Eastern Province

- June 1981, Wajir: Wajir West MP Ahmed Khalif protested that the army had killed twelve people during an operation said to be aimed at shiftas. He said at least fifty camels had been killed by the army and many huts burned. The action was justified in parliament by a minister who called the action necessary in the government campaign against shifta.

None of the families affected were awarded
compensation.

- In 1982, the bodies of 110 Somalis, who had been
  nailed to trees by the GSU, were cut down by a priest,
  who passed the information on to international aid
  organizations. This incident was confirmed to Africa
  Watch by an international aid organization. In the
  same year, GSU burned Somali settlements around
  Garissa.
- October 1987, reports of mass expulsions and killings
  in Wajir District.

SECURITY IN THE NORTH EASTERN PROVINCE

Killings, arrests and harsh security crackdowns are still reported
occasionally in the North Eastern Province, but most of the time the
isolation policy of the government keeps events in the region
unpublicized. The national press rarely reports anything from the region
other than sporadic raids attributed to bandits, shifta or poachers, or news
of development plans. Aid agencies and missionaries fear expulsion if
they speak out.

The region is visibly underdeveloped and tightly policed. All
vehicles traveling into the North Eastern Province must stop at Ekasi, a
police post before Garissa, for a security check. Vehicles receive military
escort for the journey to Garissa, Wajir and Mandera. All the NEP towns
remain extremely isolated, but Garissa is to some extent a frontier town
for traders. A concrete road has been under construction for a number
of years and appears to have been abandoned some hundred kilometers
from the town; residents suspect that the government has no intention of
completing the road for political reasons. Although the Minister for
Transport visited Garissa in September 1990 to reassure them it would
be completed by the end of the year, no significant progress had been
made at the time this report was written.

There has been little development in the provincial capital
beyond its large district hospital. The imposing structures of
administration buildings stand in stark contrast to the spread of Somali
manyattas (huts), which are often no more than domes of rags and animal
skins. Security and administration posts, including customs officials,
soldiers, police and armed escorts are dominated by non-Somali

personnel. It is noticeable that "Kenyan" is used by these personnel to describe only non-Somalis. The garrison is situated inside Garissa town, although barracks are supposed to be located at a suitable distance outside towns and populated centers. Residents told Africa Watch that there are frequent problems between soldiers and the local population, and that there have been incidents of rape, beatings and killings.

Wajir—which is located at least one day's travel by road from Garissa—shows even fewer signs of development. The residents suffer from a poor water supply and sanitation facilities, as well as extreme isolation. In regards to the education system, Wajir has the lowest enrollment rate in the country, with only 14 percent of those of school-age attending. The North Eastern Province itself has the lowest enrollment rate in the country, with only 17 percent of its school-aged population attending.[3] A letter published in the *Weekly Review* written by a reader from the North Eastern Province expresses frustration at the educational situation in the region:

> A recent special report on university admission left tears in my eyes. The report revealed that the total number of students admitted to the four public universities in 1990 was 8,866. North Eastern Province was indicated to have sent 20—that's 0.23%. This is totally absurd. More embarrassing is that one north eastern district, Mandera, failed to send a single student, while Machakos sent 724.
>
> Despite environmental hardships, the students of North Eastern Province are NOT intellectually inferior to other Kenyan students. I therefore urge the people of the province, including the North Eastern Province

---

[3] According to research carried out at the Institute of Development Studies, University of Nairobi, in 1988 the enrollment rates in the North Eastern Province were: Garissa 20 percent, Wajir 14 percent and Mandera 26 percent. Research by the Kenyatta University Bureau of Education found that there was "an alarming high transfer rate" of teachers and education officers; that there was a chronic shortage of books, and that pupils were unable, because of lack of books, to spend any time on homework. The poor development of education in the North Eastern Province was attributed to "neglect during the colonial era, a low level of economic development, and the cultural beliefs of the people."

University Students Association, Nepusa, to organize a
provincial conference to debate our educational ills. They
should come up quickly with something reliable to
reverse this dangerous trend.[4]

The government blames nomadism for the chronic lack of
development and periodically calls for it to stop. In March 1989, Hussein
Mohamed, Minister in the Office of the President, said in Wajir there was
"urgent need for the people to change their way of life from the nomadic
mode to a more settled lifestyle....Nomadic life must therefore stop to
pave way for faster development."[5] Government hostility to nomadism,
however, is matched by the aggression displayed by the security forces
towards newly-settled communities.

Wajir is tightly policed by security forces and the Special Branch,
who have a reputation for brutality. This is encouraged, according to
residents, by the isolation from other sources of administration and
authority. The Special Branch recruit as many people as possible from
the community as informers, which has created an uneasy climate.

The Special Branch has a similar hold on Mandera, the last NEP
town which straddles the Kenyan-Somali border. According to one well-
informed observer who has worked in Mandera for a number of years,
the special powers given to the security forces under the emergency laws
are fully exploited. There are periodic security campaigns, which are
never reported in the national press. According to the source, the army
cleaned out nomadic communities in the bush between Wajir and
Mandera in 1984 after the massacre, and carried out another harsh
security sweep in the same no-man's land two years later. The same
source said they had witnessed the repercussions of a number of army
scourges that involved the forced removal of whole communities from the
district.

Mandera suffers, according to this source, from the consequences
of "a strategy of under-development" imposed on the NEP by the
government. Money from the central government goes almost exclusively
to the security forces and the administration. Resentment for what is seen
as a complete disregard of the most basic services is illustrated by a

---

[4] *Weekly Review*, June 21, 1991.

[5] *Kenya Times*, March 4, 1989.

repeated complaint regarding the official plane service—a government light-aircraft bringing security and administration personnel. The uses of such a service for a population so stranded are many: emergency travel, basic supplies, medical equipment and other goods. Yet government officials are said to use much of the additional cargo space to bring in beer for government personnel, despite the fact this causes offense to many in the Moslem town. Government personnel say they consider the town a punishment posting. Cargo space is also profitably leased to the *miraa* traders (a mild narcotic; see below).

It is apparent that the population feels unrepresented and politically marginalized. During the first and second general elections, residents say officials ensured that government-nominated candidates were elected. There was an extremely low turnout of voters.

Security personnel seem determined to hold Mandera to its past in many respects—in the Special Branch office and police administration buildings, plaques remain in dedication to government officials and security men who lost their lives in the shifta war. Internal notices and posters urge Special Branch officers to be cautious socially and "never discuss business in a bar." Newcomers to the town, especially foreigners, are expected to register, although there is no such requirement specified by Kenyan immigration elsewhere in the country.

Members of the Kenyan-Somali population living in the main North Eastern Province towns, say the degree of repression is linked to the local administration—in particular, the District Officers (DO) and the District Commissioners (DC), who have the power to control or encourage police excesses on an everyday basis, and that administrators sent to the NEP are almost uniformly harsh and unsympathetic in what they consider tough and insecure postings. One Garissa resident who spoke with Africa Watch complained that the government was destabilizing the area with its policies:

> This state of emergency means the security forces can arrest, beat, rape, detain and shoot people—and for that reason the region will never be stable.

People are constantly picked up and harassed for identity papers. Beatings by the police—sometimes severe enough to cause serious injury—are considered routine. The policy to post non-Somali personnel in the North Eastern Province increases the feeling of annexation and subordination. The frequency with which the description shifta is used to arrest, detain and intimidate the population is matched by the frequency with which it is used to insult and derogate them. "Dirty shifta" is standard address from non-Somali personnel.

According to a former member of parliament from one of the main North Eastern Province towns, residents are constantly harassed by security forces on the pretext of identity checks. Officials claim their security sweeps are aimed at weeding out illegal aliens from Somalia who are able to live among Kenya's ethnic Somali population without detection. According to the former MP, residents resent being stopped by the police on the streets and in their homes, in the search for IDs. He was frequently called on to assist families whose members had disappeared.

> I would go to the station and tell them: "Look, I know this fellow. Give him his card back." Sometimes they would say "Don't interfere," sometimes they would listen. But really, there is not much anyone can do if someone is picked up by the police.

He described the Kenyan-Somali community as "very alienated." He said that the fact that the local population is regarded as shiftas or poachers by the police adminstration had been brought up in parliament by certain MPs from the North Eastern Province:

> ...[we] often raised it in Parliament—that the term shifta must not be used any more. Shifta was an anti-Kenyan movement fighting for political reasons. We had replaced the word with bandit. If government vehicles get attacked, it is like people in Nairobi robbing a bank—there is no political shifta any more. It is a way of criminalizing a whole population to justify these security measures. Kenyan-Somalis are treated like aliens in their own country.

He said he saw some development in the North Eastern province during 1979-88 but it was minimal considering how far behind the province lagged on a national scale.

> We don't get special treatment but development did reach our areas. There have been some more schools, the road was started and some few new facilities. But the

leaders are chosen by the government—elections were rigged to put certain people in power, and now they control the region. These people do not speak for the people or look after the interests of the population because they are government puppets and self-seekers only.

Malim Mohamed, brother of Chief-of-Staff Mahmoud Mohamed and the only ethnic Somali in the cabinet, attracts particular resentment; he entered parliament as one of twelve MPs nominated by the president. According to the former MP, the actions of so-called elected leaders in North Eastern province are now largely determined by the wishes of Mahmoud Mohamed, the most powerful Kenyan-Somali in the country. Few Kenyan-Somalis are in government, although they are a sizeable population of more than two million. That one of the most powerful men in the country is an ethnic Somali is not in any way representative of general political power or participation, but more akin to the policies of other leaders who have deliberately entrusted military power to members of the most vulnerable groups. Somalia's former President Siad Barre, for example, has used Ogaden refugees, and Uganda's President Yoweri Museveni has used Rwandese refugees and citizens. The vulnerability of such groups increases loyalty to the person who provides power, and minimizes alignment with opposition groups. The Kenyan government has easily created deep divisions in the ethnic Somali community by granting power to a few of the most powerless. In the North Eastern Province, co-opted leaders can be relied on to hold regular demonstrations in support of the government, particularly during security crackdowns and political crisis. They organized a number of demonstrations, for example, in favor of the bitterly resented screening exercise.

BANDIT OR SHIFTA? REBEL OR ROBBER?

Demands for the unification of all Somali-populated territory, including the Northern Frontier District, continued as the new Kenyan government took on a centralized constitution in 1964. Centralization was imposed on the NFD by Kenyan government decree under draconian laws. There was armed resistance and a battle for secession in the NFD from 1963 to 1967, and many thousands of Kenyan-Somalis were killed.

Guerrilla tactics concentrated on ambushing official convoys and personnel; whole villages were slaughtered and razed by government forces in retaliation. The government, however, deliberately downgraded what was arguably its greatest post-independence problem by ascribing so-called skirmishes to shifta. The war was perceived from the outset as the government taking necessary measures to "tame" a nomadic community which was resisting national centralization and development. Confrontation between the armed forces and the rebels was always attributed to cattle-rustling, stolen livestock, poachers and robbers—terminology heavily cloaked in cultural, as opposed to political, references. The umbrella term was shifta. It was used by the authorities to convey lawlessness and absence of political rationale. Shifta, therefore, carries two meanings:

1)   It is the official term of reference for political
        opposition in the NFD;
2)   it is a derogatory term, literally translated as bandit.

When shifta is used now by administration and security personnel, it essentially embraces both meanings.

Parliamentary calls for tough security measures against shifta and poachers continue to surface with predictable regularity, and frequent security sweeps for illegal aliens culminated in the screening exercise in 1989-90.

Periodic attacks on administration and security officials do continue in the North Eastern Province, and in neighboring provinces with large ethnic Somali populations, like Tana River District (Coastal Province) and Meru District (Northern Province). Attributed to shifta bandits, they are normally met with tightened security measures, administrative penalization and local manhunts.

•   On February 20, 1989, a driver working in the
        Ministry of Culture and Social Services was killed when
        his official vehicle was ambushed in Garissa District. A
        chief and two administration police who escaped the
        shoot-out said they were attacked by a group of about
        "twenty armed bandits—the gangsters were in groups of
        three along the road. The first group opened fire on
        our vehicle." During the same week, the councillor for
        Habaswein, Haulid Keinan, told residents of Wajir to

"report suspected bandits," assuring them that "bandits roaming the area will be wiped out completely."[6]

- In May 1989, the Tana River District Commissioner said security personnel had shot dead "one bandit" and stepped up security measures in the district. He appealed to residents to report "suspects and aliens," and "warned Home Guards to stop misusing firearms." (See chapter five, section on Home Guards.)

- In another incident at the beginning of May 1989 in Garissa District, four policemen were killed in Hulugho Division. Malim Mohamed, Minister of State in the Office of the President, called on the provincial administration to step up security. Amos Bore, Provincial Commissioner, accused the local population of "harboring bandits," saying: "It is very discouraging when the same [people] the Government strived to protect were the ones who hid the bandits." The Provincial Police Chief, Ibrahim Sallai, called for "enhanced security measures" and advocated "proper registration of area residents to help fish out suspected bandits." According to Ibrahim Sallai, "some of the nomadic pastoralists could not be identified by chiefs and were suspected to engage in banditry."[7]

One week later, the national press reported that five chiefs had been suspended indefinitely "over continued insecurity in Garissa District." The North Eastern Provincial Commissioner, Amos Bore confirmed that a chief from Modogashe division had been suspended. Residents in Garissa said the suspensions followed a "closed door security meeting" chaired by Bore. He lashed out at the local press for reporting attacks and unrest in the district: "What is the motive of the local press in over-blowing incidents that happened here?"[8] He said he had

---

[6] *The Standard*, February 23, 1989.

[7] *Daily Nation*, May 15, 1989.

[8] *The Standard*, May 23, 1989.

personally seen to it that two government information officers in the province were sacked.

In September 1989, two public buses and a police escort were attacked en route to Garissa resulting in the death of at least ten passengers. The following evening, a man suffering injuries to his hand was stopped by police on the outskirts of Garissa town. According to eyewitness accounts gathered by Africa Watch, the man "confessed to being a shifta" after being tortured in Garissa police station. Seen after interrogation in the police station by town residents—who were reportedly allowed to view the celebrated police catch—the man's finger nails were said to have been removed and he was bleeding heavily from his nose and mouth. Despite headline coverage of the ambush, the capture of this man was not reported. Africa Watch has been unable to find any evidence that he was brought to trial.

By September 26, 1989, Africa Watch obtained a firsthand report of forty men, described as Somali nationals, being held in Garissa police cells for suspected banditry and entering the country illegally. Conditions in the two cells, measuring 10' by 10', were such that there was severe overcrowding compounded by lack of food, dehydration from lack of water, inadequate sanitation, lack of ventilation and high daytime temperatures. No blankets were provided. Five women with young children were also held on charges of illegal residency. Because of the overcrowded cells, the women were kept on the floor behind the police desk without blankets and with poor access to sanitation facilities. The prisoners were repeatedly taunted by the police as shifta, kicked, hit and treated roughly.

After the enormous influx of Somali refugees in 1991, the Kenyan government warned that banditry and poaching in the North Eastern Province would worsen. To many Kenyan-Somalis, the failure of the government to distinguish between law-abiding citizens and incursions from Somalia caused deep offense. After a letter about "the Somali problem" was published in the *Daily Nation* on March 20, 1991, one man replied:

> I was surprised to read the racist remarks that banditry and poaching are synonymous with the Somali...[which]...also contains many fallacies, historical distortions and generalizations about the origins and categorization of ethnic communities in Kenya.

To separate the Somali as a distinct community from what he terms "black Africans" smacks of negative and racist stereotyping....By pointing to an Arab origin, the not-too-subtle insinuation is that the Somalis are not real Kenyans.

Unfortunately, this is the same type of mentality which pervades the upper echelons of Government and so dominates the media that the Kenyan-Somali cannot be blamed for growing up with a sense of separateness (or, in Afrikaans, apartheid).

Read the dailies, banditry and poaching are not confined to one area or a single ethnic group. As for the origins of the Somali, recent historical evidence points to their area of origin as being southern Ethiopia up to Lake Turkana. Pastoralist groups such as the Somali, Rendille and Turkana occupied Kenya long before Bantu ancestors left the Congo forest.

The question of who is a genuine Kenyan does not arise as we are a mix of various ethnic groups, a melting pot that has no place for those who thrive on absurd generalisations and negative racist cliches and stereotyping to cement their racist views.

CONTROLLING MOVEMENT: POLICING THE MIRAA TRADE

Miraa is a mild narcotic cultivated principally in Meru district, legally grown and sold. It is widely used by ethnic Somalis, who monopolize the trade nationally and regionally. The miraa trade is said to earn Meru district some one million shillings ($38,462) daily. Riding in Toyota and Suzuki pick-up trucks, the miraa traders travel mainly at night through back routes to avoid police posts and roadblocks. The leaf must be fresh when it appears on the market in the morning, otherwise it loses its strength, and traders make every effort to bypass police posts to avoid delays and demands for money.

Security crackdowns on the Kenyan-Somali community inevitably affect the miraa traders, seen as legitimate but nonetheless suspicious

black-marketeers. Their rapid cross-country movements at night attract
the attention of the security forces who try to control their movements.
The traders are regularly accused of assisting people wanted by the
security forces; transporting weapons and ammunition; smuggling ivory
and drugs; attacking security personnel; and carrying out nighttime raids
before fleeing the district. There has been no serious attempt to stop the
trade, however, because of the informal gains as well as the net
profits—namely, the extensive system of bribes levied by the security
forces and local administration. Temporary bans and restrictions on the
miraa traders' movements reported in the national papers are perhaps
the best indication of security operations in the different districts. On
October 9, 1990, when a police officer, two bank clerks and a driver were
killed in an ambush in Tana River District, the provincial police officer
launched a manhunt. No further reports appeared in the press until
October 16, when a small notice in the national press announced a ban
on miraa by the Tana River District Commissioner.[9]

During the national crackdown on poaching in the game parks
in 1989, the banning of miraa reached a crisis point for many traders
whose livelihoods depended on it. By early December 1989, deliveries to
Nairobi from Meru had suffered severe interruption and miraa traders
complained of constant harassment and threats by the security forces.
Some stopped traveling for fear of being killed by the Anti-Poaching Unit
and GSU. During that time, the security forces and the national press
made no apparent distinction between criminal elements and the rest of
the ethnic Somali community. According to the government, which
blamed poaching exclusively on the Somali community, it was a battle
against poaching; but according to the Somali community, it was an anti-
Somali campaign.

POACHING AND THE ANTI-SOMALI CAMPAIGN

Poaching in Kenya has existed ever since areas of land were
fenced off to create game parks, and increased as the monetary rewards
grew for ivory in the expanding Western tourist market. Poaching
involves partners in crime on three levels—the catching, the selling and
the buying—although the national and Western media focus almost

---

[9] *The Standard*, October 16, 1990.

exclusively on the killing of the game. In Kenya, ivory trading has been associated with official corruption at the highest levels, while the actual poaching of game is associated with the poorest and most disadvantaged sections of the population. The so-called national crisis over poaching in the parks in 1988 was not the discovery of a new phenomenon so much as the realization that poaching had gone beyond an acceptable level. Some agricultural and wildlife experts, backed up by well-placed official sources, say the real crisis for the Kenyan government was that new elements increased poaching to the extent that the official trade was unable to incorporate the excesses.

The crisis began in September 1988 when the former chair of the East African Wildlife Society, Dr. Richard Leakey, contended that the number of elephants left in the country was only 19,000, far less than the official figures. He accused the relevant ministries of "paying lip service" to protection measures. His criticisms provoked the anger of the Minister of Tourism and Wildlife, George Muhoho, who charged Leakey with trying to undermine government departments. In the debate that followed, however, there were accusations in parliament that government officials were involved in lucrative ivory trading, eliciting help from corrupt park wardens. With access to powerful and sophisticated automatic weapons, poachers operating in gangs of thirty or more are able to mow down large numbers of elephants and rhinoceroses.

From September to December 1988, the national press provided almost daily coverage of slaughtered elephants, disputes between ministers and expressed fears for the tourist industry. Kenya's economic dependency on the tourist industry for vital foreign exchange is at the heart of the concern for poaching, and provokes speculation about economic sabotage and dissident strategies. Tourist agents reported a noticeable drop in travel which was attributed to the high-profile coverage of the poaching crisis in both the U.S. and Britain.[10]

The government called the poaching crisis a "security problem" and blamed it on ethnic Somalis, with no clear distinction between the participation of illegal Somali nationals and Kenya's own ethnic Somali population. According to the government, civil war in Somalia had resulted in bands of deserters poaching with lethal weapons in Kenya, and accused Kenyan-Somalis of providing cover for renegades and

---

[10] In 1987, 78,000 American tourists went to Kenya, principally for game safaris, along with large numbers of European and Japanese tourists.

bandits. Poaching was also directly linked to the pressures of a growing population, claiming that domestic animals and nomadic communities were increasingly encroaching on the highly profitable game parks. During this time, the MP for Tana River District, Mohamed Abdi Galgalo, drew attention to senior government officers with extensive property interests in Mombasa, saying their money had come from trading in ivory. He pointed to the use of small aircraft to haul ivory out of the game parks and said it was impossible for "small men" to use such expensive means: "There is no need to harass the small man because he is merely carrying out orders from somewhere. It is somewhere that the Ministry must find out who is involved."

President Moi Announces Shoot-to-Kill Policy

On September 13, 1988, President Moi announced that poachers would be shot on sight. He gave directions to wipe out poaching with a shoot-to-kill policy in all the parks.[11] Meetings with security committees in eastern and north eastern provinces were held by Hezekiah Oyugi, Permanent Secretary in the Office of the President in charge of Provincial and Internal Security, who said "the security forces must be in total control of their areas and there should be no excuse about it." He directed that "poaching and banditry in these areas must be wiped out by whatever means." The former Director of Wildlife Conservation and Management, Perez Olindo, said his department was working very closely with the regular police force, the Administration Police, the paramilitary General Service Unit, and the defense department, to carry out the president's orders.[12] Game parks were soon being patrolled by militarized anti-poaching units and paramilitary task forces with instructions to shoot on sight. Well-armed paramilitary attachments were stationed in Tsavo, Meru-Isiolo and Garissa. Police Commissioner Philip Kilonzo commands the anti-poaching security operation.

By December 1988, figures released by the Ministry of Tourism and Wildlife reported at least thirty people had been killed in the shoot-to-kill campaign against poachers. However, reports in the national press

---

[11] President Moi's shoot-to-kill announcement was deceptive in creating the impression that it was a policy specifically introduced for a security crisis. See chapter seventeen.

[12] *Weekly Review*, September 9, 1988.

indicate the probability that many more were killed, but no official figures have been released since.

At the same time as the president directed security forces to shoot on sight anyone suspected of poaching in the parks, an assistant minister in the Office of the President, John Keen, proposed detaining anyone suspected of involvement with poaching. Hundreds of people were subsequently detained in security sweeps round the national parks.

MERU NATIONAL PARK: CRACKDOWN IN ISIOLO

In September 1988, the national press reported more than 600 people had been detained in Isiolo, northern Kenya, for security reasons. Although the government said this was linked to the poaching crisis, the large ethnic Somali community in Isiolo said the poaching crisis had increased harassment and regional tension, but had not created it. An Africa Watch representative witnessed the events in Isiolo town during the poaching crisis, which were an illustration of the extent to which the existing harassment and repression of the ethnic Somali community was incorporated into new anti-poaching strategies.

Isiolo is, in ethnic terms, a frontier town that borders on the North Eastern Province. A sizeable ethnic Somali population shares the town with a number of other ethnic groups, including the culturally similar seminomadic Boranas. The pressures caused by a rapidly growing population means competition for grazing land has become chronic, and is compounded by official restrictions on nomadic movement. Locally, access to traditional grazing grounds was drastically reduced by the creation of the Kora National Reserve in the 1970s, which was funded in part by Britain's University of Cambridge program for flora and fauna research. Thus access to vast areas of traditional grazing lands has become illegal for the communities dependent on them. It is illegal for any livestock or domestic animals to be kept in the national parks, and recent moves into the periphery of the parks by seminomadic communities searching for grazing were reported as "extensive and illegal human encroachment."[13] Pastoralists who moved from the Tana River District into Tsavo Park in the early 1980s were initially confined by the

---

[13] Ibid.

administration to the Tana River District; toward the end of the decade, however, they moved westward because of diminished grazing.

These seasonal movements of Somali nomads from the semiarid districts of Wajir and Garissa have provoked disputes over grazing rights. But evidence suggests that far from seeking solutions to what has become a serious land problem, the government has instead exploited it as a means of containing the local population. In May 1987, the government armed a local Home Guard of 200-300 non-Somalis in Isiolo with the mandate to police grazing rights and local disputes, while, simultaneously, carrying out periodic security sweeps to disarm ethnic Somalis.

Any disputes over grazing are ruthlessly put down. For example, in early November 1988, at the beginning of the poaching crisis, a significant security operation was carried out in Isiolo district. Police, GSU, army helicopters and military planes were dispatched to Kinna where grazing disputes between local Somalis and Boranas had resulted in fighting. A large number of people were said to have been killed by the security forces, but no official figures were released. When Africa Watch spoke to local residents in Isiolo, they could only say that many had been killed. On November 7, a reliable source told Africa Watch that an emergency meeting held by government officials at the District Commissioner's office considered a proposal to arm the Boranas against the Somalis.

Officials announced that all nomads and temporary settlers would be moved out of the district. According to eyewitness reports in Isiolo town, Administration Police beat up, arrested, detained and burned the homes of many ethnic Somalis. The evictions and harassment extended to settled Somali communities which were uprooted from Isiolo and Tana River District and forced into the barren, semiarid land of Wajir and Marsabit. Reports of forced relocation, and harassment of nomads continued. In January 1989, local chiefs in the Marsabit area made official complaints that injured and abandoned camels were arriving with extensive burns on their backs. Observers in the area told Africa Watch that security forces were attacking the nomadic camel trains and burning the property carried on the backs of camels. (Somali nomads transport their shelters using camels.)

There were extensive house to house (*manyatta* to *manyatta*) identity sweeps which concentrated exclusively on the ethnic Somali community. Under the new anti-poaching strategies, ethnic Somalis found they were the chief victims in the national parks; some 600 were arrested, including one person who was arrested for riding a bicycle through Meru

National Park. Members of the Kenyan-Somali community in Isiolo told Africa Watch that they were being picked up on the street by police, and any who were "hanging around" or who "couldn't satisfy the police with an account of their movements" were being arrested and jailed for a month. Some were released with a 400 shillings ($15) fine after a few days in custody. None had access to legal representation. One bus driver said he had assisted a group of about forty Kenyan-Somalis move out of Meru to Marsabit after they had been threatened by Administration Police and the military.

As the anti-poaching drive turned its attention to so-called illegal Somali aliens, identity sweeps intensified. In Isiolo, non-Somalis said there had been an influx of Somali nationals fleeing the war in the north who, they claimed, had contributed to the poaching problem. The Kenyan-Somali community confirmed this, but preferred to point out that such people were unable to get legitimate residence in a country renowned for its hostile policy to both Somalis and refugees (see chapter nineteen). Some traders in Isiolo said the Issaq refugees from the north were poaching in order to contribute money to the rebel Somali National Movement (SNM) fighting in northern Somalia. Others supported the claim that the Somali government was organizing poaching forays across the border. But the greatest concern of the Kenyan-Somalis was that the new poaching crisis was being used by the security forces to intensify harassment of the community and orchestrate the anti-Somali campaign.

By November 18, the District Officer in Meru had placed severe restrictions on miraa traders; by early December, deliveries to Nairobi had been greatly reduced. There were a number of reports that miraa traders were being arrested and their vehicles confiscated; some traders said they would have to stop trading during the crisis because they feared they would be shot as poachers. Kenyan-Somalis in Nairobi were also feeling the effects of the campaign by December, with an increase in identity checks, arrests in the main Kenyan-Somali suburb, Eastleigh, and surveillance of businesses, restaurants and shops by the Special Branch.

A Minister in the Office of the President, Hussein Mohamed, ordered "aliens with Kenyan national identity cards in North Eastern Province to surrender them immediately to the chiefs." He called on local residents to report "foreigners holding cards" and to volunteer information about "the poachers." According to members of the Kenyan-Somali community, failure to produce "voluntary information" was interpreted as deliberate withholding of information—those who do not become informers are regarded as shifta collaborators. The national press carried reports that Somalis "claiming Kenyan nationality" who had "lost" their identity cards were being imprisoned. Herdsmen who had "infiltrated the national parks" were ordered to move out immediately, and a directive was issued that all unlicensed firearms were to be surrendered to the government.[14]

At the time, Vice-President Dr. Josphat Karanja, called on North Eastern Province residents to "expose aliens who have infiltrated the country using false identities"; and Jackson Angaine, MP, said at Meru that activities of both dissidents and poachers were "aimed at undermining the Government" by sabotaging the tourist industry. He urged people to "reject the rebels and declare war against the poachers."[15] Numerous letters appeared in the national press about fear of banditry, the shifta problem and the need to root out those collaborating with the poachers. There were calls to crack down on the miraa trade, stop the smuggling on the Kenyan-Somali border and to rid Mandera of Somali currency. Newspapers carried headlines of Somali poachers being gunned down by security forces in the national parks. No distinction was made by the press or politicians between illegal Somali nationals and indigenous Kenyan-Somalis.

Reports of suspected poachers shot dead continued to be reported by the international press until late 1989; the London *Times* reported on November 22, 1989, that four suspected poachers had been shot dead in Meru National Park by the anti-poaching unit. The *Guardian* reported that wildlife rangers had shot dead six poachers in Meru national park. According to the Director of Wildlife, Richard Leakey, this included the murderers of two French tourists.[16] There was no explanation as to what evidence—if any—linked the two men conclusively to the murders. One MP, Francis Kagwima, claimed in parliament that game rangers shot and killed two primary school pupils in July 1988 in Meru National Park.[17] Leakey made every effort to reassure the country that the

---

[14] *Daily Nation*, November 27, 1988.

[15] *Daily Nation*, November 7, 1988.

[16] *The Guardian*, November 23, 1989. Two French tourists were shot and killed near Meru in July 1989.

[17] *The Times*, November 24, 1989.

shoot-to-kill policy was essentially self-defense, and said that a minister who was reported calling on the wananchi (people) to take it upon themselves to take up arms and spears to kill suspected poachers had misunderstood official policy. A shoot-to-kill policy for reasons of self-defense is, of course, already operational for the security forces and would require no presidential directive. In an interview with the *Sunday Standard* on May 21, 1989, Leakey provided details of what constituted the official policy:

> *Sunday Standard*: While conforming to the orders to shoot poachers on sight, how would you guarantee that innocent people are not shot at on mistaken identity?
>
> *Dr. Leakey*: I think this has been exaggerated. What the President has made clear is that if we come across armed gangs who intend to shoot us, we may shoot them. If we come across men who are unarmed or men who are carrying arrows and spears, we are not going to shoot. But if we come across people wandering around with automatic weapons and they threaten the lives of my officers then we will shoot.

Africa Watch has been unable to obtain official figures on the number of people killed under the anti-poaching shoot-to-kill campaign.

The poaching crisis ended in late 1989, when the phrasing of the crisis progressively turned into "satisfaction" that strict security measures in the parks had wiped out the poaching menace. International assistance helped equip anti-poaching units, including equipment from British-based firms.[18] The anti-poaching campaign successfully cut the loss of elephants from 2,000-3,000 annually to around 300 in 1989. In 1990, only thirty-one elephants were reported to have been killed by poachers. Some $150 million from the international community was sought by Leakey's office to help save the elephant population. On July 6, 1990, the

---

[18] Hopmain Limited of Kingsbury, U.K., donated powerful cordless searchlights which are capable of illuminating an enormous area for pinpointing targets up to 800 meters. Given to the Anti-Poaching Unit, Leakey said the spotlights would "make operations at night more rewarding for the strike force." (*The Standard*, September 19, 1990.)

Weekly Review reported that the morale of the security forces "has never been higher....The rangers are now armed with sophisticated firearms and modern communication equipment. They look like real soldiers in a conflict which much resembles guerrilla warfare." The dramatic reduction in poaching incidents was also a result of a ban by the Geneva-based Convention on the International Trade and Endangered Species (CITES) on ivory trading, which caused a rapid fall in ivory prices. The anti-Somali campaign, however, did not diminish. It reached a bureaucratic apex.

IDENTITY SWEEPS

Without warning, police launched what they called a "procedural operation" on May 20, 1989, to "verify legitimacy of national status."[19] Thousands of Kenyan-Somalis were picked up by police in Nairobi suburbs and slums in a daylong sweep. Police raided houses, business premises, hotels and restaurants, forcing people into police trucks and landrovers. Matatus (minibuses) were stopped en route to Eastleigh, a predominantly ethnic Somali suburb, and police forced passengers out to inspect their identity papers. The raids were concentrated on Eastleigh and Pangani, but many arrests were also made in Mathare Valley, Huruma Estate, Kariobangi, Kibera, Kawangware, Dagoretti, Kangemi, Githurai, Waithaka and the city center.

The checks affected only those who were considered as having the identifiable features of an ethnic Somali. Police stations in Pangani, Eastleigh and Kawangware were described as overflowing. At least 800 appeared in court charged with a variety of offenses; many were charged with having forged or defaced identity cards, of being in the country illegally, or of disturbing the peace. Women from Somalia who had married Kenyan men were kept in custody until they could produce a valid marriage certificate. Many marriages among the poorer sections of the community take place without a legal document, cemented only by the relevant religious requirements. At Makadara court, 423 people appeared, none of whom had legal advice or representation. Thirty-five were found guilty of illegal residency and sentenced to serve seven months with immediate repatriation after the jail term. At Kibera court,

---

[19] *The Standard*, May 21, 1989.

forty-two supposed aliens received similar sentences and repatriation orders.

Great offense was taken by the Moslem ethnic Somalis when police entered the compound of the mosque, surrounded it and arrested worshippers. The chair of the Supreme Council of Muslims, Nairobi Province, Mohammud Mohamed Adam, complained that this was a serious offense by the police, saying they had also confiscated worshippers' identity cards. The outrage of the community did force a response from the authorities; a *baraza* (public meeting and fund drive) was held in Eastleigh by the chief and government officials, where they attempted to defend their actions. According to members of the community, no one was spared interrogation—"Old women were removed from matatus to be interrogated."[20] People said their identity cards had been confiscated by police and they were told to report to the District Commissioner at their original place of birth. Officials at the baraza told the community that the government "has the right to follow suspects in all places" and issued warnings to traders that their businesses could be closed down.

There was little opportunity for aggrieved members of the community to speak out. People told an Africa Watch representative that the place was "crawling with Special Branch" and that "fear kept most of us silent." Some leaders of the community, however, warned in the national press that such action "could incite Kenyans of Somali origin against the government and thus threaten unity in the country."[21] In the weeks following the sweep, the police stations remained packed with people accused of having false identity papers, or no identity papers, and with family members and friends attempting to secure their release. According to reports received by Africa Watch, very few managed to get legal assistance.

---

[20] *Daily Nation*, May 22, 1989.

[21] *The Standard*, May 21, 1989.

16
SCREENING OF ETHNIC SOMALIS
PINK CARDS FOR SECOND-CLASS CITIZENS

On November 13, 1989, the government announced a nationwide screening of the entire Somali community. All ethnic Somalis 18 years or older—including Kenyans of Somali origin and resident Somali nationals—were given three weeks in which to present a national identity card and a passport or birth certificate at one of fifty-one different screening centers. According to the official notice: "The government advises that it will be an offence under the Registration of Persons Act, Cap 107, for any member of the Somali community to fail to appear before a legally established team within 3 weeks."

PREPARING THE GROUND

A special "Somali Probe Committee" had been set up in the Office of the President: it instructed the Department of Immigration to prepare a list of all Somalis with Kenyan papers. Immigration Department files on a number of ethnic Somalis were removed to a secret registry and a list was drawn up of those to be targeted by the Somali Probe Committee. Prior to the official announcement of the screening, the Department of Immigration wrote a letter, dated October 19, 1989, to the chair of the Somali Probe Committee, about a list of supposed illegal aliens that had been compiled by intelligence:

> It is evident that most of these Somalis holding Kenyan passports are well known businessmen [mostly transporters] who acquired their passports through either using money or some influence and thereafter embarked on an illegal exercise of poaching for other Somali nationals.

At that time, the Principal Immigration Officer, Frank Kwinga, categorically stated that:

> The Immigration Department *cannot pick on all Kenyan-Somalis* [our emphasis] with Kenyan passports but, according to records held in this office and supported by information from other organs of the government, some of the known non-Kenyan-Somalis in possession are shortlisted and their files have been moved to our secret Registry...[1]

Athough particular individuals had been identified as illegal aliens, the government decided not to confront them with due process in the courts; instead it imposed a screening exercise on the entire ethnic Somali community. The Department of Immigration was to revoke its own position and implement highly selective and discriminatory regulations against all ethnic Somalis. From March 1990, all airlines and travel agencies operating in the country were directed to refer bookings of ethnic Somalis to the Immigration Department for "smooth and quick verification" before issuing an air ticket. The letter of instruction dated March 1, 1990 from Kwinga directed that applicants' passports should be taken to the Immigration Department's headquarters at Nyayo House, Nairobi, for an on-the-spot check and clearance. This directive has been used to prevent thousands of ethnic Somalis from traveling outside the country, and has been used against Somali nationals entering and leaving. According to information provided Africa Watch, it has effectively blocked most Kenyan-Somalis from traveling outside Kenya, apart from those able to use corrupt means and personal contacts to avoid it.

DEMONSTRATIONS AND PROTESTS

The government said the screening was needed to identify illegal aliens following an influx of refugees escaping the civil war in Somali, and who had been absorbed into the Kenyan-Somali population after obtaining falsified documents. According to the government, the action was requested by leaders from the Kenyan-Somali population who were tired of being blamed for the criminal actions of Somali nationals who had entered the country illegally.

---

[1] The Immigration Department is part of the security network.

A number of demonstrations were organized by government officials and leaders in support of the screening in the North Eastern Province: these were promptly dismissed by respected leaders of the Kenyan-Somali community as puppet demonstrations. In contrast, large numbers spontaneously demonstrated against the exercise in some of the main urban centers, including Nairobi, Nakuru and Mombasa, calling it discriminatory and unconstitutional and liable to incite hatred and racial tension. President Moi condemned these demonstrations, saying a "democracy" did not mean a "free for all," and that those who criticized the screening were "either ignorant of its noble objective or outright subversive."[2]

Prominent figures who publicly condemned the screening in Kenya were penalized and hounded. Some likened the exercise to the hated old *kipande* system, a special card system used in the colonial era to control the movements of the African population (see chapter one). Ahmed Khalif Mohamed, then Secretary General of the Supreme Muslim Council of Kenya and former member of parliament for Wajir, was reported in the national press as saying "to subject only one section of Kenyan society to a selective and discriminating process will only antagonise loyal citizens." He initially refused to be screened and was subsequently dismissed from his post as Secretary General and from KANU. Mohamed Ibrahim, Kenya's only practicing ethnic Somali lawyer, has resisted pressure to be screened, but has suffered harassment by the Special Branch and was detained for two weeks in July 1990. He published an article in the *Nairobi Law Monthly* in which he said the screening exercise made him feel "like a third-rate citizen."[3]

The screening was also strongly condemned by the Kenyan Law Society which called it "unlawful, unenforceable and unconstitutional." In a statement issued by the chair, the Law Society said the screening notice was *ultra vires* Section 8 of the Registration of Persons Act, which could not be applied to communities or groups of peoples collectively but only to individuals in specific circumstances. The society said it had sent a plea through the attorney general, Matthew Muli, and the head of the civil service and secretary to the cabinet, Joseph arap Letting. There was no response to their appeal.

---

[2] *Daily Nation*, November 18, 1989.

[3] *Nairobi Law Monthly*, November 3, 1989.

DIVISIVE AND HUMILIATING TREATMENT

Despite the anger and the protests, ethnic Somalis were forced to submit themselves for screening. Thousands were arrested and summarily expelled from the country. Official sources claimed "at least 2,000 illegal aliens" had been deported by January 1990; by June it was reported that nearly 3,000 Kenyan deportees[4] were in Mogadishu, the Somali capital. Many hundreds more fled over neighboring Tanzanian, Ugandan and Burundi borders; and immigration departments in Europe and North America—particularly Canada and Britain—reported an influx of Kenyans of Somali origin destroying their documents at the airport and declaring themselves refugees. Tanzania collaborated with Kenya and returned a large number of fleeing Somalis across the border. A group of 300 were arrested in September 1990; at the time, twenty-five who were known to have fled the screening exercise were imprisoned without trial in Dar es Salaam in appalling conditions.[5]

ARBITRARY CRITERIA USED

According to those who were subjected to the screening, judgment of legitimate Kenyan citizenship depended on extremely arbitrary methods of assessment, and not on the ability to produce the required documentation which was defined as a birth certificate, a passport, national identity card or KANU membership card. Official documents were frequently confiscated by the screening teams, who claimed they had

[4] There is no suitable word for the status of the deportees. "Deportation" and "deportee" imply due legal process, which was not respected, but must be taken in context as the most appropriate description.

[5] In September, a Tanzanian woman assisting five women detainees described them to Africa Watch as being "..in terrible shape. They have had their heads shaved. Their clothes are filthy and tattered. They have no money and no one to rely on for food or medical needs. They get no medical treatment and most of them are in poor health...Most of them have children...what they get is inedible and insufficient. When we take them food, the prison guards take their share every time."

been fraudulently obtained. Questions about a person's original place of birth and family history took precedence, so that legitimate citizenship was ultimately judged primarily on:

- ability to provide full names of grand- and great-grandparents;
- ability to name clan and sub-clans;
- ability to give a detailed geographical description of the place of birth;
- ability to speak fluent Kiswahili, the national language;
- ability to answer random questions about the history and politics of Kenya;
- an "on-the-spot" identification and verification by elders and members of the Somali community.

These procedures were never officially acknowledged as the central method of identification by the head of the Screening Task Force and Rift Valley Provincial Commissioner, Mohamed Yusuf Haji, who maintained there was "nothing to fear if the right documents are produced."[6]

Contrary to these reassurances, thousands of people were failing the screening test even though they had the required documentation. Even after being deported to Mogadishu, some of these people, who had managed to hold onto their papers, continued to produce their identity cards, birth certificates and party membership in support of their case.

As the screening proceeded in Nairobi, police stations became overcrowded with those who had failed to convince the authorities of their legal status. Pangani and Kasarani police stations were described as packed. Friends and relatives attempting to secure the release of those arrested said cells were extremely dirty, poorly-ventilated and without adequate sanitation facilities—conditions which were exacerbated by overcrowding. Lack of space and segregation meant many were made to sleep on floors inside and outside the cells without any blankets or mats. Detainees relied on relatives to bring food, although many were incarcerated without the knowledge of their families.

Mahdi, a young man who initially refused to be screened but then complied because of fear and pressure from his family, told Africa Watch

---

[6] BBC interview, December 1989.

after he received his pink card in December that he "hated and despised" the exercise:

> There are better ways to get at the aliens. To me, as a Kenyan, it's an insult. All of a sudden I'm told "you're not a Kenyan" and that pains me a lot. It's like fighting a war which all along you know you're going to lose—first of all we refused to be screened, but for the ordinary man and woman, well, you just end up in jail and they can do what they like with you. There's no law whatsoever that they're using. What would happen is the way a mafia deals with someone.

> At the screening center, you have to queue. Then when you get inside they ask for your identity card. You give it and they start asking questions, like what your full name is and your grandfather's full name. I've never found it necessary to know my grandfather's full name. They write down maybe eight of these names, then ask you what tribe you are and all the clans. Some of those I didn't know, but I was lucky—there was someone who could identify me. But, if you don't have anyone to do that, then it's really bad news. If you can't get yourself identified, they lock you in a small room and then later take you to a prison.

> So it's really unfair, they judge you by small things. They are trying to say the Somalis are poachers. They are giving reasons which don't have any weight. All the Somalis are poachers? I don't think so! You see they are giving lame reasons to say that all the Somalis are bad.

> After all, is it me that let the aliens in? It's not me who allowed them in in the first place—I'm not an immigration official. They buy their way in, they're not dropped by parachute, are they? They walk in through a border post, they pay money, they live in the country, they bring money with their business, and now, after opening so many businesses, they are told "Hey, you're not to stay here." Okay, they bought ID cards, but the

corruption is not with the Somalis, it's with the government.

The screening has caused—and still will cause—problems. One old man on the screening was asking us very stupid questions—questions he himself didn't know the answer to. Like "where was the first mosque in Eastleigh built?"—and this man is from Mandera. And there is real division among the tribes now. Like me, I went to school with different Somali boys but I didn't bother asking "what tribe are you?." But today I know the difference which is no good to anyone.

I saw a number of people having problems, especially those who didn't speak Swahili. If you don't know Swahili it doesn't mean you're not Kenyan—in Loresho you will find Kikuyus who don't speak Swahili, only English and Kikuyu. The same is with us: in Nairobi, there are Somali people living in communities where we only speak Somali. The youth speak Swahili, but not the old people. But in this screening you're forced to know Swahili—because they say if you don't know, you're not a Kenyan.

Women, who made up more than half of those deported, were at a particular disadvantage where language is concerned. Although Kiswahili is the national language and is estimated to be spoken by some 70-80 percent of the population, many people do not speak it as their first language and a number of communities only speak a local language or a dialect of Kiswahili. Kiswahili has spread through education and trade, but a large proportion of the Somali community living in the North Eastern Province only speak Somali. In Nairobi, many women from the Somali community are unable to speak Kiswahili, largely because of their reduced educational opportunities and the fact that they are less likely, in the urban centers, to be involved in large-scale trading and transporting networks.[7]

Mahdi commented on the predicament facing women:

In most cases, it has been women who are jailed. Men are not caught in big numbers because they know their way out. They are confused about the women—they have jailed women who are from Kenya and women who are from Somalia because they only speak Somali. They don't differentiate because they think once they speak Somali they are all from Somalia.

Women are jailed mostly because in the screening they have all men screening both men and women. They don't have a certain section for women alone. That's bad because you know our women are shy; they can't talk loud and complain about what's being done to them. So the officials just say, okay, you go inside and she cannot defend herself. The best a man can do for her then is to get her out by paying a bond. But the police refuse this as well. The reason they have done this is because they know some men bring a wife from Somalia. Now when he brings her to Kenya and marries her, doesn't that mean she's Kenyan? But no, they harass you, even if you've got kids.

With us, women are the community. So they should keep the language so they can teach the children. But if she gets Swahili then the language is gone—that's why there is a difference. We think the women are going to bring up the children so she has to know Somali. They don't speak Swahili because it is their role to concentrate on Somali tradition, Somali language.

---

[7] In contrast, women do much of the trading from the North Eastern Province into Somalia. Even during full-scale civil war, women traders regularly traveled by foot and vehicles to bring clothes, perfume, stationery, shoes etc. from Mogadishu. The only language used in this network is Somali.

The fact that under Kenyan law, marriage to a Kenyan makes Somali women eligible to be considered Kenyan citizens, was not recognized during the screening. Marriage ceremonies recognized in the Somali community were not necessarily recognized by the state. Many of the poorer members of the community married by religious ceremony, without obtaining an official license. Somali women married to Kenyan citizens also had problems being identified by elders and other members of the community. According to some accounts, this vulnerability was at times compounded by personal rivalries and family disputes associated with polygamy[8]—exploiting the opportunity to get rid of unwanted wives and rivals. In addition, women reportedly had more problems securing people who could vouch for their ancestry because women normally move away from their place of birth into the town or village of their husband. For these reasons, many women were immediately arrested and deported. The tragic consequence of these detentions and deportations was a large number of abandoned children. Africa Watch spoke to one woman named Bilan, who described how she came across six abandoned children:

> I was walking on the corner of 6th Street [in Eastleigh] when I heard a loud cracking noise, so we investigated. It was coming from a house near the street. We could hear crying inside, and someone pushing against the door. We looked through a window and there were six children, all crying and calling for someone to come. The eldest—who was about nine—told us the police had come early in the morning and taken the mother away. The police told them to stay in the house and they would send someone to help them. Then they shut the door on the children, who remained locked inside. That was four or five hours ago, and there was a small baby there being held by her sister.
>
> My friend said we would have to leave them. At that time there were so many of these children without their mothers. But I couldn't leave those children so I told her we must find someone. First, I took them all home to my

---

[8] Polygamy is common among the Kenyan-Somali community, permitted under Islamic law.

mother who told me I was mad—how was I going to find
someone when everybody was in trouble and there were
so many kids around, she said. But I told her to wait, I
think I can find one of their relatives.

So I went to one woman who said yes, I think they are
relatives of so-and-so. I went to that next woman, who
said yes, we know their aunt—and it went on like that
until I found an aunt who said she would have them.
Although she had four of her own children and said she
was expecting the police to come for her any day, but she
told me, if they come, we will all go together.

Africa Watch interviewed a number of people who said they knew
of children abandoned and families separated. One family of seven
children, between 18 months and 12 years of age, reportedly stayed in
the house for two days waiting for their mother to return. They were
discovered by a neighbor who called by chance. The mother had been
arrested at the screening center, detained for three weeks, and then
deported without any opportunity to see her children. The father, a
transporter working in Uganda and Sudan, was not present during the
screening exercise and was unable to defend what other members of the
family insist was his wife's legitimate Kenyan citizenship. Another
woman—who later managed to return to her family—told Africa Watch
that she was stopped without her screening card at a shop one morning
and taken directly to Embakasi police camp where people were held
before being deported. After more than three months she was reunited
with her five children, all under the age of nine, who had been discovered
by a neighbor and taken to relatives.

NO DUE PROCESS OF LAW

All but a small number of businessmen were deported without
any legal representation, consultation or trial. According to one lawyer
who visited the police stations at the time of the screening, people were
not properly charged. He told Africa Watch that:

...the police were not holding those people on any charge
under the Penal Code and there was often no option of

a police bond. They were only holding on behalf of
Nyayo House and using Special Branch powers to detain.
I saw no details recorded in the Occurrence Book—there
were serious departures from police regulations.

Police were said to be obstructive to those attempting to provide
legal assistance. On the few occasions the cell registers were made
available to lawyers, the basis of detention was simply recorded as
screening. Such a charge has no legal validity or constitutional
foundation. Lawyers who were called in to represent certain businessmen
say other people in custody were astonished that lawyers could be used.
The same lawyer continued:

> ...they believed entirely in the power of the government
> and were convinced that lawyers couldn't be involved. In
> fact, many believed that taking a lawyer would make
> their case more difficult, and had been told that
> everything would be solved by the government "in a
> proper manner." They had been convinced that lawyers
> would only damage their case.

Friends and relatives of those in custody said no one believed
they would actually be deported; they regarded it as a threat, but not a
possibility. Most believed that their own case was simply a mistake which
would be sorted out. They pointed out they had gone to the screening
panels because they were confident of their documentation.

POLICE HARASSMENT

Ethnic Somalis have suffered constant harassment and
discrimination from the police; this exercise, said some, was only
distinguished from other procedural operations by its scale and
uniformity. Police behaved as if they had been given special license to
persecute the Somali community during the screening exercise, forcing
entry into homes and businesses, arresting people on the streets and
detaining without charge or trial. Many people complained of harassment
by police. One woman told Africa Watch what happened when police
came for her uncle:

Two policemen came into the house and told my uncle to come with them—we knew what was going to happen to him. They told me to shut up and started to push him out of the house. I told them they were wasting their time—then they said to me, "and I suppose you are the one to get him a card?."

Then they threatened me. They had guns, and one was pointing it at me saying he would shoot me. I said he would never get away with it, that my father and brothers had guns and would kill him for it. The police were very angry—"you dirty shifta." They kept saying, "don't you have any respect?" Then they took my uncle out and said they would come back and deal with me later. They said they wanted to teach me how to respect the police.

The next day they came back for me, but I had gone to my aunt's house. The police told my mother they had come to teach me a lesson, that two or three nights in the cells would teach me respect. They told her they would get me at any time.

But I moved in with my aunt. I heard they came for me nearly every day, sometimes late, always threatening my family. They said they would get me when I came home. After some weeks I left the country.

In another account, a student described to Africa Watch how identity searches by the police stopped people from going out on the streets at night, as if there was an official curfew, but that no one felt safe in their homes either.

The Kenyan-Somalis have had problems with the police for a long, long time—then occasionally, like now, it gets big and grabs the headlines, then the next day it's gone again—but not for us. This has been the worst, especially this house to house, lodge to lodge search. That's really bad because the Kenyan police don't have a disciplined way of approaching anyone—they just come in a rough

manner: "what do you have here?" You see, they always
come as if they're sure you *don't* [original emphasis] have
the documents—just walking straight into your house and
pushing you into the kitchen. They look under beds, in
cupboards; we don't even know what they're looking for.
When they start walking into your house then they are
ruling in your house. That's too much.

In the North Eastern Province a number of threats were made by
the Screening Task Force that there would be house to house checks by
the security forces if people did not observe the screening deadline.
Screening in the NEP was extended three months beyond the original
deadline because of poor attendance at the twenty-six screening
centers—which the government attributed to nomadism. By March 11,
1990, the *Kenya Times* reported that only about 50,000 people had
registered in the NEP. The Garissa KANU branch chair, Aden Nuno, said
the exercise should be extended until the end of March when a "manyatta
to manyatta registration campaign" should be launched. He also told
KANU youthwingers "not to rest after the exercise but to liaise with the
security personnel and report those they suspected had been registered
through dubious means."[9] One Garissa resident told Africa Watch:

Every Kenyan-Somali is unhappy about this screening,
even those puppet leaders here in the North Eastern
Province. They're just doing it to please someone. Our
pockets are really full now—Somalis have to carry three
cards: national ID, the screening card and the KANU
card. The police can get you for any of them and you'd
be in big trouble. They can do anything—the police are
getting out of control completely. They're after
Somalis—if they see you on the street they just call
you—hey! Come here you! You, shifta! I've been stopped
a number of times—since the issue of the poaching
started it's been very serious. They'll call you wherever
you are and you must give them your cards; then they
start telling you you're a poacher. They say—"you, you're
all poachers; you're shifta"—ugly things which make you

---

[9] *Kenya Times*, March 11, 1990.

angry but you can do nothing about it. It's like they're trying to put us in a corner. They're trying to nail us with something. They're trying to prove we're all poachers, that is one thing, and that we are all aliens. If you look at that reasoning—well, even a fool can differentiate. Now it's the Somalis, but it'll go on and on and tomorrow there will be justice for no one. That's where it's heading for.

DEPORTATIONS

Those who failed to get a pink card were detained—some for nearly a month—and then transferred to Embakasi Police College, Nairobi. Some thirty cases had been filed in an attempt to stop the deportations, but most of the applicants abandoned their case or fled the county. Only four cases were brought to court.

Mohamed Kanyare Afrah and Yusuf Osman Gabayare, businessmen, filed applications in court on December 15, 1989, on the basis that they had documentation which proved they were bona fide Kenyan citizens. Mohamed Kanyare Afrah's citizenship was under scrutiny before the screening exercise started; his name was at the top of the list provided by the Department of Immigration to the Somali Probe Committee. Lawyers were unable to obtain a court order to allow them to take the necessary action to stop the commissioner of police and the principal immigration officer from proceeding with summary deportation. Dr. John Khaminwa had served the affidavit and obtained a court order that stayed the deportation of the two men, but the attorney general was unavailable to complete the procedure.

Dr. Khaminwa made a last minute attempt to secure due process by going personally to the attorney general's home on December 16, but was refused entry with the comment from the attorney general that "my home is not an office and I can't be served official documents there." By that time, Kanyare and Gabayare had been taken to Liboi, on the Kenyan-Somali border. Khaminwa went to court on December 18 in an attempt to commit the commissioner of police and the principal immigration officer for contempt of court, but the state council argued that the government was unaware of a court order at the time of deportation. The court said the two men had already been deported and were no longer within Kenya's jurisdiction. Africa Watch has since determined that the two men were in fact still within the Kenyan border at the time of the ruling, but that no effort was made to return them to Nairobi or to halt deportation.

Another businessman, Ahmed Hersi Farah, filed an application on December 20 with an order made for stay of deportation on January 15, 1990. The attorney general said Farah had already been deported by air—in fact he was in Liboi with Kanyare and Gabayare after the Somali Government refused to accept his expulsion by plane.

EMBAKASI POLICE COLLEGE
INTERNMENT AND DEPORTATION

Embakasi Police College is a paramilitary style camp on the outskirts of Nairobi. The first group of about 500 women, men and children were interned at Embakasi to await deportation. A small number of tents had been erected, but most were without adequate shelter and food. Witnesses describe the anguish and misery of the deportees—particularly those who had been separated from children—and the constant appeals to family members to arrange for their release. Access to family and friends was abruptly stopped after three days, and army trucks arrived in the camp to take the deportees to the border zone. Panic ensued when people were forced on to the trucks and many tried to resist. Ambulances were later brought for people apparently suffering from head injuries and broken limbs.

The trucks traveled by night, reaching Garissa early in the morning. Garissa residents say army jeeps, landrovers and a helicopter provided an armed escort to the convoy of about fifty vehicles. Apart from one short break outside Garissa town, the people endured about eighteen hours of travel, packed into the trucks without water or food during daytime high, desert-like temperatures. They reached Liboi at around 6:00 P.M., and were taken directly to an internment area at the border post.

Military personnel and the General Service Unit kept the group under armed guard in the wire-enclosed compound of the border post office. Kenyan military personnel negotiated with Somali border officials to take the group into Somali territory. After three days they were accepted, apparently by instructions issued from Mogadishu.

Two of the businessmen on whom the press had focused were brought to the border in a separate police van and held separately under armed guard. Kanyare was known to be wanted by the Somali government for alleged anti-government activities. The shock of summary deportation, for all the deportees, was accompanied by great fear for their fate in a country divided by civil war. Africa Watch obtained a firsthand account from one of the deportees at the border:

> After a few days, a captain from the Somali army came to negotiate our journey to Somalia. We were taken over the border late one night. The captain gathered us all together and gave us a long lecture about the insecurity in the area and the food shortages. One of the passengers had money on him and used it to buy meat for everybody, but that did not last long. The captain would order his soldiers in front of us to "take animals by force from the local nomads." He would tell them "shoot them in the legs if they resist." Many people refused to eat the food on account of this.

> We were eventually allowed to go into [Dobley] town which was completely deserted. The civilians who normally live there, who are Ogaden, had fled after the army drove the SPM[10] out. Even though the SPM was not in the area, the soldiers were always firing their guns. The captain refused to give us our exit papers, which some people had received, until transport for us arrived from Mogadishu. But we could not wait because conditions were so bad. The area is very bad for malaria and many people got sick but there were no medicines. Anyone who could find the money to pay for the bus left but of course most people had no money on them.

The majority of the deportees continued to protest they were not Somali citizens and produced their Kenyan national identity cards and other documentation. They became distraught at the prospect of being transported to Mogadishu. Once in Mogadishu they were put in a camp in the compound of the Ministry of the Interior building. Eyewitness accounts described the situation of the deportees as pathetic, without

---

[10] Somali Patriotic Movement, fighting in southern Somalia.

shelter and without humanitarian assistance. The group consisted mainly
of women—some of them in an advanced state of pregnancy—and some
men and children, including small babies. They were divided into family
units. Independent witnesses say the extent of the psychological distress
was manifest, including the confusion of the children, and the desperation
of adults to return to their families and property in their home country.
At least three died from lack of food, shelter and medical assistance.

Somalia's only human rights lawyer, Dr. Ismail Jumaale, reported
before his death on July 22, 1990, that deportees from Kenya began
arriving in January in groups of 100-300, and were still arriving in June
although the Somali government had refused to accept any more.
Jumaale had over two thousand such cases on file. He said about one
hundred initially proved to be Somali citizens, and left to seek assistance
from friends and relatives. But the remaining group continued to insist
that they were Kenyan citizens and none sought refugee status nor
claimed Somali citizenship. Many were unable to communicate adequately
in Somali and all continued to produce Kenyan national identity cards,
passports and party membership cards as evidence of their status.
Jumaale composed a dossier of the cases and presented it to the Ministry
of the Interior in April. An investigating committee verified that these
people were not Somali citizens.

The situation of the Kenyan-Somali deportees was unique—not
refugees, exiles, deportees nor fugitives—but simply stateless. The
inability of international organizations to categorize them left them
without any real assistance. United Nations Under-Secretary General,
Abdulrahim Farah, visited the Embakasi camp after coming under
pressure from independent witnesses. He promised to take action through
quiet diplomacy and instructed the UN to do everything possible to assist
the deportees. No assistance was forthcoming, however, other than some
food parcels from the United Nations Development Program. Other
international aid organizations said they were hampered by limited
resources. The Secretary General of the Organisation of African Unity
(OAU), Salim Ahmed Salim, said he would speak to Kenyan and Somali
ambassadors but said the OAU had no powers to act on their behalf.
Africa Watch wrote to the secretary general, pointing out that a group of
African people expelled from their country and currently stateless in
another African country to which they had been forcibly deported, had a
right to expect a humanitarian response from the OAU.

Jumaale wrote to the Kenyan government asking why these
people were made stateless. He asked why the deportations were carried

out without due process of law, leaving family and properties in Kenya. A copy of the letter was circulated to the Kenyan press by Jumaale, but it was not published by any of the national papers. He also sent an open letter to Kenyan lawyers, dated March 27, 1990, appealing to them to intervene with the government. He wrote:

> In my capacity as a lawyer who is concerned with the question of Human Rights, I have been approached by more than 1,500 persons who are complaining of unjust and illegal deportations from Kenya, a country [of which] they claim to be its citizens.
>
> For some time now, in collaboration with some international agencies, I have been investigating this matter and have established that the majority of these people do possess the following documents which testify to their Kenyan citizenship:
>
> a) Kenyan Identification Card;
> b) KANU Party Membership Card;
> c) Kenyan Birth Certificates;
> d) Kenyan passports.
>
> The Life Membership to the KANU Party were issued to these people by the State President.
>
> It is important that during the screening operations no considerations were given to the possession of these documents. Almost all the deportees were picked up and removed by the Kenyan police. Despite being discriminatory and unconstitutional, this action poses some questions.
>
> Was it not proper to take those involved to law courts and prove to them the nature of the crimes they had committed to deserve expulsion from [their] home country? Was it not also in the event that the decision to deport them had been made, [fair] to allow them to remain in Kenya enough time in order to place their property under proper care? Most of those concerned do

not know the fate of their children and wives left in Kenya.

These people are being accused of being ethnic Somalis... the fact that the North East Province is inhabited by Somalis has been overlooked. Somalis who originally came into Kenya from Somalia live in Kenya as one of the many other ethnic communities and had acquired their nationality in accordance with the constitution of the State.

What is the significance of treating ethnic Somalis differently from other ethnic groups anyway? Like issuing them with special ID cards and other documents. Are the authorities engineering another "Separate Development Scheme" in a black African country?

Jumaale illustrated the flagrant breach of law by pointing out that Ahmed Hersi Farah was deported after a Kenyan court decided he was a genuine citizen.

CLIMATE OF PERSECUTION AND FEAR

In practice, the screening exercise was never officially brought to an end, although government officials said it stopped in March 1990. It has, instead, become institutionalized because all ethnic Somalis over the age of eighteen are expected to have obtained the pink card in order to participate in almost every sphere of life. The cards are essential for the purpose of all state services and bureaucracy, including education, trade, land and financial transactions, and for internal and external travel.

House-to-house searches, loss of family, harassment of businesses and traders and arbitrary arrests on the streets characterized the sort of persecution experienced throughout the Kenyan-Somali community in the main urban centers. Seven thousand ethnic Somalis in Mombasa went into hiding according to the Coast Provincial Commissioner, Simeon Mung'ala.[11] In the North Eastern Province even greater use was made

---

[11] *Kenya Sunday Times*, December 3, 1989.

by the security forces and administration of the emergency legislation. Strict and frequent identity checks, restriction on trading and employment, and a blanket policing of movement intensified under the screening. Whole communities were being "internally deported" to areas designated by local officials and security personnel. In February, 400 families[12] were moved from the Tana River district across the Somali border.

AFTERMATH

If the government's goal was to expel illegal aliens from the ethnic Somali community, then the exercise was a decisive failure. Many of the people who were forced to flee Kenya during the height of the screening exercise have returned to the country. Some who were deported to Somalia made their way back to the border. Widespread corruption in the security forces and the administration made a mockery of the exercise, despite government claims that it had been a great success.

But the aftermath is not just a feeling of deep resentment and insecurity in the Kenyan-Somali community. Some of the victims of the exercise now live a clandestine existence in their own country, unable to leave their homes for fear of discovery. Africa Watch interviewed one such person:

> I don't known how it all happened. I went to the Screening Center and presented all my documents. The elders were there and a group of people inspecting the documents. The elders knew me well and two of them signed my papers.
>
> Then someone came and said "I know this man; let's not give him a card"—then left the room. Everyone was surprised, but I was taken to Pangani Police station. Even then, I was not worried and I just told my son, who was outside, to go home and I would come soon. In Pangani I was not under arrest, just held with about twenty-five

---

[12] A conservative estimate would put this number at around 4,000 people.

other people. It was filthy. They keep about fifty people
in one cell—no sanitation, no light and you can't stretch
your legs. The food was just one piece of bread and one
mug of tea in the morning. In the evening we got one
small dish of *ugali* [maize meal]. The police were
bad—not at all civil—said we had no rights anyway and no
food was allowed to be brought from family.

They took some away to Kasarani [police station], which
was a little better—but the cells are the same condition
and the police beat anyone who speaks. On one occasion,
they put me in a small room and just beat me down to
the floor. I still thought it was a mistake and soon
someone would come and release me.

Then I was taken to Embakasi where all the people had
been collected for deportation. They had built about 100
tents and so there were about six to every one of those
small tents. There was no sanitation, people just had to
do what they could to try and keep clean. We got food
twice—just bread and ugali. The children there were
crying a lot because there was nothing for them. We had
to buy cartons of milk for the children from outside. We
were guarded by Administration Police which wasn't too
bad because they didn't interfere with us—just guarded
us.

At around 6:00 P.M. one day about twenty-five army
trucks came. They made us get into the trucks and put
about twenty-five of us in each truck, guarded by four
Administration Police. We pleaded with them to give us
a chance to tell our children and family where we were
going but they refused. No one was allowed to see us.
The trucks started moving towards Garissa.

One old man in my vehicle had asthma and a kidney
problem; he was always needing to urinate. But they
refused to let the vehicle stop, they just held his
shoulders and made him do it from the side while the

vehicle was driving. We all felt very bad for him—I've never seen anything like that.

At Garissa the next day, about 9:00 A.M., we got tea and a five minute break, then started moving again to Liboi, followed by two army helicopters. We arrived around midday and they put us in an open area surrounded by wire at the border.

That place was terrible. There was no shelter through the day, not even at midday. Anyway, people were treated just like animals by the army and the Administration Police. Because there was nothing—no shade, no food, no water or sanitation—the women started throwing tins at the police. They were beaten up with sticks.

We were there for two days. They gave us food once, which was just two cans and one packet of biscuits. The children were getting in a worse and worse state—crying and vomiting, some had diarrhoea. We asked some of the police to get water for the children. They did; but it was dirty water.

The Somali army came after two days—a captain and two lieutenants. They talked with the Kenyan army and said they would take us. We said, "before you take us, please let us take our families and children and properties as well." I had left my family and my shops and even my vehicle. Everybody was like that. Anyway, some people had trucks and vehicles ready for them at the screening place in case they had to make a run, but I had just put my son in and told him to go.

The trucks came and took us to Mogadishu. In Mogadishu we went to Dr. Jumaale, a group of us, and he collected all the information and opened a file. There was no food in the camp at all—we just relied on people taking pity on us. Some left and went to find relatives. This camp was only about 100 meters square and there

were about 300 women and children there as well as the
men. We let the children stay inside the trees where
there was some shade.

Anyway, I got what we called [a] "letter of deportation"
from the Somali government saying what had happened,
and I went with it to Mandera, back to the border. At the
border, Kenyan immigration gave me a one month visa
because I told them I must sort everything out. Then I
went to Immigration at Nyayo House to get an
extension; but the official there said the immigration
people at Mandera were wrong and I wasn't entitled to
a visa at all. I told him I need three months to collect
everything—my family and properties—but he said no and
called the police. They put me in a cell then took me to
Langata police station.

Langata—well—it was terrible of course, with about
twenty people in a small cell. If you're sick and call for
assistance, they never reply. They beat people all the
time—sometimes on order, sometimes just to satisfy
themselves. I was in there for fourteen days. They told
me I can't have a lawyer, that I'm not authorized to call
or appoint a lawyer. I argued but they said we have no
rights; they said we had no right to "interfere with the
immigration authorities." They told me they would
deport me at their own convenience. Then, one night at
around midnight, they came for me and took me to the
Garissa bus stop in Eastleigh.

Mohamed (not his real name) bribed the police to leave him at
the bus stop. He described how people deported to Somalia used
whatever means they had to get back into Kenya. Most, he believes, have
managed to return; and most have managed to trace missing family
members. Children whose parents had been taken were mostly being
looked after by next-door neighbors in the belief that one day the parents
would manage to return. Many of the families that remained, however,
complained of continued police harassment. Mohamed said:

Now I have no ID—all my documents were taken by the screening officials—so I just stay with my family at home. I can't make any movements or work or set up business or even draw money. I'm very much alone, and I spend my time wondering how I'm going to work, how am I going to feed my family? I don't have the liberty to work and live properly. I lost about 1 million [Kenyan Shillings equal to $38,462] with my business. I can't even use a bank.

Police are on ID patrols in streets everywhere. But they don't know where I am because I hide in different houses. I don't think they'll ever leave us alone—it's become a business now. If you don't have ID you give money. You have to buy from the screening people and immigration—something like this, it can go on forever. There's so much discrimination against Somalis here. It's an everlasting problem with no end. No one knows what to do.

But then I think, surely there must be a solution. Am I a refugee?—I don't even have documents to travel with; the government will never accept if I apply for documents. And if we give our names? Even if we give our names to organizations to ask for help?—of course, we will be arrested. Whenever they see a Somali, they have to harass you. And if you lose your card, you can't get a replacement because who can dare to go to the authorities? If you lose it, you go to jail. If you're lucky, then you bribe. Look at my life: if anyone comes to my house, I have to hide. I spend all my days hiding; listening for noises and voices—following my fear to different houses. I think my life is in danger.

On June 14, 1991, police began another roundup of ethnic Somalis in Nairobi. In what was described as "an obviously calculated operation" by one eyewitness, police and plainclothes officers raided hotels, guest houses, restaurants, bars and houses and seized people of Somali nationality. The majority of those arrested had visitors' visas issued by the Immigration Department, which gave them the right to stay in the country. Eyewitnesses said the operation swept through all areas of the city causing panic, and thousands were held in police stations overnight before being taken to Embakasi Police College.

17
THE SHOOT-TO-KILL POLICY

In practice, Kenyan police have a shoot-to-kill mandate, but this has not been officially sanctioned as a nationwide government policy. Official policy is a patchwork: there is a shoot-to-kill policy in the gameparks (see chapter fifteen), in the North Eastern Province, on the borders, and a shoot-to-kill policy was introduced during the July demonstrations. There is an increasing unease about the frequency of police killings, especially those where the suspect is unarmed and constitutes no threat to the public or to the security officers. The following cases illustrate the circumstances in which people have been shot dead by police officers.

•   Raymond Ang'awa, a 17-year-old schoolboy from Kariobangi South, Nairobi, was shot dead by police on April 5, 1990. An officer has been charged with his murder but has not yet come to trial. According to eyewitness accounts, three uniformed police and one plainclothes policeman on patrol in the area started to chase a group of youths who were standing near a kiosk in the Kariobangi suburb. An eyewitness living near the kiosk described the shooting:

Raymond ran towards our gate but he tripped and fell down. The uniformed policemen caught up with him and shot him several times while on the ground. I could not believe my eyes. The fallen boy was sprayed with bullets—I started shouting, and people were running down the street towards us. One policeman grabbed Raymond telling him to stand up or I'll finish you. The boy tried to stand but was unable to. Then they let go of him because they realized that the crowd were about to confront them, and told the one who

had shot the boy to disappear, leaving two
uniformed and the other one.[1]

    The boy was shot fifty meters from his parents
house in the company of his friends. No one knew
what crime the police suspected him or the other
youths of committing. Raymond died on arrival at the
Aga Khan Hospital.

- The public killing of an escaping prisoner in central
  Nairobi was witnessed by crowds on October 23, 1990.
  A young man broke free from prison guards as he was
  escorted from the court to the prison van. He was shot
  once as he bent to get through the wire of the Law
  Court parking lot, but managed to continue running
  some distance before a prison guard shot him several
  times, including fatal shots to the body and head. The
  prisoner was on remand for a petty offense and had
  not been sentenced. Police and prison guards refused
  to release his name to the press.

- A farmer in Kiambu, Stephen Karanja was arrested on
  April 8, 1987, in connection with police investigations
  into a robbery. He was shot dead by a police
  officer—allegedly in a nearby forest—on April 12 and
  buried at an undisclosed location. His family was not
  notified of his arrest, death or burial. After his wife
  filed a habeas corpus in June, Judge Derek Schofield
  ordered the police to find the body. In spite of an
  exhumation at the spot where the police said the body
  had been buried, they were unable to produce it. The
  police were said to be looking for "a male body with a
  bullet hole in his forehead."[2] The body has never
  been produced. After Judge Schofield threatened the
  Director of the Criminal Investigations Department
  with contempt of court for failing to produce
  Karanga's body, former Chief Justice Miller transferred
  the case to another judge.

---

[1] *Sunday Standard*, April 8, 1990.

[2] *Weekly Review*, August 7, 1987.

REPORTING CASES

In 1990, there were fifty-three reported cases of people shot and killed nationwide by police and prison guards (see below for list). This is not an accurate reflection of the number of people killed by the security forces because many cases—particularly in the provinces—are not reported by the national press. This is readily conceded by the Nairobi police chief, Godfrey Kinoti. When he was interviewed by the *Weekly Review* on November 16, 1990 about the "alarming increase" in the number of suspected criminals shot dead by police in Nairobi, Kinoti said that "the rise in the number of police shootings of suspects reported in the media may be attributed to the media becoming more active in reporting such incidents."

The number of police killings has increased as the force becomes more heavily armed and with more sophisticated weapons. After the 1982 attempted coup, the police force was reinforced with a new issue of firearms and older model rifles were replaced with up-to-date equipment, including submachine guns and G3 rifles. Before 1982, many police patrols carried only batons and handcuffs. During their six months' basic training, all police recruits are taught to use firearms, and learn basic relevant laws; but critics maintain this training is inadequate for such a large, well-armed police force.

A RIGHT TO KILL?

According to the Constitution, a police officer has the right to shoot and kill a suspect "in exceptional circumstances." In Section 71, 2(b) it is stated that:

> A person shall not be regarded as having been deprived of his life in contravention of this section if he dies as the result of the use of force to such an extent as is *reasonably justified* [emphasis added] in the circumstances of the case, in order to effect a lawful arrest to prevent the escape of a person lawfully detained.

The qualification "reasonably justified in the circumstances" has been open to interpretation. Section 28 of the Police Act is more specific as to the circumstances under which a police officer may lawfully use firearms:

> A police officer may use arms against (a) any person in lawful custody and charged with or convicted of a felony, when such a person is escaping or attempting to escape; (b) any person who by force rescues or attempts to rescue another from lawful custody; (c) any person who by force prevents or attempts to prevent the lawful arrest of himself or of any other person.

Parliament sanctioned the shoot-to-kill policy in the game parks in 1988, but the issue of a nationwide policy has not been debated since 1980. In 1980, former Attorney General Charles Njonjo, was asked in parliament about the circumstances under which policemen were empowered to shoot when dealing with suspects. He replied: "the police have my authority to shoot-to-kill." When criticised by some MP's, Njonjo said that the practice of shoot-to-kill was consistent with the country's legal system, and justified it on the grounds that "we do not want people threatening our lives...we do not want to live in fear and have our homes protected like prisons because of insecurity."[3]

Two months after Njonjo gave this statement, certain members of parliament pressured the new attorney general, James Karugu, to articulate his views on the policy after police gunned down Alfred Bengo Ong'eta, mistakenly identified as a criminal. MPs Koigi wa Wamwere, Nakuru North, and Abuya Abuya, Kisii, put forward motions in parliament to rescind Njonjo's shoot-to-kill order. Karugu decreed that:

> Our police have received instructions about the law on this subject and nothing I say here is intended to deter them in their war against crime. But I must remind them, however, that there is a presumption in law that every person intends the natural consequences of his acts. Therefore they must know that they are accountable for their acts as individuals. They must remember that shooting to deprive a person of his life is an extreme step that can only be justified by extreme circumstances.

---

[3] *Daily Nation*, March 26, 1980.

Although he stressed that "the use of a firearm by a trigger-happy policeman would be illegal," he did not sufficiently clarify to what extent a shoot-to-kill policy was in fact operational. He strongly defended a shoot-to-kill policy against armed and violent robbers, saying in such circumstances "a police officer would not only be justified but bound by law to use such force as is reasonable in the circumstances."[4]

INTERNATIONAL STANDARDS

International standards on use of firearms asserts that: "Law-enforcement officials, in carrying out their duty, shall, as far as possible, apply non-violent means before resorting to the use of force or firearms." The United Nations also recommends that governments should: "Specify the circumstances under which law enforcement officials are authorized to carry firearms and prescribe the types of firearms and ammunition permitted"; and "Ensure that firearms are used only in appropriate circumstances and in a manner likely to decrease the risk of unnecessary harm."[5]

Since the parliamentary debate in 1980, there have been no further interpretations of the shoot-to-kill policy. When asked about it in relation to the shooting of Raymond Ang'awa (see above), the Commissioner of Police, Philip Kilonzo, said it was "specified by law"[6]. President Moi publicly condemned the shooting, saying the officer responsible would answer for the "callous and shocking act." The officer was charged with murder, but the case has not yet been heard.

In other less publicized cases, public anger has provoked scenes of mob justice, threatening the life of the police officers involved. In June 1988, for example, a suspect was caught by two police officers. He was handcuffed and marched down a main Nairobi street before one of the

---

[4] *Daily Nation*, June 19, 1980.

[5] Conclusions and recommendations, Interregional Preparatory Meeting for the Eighth United Nations Congress on the Prevention of Crime and the Treatment of Offenders, September 1990.

[6] *Sunday Standard*, April 8, 1990.

policemen opened fire, killing him with three bullets. The police officer barely escaped a large crowd.[7]

SHOOTING-TO-MAIM

According to Kenyan law, when the police intend to prevent a suspect from fleeing arrest, they are required to shoot-to-maim. Section 28 of the Police Act contains a provision on the use of arms, according to which:

> Arms shall not be used as authorized unless the officer has reasonable grounds to believe that he cannot otherwise prevent escape, and unless he gives warning to such person that he is about to use arms against him and the warning unheeded.

> The officer must have reasonable grounds to believe that he or any other person is in danger of grievous bodily harm or that he cannot otherwise prevent the rescue or as the case may be to effect arrest.

It is unlawful for a police officer to shoot if the person escaping is a minor offender and poses no threat, even if there is no other way to affect arrest. A person in custody must have been charged with a felony before shooting is considered justifiable. The shooting of a fleeing suspect, however, is common practice. There have been many reported cases of unarmed petty thieves shot whilst fleeing.

According to Nairobi Police Chief Kinoti, Kenyan police are trained to immobilize, not to kill; the evidence, however, proves otherwise. In most reported cases, suspects are shot in the head or back whilst fleeing. No police officer was reported killed or wounded during the most intense period of police killings in 1990, when in October alone there were fifteen reported killings by police in Nairobi.

There have been other incidents of police flagrantly abusing their firearms to shoot and kill merely for disobedience, or when someone fails to follow their instructions or meet their demands. In May 1991, for

---

[7] Africa Watch interview.

example, an Administration Policeman shot at a matatu driver when he refused to stop.

SHOOTING TO KILL AT THE BORDER

According to anonymous testimony given to Africa Watch by a security official, a shoot-to-kill policy is in operation on the border regions, justified as defense of the nation. However, the army and security forces frequently fail to distinguish between those who are hostile intruders, and those who are merely carrying arms for the purpose of defending themselves and their livestock. In the North Eastern Province, the security forces can use shoot-to-kill with impunity.

Police officers have been charged with the murder of innocent civilians, as in the case of Raymond Ang'awa, but these are the exception rather than the rule. The list below which details recent cases involving the shoot-to-kill policy has been compiled on the basis of information contained in the national press. The list indicates the necessity for the government to clarify it's shoot-to-kill policy and to introduce—and abide by—far stricter measures of discipline for its security forces on this issue.

TABLE 2
SHOOT-TO-KILL CASES FROM JANUARY 1990 TO MAY 1991

Date	Circumstances
January 3, 1990	A suspected gangster was shot dead by police when a gang of five men stormed into the residence of the Nyanza Deputy Provincial Commissioner. The two policemen on guard shot and killed one man, while the others escaped.
January 17, 1990	Two suspected robbers were shot following a chase in Nairobi.
January 29, 1990	Two Somali bandits shot dead in a shoot-out with security officers in the Kilifi District/Tana River border.

February 21, 1990	A suspected Ugandan cattle-rustler shot dead in the Gituamba area along the slopes of Mount Elgon in Trans-Nzoia District.
February 26, 1990	A man mourning the death of Robert Ouko was shot when GSU and riot police opened fired on mourners at the Moi Stadium in Kisumu. It was reported that he was beaten by security men and died the following day at the New Nyanza General Hospital.
April 2, 1990	Bandit killed by security forces in Tana River District.
April 10, 1990	Seventeen-year-old schoolboy shot dead by police who tried to disperse a group outside the boy's home on the Kariobangi South Estate, Nairobi.
April 26, 1990	Two men shot dead and a third wounded after a watchman told the police that the men were "behaving suspiciously" in a Nairobi shopping center in the Westlands area.
May 2, 1990	Bandit killed by security forces in Garissa, about nine kilometers from the Somali border, after a gang allegedly attacked the Aruma Adminstration Police camp.
May 8, 1990	A suspected car thief was shot dead by police in Outering Road Estate in Nairobi.
May 9, 1990	A gangster was shot dead by police after he and three others had reportedly robbed an Asian wholesaler of 5,000 shillings ($192) on Keekokork Road, Nairobi.
May 28, 1990	Two suspected bandits "from a neighboring country" killed by security personnel in Garissa, reported by Garissa District Commissioner Francis Sigei.
June 12, 1990	Three remand prisoners shot dead in Bungoma by police as they were allegedly trying to escape. Six other prisoners were wounded.
June 14, 1990	Two suspected robbers shot dead by police in Mombasa.

June 25, 1990	Two suspects shot dead by Bungoma police in Mount Elgon area.
June 28, 1990	A member of a gang allegedly terrorizing motorists along Nairobi/Mombasa road shot dead by police.
July 11, 1990	Three suspected robbers were shot dead by police in Murang'a.
September 22, 1990	Meru police shot and killed a man they suspected of being the leader of a gang which they claimed had been terrorizing residents.
October 16, 1990	Police shot and killed five robbers (one woman and four men) outside Ngarai Brilliant Hotel. They had allegedly broken into Zodiak Fashion Shop on Keekorok Road and stolen goods worth 123,375 shillings ($4,745). A sixth person escaped.
October 30, 1990	Nairobi police gunned down and killed three suspected robbers and seriously wounded two others after a car chase through the city center.
October 31, 1990	Two suspected robbers shot dead by police in the Kariobangi South Estate, Nairobi.
November 2, 1990	Suspected gangsters shot dead by police in a Nairobi city estate.
December 14, 1990	Man shot and wounded by a stray bullet as police fired shots to disperse group of protesting students at Laikipia College Campus, Naivasha. Gitahi Ngaruro, Assistant Minister for Agriculture, and James Mwaura, Nakuru acting District Commissioner, said man was shot dead. Peter Oloo Aringo, Minister for Education, denied the death.
December 17, 1990	A watchman guarding a restaurant in Limuru was shot dead by an Administration Policeman. Police officer charged with the murder.
December 27, 1990	Police killed leader of a six-man gang which had allegedly killed four people in Meru.

December 27, 1990   Police killed gang leader in Elburgon township.

December 27, 1990   Policeman beat farmer to death after arresting him
                           while shouting at Kilome Trading Center in Mukaa
                           Location of Machakos District. The police officer was
                           arrested.

February 2, 1991   Police shot and killed a man at Kencom bus stop in
                           Nairobi after chasing him through the streets. He had
                           allegedly tried to steal a bag.

March 17, 1991   Ugandan bandit was killed by police in Busia.

March 18, 1991   Two armed robbers killed by police after a gang stole
                           300,000 shillings ($11,538) from a house.

March 20, 1991   Two suspects, thought to be part of the gang that took
                           part in the above robbery, shot dead by police
                           following an abortive robbery in Nairobi South C
                           Estate.

May 3, 1991   Police shot and killed a man suspected of being the
                           mastermind behind a number of robberies in the
                           Kakamega District.

May 16, 1991   Nakuru police shot and killed one of six gangsters
                           who had reportedly robbed several petrol stations in
                           the town.

18
NORTHERN KENYA
A VIOLENT OCCUPATION

The dry plains northwest of Lake Turkana and the semiarid regions of northern Kenya have been the settings for some of the most vicious security operations mounted by the government. Ruled under a state of emergency as part of the Northern Frontier District until 1963, northern Kenya is a volatile and isolated region characterized by cattle-rustling and border disputes. In July 1989, a border dispute culminated in the massacre of at least 500 civilians and the annexation of some 14,000 square kilometers of territory by Kenyan security forces.

The fluidity of the Kenyan, Sudanese and Ethiopian borders has led to frequent disputes and changes of allegiance at the local level. At times, the scale of these regional conflicts has led to national disputes and retaliatory forays by national security forces. The Kenyan government, for example, has often accused the Ugandan government of invading its territory, although district officials on both sides of the border consider armed groups as part of normal cattle-rustling and maintain close cooperation.

The government arms sectors of the population and depends on them to protect its interests at the border, and, according to information given to Africa Watch, a shoot-to-kill policy is in force.[1] In some areas, the government has resorted to handing out more weapons locally, contradicting its policies aimed at reducing them. More guns have been given to the regional Home Guard and militia. More stringent penalties have been introduced to control illegal weapons in an attempt to reduce their number, and to contain powerful local groups. The proliferation of sophisticated weapons has made it necessary for some nomadic and pastoralist communities to acquire guns for defensive purposes; but this in turn makes them a legitimate target according to the security forces.

Much of the instability in the region has resulted from the availability of rifles and automatic guns since the late 1970s. The replacement of traditional weapons by modern equipment has changed

---

[1] Africa Watch interview with an anonymous member of the security forces.

the dynamics of cattle-rustling, and has led to the rise of well-equipped groups of up to 200 to 300 raiders. These small armies, known locally as *ngoroko* (another term for bandit), are often led by former members of the security forces who use their military training to maximize the use of automatic weapons.[2] Many such groups survive almost exclusively on raiding and banditry, and are detached from the local community. Traditional cattle-rustling—normally carried out to increase depleted herds or to acquire animals for celebration and ritual purposes—has now become a significant security risk.

PUSHING THE BOUNDARIES

In 1988, the Kenyan government took advantage of events to unilaterally redraw the map by annexing an area of some 14,000 square kilometers of Sudanese territory, known as the Elemi Triangle.[3] The first indication that Kenya was interested in the area—which reportedly may have reserves of oil and minerals—came after President Moi visited the region in May 1988. In July 1988, a large cattle raid on the Kenya, Sudan and Ethiopia border escalated into a major retaliatory action by the Kenyan security forces. At least 500 civilians were massacred by the security forces, who used helicopter gunships and jets to strafe villages in territory subsequently annexed by Kenya.[4] By January 1989, Kenya had

---

[2] Large-scale raids have been known to use rocket-propelled grenades and automatic machine guns. Many weapons were taken from neighboring Uganda as the regime of former President Idi Amin collapsed in 1979-80. In 1980, Turkana from Kenya mounted a coordinated attack on Ugandan police posts and undertook raids as far as 200 kilometers inside northern Uganda. Thousands of weapons were brought back into northern Kenya, captured from the fleeing Ugandan soldiers. Some 250,000 head of cattle were also brought into northern Kenya, including diseased and infected herds. As a result, thousands of cattle in Kenya died in 1980.

[3] The Elemi Triangle borders on Ethiopian territory as well.

[4] An estimated 200 participants in the raiding group were killed as well as 500 civilians. Interviews given to Africa Watch by local residents in northern Kenya, medical personnel, aid officials and church members were on an anonymous basis. These sources have given different estimates of the number

completed official annexation and the *Kenya Times* ran front page stories calling for the banning of maps which showed the area to belong to Sudan.

THE KIBISH MASSACRE

On July 28, 1988, a large group of well-armed Nyangatom[5] raiders moved through the disputed Elemi Triangle, attacking and raiding the Mirele,[6] and into southern Ethiopia where they took a large number of cattle. Returning from an attack on Koroko, they moved north of a Kenyan police post and picked up some Turkana cattle. The raiders—"very heavily armed with automatic guns and possibly mortars"[7]—then encountered Kenyan police from the Kibish police post who had been sent to intercept them. The Kenyan police were poorly matched against such an army and soon ran out of ammunition. Fifteen Kenyan police were killed immediately; four were reported in the national press as having had their throats cut. Some police were taken hostage and uniforms and weapons were seized. Ethiopian security forces, assisted by herders who had lost their cattle, pursued the raiders who retreated into the hills. The Kenyan government was alerted, and on July 29, 1988, the District Commissioner from Lodwar, the provincial capital, was flown to Kibish.

---

killed, but all independent accounts put the number above 500. As there is no conclusive evidence for a higher figure, Africa Watch has taken 500 as the most conservative estimate, but believes more than this number were probably killed.

[5] Nyangatom is the Ethiopian name for a small group (about 5,000) of semi-pastoralists living primarily in the Lower Omo Valley. These people are known to the Kenyans as the Dongiro. They are part of the same ethnic grouping as the Kenyan Turkana, the Ugandan Karamojong and the Sudanese Taposa.

[6] The Mirele, also cattle owners and semi-pastoralists, live primarily inside the Kenyan border: they are known as the Dassenetch in Ethiopia.

[7] Information from anonymous testimony given to Africa Watch and corroborated by a member of the security forces involved who described the raiders as "carrying very powerful and sophisticated Soviet-made weapons."

The response by the Kenyan government was dramatic. More than fifteen transport planes flew in military supplies, equipment and GSU units to Kibish. Ground reinforcements were sent in on August 1 and 2. Eleven GSU vehicles, three armored personnel carriers and ten army trucks traveled through Lodwar at night, and did not return until August 15. Lodwar provided 8,000 liters of fuel for the action, at the request of the District Officer. Two jets made more than thirty trips from positions in North Kachodo. After the first report in the national press about the police killings, there was a news blackout.[8]

It is estimated that at least 200 raiders were killed when attacked by Kenyan helicopter gunships and paramilitary forces. Helicopter gunships then went on to attack the Kibish settlement, which had reportedly already been strafed by the two jets. At least five small villages were strafed by the Kenyans inside the Ethiopian border, including Nakua settlement.

Many hundreds of people are said to have been killed in the attack. Injured security personnel flown to Lodwar hospital and on to Nairobi claimed "nearer a thousand" had died. A Lodwar surgeon was provided with a military uniform and flown to Kibish during the first week. He was afterwards given immediate leave. From July 29 to August 15, there were many reports of deaths. A highly-placed official in Lodwar said that Kenyan troops had also carried out a retaliatory massacre in a Sudanese Taposa village.[9] The killings at Kibish have never been officially acknowledged.

THE ELEMI TRIANGLE

Soon after the massacre, on November 1, 1989, Kibish was officially opened by Kenya as a new division. The official annexation of the territory triggered an angry response from the Sudanese government,

---

[8] Two BBC reports confirmed movement of Kenyan paramilitary units and aircraft in response to clashes in the Elemi triangle.

[9] The attack came at a time when the rebel Sudan People's Liberation Army (SPLA) had taken control of much of the adjacent Sudan border. The SPLA, which was receiving food and logistical support from the Kenya government, said many of the Taposa were government militia.

and diplomatic relations were temporarily broken. The area, however, was surrounded by territory controlled by the Sudan People's Liberation Army and there was little the Sudan government could do beyond making diplomatic protests.

A month before Kibish officially became Kenyan territory, former British Minister for Foreign Affairs Sir Geoffrey Howe, flew to Lodwar to inspect development projects funded by the European Community (EC). This included inspection of the Turkana Rehabilitation Project (TRP), which played a major role in "Kenyanizing" the Kibish area.

As part of the TRP, a Kenyan population was moved into Kibish through a resettlement scheme. Turkana settlements in northern Kenya were each requested to send ten to fifteen people for resettlement in Kibish, and families who moved into Kibish were provided with small numbers of livestock. The TRP was EC funded, and managed by a Norwegian administrator in Lodwar. After resettlement began, initially under the supervision of expatriate personnel, the project was Africanized. Kenyan personnel took over the management of the project at Kibish in 1988, as well as the Turkana Water Project.

A major reshuffle in provincial and district administration followed the annexation of Kibish. New district commissioners and district officers were brought in at Lokitong, Kibish Division, and local chiefs were replaced. The building of fifty government houses and offices in Kibish began soon after the massacre—a GSU camp, a Kenyan police camp and an Administration Police camp were built, as well as administration offices. The EC provided food for work in the area, and the Norwegian Development Agency (NORAD), established a new bore hole.

BACKGROUND

Imposing Rule

The small, original population of the Kibish people, the Nyangatom, was estimated to be between 2,000 and 3,000 individuals. After the demarcation of the frontier in 1907 by the colonial government, Nyangatom communities planted sorghum inside the Kenyan border. They were gradually pushed back by the Turkana, who were under attack from the British colonialists. Up to the 1940s, the British mounted a series of bloody campaigns against the Turkana to force them to lay down their weapons. Over 250,000 head of cattle were seized by the

British in their efforts to subdue the communities, which, according to research carried out in the area, effectively institutionalized cattle-rustling.

Ruled under a state of emergency like the rest of the Northern Frontier District, the area was left administratively isolated by the British. It was regarded as a buffer zone and served to hold back Italian expansion and protect the "White Highlands." Kibish was officially Sudanese and Ethiopian territory, but the Kenyans retained a police post inside the region which they had administered for the Sudanese in 1939.[10] By 1942, the Turkana were allowed by the British colonial government to graze their cattle up to and into the Elemi Triangle, and along military posts known as "the red line." In the mid-1960s, Lake Turkana rose and flooded agricultural land, forcing back the Turkana once again.

Cattle-rustling, skirmishes and shifting alliances have since characterized the region—problems compounded by the introduction of sophisticated weapons.[11] The policy of the newly independent government was to increase the number of Home Guards for defensive purposes. Turkana Home Guards are now given a rifle and twenty-five bullets, and are answerable to the police administration. They have no distinguishing uniform, but can be called upon at any time to assist the security forces. Different areas have different means of mobilizing Home Guard units. In many areas the Home Guards are disciplined and respected elders of the community employed to patrol rather than fight; in other areas, particularly border regions and destabilized regions, Home Guards are more akin to a militia, first to be sent into trouble spots and subsequently backed up by the security forces, if necessary.

Lokichokio, 1988

The Kibish raid came only three months after a major security operation nearby on the Kenya-Sudan border. On April 13, a dawn raid on thirty settlements in the Lokichokio division of Turkana district resulted in 192 villagers killed and fifty injured. The rustlers were well-

---

[10] The territory was handed over to Kenyan administration by the British while new border posts were being set up along the Ethiopian border.

[11] At least 5,000 to 6,000 people have been killed as a result of cattle-rustling in the last fifteen years, according to the findings of cattle projects in the region.

armed, carrying automatic and semiautomatic weapons. Four hundred raiders retreated across the Sudan border with an estimated 3,500 head of cattle, sheep and goats. The Kenyan security forces responded with retaliatory killings.

It reportedly took two days for the news to reach the government in Nairobi. The GSU, Administration Police, regular police and helicopter gunships were sent to retrieve the livestock. This was done by using helicopters to ferry groups of Turkana militia (Home Guards and stock-owners) over the top of the stolen livestock and positioning them in a line behind the retreating raiders. The gunships were used to shoot the raiders, scattering the group and killing some forty people.[12] According to Rift Valley Commissioner Yusuf Haji, twenty more were killed by Home Guards. The livestock were then driven back into Kenya by the Turkana. According to information given to Africa Watch, the Turkana, in collaboration with the Kenyan security forces, took livestock from other settlements and villages on their way back. At least 200 Sudanese villagers were killed in retaliation for the raid.

Follwoing the raid on April 22, GSU and regular police officers were posted to the border area and the Provincial Security Committee and the Provincial Commissioner flew to the area to "improve security."[13]

Under President Moi's government, more attempts have been made to co-opt the Turkana community into the administrative structure and to develop the region. The first three Turkana district officers were trained and appointed in 1989, and the number of recruitment drives for the security forces has increased significantly in northern Turkana since 1982.

Guns, Gold and Power

Measures aimed at reducing the number of illegal weapons resulted in an amendment to the Firearms Act in August 1988. The amendment introduced stringent penalties for offenders, making illegal possession of a gun punishable by a maximum of fifteen years' imprisonment and a minimum of ten with a fine of 20,000 shillings

---

[12] Ministerial statement by Minister of State, Office of the President, Laban Kitale, issued on April 17, 1988.

[13] *African Defence*, June 1988.

($769). A firearms certificate became mandatory for all firearms, and possession of an air rifle became illegal. The law also imposed stricter use and custody of firearms by security officers. (See chapters five and seventeen.)

The proliferation of illegal weapons, however, is also linked to gunrunning for the gold trade. Gold comes primarily from southern Sudan,[14] but is also found in the Turkwell Gorge and areas of northern Kenya. Guns and gold, together with administrative isolation, have led to personal political fiefdoms in some communities—powerful local officials and politicians who are able to exploit the lawlessness.

Pokot, 1984

A major disarming operation was carried out in Pokot in mid-1984. An influx of arms from the Ugandan border had increased banditry, and the proliferation of weapons coincided with an expansion of settled communities in the pastoral territories of the Pokot people. The government delivered a number of ultimatums to recover weapons from the local community which generally went unheeded—there was genuine fear of arrest among the locals who had been subjected to numerous security sweeps by the GSU. Guns had also been incorporated into the lifestyle of the pastoralists and were coveted for defensive purposes; some weapons were buried to avoid confiscation. According to the *Weekly Review*:

> By 1983, Pokot was so flooded with illegal guns that the state carried out a six-month major security operation to disarm the people. The government, using helicopters combed the area but never completely got rid of the problem as the Pokot were unco-operative.[15]

After issuing an ultimatum in mid-1984, the GSU and police rounded up most of the livestock in the region and moved them to makeshift compounds. Some of the livestock subsequently died because

---

[14] Gold is mined in the Kapoeta region by the Taposa people who attempt to sell it to Kenyans, together with weapons, especially when there is a scarcity of food.

[15] *The Weekly Review*, August 19, 1988.

of lack of grazing and water. Low-flying helicopters were used to intimidate the pastoralist communities and settlements. It is widely held that the GSU shot at communities and that there were some deaths. No figures, however, have been released. Some weapons were recovered, but the operation was abandoned within a month—apparently because of the adverse publicity the recent Wajir massacre had attracted.

Katilu and Amolem, 1980

In 1980, GSU units were sent into Katilu, on the Turkwell River, and Amolem, on the River WeiWei, following a large raid on cattle in southern Turkana. During the cattle raid, which had pushed into Baringo district, some cattle belonging to the president were also stolen.

Hundreds of civilians were taken by security forces to the local airstrip. Eyewitnesses say some civilians were shot dead while trying to escape. Men and women were beaten and forced to lie down on the airstrip. GSU soldiers ran over people in heavy army shoes, beat their buttocks and kept them on the airstrip overnight. A local chief was tied to a government-owned landrover and dragged out of the village. He disappeared, but his death has never been officially acknowledged. All the security personnel involved had camouflage uniforms without numbers, and there were no license plates on the government vehicles used.

Many people were treated at the local dispensary for injuries caused by the heavy, studded boots of the GSU, and the beatings. Two days later, GSU officers returned and stripped the dressings from the injured before forcing them again on to the airstrip. Many people were again beaten and assaulted by the GSU before they left. According to aid agency sources, photographic evidence of the dead and wounded was given to the Norwegian embassy, but no official figures were ever released. The government did not officially acknowledge the attack.

Attempts to limit the number of illegal weapons were increased after the 1982 coup attempt. In Ortum, six men were summarily shot dead in a shop in 1983 after being accused of making firearms. GSU units stepped up security sweeps in arbitrary intimidation of the local settlements and villages; homes were raided, and beatings and rapes were reported as commonplace.

19
REFUGEES
A DANGEROUS SANCTUARY

The government's attitude toward refugees is often flagrantly hostile. Various illegal and callous strategies have been used to discourage people from seeking sanctuary inside Kenya's borders, including harassment and assault by the security forces and deliberate deprivation of emergency supplies.

Before the events of 1991, which produced a catastrophic number of refugees in the Horn of Africa, Kenya had a relatively small official refugee population of around 10,200. This, despite being surrounded by refugee-producing countries. Government hostility to refugees is overt and well documented, including public speeches by President Moi directing his security forces to get rid of particular groups of refugees. The government regards refugees as a security problem; its policies are therefore decided by political, rather than humanitarian considerations.

In many cases, refugees arriving at the borders are intimidated and obstructed by the security forces before they have the opportunity to register with international organizations; some have been beaten and killed. Consequently, Kenya has developed a notorious reputation amongst its neighbors for its treatment of refugees, its summary deportations and purges. Wherever possible, refugees avoid it as an escape route.

During the first half of 1991, however, Kenya's refugee population increased tenfold. Never before in its history has Kenya had to provide for so many refugees. The impact on Kenya was such that President Moi uncharacteristically called a press conference to appeal for international assistance. In June, the Minister for Home Affairs and National Heritage, Davidson Kuguru, estimated that there were 100,000 refugees in Kenya, of whom 60,000 were Somalis.[1] In May, there had been a large influx of Ethiopians.[2] Kuguru anticipated that the number

---

[1] Many thousands of Somalis fled to the Kenyan and Ethiopian borders when former President Siad Barre was ousted and civil war escalated in December 1990.

[2] Former President Mengistu fled Ethiopia as a rebel coalition advanced on Addis Ababa in May 1991.

of refugees in Kenya could reach half a million by the end of 1991 if political conflicts were not resolved in Ethiopia and Somalia.

DETAINING REFUGEES

Somali refugees who began arriving on the coast in January 1991 were frequently detained on board their vessels as Kenyan authorities refused to allow them to disembark, which led to many deaths, as overloaded boats capsized and vital relief was withheld.[3]

In March, more than 140 Somali refugees drowned when their boat, the MV *Christian*, ran aground off the Malindi coast. Most were women, children and the elderly. The boat had a capacity of fifty but was carrying over 700. One hundred and forty-five bodies were buried in a mass grave in Malindi, and forty others were reported missing.

Officers dealing with the arrivals told the refugees only Kenyans, Ugandans, Tanzanians and Somali passport holders with visas to a third country would be allowed to enter Kenya. In an interview with the *Daily Nation*, an official said "the others will have to go back to the vessel until the goverment decides what to do with them".

Many of the refugees arriving by boat were thereafter detained on board despite some death and terrible conditions from overcrowding. In March, 450 refugees were not allowed to leave the MV *Raas Kambooni* until an autopsy was carried out on a five-year-old girl who had died on the ship. The captain, Abdulakadir Khayre, said the refugees had not received any food or water since arriving in Kenya, and added that he had been buying them provisions with his own money. He said two or three of the refugees still had bullet wounds and needed medical attention, and wrote a letter to the Kenyan authorities, the Immigration and Port Health departments, the United Nations High Commission on Refugees (UNHCR) and harbor master drawing attention to the plight of the refugees: "The refugees are suffering. For 450 people to stay and sleep in one place for days and nights is just unimaginable. On top of that, they have no food to eat or water to drink." The refugees were allowed to disembark after eight days when the autopsy showed that the girl had died of natural causes.

---

[3] Information has been compiled from reports in the *Daily Nation*, unless otherwise indicated.

By the end of March, about 800 refugees were living in boats off Mombasa awaiting clearance to enter Kenya. Journalists were banned from entering the port, but reports from the crews and Somali nationals in Mombasa indicated that conditions on the boats were appalling. Some of the boats reportedly had no toilet facilities, and another child is said to have died on board because of overcrowding. Refugees developed diarrhoea.

In April, as the number of refugees arriving in Kenya continued to increase, a boat carrying 850 refugees (320 of whom were Yemeni nationals) arrived. The MV *Boolimong* had been refused permission by the Kenyan authorities to dock either at the Kilindini port or Old Port of Mombasa. It was anchored eight kilometers from the Mama Ngina Sea Drive for a week. A member of the Institute of Islamic Culture, Feisal Sherman, visited the boat and claimed that the refugees were starving and living in "pathetic and sickening conditions." The refugees were treated for diarrhoea, vomiting, dehydration and headaches. The boat was eventually allowed to berth at Kilindini, ten days after it had arrived.

Permission to dock at Kilindini was also refused to an Italian vessel, the MV *Kwanda*, unless alternative destinations were found for the 700 Somalis on board. The ship's captain reportedly pleaded with the authorities to enter the port as they were suffering squalid conditions. There was a dire shortage of food and medical supplies. Sick refugees had to hold out for days without treatment. Eleven babies had been born on the ship, one of whom died. Another, an eight-month old child, died whilst the boat was anchored at sea.

At a press conference, the Coast Provincial Commissioner, Simon Mung'ala, said that the Kenyan authorities view was that "these people are just travellers from Somalia who are on transit to a destination we do not know."

The UNHCR representative in Kenya, Sylvester Awuye, attempted to clarify the status of the boat refugees. However, the Ministry of Foreign Affairs and International Cooperation issued a statement which said that the 700 Somalis on the Italian vessel would not be allowed to stay in Kenya as refugees as there were already "very many Somalis in the country."

Africa Watch received reports that on May 21, 1991, the Lamu district authorities rounded up Somali refugees and boat owners with their staff, and forced them on board the MV *Koyama*, which was towed by the Kenyan naval patrol ship, Madararka, to Magakoni naval base near Lamu. Other refugees from Fasa and Kilakistini islands were also forced on board so they could be deported to Somalia. On May 24, sixteen refugees died when their boat capsized. On May 25, the Kenyan patrol ship transferred forty-eight refugees, most of whom were women and children, onto a leaking fishing boat with broken engines: it capsized immediately, killing twenty-one of the refugees (see appendix E).

In June, the Kenyan press reported that security forces in Lamu confiscated seven Somali boats that had been used to bring in hundreds of refugees. Some of the boats were held back for lack of safety, because the vessels were not considered seaworthy. Others were detained on security grounds, to prevent the boats from bringing in more refugees.

THE CAMPS

The boat refugees who were allowed to disembark were taken to Jomo Kenyatta showground in Mombasa. By April, it was estimated that almost 10,000 Somalis were living in the showground without any proper amenities. The Secretary General of the OAU, Dr. Salim Ahmed Salim, visited the showground in April and was told by the refugees they felt "bitterness" towards the UNHCR because of the conditions.

A new refugee camp was constructed at Utange on a fifteen acre site donated by the Kenyan government which became known as the Mogadishu Camp. Only 159 shelters provided for less than a quarter of the 8,000 refugees. Conditions deteriorated further when heavy rains hit Mombasa at the beginning of May. There was an acute shortage of food—some refugees claimed they had not received anything to eat for a week. In addition, two of the three water taps in the camp did not work. Some refugees were forced to travel five kilometers to Utange shopping center to get water. Journalists were refused access to the camp but published reports indicated that two children had died of diarrhoea. A UNHCR official described conditions as bad.

SURVIVING THE BORDER: LIVING IN NO-MAN'S LAND

Since April 1989, significant numbers of Somali refugees have attempted access to Kenya at the border with Somalia, next to the North Eastern Province. They have been forced out of makeshift camps back into Somalia by the Kenyan security forces (see below, Forced Repatriation of Somali Refugees). Caught between two hostile security forces, many thousands of refugees have taken on a furtive and dangerous existence in the inhospitable semiarid no-man's land straddling the border.

In May 1991, journalists working for the official Kenya News Agency reported an estimated 100,000 Somali refugees living on the border. They witnessed 20,000 settled under bushes, waiting for relief supplies as their own food stocks were depleted. In urgent need of food, medicine and shelter, most had sold the last of their possessions to buy food or to obtain money. Kenyan News Agency journalists reported that sick women and children risked imminent death if they did not receive urgent medical treatment. Journalists told Africa Watch that these people were subjected to attacks from both Kenyan and Somali security forces. Reports of beatings, arrests and incidents of shootings of refugees persisted, although no impartial observers confirmed this. In Mandera and Liboi, there were reports in April 1991 of refugees harassed and beaten by security personnel in makeshift camps established by the Kenyan Red Cross. Most refugees were prevented from entering Kenya and remained trapped between the Kenyan and Somali security forces along the border.

In May, police in Garissa rounded up Somalis in a crackdown on illegal aliens in the district. A police spokesman said those arrested were Somalis who had failed to register with the UNHCR. They were taken to the refugee camps at Hulugho and Liboi until their status could be determined. The Garissa District Commissioner, Francis Sigei, said that the crackdown on illegal Somali immigrants would continue, and that locals found harboring them would be charged in court.

REFUGEE POLICIES

The Border

Although Kenya is a signatory to the United Nations Convention Relating to the Status of Refugees, thousands of refugees have been attacked on Kenya's borders by the security forces, without any concessions to the legitimate rights of these people to apply for registration as bona fide refugees. Refugees attempting to enter Kenya have described incidents to Africa Watch where people have been beaten, starved, interrogated, arrested, imprisoned or handed over to the security forces of the country from which they are trying to escape. In some incidents, refugees have been shot on Kenyan territory by Kenyan security forces or the persecuting foreign forces.

Sudanese Refugees

The Kenyan government effectively stopped an influx of displaced Southern Sudanese by establishing cooperative security procedures with the rebel Sudan Peoples Liberation Army, who now control all territory adjacent to the northern Kenyan border (see chapter eighteen). Kenya insists it only provides humanitarian aid to the SPLA. There is at least one SPLA camp in northern Kenya, for soldiers receiving food and logistical support, but no evidence has been produced to indicate this is a training camp. SPLA security officers are posted in Lockichokio, northern Kenya, to control and monitor any cross-border movements of the Sudanese population.

According to a small group of non-SPLA southern Sudanese refugees in Nairobi, their refugee status is under constant threat. One Sudanese refugee who spoke to Africa Watch, said they are forbidden to travel to northern Kenyan unless approved by SPLA security officials based in Nairobi. This refugee said that members of the non-SPLA community are frequently required to report to Kenyan CID and Special Branch to preserve their refugee status.

People attempting to flee the SPLA-held areas are unable to get access to Kenya. On the more remote border with Sudan, the Home Guards and the security forces discourage attempts to cross into Kenyan territory, as well as making the occasional retaliatory raids across the mutual border (see chapter eighteen). According to information given to Africa Watch, Sudanese refugees who have crossed into northern Kenya have been taken to SPLA security officers, not to an internationally recognized organization. In 1988-90 significant numbers fled southern Sudan as the SPLA took territory near the Kenyan and Ugandan border. At least 20,000 refugees fled into Uganda—despite the fact that the Ugandan government is also considered sympathetic to the Sudanese rebels—while less than 100 were registered as refugees in Kenya.

Ugandan Refugees

Kenya's policy toward Ugandan refugees is determined by political considerations: President Moi periodically encourages antagonism towards Uganda's present government by publicly accusing it of attempting to destabilize Kenya. He has frequently accused Ugandan

President Museveni of assisting dissidents, training rebels, and allowing armed incursions across the border.

Beginning in 1985, a minority of politically-active Ugandan refugees have received encouragement and even sponsorship from the Kenyan authorities. Previously, from 1980 to 1985, Kenyan security agencies cooperated with former President Milton Obote, to forcibly return politically-active exiles into custody in Uganda, where they sometimes faced death. All Ugandan refugees, however, lead a tenuous existence in Kenya. Since 1986, there have been a number of documented purges of registered Ugandan refugees who were summarily deported to Uganda.

Crossing into Kenyan territory is easy on the porous border; but a person presenting himself or herself as a refugee to security personnel faces dangerous consequences. A refugee risks being arrested as a spy, beaten or returned to the Ugandan authorities. During times of active hostility, the national press has carried reports of Ugandan people shot in the border regions as suspected cattle-rustlers (see chapter eighteen). Most Ugandan refugees who were legitimately registered with the UNHCR managed to cross the border at the height of the previous civil war, before President Museveni took power in 1986. One such person, James, came to Kenya in 1985 and described to Africa Watch his experience at the border:

> I crossed with a group of women and children near the border post, and we were discovered by the Kenyan police. They took us to the police station—at that time there were a lot of people crossing so they were used to refugees like us. They separated the men out and kept us in the station. We had to answer a lot of questions, and some were taken away. I don't know what happened to them. But there were about ten young men, like me, who stayed with the police for about two months. We had to wash for them, cook for them, clean—things like that. Then another group were brought to the station and we were transferred to Nairobi.

According to Ugandan refugees in Kenya, Kenya no longer accepts Ugandans seeking refugee status at the border, and is making every attempt to expel those registered with the UNHCR.

Somali Refugees

Kenya has held back a wave of Somali refugees since 1988, when the forces of former President Siad Barre killed thousands of civilians in response to escalating armed conflict initially in northern Somalia. Although most of the northern refugees fled into camps in Ethiopia, a significant number also sought entry to Kenya. Officially, Kenya took a negligent number of registered refugees, but thousands of businessmen and their families took advantage of the entrenched corruption to buy Kenyan ID papers. This "paid-up" intake was characteristically urban and wealthy, and most had family contacts among the Kenyan-Somali population.

In 1989, there was a second influx of refugees when civil war spread to southern Somalia, adjacent to Kenya's North Eastern and Tana River provinces (see chapter fifteen). Every effort was made to repulse these refugees, the majority of whom were poor and nomadic. Throughout 1989, thousands of refugees arrived at the Kenyan border. Initially they attempted to present themselves to the Kenyan authorities to be taken in as registered refugees, but as the response of the Kenyan authorities became increasingly brutal, the refugees avoided border guards and lived as a stateless community on the vast, inhospitable no-man's land between the two countries. They were subjected to attacks from the Kenyan and Somali forces, and many were eventually forced to return to southern Somalia where thousands of civilians later died as a result of civil war.

As described earlier, the third influx of Somali refugees came in early 1991 after rebel forces succeeded in ousting former President Siad Barre and took the capital, Mogadishu.

The Kenyan government found it expedient to cooperate with Barre's regime when it came to its own Kenyan-Somali population. Through "good neighborly" relations with Barre, the government secured cooperation to prevent cross-border support for anti-government movements. The Kenyan government, likewise, refused assistance to anti-Barre Somali forces who attempted to use facilities on the Kenyan border to sustain guerrilla attacks in southern Somalia. Consequently, the reception of those seeking refugee protection has been highly discriminatory. As the Somali civil war disintegrated along clan lines, refugees at the border were vetted according to their ethnic group, rather than on the basis that they were civilians at risk.

Forced Repatriation of Somali Refugees After the Dobley Massacre

The best-documented incident of forced repatriation on the Kenyan-Somali border occurred in November 1989, when some 3,000 refugees were effectively starved out of Kenyan territory and subsequently forced back across the border at gun-point.

The refugees arrived at the border on September 20, 1989, after Somali troops attacked Dobley, a small Somali town held by the rebel Somali Patriotic Movement. Four Kenyan border police were also killed when six armored cars driven by the Somali army pursued fleeing civilians into Kenyan territory. Refugees were initially treated roughly by the Kenyan authorities, and were threatened by the local district officer, but they refused to return to Dobley. The refugees described a massacre in the town, which left bayonetted corpses lying in the deserted town, many with their throats cut. Many nomads were also killed as the Somali army cleaned up the surrounding region after occupying the town. The situation of the refugees improved when the Kenyan government reacted angrily to the killing of its four policemen and the brief incursion of the Somali army into Kenyan territory. After visiting the site, reporters from the national press wrote of "genocide...claiming upwards of 150 citizens." President Moi pledged to assist the refugees.

The refugees enjoyed a temporary reprieve between September 22-25 when Army Chief of Staff, Mahmoud Mohamed, visited Liboi with Commissioner of Police, Philip Kilonzo, and a government delegation. Harassment ceased and the refugees were moved to a more sheltered site near the police compound. The refugees formed a committee to liaise with Kenyan officials and to make arrangements to be taken to the UNHCR in Nairobi. Three of the most severely injured Somali refugees were flown to Garissa District Hospital—a girl of seven with multiple gunshot wounds, a young woman of sixteen with a shattered lower leg, and a woman with gunshot wounds in her arm and thigh. At least twenty other injured refugees failed to receive urgent medical treatment for bullet wounds—including a young girl with gunshot wounds in her thigh; a young man shot through the bladder; and others suffering from bullet wounds in the throat, arms and legs. Two trucks were made into temporary shelter for the most severely injured, whose injuries quickly became septic.

On September 25, however, the refugees were surrounded by armed guards and were refused access to the town, which they depended on for food and water. Thereafter, the refugees received no rations of food other than a few provisions brought to them by sympathetic people from the town. Two children and three women were buried in Liboi, who were said by the other refugees to have died from starvation. Despite requests from international agencies, including the Kenyan Red Cross and the UNHCR, the government refused to allow food, shelter and medical provisions to be taken to the refugees.

Kenyan officials made repeated attempts to persuade the refugees to return across the border, despite their expressed fears of death and arbitrary reprisals. The Kenyan army and border police constantly harassed the refugees in an attempt to intimidate them into returning. Some women were removed from the site by the Kenyan army and taken into the army area. Reports of rape resulted in the eventual arrest of an army officer. Beatings and harassment continued and three of the refugees were arrested for inciting resistance to forced repatriation. One of the men arrested wrote a letter from the border:

> On Thursday September 28 they tried to repatriate us. Soldiers and lorries were brought. We were given only some minutes to collect our things and leave. The previous night we decided to write a letter to the DO. We said in the letter:
>
> 1) As from today we will start fasting, only the sick and children are exempted from it.
>
> 2) We will remain seated and continue fasting until a UNHCR representative comes to us.
>
> 3) We will only speak to the UNHCR.
>
> 4) We requested medicine/treatment for the sick and wounded.
>
> We then started to sit down and not move. We said even if beaten, not to resist. They picked up three of us. Released two and kept one for three days in prison. The refugees are still there. Some of course have run away as a result of the threat and beating. The situation is critical. We told them to take one of us to Nairobi to the UNHCR. But they are not willing.

The Kenyan army managed to forcibly return sixty of the refugees in fifteen vehicles on September 28. According to eyewitness accounts, the refugees lay on the ground and locked arms in an attempt to resist, but armed soldiers forced them into the back of vehicles at gunpoint. Of the sixty, eighteen were subsequently reported executed in Dobley and forty-two imprisoned in the regional capital, Kismayu. An increasing number of refugees dispersed into the bush to search for food and water, and eventually the remaining few were forced back across the border. Most of the refugees had fled to the Kenyan border twice before, during April and July of the same year. On all occasions the refugees say they were beaten and threatened by Kenyan security personnel and officials.

The sudden change of policy, after initially offering sanctuary to this group of refugees, came after a visit by high-level Somali officials to Nairobi and the border area. In exchange for policing rights up to Dobley town and for the opportunity to inspect the hardware of the Somali army, Kenya agreed to repatriate the refugees immediately.

Registered Refugees: No Guarantees

Accepted refugees are first taken to the Nairobi offices of the UNHCR and temporarily registered while vetted by the Ministry of Home Affairs, Immigration Department and the Special Branch. Refugees say screening by the Special Branch is gruelling and is the most decisive in its outcome. According to its mandate, the UNHCR is unable to register a refugee unless passed by the Kenyan authorities and cleared by the Special Branch. The organization has no power to offer protection to refugees who are arrested or deported during interrogation.

After clearance, a refugee is transferred to the Thika Refugee Camp[4] where he or she stays until permanent refugee status has been granted. The refugee camp is situated a few kilometers outside Thika town and subject to strict security measures. Since 1989, refugees from the camp say a permanent armed guard of Administration Police control movement to and from the camp. Medical facilities are said to be extremely poor, forcing refugees to rely on local amenities. One refugee said he was aware of at least two people who had been refused access to the town for vital medical attention, and of another who was too sick to walk the distance. Pleas to the UNHCR to set up a medical center have

---

[4] About 60 kilometers outside Nairobi.

proved fruitless. One refugee told Africa Watch that the atmosphere and conditions of the camp make it "more like a detention center" and said he had seen a number of refugees beaten for attempting to go into the town for food.

After permanent refugee status has been granted, refugees are able to seek accommodation, employment and education. Even at this stage, there is little sense of security. Grants for vocational courses for refugees have been substantially reduced and employment opportunities are extremely limited, given the severe unemployment situation in the country as a whole. In December 1989, student refugees staged a sit-in protest when financial support for certain courses was inexplicably withdrawn, leaving many refugees indebted to landlords and unable to continue with their qualifying exams. According to the director of one of the educational organizations, the Kenyan government had withheld grants while the validity of certain registered students was under scrutiny. He attributed the problems to "the Ugandan intake," claiming some were illegally pursuing studies. Refugees who faced eviction and financial disaster because of this action said they found no solace at UNHCR. According to the refugees, they were offered no help. A spokesperson for UNHCR confirmed to a member of the international press corps in Nairobi that some allowances had been suspended while the organization reassessed the status of some of the refugees.

The willingness of the government to use refugee communities as political scapegoats makes Kenya a dangerous sanctuary. In 1990, all registered refugees, as detailed above, faced the threat of deportation as the security forces purged the refugee community on the instructions of President Moi. The Kenyan govenment's actions are in clear breach of its obligations under the United Nations Convention Relating to the Status of Refugees, to which it is a party, and the Protocol relating to the Status of Refugees to which it is a signatory. Protests made by international human rights organizations and aid agencies to the Kenyan government about its failure to respect these treaties have met with dismissal and anger. The Kenyan government's refusal to honor international, humanitarian standards regarding refugees is further illustrated by the persecution it metes out to Kenyan refugees and exiles abroad.

Kenyan Refugees: The Shadow of Fear

The Kenyan government denies there are any Kenyan refugees, but the numbers of Kenyans seeking asylum in Britian, Canada, Scandanavia and the United States have increased since 1988. In Canada,

214 Kenyans applied for asylum in 1990, compared with 181 in 1989 and 60 between May 1986 and December 1988.[5] In the United States, there were fifteen applicants in 1990, compared with 3 in 1989 and 3 in 1988.[6] In Britian, there were 11 applicants in 1988 compared to 16 already submitted in the first six months of 1991.[7]

Kenyans have also fled into neighboring Tanzania and Uganda, where they make urgent attempts to seek an alternative country of asylum because of fear of persecution and abduction by the Kenyan security forces. A number of Kenyan refugees arrived in Uganda and Tanzania between July-December 1990. In January 1991, there were reports of a Kenyan student abducted by Kenyan security agents in Kampala. The student was later returned to the UNHCR.

In 1990-91, Africa Watch received detailed information from lawyers in Canada, the United States and Britain on Kenyan citizens seeking refugee status. These included accounts of people who had been tortured by the security forces and accused of belonging to the Kenya Patriotic Front (KPF); ex-detainees, political prisoners and multiparty advocates who were persecuted in the 1990 political crackdown (see chapter three); and Kenyan-Somalis who suffered on account of the screening exercise (see chapter sixteen).

REFUGEE PURGES

The tenuous existence of refugees—even after registration with the UNHCR—is documented in the number of purges carried out against Ugandan refugees, and, in 1990, against Rwandese refugees.

In 1986, thousands of refugees, mostly Ugandans, were rounded up by police in a campaign to expel illegal aliens. In September, police

---

[5] According to the Immigration and Refugee Board of Canada, Convention Refugee Determination Division, there were 37 applicants between January and July 1991, 214 in 1990, 181 applicants in 1989.

[6] According to the Statistical Division of Immigration and Naturalization Service, USA, 8 applications were filed in the first six months of 1991, with 16 cases pending.

[7] Information from the Immigration Department, Statistical Division, Britian.

arrested many registered refugees in Nairobi, Kisumu and Busia after raiding nightclubs, bars and hotels, and carrying out ID checks on the streets. Six hundred illegal aliens were picked up in Kisumu and eighty-seven Ugandans were summarily deported at the border. In Busia, 400 people were arrested after local chiefs reportedly ordered landlords to evict refugees or face prosecution. Similarly, in March 1987, Kenyan police arrested more than 200 people in Kitale as illegal aliens, including Somalis, Ethiopians and Ugandans. Public transport was stopped and searched between Isiolo and Marsabit. Several hundred people—mostly Ugandans—were reported to be facing deportation.

The most recent crackdown was effected in November 1990, when President Moi ordered all Ugandan and Rwandan refugees to leave the country. Police sweeps were carried out in most of the major towns and those arrested were kept in police custody for some time before being charged with being in the country illegally. The majority of those who appeared in court were Ugandan, others were Rwandese. Ethiopian, Somali, Burundi and Tanzanian refugees were also picked up. A Ugandan student, brought into the UNHCR offices from court by the police, described what happened:

> I was arrested on the way to college where I do a course in Spring Valley. There were two APs [Administration Police] who took my ID and tore it up. I was taken to the Spring Valley police station and put in a cell. There were over fifty people in a cell 10' by 20'. All of us were standing and we had to remove our shirts to survive. One person was really suffocating. The police treated us very harshly. Some were beaten, slapped around and kicked, and some were beaten on their knees as they sat down. Their knees were really damaged from the clubs. Yesterday we were taken to court in Kibera, about fifteen of us—the rest were all charged with drunk and disorderly behavior. The refugees were eventually put in a line and given a roll call and told we would go to court again the next day. At about 3:00 P.M. we were taken by police officers to UNHCR and we were told that we refugees are no longer the property of the Kenyan government, who can't be held responsible for what happens to us.

Refugees told Africa Watch how APs and KANU youthwingers came to their homes to look for illegal residents immediately after the presidential directive. Crowded into the offices of the UNHCR in the hope of protection, refugees described how local youthwingers identified the homes of refugees to the police. Although most refugees could produce identity papers, they were subjected to police violence, confiscation of property and extortion. Youthwingers and police illegally forced entry and destroyed or confiscated identity papers. Some reported incidents of rape and sexual harassment by the youthwingers.

Before deportation, many of the refugees spent a number of days in police custody without access to either lawyers or family. Conditions were described as very poor, exacerbated by chronic overcrowding. One family of fourteen, including three children under the age of five, described their two nights in police custody:

> We were picked on Saturday [the day of President Moi's speech]. There were about eight police and youthwingers. They didn't show us any identification, but just walked into our home. They told us we are all under arrest. We went with them to the police post at Ong'ata Rongai where we were put in a cell together with some Kenyans—about twenty-five of us. They denied us food and water. We didn't even have anything for the children. When we asked for food they beat us—slapping us on the face, kicking us, as well as drawing their guns and threatening to shoot us.
>
> In the morning we were taken to court without even receiving a mug of tea. In court we were told our IDs are fake and they took us back to the police station. This morning we were given some tea and brought to UNHCR. Even the children had nothing—but when we tried to give money for food to some of the officers who seemed a bit sympathetic, it was taken from us.

One Rwandese woman expressed great concern for her brother who, she said, had been thrown in jail for political reasons when the directive was issued:

My brother was picked up off the road and taken to
Langata police station on Sunday. We've been here as
refugees for twenty-five years—we schooled here, worked
here and lived here, and we are proud of that. But now?
How can I even go to my brother because I'll be arrested
with him. We have to find people to take my brother
food. I don't understand how they can arrest him and
lock him up like that. How can he go to Rwanda now,
there is civil war?

We have all the right documents and cards. Alright, if
they want us to go, we must go...but they should find us
a place to take us if they don't want us here. An
alternative place must be found and they should put us
all together in some center to assist us; not just picking
us up and putting us in cells.

Why after twenty-five years do we end up in cells and
told to pack our things and leave? We need time to leave
if we have to go. They should release people and get
them all together, instead of some in Kabete police
station, some in Langata, some in Pangani, some in
Dagoretti. We won't go to Rwanda, but at least they can
settle us somewhere else properly.

The exact number of refugees forcibly repatriated as a result of
this directive is not known, but at least one thousand are known to have
reached the Ugandan border in a specially-assigned train. On October 26,
a train heavily guarded by armed APs and GSU left Nairobi station with
about 500 refugees. "Reserved for Vagrants" notices were posted in
carriages, and refugees were brought directly to the train from police
custody and court cells. According to the refugee community in Nairobi,
another train left during the night on October 25 with a similar number
of refugees. Both trains picked up more illegal aliens from other major
towns en route, like Nakuru and Eldoret, before reaching Busia on the
Kenya-Uganda border.

At the border, the Ugandan border police and immigration
officers took the refugees to a police compound for screening and alerted
the Ugandan government. According to the Ugandan government, all
recently repatriated refugees had to be screened for criminal elements

and rebels. They were taken to an army barracks and then transferred to a camp in Tororo town.

Some Ugandan refugees saw this as tantamount to a death sentence, and said they would be prepared to do anything to avoid being returned. On October 30, twenty refugees broke into the Thika camp to seek protection from the crackdown.[8] In a letter sent to Africa Watch, another Ugandan refugee said:

> As I am writing to you now I am 20 days staying in Kenya illegally because they refused to renew my pass. I was told I am no longer eligible to stay in Kenya, and that I had better go back to my home country. There is nothing I can do. Since this all started, we are having our documents confiscated. There is nothing coming from the UNHCR—you go to them and they just give you a another letter which is thought to be illegal by the Kenyan authorities. So what can one do? As for me, I have two options in mind: if the worst comes to the worst I shall go and hand myself to the Ugandan authorities of course with the knowledge of being killed or detained. Or, I will fight the arresting officers here in Kenya so that I can be sentenced to some time in prison. By the time I finish the sentence, I can hope that things have changed.

THE DOUBLE BURDEN

Representatives of Africa Watch both in the United States and in Britain have interviewed numerous Kenyans who have provided information about the efforts of the authorities to monitor their movements and threaten those perceived as critical of the government, to disrupt scholarships and to encourage them to spy on each other. Lawyers in the United States and Canada have also told Africa Watch that Kenyan security officials routinely follow, harass, threaten and, in some known cases, photograph Kenyans abroad seeking refugee status. These refugees fear for the lives of their families and relatives at home as well

---

[8] *Kenya Times*, October 31, 1990.

as for themselves. A lawyer in Canada has documented the threat made by Kenyan security officials to kill the father of one Kenyan applying for refugee status. The Kenyan government has devoted increasing resources to monitor the activities of Kenyans abroad (see chapter five).

Continued harassment by the security forces has a devastating effect on a person's life, when they are already vulnerable and trying to find protection. The double burden of fear is described in anonymous testimony given to Africa Watch by a woman who fled Kenya after being raped and tortured by the Special Branch:

> Now I am terrified of people coming after me, and I wake up frequently during the night to check the door is locked. I never feel safe—I am always on the look-out because of my fear. When I smell deodorant similar to that of the men who raped me, my body shakes. I get stomach pains and headaches often. I see many reports of rape in this country and it has made me feel I am in a dangerous country for being raped. Generally, I prefer to be alone now because there is no-one I can trust to talk to and I fear the Kenyan spies.

KENYAN GOVERNMENT'S HOSTILITY TO REFUGEES IN CANADA

The Kenyan government has shown intense hostility toward the presence of Kenyan refugees in Canada, whether they are political dissidents, self-proclaimed members of MwaKenya or ethnic Somalis seeking refuge from the screening exercise. When screening of ethnic Somalis was introduced in Kenya, Kenyans and Somalis living in Canada organized a series of protests. The Kenyan government was sharply critical of the Canadian government for allowing the demonstrations (see chapter sixteen). KANU officials organized anti-Canadian demonstrations in Mombasa and the North Eastern Province, and President Moi demanded an apology from the Canadian government for allowing the protest against the screening to go ahead and blamed the government for allowing the demonstrations to be televised. President Moi said that Kenyans who went to Canada and claimed refugee status would be "dealt with harshly." In one case, the Immigration and Refugee Board accepted that this statement by President Moi was sufficient basis for giving a person from Kenya refugee status.[9]

Nevertheless, according to information passed to Africa Watch by Canadian lawyers, the Canadian government imposed visa restrictions on Kenyans to stop legitimate refugees from coming to Canada after the screening exercise began (see chapter sixteen).[10] The Canadian government agreed to return Kenyan refugees on the condition they would not suffer recriminations at the airport. Human rights organizations expressed concern that this was not a sufficient safeguard against abuse. As decisions on refugee claims are made individually for each claimant, there has been considerable inconsistency in the way Kenyan refugees have been treated in Kenya. Some claimants have been accepted, others rejected and sometimes even deported to Kenya. In a letter to Africa Watch, a lawyer representing a Kenyan seeking refugee status, described the action taken against Kenyan refugees:

> The Kenyan embassy in Canada has been photographing Kenyans' protesting here, sending agents to meetings of the Kenyan Canadian association and issuing death threats to the families of refugees claimnants remaining in Kenya.

He said his client was afraid to reveal the fact he was Kenyan because of his fear that he would be deported to Kenya. He refused to admit he was Kenyan, in spite of the fact the Immigration department was holding his Kenyan passport. The Canadian High Commission in Kenya asked the Kenyan government to verify the citizenship of the claimant. The senior assistant immigration officer, John Nangurai, from the immigration department of Kenya confirmed that the claimant was a Kenyan citizen, and also confirmed that the claimant's father and mother were Kenyan citizens. Africa Watch has obtained evidence of the harassment of this applicant's immediate family. The father of the claimant was summonded by the same senior assistant immigration

---

[9] Immigration and Refugee Board of Canada, Convention Refugee Determination Division, File U90-02024, Decision dated January 31, 1991.

[10] Canada annually gives the Kenyan government $42 million in aid.

officer to "explain the whereabouts" of his son. An affidavit was made by
a Canadian lawyer on the subsequent persecution of the father:

> As a result of his son's interaction with the Canadian
> government and the subsequent communication from the
> Kenyan Department of Immigration to him he is afraid
> of the Kenyan government. The father stated that he is
> too afraid to go in to see the authorities at the Kenyan
> Department of Immigration because he thinks that they
> will detain him. The father.. sent a friend in to make
> arrangements with the Department of Immigration to
> enable him to travel to Mecca...however, his friend was
> told that there was a problem with the father's file and as
> a result nothing could be done for him.

The Kenyan government maintains, however, there are no
Kenyan refugees but only people who have gone into a voluntary exile.
Political exiles, like writer Ngugi wa Thiongo, human rights lawyers
Gibson Kamau Kuria and Kiraitu Murungi are referred to by the Kenyan
government as self-exiles and have been harshly condemned by President
Moi and other politicans. To a great extent, this definition has been
accepted by countries like Britian, whose close links with Kenya prevents
recognition of the seriousness of persecution in Kenya (see chapter
twenty). Africa Watch has received letters from British lawyers
representing Kenyan-Somalis seeking refugee status who challenge the
Foreign Office view that, although there have been grounds for concern,
Kenyan-Somalis are no longer discriminated against.

20
BRITISH POLICY

Britain has traditionally kept silent on the human rights situation in Kenya, even when other Western governments have voiced their concern. Stubbornly ignoring evidence of a poor human rights record, the British government continues to regard Kenya as stable, peaceful and economically successful. Diplomats in Nairobi make no secret of the fact that the British government considers President Moi a safe option, even after taking into account human rights abuses and political discontent. The Kenyan government is rarely judged on its own merits, but always comparatively "it is better than its chaotic neighbors" and speculatively "what comes next may be worse."

Strong commercial ties have been maintained between the two countries, and Kenya has been held up by the British as a role model for the rest of Africa. Seen as worthy of development assistance and an ideal place for investment, Kenya is the largest recipient of British aid in Africa and the second largest in the world. Since independence in 1963, Britain has given more than £500 million in bilateral aid to Kenya.

President Moi's pro-capitalist stance and relative economic success account for at least some of the privileges and favor Kenya enjoys in the West. Britain's first concern in Kenya is to protect its commercial interests, trade and investments of development aid—human rights and democracy are secondary. Consequently, recent British policy linking the allocation of aid to human rights and political reform, becomes contradictory and ambivalent when applied to Kenya.

For Kenya, the consequence of receiving so much foreign finance is that the West is concerned to maintain a secure environment for its continued economic investment. This is the West's yardstick for stability. If protests against the one-party system continue in Kenya, Britain may be forced to concede that its interests would be best served by encouraging moves towards a system that guarantees respect for human rights, rather than a nationwide revolt.

LINKING AID TO DEMOCRACY

In June 1990, the British government set new conditions on aid distribution that indicated an unprecedented willingness to take an active role in promoting human rights. The stringent political and economic conditions that would in future be attached to British aid were specified by Foreign Secretary Douglas Hurd, who said: "Countries tending towards pluralism, public accountability, respect for the rule of law, human rights and market principles should be encouraged. Governments who persist with repressive policies, with corrupt management, or with wasteful and discredited economic systems should not expect us to support their folly with scarce aid resources."[1]

A few days later in Kenya, the outgoing British High Commissioner, Sir John Johnson, gave reassurances that aid to Kenya would not be affected. He said: "I can speak for British government policy in Kenya. There has been no intention to cut down aid to Kenya."[2] In the same week, he announced a British government grant worth £3.14 million for the Kenya Railways Corporation.

In July, events occurred in Kenya which were to test Britain's recently articulated commitment to human rights when Kenyans attempted to attend a rally calling for an end to the one-party system of government. In spite of blatant abuses by the Kenyan government (see chapter four), Britain remained uncritical. The British High Commissioner visited President Moi to express Britain's concern over detentions, but details of the meeting were never made public. Mr. Hurd later defended such private approaches to governments saying that in certain cases "we will find the government in question more amenable to private representations, so that it is not seen to lose face."[3]

In London, the former Secretary of State for Foreign and Commonwealth Affairs, William Waldegrave, visited the Kenyan High Commissioner, Dr. Sally Kosgei, to express Britain's anxiety over the recent events. A Foreign Office official characterized the half hour meeting as "friendly," though Waldegrave had urged the early release of political detainees.

When questioned in the House of Commons about Britain's response to the recent arrests without charge of former cabinet ministers

---

[1] *The Independent*, June 7, 1990.

[2] Speaking in a Voice of Kenya TV conference, June 12, 1990, reported in the *Daily Nation* on June 13, 1990.

[3] *Crossbow*, October 1, 1990.

Kenneth Matiba and Charles Rubia, Waldegrave replied: "There are real causes for concern including the detention of critics of the Government which are bound to worry the friends of Kenya. The Kenyan Government are well aware of our views on these matters."[4] Yet this concern was not translated into any action against the Kenyan government: indeed these views, and the manner in which they were conveyed, apparently prompted nothing other than gratitude from President Moi who thanked Britain's former Prime Minister, Margaret Thatcher, for "ignoring those who were urging her to criticize Kenya."[5]

Meanwhile, in protest over the brutal action taken against supporters of the multiparty system, Norway, Denmark, Finland, Iceland and Sweden threatened to cut aid of about £50 million. The U.S. warned that aid to Kenya would be frozen unless steps were taken to respect human rights. In Britain, it was reported in the *Independent* that the Foreign Office said there were "no plans to review aid in the light of concern at the Kenyan Government's actions."

As new evidence continued to reach human rights organizations of the extent of the Kenyan government's killing of the pro-democracy demonstrators in July, a British parliamentary delegation visited the country. After an eight-day visit—during which the visitors did not meet any members of the opposition nor seek a first-hand assessment of the human rights situation—the delegation concluded that Kenya was peaceful, stable and democratic. They said they had seen "no evidence of political repression."[6] Yet in that same week, Charles Kuria Wamwere, brother of an exiled former member of parliament, was jailed for four years after pleading guilty to belonging to a clandestine movement, the Kenyan Patriotic Front. He had been held incommunicado for thirteen days before admitting to the charge. He was denied any legal representation and it is widely believed that he was tortured to obtain a confession. House searches, police harassment, arrests for sedition, and torture were common practice at the time of the visit. Yet, Frank Haynes,

---

[4] *Hansard*, vol. 176, no. 1531, July 17, 1990.

[5] *The Times*, July 27, 1990.

[6] *The Guardian*, September 20, 1990.

leader of the delegation, said that as legislators in the U.K. they would do whatever possible to help Kenya "regardless of what is happening now."[7]

The visit prompted an open letter from the daughter of detainee Kenneth Matiba, Susan Matiba, who criticized the delegation's intention to inform the British government that Kenya was democratic and deserving of more assistance. She wrote: "My father languishes in detention right now sleeping on a cold cement floor and fed on a substandard diet, in solitary confinement—for having dared exercise a constitutionally guaranteed human right." She questioned the implications of the fact that the British delegation had apparently been flown to the country at the expense of the Kenyan government and had failed to meet with anyone other than party officials and party representatives.

It was against this background that Douglas Hurd reaffirmed his commitment to using aid as a lever to promote human rights. In October 1990, he wrote: "We will reward democratic governments and any political reform which leads to greater accountability and democracy. The corollary is that we should penalise particularly bad cases of repression and abuse of human rights... We should be clear that we are not only talking about freedom from poverty and hunger, but freedom from the fear of torture and arbitrary arrest. We must underline to aid recipients that the two are complementary."[8]

Two weeks later another parliamentary delegation went on a fact-finding mission to Kenya. Upon arrival, the delegates made it clear that they were not there to see Kenya's human rights track record but to see how Kenya used aid from Britain.[9] There was no indication that Mr Hurd's recommendation that human rights be introduced into the aid dialogue would be implemented, though during the visit the delegates did appeal to the Kenyan government to release three detainees—Kenneth Matiba, Charles Rubia and Raila Odinga. They also met with some forty people representing various political opinions. However, at the end of the visit, they concluded that Kenya was a "symbol of stability" in a region of turmoil and that they would seek a "forum from which to correct the

---

[7] *Daily Nation*, September 12, 1990.

[8] *Crossbow*, October 1, 1990.

[9] Summary of World Broadcasts (SWB), October 16, 1990.

distorted picture of Kenya portrayed by some sectors of the British press."[10] They also remarked that Kenya had a "lively and free press" which was a good foundation for any democratic country.

In December 1990, one of the delegates, Michael Colvin, asked in parliament for confirmation that Britain would continue its aid program to Kenya which he said had shown considerable improvement in its human rights record over the past few months. The Minister for Overseas Development, Lynda Chalker, confirmed that as Kenya was implementing structural adjustment programs and had a good economic record, it would continue to receive aid from Britain. She said: "We seek to give humanitarian aid irrespective of the behavior of the government."

In the same month, the U.S. Senate froze the disbursement of $15 million in economic and military aid unless Kenya stopped physical abuse of political detainees, brought detained persons to trial, and restored freedom of speech.

Exactly one year after the British government's 1990 statement linking human rights and democracy to aid, Chalker visited Kenya where she expressed views that directly contradicted this policy. She said Britain "had no intention of dictating what kind of political systems to adopt" and that "every country should be left alone to determine its own destiny and an acceptable political change conducive to the socio-economic needs and expectations of its people."[11] She did, however, stress the importance of an open socioeconomic society to enable governments to encourage privatization of public firms.

In light of this statement, together with the fact that there is no evidence to show that British aid to Kenya has altered or been reassessed since June 1990, it is difficult to avoid the conclusion that official statements of intent have little bearing on actual government policy toward Kenya. In spite of a steady flow of highlevel visits from Britain to Kenya, there have been no attempts to gain an accurate assessment of the human rights situation nor has there been any convincing response from Britain to political persecution in Kenya.

On March 26, 1991, Vice-President George Saitoti, headed a Kenyan delegation in addressing an all-party parliamentary group in London. The group was chaired by Lord Greenhill, and was composed of Alan Beef, Kevin McNamara, Timothy Raison, Lord Seebohn, Andrew

---

[10] SWB, October 18, 1990.

[11] SWB, June 6, 1991.

Wouth, Bowen Wells and Jim Clerk. Professor Saitoti focused on what he called the "miracle" of the Kenyan economy and recent growth figures. When he mentioned that Kenya had been criticized for its human rights problems, he described this as an "international conspiracy." He said the KANU Review Committee had been a great exercise in democracy "from top to bottom." On demands for political reform, he described the editor of the *Nairobi Law Monthly* as a "criminal." Saitoti's further remarks made about Jaramogi Oginga Odinga as a "well-known communist," coup-plotter and arms smuggler, have since prompted Odinga to take court action to sue the vice-president.

The response of the parliamentary group was generally supportive of Kenya. Sir David Steel, however, said that there were incidents in Kenya which caused alarm, and referred to the harassment and detention of Gitobu Imanyara.

The failure of the British government to take a stand on Kenya's political and human rights record was addressed by the *Times* in an editorial in June 1991. The editorial called for a suspension of aid to Kenya. In a reply to the newspaper, Kenyan High Commissioner Kosgei, cited the fact that refugees were fleeing to Kenya from neighboring countries as proof of her government's entitlement to continued foreign assistance. She referred to the World Bank when answering the *Times'* charge of nonaccountability and expressed her belief that pluralism can flourish with a one-party system. She made no reference to human rights.

In March 1987, President Moi arrived in Britain having cut short a visit to the U.S., apparently irritated by congressional and state department concern over allegations of police torture of political detainees. In Britain, however, no mention was made of human rights abuses nor of other countries' obvious concern. On the contrary, Britain endorsed its approval of Kenya by signing a £50 million aid agreement.

THE THATCHER BLESSING

The following year, the former British prime minister, Margaret Thatcher, visited Kenya and made a public statement on the human rights situation which completely exonerated President Moi. She said that he was "just as concerned at any abuses of human rights as anyone else would be." She assured the president in private talks that she felt "Kenya's human rights record is good" and that she had "faith in the President's assurances that any abuses will be corrected."

Not surprisingly, during the visit Moi did not press Thatcher on her opposition to sanctions in South Africa. Unlike other former colonies of Zimbabwe, Ghana and Nigeria, the Kenyan government has consistently remained mild in its criticism of Britain's position on sanctions. Whilst in Kenya, Thatcher announced a new aid package worth £20 million.

In 1989, the amount of bilateral aid received from Britain was £53,941,000, almost 11 percent of the total for sub-Saharan Africa. In the same year, Britain spent £9,596,000 on Aid and Trade Provision in sub-Saharan Africa: of this, Kenya received £7,871,000.[12]

Substantial British funds also reach Kenya through Britain's contribution to the multilateral agencies including the World Bank, the European Community and the African Development Bank. In 1988, gross development aid from all multilateral sources to Kenya was £70 million, of which Britain's share was £7 million.[13]

COMMERCIAL TIES

Kenya's economy is now a dependent one, being one of the highest recipients of Western aid in the world. With the current decline in its domestic economy, foreign aid is playing an even more important role in Kenya's economic survival. In 1979, overseas aid accounted for only 35 percent of the Kenyan government's development plan; in 1990, the figure was nearly 90 percent.[14] In theory, this implies an increase in influence for aid donors: Britain has so far been reluctant to use this influence to promote human rights.

Britain is the largest foreign investor in Kenya with investments valued at around £1.5 billion. Many British industries have had bases within Kenya since independence and new companies continue to be attracted there. During the first five months of 1990, trade missions from nearly seventy British companies visited Kenya. Despite competition for

---

[12] Overseas Development Administration (ODA), *British Aid Statistics, 1985–89*, London.

[13] ODA, *Britain and Kenya: Partners in Development*.

[14] *Economist* Intelligence Unit, *Kenya Country Report*, no. 3, London, (1990).

business from Western Europe, Japan and the U.S., Britain still remains
Kenya's chief supplier of manufactured goods.

Britain is also Kenya's biggest trading partner. Since
independence, with the exception of a few years, Britain has consistently
been Kenya's largest export market: in 1989, exports to the U.K.
constituted almost 20 percent of all Kenya's exports. Britain has also
remained the major source of Kenya's imports: in 1989, nearly 19
percent of all Kenya's imports were received from Britain.[15] The total
value of trade between the two countries in 1989 was valued at almost
£360 million.

Obviously, there is a major economic incentive for Britain to
maintain good relations with Kenya. As long as Kenya's economic
performance remains so much better than most other African countries
and remains a focus of British aspirations, there is little evidence to
suggest that the government will use aid as a lever to promote human
rights.

MILITARY AND STRATEGIC TIES

Britain's lack of resolve in pressing for democracy and human
rights is further influenced by the desire to maintain strong military links
between the two countries. Kenya is an important strategic ally of Britain.
This importance has diminished recently with the reduced threat of Soviet
expansionism in Somalia and Ethiopia. However, Kenya's support of the
coalition forces in the Gulf War enhanced its strategic position and won
praise from Britain.

Britain has enjoyed close military and security links with Kenya
since the time it was a colonial power. In the 1960s, Britain was
instrumental in setting up Kenya's armed forces when it provided aid in
the form of weapons, equipment and training. The Kenyan army was
derived from the indigenous armed force set up by the British to protect
their interests in East Africa. After independence, many British officers
were asked to stay on with their former regiments in the belief that this
would ensure stability and continuity in the new army. A British general
continued to serve as Army Commander and Chief of Defense Staff until
1969.

---

[15] Ibid (provisional figures for 1989).

In 1963, Britain gave 3.6 million in U.S. dollars to help establish the Kenyan navy. Officially inaugurated in 1964, the navy only became fully operational in 1976 when Kenyan cadets had finished being trained in Britain. A British officer remained in command until November 1972. The Kenyan Air Force was established in 1964 with aid and training from Britain.

Britain has long been an important supplier of arms to Kenya, which does not have its own arms industry. In the early 1980s, all Kenyan naval vessels were of British origin, many of the Kenyan Air Force's aircraft were made by the British Aerospace Corporation, and Britain was the source of much of the army's equipment.

A number of British military advisers and civilian technical representatives remain in Kenya. Mombasa provides Britain with an important refitting and resting post. Two thousand British infantry troops go to Kenya each year to carry out military training and exercises. Kenyan officers continue to train and be educated at British military academies.

Like the military establishment, Kenya's police force also grew out of various security forces that were set up by the British during the colonial period. Development aid from Britain is now allocated to projects which assist the Kenyan police, such as training, telecommunications systems and the provision of equipment. Scotland Yard is on occasion requested to assist the Kenyan police with investigations: most recently, they participated in the inquiry into Dr. Robert Ouko's death and that of Julie Ward, a British national who died in Kenya.

THE SPECIAL RELATIONSHIP

Relations between Kenya and Britain have remained cordial and friendly since independence. Apart from the commercial and military ties, there are a wealth of personal contacts and relationships that bind the two countries. Kenya has the second largest number of British expatriates in Africa. Each year over 400 Kenyans are awarded places to study in Britain under the Technical Co-operation Training Program, with up to 900 participating in the program in the U.K. at any one time. Many more are in Britain as postgraduate students. There are parliamentary exchanges between the House of Commons and the Kenyan parliament, and regular highlevel visits.

Britain is in an ideal position to address the human rights situation in Kenya. Unfortunately, it has been too preoccupied with protecting its economic interests to take effective action. In its eagerness to maintain good relations with Kenya, Britain turns a blind eye to human rights abuses and continues to back a government which is becoming increasingly repressive. In its efforts to always portray Kenya as peaceful and stable, Britain ignores political persecution and the lack of democracy. Periodic requests from British parliamentarians to release political detainees are token gestures of concern. If Britain wants to prove its commitment to democracy and pluralism, it should implement the June 1990 policy statement and suspend aid to Kenya until there is a genuine improvement in the human rights situation.

21

UNITED STATES POLICY

Over the last year, the United States government has increased its efforts to address the deteriorating human rights situation in Kenya. Since the crackdown on multiparty activists in July 1990, the U.S. has shifted away from the habitual silence that previously characterized its human rights policy towards Kenya, and has issued strongly-worded protests against violations by President Moi's government. To a large degree, this recent focus on human rights by the administration is a result not only of events in Kenya but also of pressure from Congress, which has been an outspoken critic of Kenya for years, as well as a recently active U.S. Embassy in Nairobi.

Unfortunately, this current willingness of the U.S. government to protest human rights abuses has, at several crucial junctures, been undermined by conciliatory gestures toward the Kenyan government. The administration apparently sees a conflict between human rights advocacy and other U.S. interests, and its attempts to compensate for its outspokenness on human rights have undermined its efforts. In attempting to ensure smooth relations with Kenya, the administration has sometimes made the mistake of offering economic rewards to an unpopular government which undercuts those Kenyans who are attempting to establish a foundation for a stable, democratic government, based on the rule of law.

For years the United States viewed Kenya as a stable and moderate African ally. Its anti-Soviet foreign policy and Western-oriented economy helped Kenya to become by 1990 the largest recipient of U.S. aid in sub-Saharan Africa. For fiscal year 1991, the Bush administration requested a total of $53 million in aid to Kenya, including $8 million in foreign military financing, $1.175 million in military training, and $7 million in economic support funds. This friendly relationship has also included a strategic dimension. Beginning in the late 1970s, the United States became increasingly concerned about Soviet influence in the Horn of Africa and the security of supply lines for Middle Eastern oil. The U.S. saw Kenya as a potential staging point for U.S. forces in the Indian Ocean, and as a result the U.S. signed the Facilities Access Agreement with Kenya in June 1980. The agreement provided for overflights, landing rights at three airfields, and port of call rights at Mombasa. Accompanying the agreement was an increase in U.S. military assistance, from a level of $20 million in 1980 to over $30 million in 1982.[1] With this agreement, the U.S. began to outdistance even the United Kingdom as the major supplier of arms and military equipment to Kenya. Since the agreement, the U.S. has maintained only a minimal number of personnel in Kenya and has not established a permanent military presence, yet it has regarded Kenya as an essential part of the Central Command, previously known as the rapid deployment force. Although the Soviet influence is no longer a factor, the instability in the Horn is likely to ensure Kenya's continued importance to the U.S. government.

THE REAGAN ADMINISTRATION

Throughout the 1980s, despite a steady erosion of human rights, the United States did not often publicly push for improvements, even when unambiguous statements of policy were called for. For example, in Nairobi in January 1987, while the Kenyan government was engaged in a major crackdown on alleged members of Mwakenya, former Secretary of State George Shultz spoke in glowing terms of U.S.-Kenyan relations and assured Kenya of continued economic and military support. He never mentioned human rights issues.

Members of Congress were far more critical. Barely a week after Secretary Shultz's visit to Nairobi, Congressman Howard Wolpe, then Chairman of the Subcommittee on African Affairs of the House Committee on Foreign Affairs, held a press conference in Nairobi and condemned the serious erosion of democratic rights in Kenya. Congressman Wolpe cited many instances of intimidation of political opponents by the Kenyan security forces, observed that freedom of expression was under serious threat, and cautioned that this situation could ultimately damage Kenya's friendly relations with the United States.

The Reagan administration's silence on human rights issues was broken on a few occasions. The State Department issued a strongly-worded protest in 1986 when allegations concerning the torture of political prisoners surfaced. The U.S. also objected to Gibson Kamau

---

[1] Harold Nelson, ed., *Kenya: A Country Study* (Washington, D.C.: The American University Foreign Area Studies, 1984), p. 227.

Kuria's detention in March 1987. President Moi's strategy in detaining Kuria—to silence him and to provide an example for other would-be dissidents—ran aground when Moi visited Washington, D.C. shortly thereafter. During his visit, the State Department issued a protest which stated that reports of the torture of political prisoners "raise serious questions of human rights abuses." The statement also called on the Kenyan government to "investigate these most recent allegations, make the findings public" and take appropriate action if investigations confirmed that abuses were still occurring.[2] This criticism, combined with persistent questions raised by Congress, so angered President Moi that he abruptly curtailed his visit. The negative publicity apparently worked. Although the Kenyan government continued to target alleged members of Mwakenya, by mid-1987 the number of arrests and allegations of torture declined. In addition, nine political detainees were released in December 1987 and February 1988, and at least twenty convicted political prisoners were released after serving their sentences or were released after having their sentences reduced on account of good behavior.

Unfortunately, the Reagan administration failed to build on its criticism of the Kenyan government and to construct a coherent policy regarding human rights in Kenya. In fact, after March 1987, the U.S. did not publicly condemn any further violations by President Moi's government. Such serious developments as the screening of ethnic Somalis, the increase in the amount of time police can hold suspects in incommunicado detention, the loss of judges' security of tenure, the banning of three independent news magazines, and persistent reports of torture were virtually ignored by the Reagan administration.

The U.S. Embassy in Nairobi followed Washington's lead, keeping a low profile on human rights issues and taking little initiative in seeking out information about abuses and bringing them to the attention of the Kenyan authorities. Ambassador Elinor Constable intervened privately on behalf of individual Kenyans, such as the jailed historian Maina wa Kinyatti who was married to an American, and Gibson Kamau Kuria and responded to inquiries from Congress and human rights groups. Had the Embassy's intervention been broader in scope, rather than focusing on a few individual cases, it would undoubtedly have achieved greater results.

---

[2] Blaine Harden, "Kenya Says Lawyer Joined Rebel Group; Attorney in Torture Case Accused of Subversion," *The Washington Post*, March 14, 1987.

In the mid-1980s, the Kenya chapters of the State Department's annual *Country Reports on Human Rights* did little to compensate for the administration's general neglect of Kenyan human rights problems. The *Country Reports*, which catalogue and protest human rights abuses around the world, generally understated the severity of human rights problems in Kenya, while sometimes accurately reporting on isolated instances. For example, the 1986 and 1987 *Country Reports* consistently downplayed the use of torture by the Kenyan authorities. Rather than stating in its own voice that torture occurs, the State Department conceded only that "[t]orture has been cited in the Kenyan press and has been noted by human rights organizations and in the international media." The 1987 report distanced itself from the claims even further by stating that: "[i]solated reports of police torture do not suggest that torture is commonly practiced, but rather indicate that physical abuse and degradation are occasionally carried out by some persons without official government sanction." Apparently, though inexplicably, the State Department deemed it unnecessary to conduct its own investigations into the reports of torture.

The *Country Reports* also underestimated reports of arbitrary arrests and disappearances and downplayed the significance of the 1988 constitutional amendments. For example, the 1988 report, while accurately describing government control over journalists, failed to note in detail the persecution of Bedan Mbugua, the editor of *Beyond*, and the official harassment of Gitobu Imanyara. In another example, the 1989 report corrected some of these imbalances, but seriously underplayed the discriminatory and repressive nature of the screening of Kenyans of Somali origin.[3]

THE BUSH ADMINISTRATION

By the spring of 1990, the beginnings of a coherent U.S. human rights policy emerged, partly due to Smith Hempstone, President Bush's appointment as the new U.S. Ambassador in Nairobi. In a move which

---

[3] For a more extensive analysis of the State Department's country reports see *Critique: Review of the Department of State's Country Reports on Human Rights Practices for 1988* (New York: Lawyers Committee for Human Rights and Human Rights Watch, various years).

surprised   many   observers—apparently   including   the   State
Department—Ambassador Hempstone, formerly an African-based U.S.
reporter and an editor of the ultra-conservative *Washington Times*, adopted
a policy of outspoken identification with the goal of multiparty
democracy.   Upon his arrival in Nairobi, the Ambassador began to invite
human rights advocates and proponents of multiparty rule to gatherings
at the embassy. In a May 1990 speech before Kenyan businessmen,
Ambassador Hempstone stated that Washington would give preference in
its dispensation of foreign aid to those nations that "nourish democratic
institutions, defend human rights, and practice multiparty politics."[4]
The statement outraged President Moi and provoked a chorus of
condemnations from members of KANU.   The day after Ambassador
Hempstone's speech, President Moi pointedly noted that Kenya was a
"sovereign state and equal to other states and does not require any
guidance from outsiders on how to run its affairs." Days later, Cabinet
Minister Elijah Mwangale publicly accused the U.S. of engaging in
treason by pouring money into dissident activities.[5] The *Kenya Times*
perhaps best summed up the reaction of the Kenyan government in a
front page editorial which stated: "Shut Up Mr. Ambassador."

In Kenya's case, Washington at first kept up the momentum
started by Hempstone by issuing timely and strongly-worded protests
condemning the July 1990 arrests of prominent human rights and
multiparty advocates. According to a statement protesting the arrests of
Kenneth Matiba and Charles Rubia:

> We are distressed by the detention without charge in
> Nairobi during the past two days of Kenneth Matiba and
> Charles Rubia....These actions can only serve to tarnish
> Kenya's image in the international community. We call
> on the government of Kenya to accord these people due
> process. We further urge the Kenyan government to

---

[4] Jane Perlez, "U.S. Envoy Steps Into Political Firestorm in Kenya," *The New York Times*, May 6, 1990.

[5] "U.S.-Kenyan Dispute Grows a Little Testier," *The New York Times*, May 9, 1990.

allow its citizens the right to express opinions freely and
to assemble peacefully without hindrance...[6]

Unfortunately in the same period, the administration's response
to the massive crackdown against demonstrators which resulted in the
death of at least 100 people at the hands of security forces, was
inappropriately tepid. Appearing to suggest that demonstrators had been
responsible for the violence, the Administration stated:

We regret the violence and trust that restraint will be
shown by all, as the Government of Kenya attempts to
restore order.

The State Department continued to undercut itself. On July 5,
1990—only days after the Kenyan government swept multiparty
campaigners and human rights activists into jail—the U.S. signed an
agreement that would have allowed the Kenyan government to receive
$5 million in military assistance. Congressional leaders reacted angrily
and demanded a suspension of foreign aid, including the $5 million.
After weeks of bargaining with Congress, Assistant Secretary of State for
African Affairs Herman Cohen reluctantly agreed to suspend delivery of
this military aid, but continued to press Congress to provide portions of
non-military assistance. Partially due to Congress's anger over the $5
million, Kenya released lawyers John Khaminwa and Mohamed Ibrahim
in July 1990.

Secretary Cohen visited Nairobi in August 1990, in an attempt to
repair what Washington saw as the damage done to U.S.-Kenyan
relations by Hempstone's high public profile—which included providing
sanctuary in the U.S. Embassy to Gibson Kamau Kuria. The visit dealt a
severe blow to the entire human rights community in Kenya, and, by
extension, in Africa as a whole. When asked about U.S. backing for
multiparty democracy, Cohen responded that "while the United States
favors a multiparty system, who are we to say that it is good for
everybody?"[7] This suggested that Africans were somehow to be treated

---

[6] State Department Daily Briefing, July 6, 1990.

[7] Jane Perlez, "With Care, U.S. Presses Kenyans to Open Their Political Process,"
The New York Times, August 6, 1990.

differently from people struggling for democracy in other parts of the world. Cohen also commended the deliberations of the KANU Review Committee, and told the press that "the people of Kenya, under the leadership of President Moi, are now in the process of making some important decisions about their own political future." Cohen pointedly refused to meet privately with the most prominent critics of Kenya's government, although he met with a few less well-known individuals associated with the pro-democracy movement who were invited to an embassy function along with government officials.

The significance of Cohen's visit cannot be overstated, coming as it did on the heels of brutal measures to contain pro-democracy protests. In regard to the detentions that occurred in early July, Cohen claimed that he had "discussed recent events in Kenya" with President Moi, but that he was "not at liberty" to reveal what Moi had said about them. However, Cohen's otherwise warm relations with President Moi's government left serious doubts in Kenya as to whether human rights concerns were raised with a sufficient degree of seriousness, even in private discussions.

In contrast to the conciliatory approach adopted by the Bush administration, the U.S. Congress demonstrated its concern in the foreign aid appropriations act for fiscal year 1991, passed and signed in November 1990. Initiated by Senator Edward Kennedy and included in the bill by the chair of the Appropriation Foreign Operations Subcommittee, Senator Patrick Leahy, Section 597 of the foreign aid act required President Bush to certify that the Kenyans had met the following four human rights conditions before releasing an estimated $7 million in economic support funds and $8 million in foreign military financing aid: 1) take steps to charge and try, or release all prisoners, including those detained for political reasons; 2) cease any physical abuse or mistreatment of prisoners; 3) restore the independence of the judiciary; and 4) restore freedom of expression. To emphasize Congress's concerns, Senator Leahy and his staff led a delegation of five other Senators, including Al Gore and Barbara Mikulski, on a trip to Nairobi in November 1990. While there, Leahy made strong representations on behalf of imprisoned democracy advocates and reiterated the concerns expressed in the foreign aid appropriations act.

Another $5 million setback to the U.S.'s improving human rights policy occurred in early February 1991, when the Bush administration rewarded the Kenyan government with military assistance. To avoid the human rights conditions on 1991 foreign aid funds for Kenya, the State

Department instead drew the $5 million from 1990 assistance already in the pipeline, which Congress had withheld after the crackdown in July 1990. The administration justified the grant on several grounds. Contrary to a common perception in the U.S., the administration did not state that aid was granted because of Kenya's support for the U.S. during the Gulf War. The administration publicly justified the aid grant on "marginal improvements" in human rights. At a March 12 press briefing, the State Department's Richard Boucher stated that the assistance was provided "to acknowledge limited steps that have occurred in the area of human rights..." He cited new limits on the president's authority to dismiss judges, the reinstatement of secret balloting in primary elections, and the deliberations of the KANU Review Commission.

In fact, the aid grant was a reward for Kenya's support in other political and military respects. First and foremost, President Moi helped the U.S. deal with the embarrassing problem of several hundred Libyan prisoners of war in Chad who the U.S. had been arming and training to use against the Qadhafy regime. When the Habré government in Chad fell to forces friendlier toward Libya, Kenya agreed to provide refuge for the prisoners, who were hastily evacuated from Ndjamena by the U.S..[8] The Kenyan government also assisted the U.S. by helping to evacuate Americans from Mogadishu and Khartoum, who were thought to be at risk respectively because of the impending collapse of Siad Barre's government in Somalia and support for Iraq in Sudan.

Congressional leaders once again reacted with sharp disapproval toward the administration's overtures to the Kenyan government. Within weeks of the granting of the aid, Senators Paul Simon (the chair of the Senate Subcommittee on Africa), Nancy Kassebaum (the ranking Republican on the Africa subcommittee), and Patrick Leahy issued sharp rebukes to the State Department. Senator Kennedy introduced a new resolution calling for a suspension of all assistance to Kenya. In the House, Representatives led by Howard Wolpe badgered Secretary Cohen about the decision during congressional hearings on the administration's foreign aid request for 1992.

---

[8] Interestingly, in May 1991, despite accepting $5 million as a reward for their assistance, the Kenyan government decided that it would no longer accept the Libyan POWs and those who decided not to return to Libya were accepted into the U.S. as political refugees.

Only days after the administration's gesture of support, the Kenyans authorities arrested Gitobu Imanyara. The State Department, which was acutely embarrased by the jailing of Imanyara, responded with a strongly-worded statement issued simultaneously in Nairobi and Washington:

> The United States government is dismayed by the arrest on March 1 of Nairobi Law Monthly editor Gitobu Imanyara. This step, which is clearly in retaliation for material appearing in Mr. Imanyara's publication, is another denial of freedom of expression in Kenya.
>
> The United States calls upon the government of Kenya to release Mr. Imanyara without delay and to move to correct other outstanding human rights problems, including detentions without charge and other abuses. We urge the government of Kenya to move promptly towards greater respect for human rights.[9]

At a Congressional hearing in May 1991, Secretary Cohen said that he felt personally betrayed by the incident.

Congress responded to Imanyara's arrest with an outpouring of congressional cables, letters and phone calls urging the Kenyan government to release Imanyara, as well as Kenneth Matiba, Charles Rubia and Raila Odinga, and to take other steps to improve serious human rights problems.

In late March, Ambassador Hempstone made waves again after a meeting in late March with Matthew Muli, then the Kenyan Attorney General. At the meeting, Hempstone inquired about the health of Matiba, Rubia and Odinga, who at that time were detained without charge and requested that the attorney general tell him when and where the three men had been able to meet with their families, doctors and lawyers. Following the private meeting, Ambassador Hempstone told the Kenyan press exactly what had transpired, reiterating his request for details on the well-being of the prisoners. Kenyan officials were outraged at what they considered a breach of diplomatic protocol and the Kenyan

---

[9] Press release from the U.S. Department of State, Office of the Assistant Secretary/Spokesman, March 1, 1991.

parliament predictably devoted a session to railing against Hempstone.

Congressional scrutiny has been the most consistent U.S. voice for human rights improvements in Kenya, including the release of Kenyan detainees and the initiation of other positive changes. While Congress debated conditions for Kenya's aid in fiscal year 1992, the Kenyan authorities saw fit to release Kenneth Matiba, Charles Rubia and Raila Odinga. Worries about their deteriorating health were certainly a factor in the release of these prisoners, but the aid controversy was also an important factor. Congressional attention has also been helpful in securing the releases of Gitobu Imanyara and Rev. Lawford Ndege Imunde[10] and in encouraging legislation which reduced some of President Moi's influence over the judiciary and abolished queue-voting by the KANU Commission. This legislation provided Kenyan diplomats in the United States with an opening to argue that Kenya was indeed improving its human rights record, but the argument has apparently fallen on deaf ears. The U.S. administration has stated several times recently that more serious human rights improvements are needed. As of July 1991, the administration had made no attempt to certify that the conditions imposed by Congress had been fulfilled.

Washington is at a crucial point in its relations with Kenya. The administration can choose to build on the momentum created by Congress and by its own Ambassador in Nairobi, and develop a policy which consistently and constructively seeks to advance human rights in Kenya. The beginnings of such a policy were evident in 1990, but they were unfortunately undercut by simultaneous extensions of support toward the Kenyan government. As the Kenyan reaction to past public comments have shown, the government is susceptible to American criticism.

The alternative to this policy, to continue to send conflicting messages to the Kenyan government, will inform the repressive forces entrenched there that U.S. economic and strategic considerations

---

[10] This congressional attention has not gone unnoticed by human rights activists in Kenya. In a March 1991 letter to Senator Bob Graham, a human rights lawyer in Kenya stated that: "On behalf of the pro-democracy advocate in Kenya...we wish you and your colleagues in Congress to know how heartened we all felt on seeing a copy of your statement to President Moi" which protested the arrest of Gitobu Imanyara.

ultimately outweigh concerns for the people of Kenya themselves. More importantly, it will convey the same message to those Kenyans who have courageously confronted the government in the belief that the U.S. would come to their support.

22

RECOMMENDATIONS

Africa Watch calls on the Kenyan government to implement the following changes with immediate effect in order to meet its international legal obligations:

- Reaffirm the right of free assembly under Kenyan law, and permit nonviolent demonstrations on matters of national concern to proceed without violence or threat of violence from members of the police and security forces. Abolish laws making meetings of three or more illegal;

- Launch an independent and public investigation into the circumstances surrounding the deaths of demonstrators on February 23, 1990, and July 7, 1990, and on other occasions when people have assembled to protest in a nonviolent fashion. Bring to trial any members of the police and security forces against whom there is evidence of the use of excessive violence;

- Reaffirm the right of freedom of expression as provided by the constitution, and allow all Kenyans to speak freely and publicly, publish their opinions in print or transmit them over electronic newsmedia, and travel within the country and to and from Kenya without restriction or threat of violence, to them, their families, their associates, or others who share their views;

- Allow the public to exercise the constitutional right to vote, whether a member of KANU or not, without fear of intimidation and physical assault to either themselves or family members;

- Restore parliamentary freedoms and prevent intimidation of MPs, including their expulsion from the party, harassment and interrogation by security personnel, use of economic penalties;

- Guarantee the protection of constitutional rights to nonparty members and put an end to coercive

recruitment tactics; recruitment quotas for local
officials should cease;

- Cease police harassment of nonparty members;
- Restore all rights, privileges and licenses which have
  been suspended by KANU disciplinary action;
- Clarify the role and mandate of KANU youthwingers.
  They should not under any circumstances be allowed
  to act as a police force;
- Publish the full report of Inspector John Troon into
  the circumstances surrounding the killing of Dr.
  Robert Ouko, launch a further independent and public
  investigation into any details remaining unresolved,
  and bring to trial any individuals against whom there is
  any evidence of illegal behavior;
- Cease the intimidation of the clergy and the
  interference with their efforts to carry out their
  pastoral duties;
- Launch a public inquiry into the suspicious
  circumstances surrounding the death of Bishop
  Alexander Muge;
- Remove restrictions on publications that have been
  banned, including *Financial Review, Beyond,* and
  Development Agenda. Allow editors and publishers to
  operate without sanction or threat of sanction;
- Restore fully the independence of the judiciary. The
  government should cease the practice of using
  expatriate judges on contract to achieve politically-
  motivated decisions. The government should ensure
  that all Kenyans enjoy the rights enshrined in
  international standards. That is: the right to a public
  trial before an independent and impartial tribunal; the
  right to be presumed innocent until proved guilty; the
  right to be tried within a reasonable period of time;
  the right to have legal counsel of one's choice and to
  have adequate time to prepare a defense; the right not
  to be compelled to testify or confess guilt and the right
  of appeal;
- Cease the practice of convicting detainees on the basis
  of uncorroborated confessions. Where either the
  detainee or their lawyer asserts that the confession was
  obtained under duress, it should be regarded as null
  and void;

- Inform all detainees and prisoners of their right to consult a lawyer of their choosing, and respect that right;
- Cease the intimidation of detainees who choose to exercise their legal right to consult a lawyer; and establish a system of legal aid for defendants;
- Ensure that appeals go forward as a matter of urgency without delay, to prevent sentences being served before appeal is accepted;
- Abolish detention without trial. Bring all detainees before a court to be charged within 48 hours of their arrest;
- Abolish the holding charge that allows security forces to hold suspects while further investigations are conducted. If the prosecution does not have enough evidence to bring charges, suspects should be released without further delay;
- Ensure that bail again becomes a constitutional right. It should not be used by the state to punish by holding suspects for long periods in remand in conditions similar to those for political prisoners;
- End the harassment of ex-detainees and political prisoners and allow them to enjoy full rights as normal citizens by ceasing interference with employment opportunities and studies and putting an end to surveillance by Special Branch and other security forces;
- End reprisals against families and relatives of persons detained on political charges. Allow them to enjoy the rights they are entitled to, and cease the additional unnecessary suffering prompted by denying their visitors' rights, withholding information or subjecting them to humiliating and obstructive behavior by the authorities;
- Repeal all sedition laws. Establish a commission to investigate the abusive use of charges of treason, subversion and breach of the peace;
- Cease all forms of physical and psychological torture: allow legal access to detainees held in police and Special Branch cells and unofficial detention centers;

- Permit and facilitate independent public investigation into the practice of torture within Kenya's detention centers, and prosecute any individuals against whom there is evidence that they have either practiced torture or condoned it;
- Ensure that people charged with treason or on charges related to treason obtain a fair trial in accordance with internationally recognized standards. In particular, their complaints of torture, denial of medical attention and interference with their right to legal counsel should be investigated without delay and corrective action taken;
- Cease the routine physical and psychological abuse of prisoners by guards and by convicted prisoners who are allowed to act in a supervisory role;
- Allow the International Committee of the Red Cross (ICRC) which operates under rules of strict confidentiality to visit all prisoners held on political grounds;
- Improve living standards and medical care in prisons so as to be in accordance with international standards and Kenyan law;
- Permit and facilitate an independent public investigation into the abuse and deaths of inmates in Kenya's prisons, and bring to trial individuals responsible for the death or ill-treatment of prisoners. Observe requirements for registering suspects;
- Establish an independent commission to assess the losses suffered by Kenyan Somalis caused by the screening program, including both property lost and disruption caused by the process; return all confiscated property, and award full and unconditional compensation as soon as is reasonably possible;
- Abolish the special privileges and immunities granted to game wardens and other members of government forces to shoot-to-kill anyone suspected of illegal poaching activities. Pre-existing Kenyan law provides adequate security for such government officers under the right of self-defence. The shoot-to-kill policy should be replaced by rules of engagement which clearly

establish that members of the security forces will only use lethal force in proportion to the threat posed to them or to others;

- Reaffirm that all sections of the government forces, including the police, Special Branch, Criminal Investigations Department, General Service Unit,the Administration Police and amongst others, the Home Guards, are subject to the law and not permitted to engage in excessive or indiscriminate violence;

- Launch independent public investigations into incidents of violence which have occurred during disputes over land, including the clearances of squatter areas and informal markets in and around Nairobi. Bring charges against any members of government forces where there is evidence that they have used excessive or indiscriminate violence, or were implicated in planning and implementing evictions that are either illegal or carried out in an illegal or violent manner;

- Institute a commission of inquiry into illegal land acquisition, the problem of landlessness, land registration and squatter status. Register all squatters. Respect the findings of the investigations regarding ownership of land, and pay full and immediate compensation to individuals who have been deprived of land, assets or income as a result;

- Launch a public investigation into the massacre at Wajir in 1984 and other incidents of deaths at the hands of government forces in the North Eastern Province. Bring to trial any individuals against whom there is evidence that they have been involved in such killings;

- Repeal the emergency powers which the government enjoys in North Eastern Province;

- Reaffirm that all Kenyans, regardless of ethnic background, are equal before the law, and that discrimination on the grounds of ethnicity by any individual or body, public or private, is illegal and unconstitutional;

- Abolish the requirement that all Kenyan citizens of Somali ethnicity be required to carry special identification;
- Permit and facilitate the immediate return of all Kenyan-Somalis who were illegally expelled from the country. Restore the citizenship and rights of those illegally stripped of Kenyan citizenship;
- Allow refugees to register according to international law without difficulty and facilitate their protection by ending the harassment of refugees at the border and the arbitrary expulsion of refugees. Allow all registered refugees to live without fear of being killed, imprisoned and intimidated by security forces. Conduct a public inquiry into the massive corruption which allows security forces to extort bribes from refugees;
- End abuses against women through arbitrary and so-called prostitute police roundups. Women should not be subjected, for harassment purposes, to forcible examinations concerning sexually transmitted diseases.

APPENDIX A
A VERY KENYAN TALE
THE STORY OF ODUOR ONG'WEN

I was born on September 14, 1960, at Udenda Village in West Alego location of Siaya District in Kenya. Both my parents were peasants and my father died in 1976. I have four brothers and two sisters, among whom only my eldest brother works. After passing my examinations with three principles and one subsidiary, I was admitted to the University of Nairobi in the Faculty of Science where I studied computer science and operations research as majors and chemistry as minor (1980-84).

Upon joining the University of Nairobi in October 1980, I was elected as representative of first year students to the Faculty Board, the governing body of the faculty. In 1980, the government had banned the student union, the Nairobi University Students Organization (NUSO) and, apart from representation at faculty boards, there were no democratic and independent student organizations to articulate student interests. We began agitating for the unbanning of NUSO and in November 1980 we elected an interim committee to work for the launching of an independent student association. It was from this time that Special Branch began keeping me under surveillance.

In April 1981, the government barred Oginga Odinga, a former vice-president and leader of the only post-independence opposition party, from taking part in parliamentary by-elections. I, with other students, led a student demonstration against this decision. On the same evening of the demonstration I was arrested by the Special Branch and questioned at their offices at what was then known as Carpet House (now offices of the *Kenyan Times* newspaper) for two consecutive days. During the arrest, I was threatened with torture but was not physically tortured. I was later released with strict warning not to tell anybody. However, I could not hide this illegal detention and I talked about my ordeal with the students.

On May 16, 1981, there was once again a massive demonstration by the students against the barring of Mr. Odinga and a candidate in Busia South constituency, a Mr. Diffu, from contesting the by-elections. The demonstration was also in support of doctors who had embarked on a nationwide strike demanding improved working conditions. The state expelled all the known members of the interim committee. The paramilitary police, the General Service Unit (GSU), was sent to raid student halls of residence at 1:00 A.M. where many students were injured from either police beatings or from "accidents" while jumping from upper floors of their halls. After the police had occupied the university campuses for four days, the university was closed on May 18, 1981.

Following the closure of the university, all students were ordered to report to their area chiefs. I was, however, summoned by the Special Branch at Busia where I made three statements to the political police. I was made to report to the Special Branch twice a week for the entire duration of the university's closure.

The university was re-opened in August 1981 and the students continued with their legal struggle to have an independent student organization. I was at the center of these democratic struggles. The Special Branch intensified their surveillance of me and between August 1981 and March 1982 I was arrested on three occasions where I was questioned and released.

On February 16, 1982, the students succeeded in securing registration of the Students Organization of Nairobi University (SONU). I was elected onto the Student Representation Council (SRC) which was the executive body of SONU. In May 1982, SONU took a strong stand against bulldozing the country into one-party dictatorship and against arbitrary arrests and detentions of lecturers and other Kenyans. Two days after we had issued a statement opposing the introduction of de jure one-party rule, my university room at Dag Hammarskjold hall, room 235, was raided and thoroughly searched in my absence. I came from lectures to find the room turned upside down.

Between May and August 1982, special surveillance of me was intensified. I even managed to identify two of them, whose names were Mr. Busuru and Mr. Obara.

On the night of July 27, 1982, after I had addressed the students on the changes government was introducing into the loan scheme, I was once again arrested, questioned and threatened. I was released around 3:00 A.M. and warned not to address further meetings and not to tell the students what had happened. I defied those unlawful orders and went ahead to address similar meetings at Kenyatta University College on July 28, 1982, and Kabete Campus on July 30, 1982.

On August 1, 1982, there was a coup attempt by personnel of the Kenya Air Force. The university was closed the following day. I went to my rural home (Udenda). On August 9, 1982, I received a summons from the Siaya Special Branch office to report there immediately. I went to Siaya Special Branch offices on August 10, 1982. I was questioned for five hours, then released.

On August 16, 1982, Special Branch personnel came for me at Udenda. The time was 2:48 P.M. and they dragged me from lunch into a landrover, registration number KVB 014, and sped away with me to Siaya. They were four in number and armed. I was booked at Siaya Police Station where I stayed overnight. The following day, August 18, 1982, I was taken to Kisumu Provincial Special Branch headquarters, where I was questioned for seven hours and then locked in a cell. The cell had no blanket. I stayed there for two days and two nights. On August 20, 1982, I was taken to Nairobi (Carpet House) Special Branch headquarters with six other people. The same night we were taken to GSU Training Camp at Embakasi on the outskirts of Nairobi. We were detained at Embakasi GSU Training School, Sungura Dormitory, illegally and incommunicado for forty-two days, from August 20–September 30, 1982.

During the forty-two days of detention at Embakasi we were subjected to a lot of physical and psychological torture. We were made to lie on our backs on sisal mat with legs straight and arms alongside the body for 12 hours (from 7:00 A.M. to 7:00 P.M.). No talking was allowed and even when one wanted to go to the toilet, he was not supposed to speak but only raise up his hand and be escorted to the toilet at gunpoint. We bathed only once a week and meals were irregular.

We would be called one by one for interrogation at the Commandant's office. The interrogators were Special Branch officers, CID officers and a contingent of GSU personnel whose duty it was to beat those they considered obstinate in order to extract confessions. During this period of detention I was thoroughly beaten on three occasions on the orders of a CID officer by the name of Peter Mutua Sila. I did not confess.

On September 30, 1982, I was taken to court and charged with sedition. The substance of the charge was that on August 1, 1982, I "took part in a demonstration, the purpose of which was to excite disaffection against the government of Kenya as by law established." I was not required to plead to the charge as consent to prosecute had not been obtained from the attorney general—I was then condemned to Remand and Allocation Prison at Industrial Area, Nairobi. The consent never came until January 1983.

During this time in prison, we were subjected to worse treatment than convicted prisoners. Body searches were conducted on us twice daily and this was done in the most humiliating manner. We university students numbered sixty-seven. We were denied bail pending appeal.

Some had denied the charges, and others, including myself, had not even pleaded—but we were subjected to the most humiliating treatment.

All sixty-seven of us were kept in Block E and in cells measuring six feet by six feet. The cells were poorly ventilated and in each cell there were between six and eight prisoners. We had no bedding except two torn blankets each and were not allowed to go to the toilet—relieving ourselves in the chamberpots inside the tiny and crowded cells. We were locked inside the cells almost 24-hours-a-day, except a five minute spell during which we took our meals and ate inside the filthy, crowded cells. The blankets were heavily lice-infested and we were not given time to have them sprayed with disinfectant or to air them out in the sun.

Meals were half-cooked and consisted of porridge (served at 6:00 A.M.), beans with ugali (served at 9:00 A.M.) for lunch and supper comprising ugali with decaying kale vegetables (served between 11:30 A.M. and noon). The ration for remand prisoners was half that of convicted prisoners, which in itself is very little. We were denied any reading materials, toothpaste, soap and medical treatment.

Special Branch officers visited the prison from time to time to threaten us individually to plead guilty to the framed-up charges. The state failed to persuade us into pleading guilty and could not find people they could convince to falsely testify against us. They isolated six students they had found collaborators to testify against: and the remaining sixty-one of us were released—of course, explained as the magnanimity of "His Excellency Mtukufu Rais Daniel arap Moi, the ever merciful, mindful of all Kenyans' welfare and lover of the youth." We were released on February 23, 1983, and had to report to the university and sit examinations on March 1, 1983.

Immediately after examinations in March, the university was closed again until October 3, 1983. A few days after the university was re-opened, a Special Branch officer, a Mr. Ondiek, approached me to try and persuade me to abandon my role in the leadership of SONU. I rejected this suggestion. On November 16, 1983, I was elected its Secretary General. I continued to be subjected to constant police harassment and threats throughout my office as the SONU Secretary General, the most serious being my arrest in April 1984 just a few days before the beginning of my final year examinations. I had just returned from a two-week visit to the Soviet Union, Czechoslovakia and Bulgaria during which I had attended an Executive Committee meeting of the International Union of Students (IUS) in Prague and the 14th IUS Congress in Sofia. My crime was visiting a socialist country.

After completing my studies at the University of Nairobi, I was posted to Kipsigis Girls' High School in Kericho District as a teacher. This was in August 1984. During the same month, one of the Special Branch personnel who had been deployed to secretly monitor activities of students and lecturers, a Mr. George Okumu, was transferred to Kericho. From September 1984 to April 1986, there was constant interference with my mail. I got evidence of this when after my arrest when I was taken to Nyayo House, Nairobi. The Special Branch officers showed me one of my telegrams they had intercepted. I was also shown application for scholarship forms from the IUS in which I had asked IUS to send for two expelled students from the University of Nairobi, Karimi Nduthu and Philip Trop arap Kitur.

In February–April 1985, there was a crisis at the University of Nairobi. This crisis was sparked off by arbitrary expulsions from the university of five students and the withdrawal of many scholarships. Students in all the campuses of the university, as a result, staged a week-long peaceful sit-in culminating in a prayer meeting on February 10, 1985. The police, under the command of the current Commissioner of Police, Philip Kilonzo, stormed the prayer meeting and bloodily shot a number of students. Five students were arrested during the fracas, among whom was former SONU chairman, Julius Mwandawiro Mghanga. Another student was taken for Tirop arap Kitur and also violently arrested.

Tirop himself managed to escape the dragnet and, in company of another expelled student, Karimi Nduthu, came to stay with me in Kericho. I tried to help them secure scholarships to finish their degree courses through the IUS scholarship scheme. During the trials that followed the student arrests, I helped in raising funds for the students' legal defense. I was thus arrested in March 1985 and threatened that I would be charged with inciting students. I was released after being held in Nakuru Police Station for two days.

In the same month of March 1985, students of Kipsigis Girls' High School staged a play entitled "Now What?" written and directed by me during the Kenya Secondary School Drama Festival. The play was banned after winning both at subdistrict and district levels. As a result, the Special Branch officers again visited me in the school and questioned me.

On March 27, 1986, President Moi made a stopover at Kipsigis Girls' High School where I was teaching. He was on his way to Kisis Teachers' College to officiate at the college's graduation ceremony. While addressing students and teachers of Kipsigis Girls, President Moi unleashed a very scathing attack on me, claiming that I was just teaching students "politics of subversion." Hardly two weeks later, on April 14, 1986, I was arrested.

On April 14, 1986, at 4:30 P.M., five Special Branch officers, namely Superintendent Chukri, Inspector Kimeto, two other officers and a driver came to Kipsigis Girls' High School, and Superintendent Chukri told me that he was under instructions to take me to a place he "did not know." When I asked him whether I was under arrest, he refused to confirm or deny it. He simply insisted that he had been instructed to take me. He said before that, they would like to search my staffroom desk and my house. The search in both places lasted four and a half hours and was done in the presence of a friend of mine and a teacher at Kericho High School. During the search the police took with them a number of my personal correspondence, newspaper cuttings and a few books like Ngugi wa Thiongo's *Devil on the Cross, Barrel of a Pen*, A. M. Babu's *African Socialism or Socialist Africa?*, Fanon's *Wretched of the Earth*, Freire's *Pedagogy of the Oppressed* and a few works of Marx, Engels and Lenin. They also confiscated a completed manuscript of a book on my detention (August 1982 to February 1983) and a few articles I had written for local newspapers. They had a white Subaru saloon car.

At 9:00 P.M., I was taken to Kericho Police Station where a big cell was emptied of its inmates and I was locked in. I was denied supper and was not given any blanket: I slept on the cold cemented floor.

The following day at about 5:15 A.M. Supt. Chukri and another officer, plus the driver of the day before, came for me and drove me to Nakuru in the same Subaru car. At Nakuru I was taken to the provincial Special Branch officer, Senior Superintendent Rono, who asked me a number of demeaning questions, slapped me and even attempted to spit on my face.

At 8:17 we left Nakuru with the same police officers and I was driven to Nairobi where I was booked at Muthangari Police Station at 11:20 A.M. Up to this time, I had not eaten anything since my lunch the previous day.

I was kept at Muthangari until 9:27 P.M. when three people came for me in a white landrover...I was led into the vehicle, blindfolded and ordered to lie on my back on the floor of the landrover. I was driven for a long time about the streets of Nairobi, apparently to confuse me, then finally taken to a small underground cell measuring about eight feet long by five feet wide, painted dark and very dimly lit. It had no ventilation and was mechanically air-conditioned. The cell had a mattress and one old blanket. After I had got rid of the blindfold, I complained about being denied food for over 30 hours. I was then again given cold ugali and sukumawiki (kale).

As the cell was dark, only dimly lit by starlets of faint light from one of the walls, it was not possible to distinguish between day and night. My only way of measuring time became the change of guards, which was done every six hours.

The next day, in the morning hours, I was blindfolded, led by the hand out of the cell and into an elevator which took me many floors up. After being led out of the elevator I was dragged up another set of stairs—a very punishing experience for a blindfolded man.

I was led into a room where, on removal of the blindfold, I found myself before a panel of twelve men. The head of this panel, I came to learn, was James Opiyo. Others on the panel were a Mr. E. Mjomba, a Mr. Wachira and a Mr. Waweru.

The panel began questioning me on a wide range of issues, including who my friends were; which politicians—local and international—I admired and who I was in touch with; my alleged role in MwaKenya; my family background and why I refused to heed their order when they told me to abandon student leadership while I was student at the University of Nairobi. They also questioned me on why I joined students in raising funds for legal defense of a former student leader, Mwandawiro Mghanga.

I answered as truthfully as I could recall. When I denied association with MwaKenya, the panel ordered me to take off all my clothes, to which I had no choice but to comply. They then ordered me to put my right forefinger on a point on the floor and spin around it very fast. I did. After about three minutes of spinning around the point, I began to feel dizzy. One of the interrogators then pushed me and I banged my head on the hard floor very hard and painfully. They then ordered me to perform 100 push-ups. I was still feeling dizzy and my banged head was also paining. But I had to comply. After doing about thirty-five push-ups I could not continue any more. The panel insisted that I proceed, but I had no more energy left to continue. Then all the twelve men descended on me with wood from broken table and chair legs while some had big tire treads. They beat me up until I lost consciousness. I do not know how long I lapsed but when I regained consciousness, Opiyo ordered that I be taken to the swimming pool for water treatment. I did not know what this meant and thought they were

sorry for beating me to unconsciousness and were thus ordering the
sentry to take me to a real swimming pool for recovery. I was allowed to
put on my clothes, blindfolded and led out, down a staircase and into the
elevator. When the elevator stopped at the basement I was led out, the
blindfold was removed and I was ordered to take off my clothes, I was
once again stark naked.

I was then ordered into another cell, similar to the one I had
slept in the previous night and told to stand against the farthest wall
looking at the door. I was surprised and caught off guard when a jet of
very cold water was directed at my eyes from a fire hose. The water was
under very high pressure and very cold. It hit me harder than a blow.
The jet continued even after I fell down until the water level in the cell
reached about three inches high. The door was then locked and a fan put
on to maintain the low temperature of the water.

I was left in that water for five consecutive days without food.
While in the water, I was not allowed even to go out to answer calls of
nature. I was thus forced to relieve myself in the water. After about three
days, the water turned corrosive and the skin of my feet began to itch.
Every six hours, as the police sentries changed guard, I was hit by the
cold jet of water for about one minute. After five days, I was asked
whether I was ready to talk, and I told my captors that I had always been
ready to talk. I was removed from the water, ordered to put my clothes
on, blindfolded and taken upstairs to the panel again. This second
appearance I met only eight of the panelists. They began questioning me
on the same line as the first interrogation. I insisted I was not going to
participate in their interrogation while I was so hungry and weak. They
tried to intimidate me but I stood my ground. Realizing that their threats
were an exercise in futility, they ordered a meal for me—ugali and
meat—which I could not eat since it was solid and I had been starved for
close to one week. They then brought fresh milk which I drank, then they
ordered that I be taken to rest.

I rested in a dry cell for a full day. The following day I was
blindfolded again and taken before the panel of eight. I once again
refused to admit the false allegations that I was involved with MwaKenya.
I was, as on the other day, made to remove all my clothes and do push-
ups. I was still very weak and could not manage even ten. So, as on the
previous occasion, I was beaten up. After some beating, Opiyo ordered his
panelists to halt the beatings and they stopped. I was then told to sit on
the floor stark naked with my legs stretched wide apart. I sat but refused
to stretch my legs. I feared that they wanted to castrate me. Then three

of the officers came and one held me by the hands while two stretched my legs. I attempted to resist but was overpowered. Held by a strong man, and with legs a-stretch, I was helpless. At this juncture one of the officers left and after a short time came back with a woman.

The woman began rebuking me and making unrepeatable comments, including the fact that I was not circumcised. It was after the woman's mention of circumcision that one of the panelists, Mr. Wachira, drew out a sharp knife, came and held my penis, threatening to circumcise me, unless I talked. I refused to budge. After some time, realizing that they were not making any headway, they left me and ordered that I put on my clothes before being led into another room which had only a chair. As usual, I was blindfolded as I was moved from one place to another.

I was kept in the isolated room for something like an hour before I was once again blindfolded and taken back to the interrogation room. When the blindfold was removed, I realized the panelists were twelve again. Also there was an empty chair next to mine. About one minute later a friend of mine was brought in blindfolded, made to sit and blindfolds removed. My friend was then asked to narrate "how we had attended a MwaKenya Congress" together. Without batting an eyelid, my friend began narrating how he had gone to Karatina for the congress and met me there, seated among the leaders—in front—and how he later left as we, the leaders, went to another venue for another meeting. I was shocked at how eloquently this man lied. But I did not hold it against him. I knew he could not stand the torture anymore. The day these Special Branch officers were alleging I had attended MwaKenya Congress (March 1, 1986), I was involved in two official functions, both in Kericho—hundreds of miles from Karatina. In the morning of that day, I had officiated at a district cross-country meeting at Kericho High School and in the afternoon I was the master of ceremonies at district drama festival at Kipsigis Girls' High School. I told my interrogators these facts but apparently they were not interested in the truth.

Then they brought another of my friends from Kericho, who refused to join them in their conspiracy of lies against me. He was whisked away very fast when he refused to corroborate lies. They had threatened they would bring another friend, but they changed their mind and only ordered me to remove my clothes. They began beating me to admit the allegations. The beatings concentrated on my joints and the soles of my feet where the skin was peeling off due to the long stay in water. Other allegations they wanted me to admit included the fact that

I attended a MwaKenya oathing ceremony on November 23, 1985, allegedly held somewhere on the outskirts of Nairobi. This was in spite of the fact that on November 23, 1985, we had a parents' speech and fund-raising day at Kipsigis Girls' School where I was the master of ceremonies. They also wanted me to admit that at 2:00 P.M. on January 2, 1986, I attended a MwaKenya meeting at Imperial Hotel in Kisumu, despite the fact that we had a staff meeting at Kipsigis Girls' High School of which minutes were available.

I was once again taken down and kept in water without food or toilet facilities for four days. On the fourth day I collapsed. By this time I had lost my voice and was very weak. I was removed from the water. I woke up to find myself in a dry cell lying on a mattress, and I was given hot milk to drink. For three consecutive days I was sent emissaries in the cell to convince me to accept the allegations, but I refused.

On April 26 (as I saw on the watch of one of the officers), Opiyo called for me at a small office where I found them with a person he introduced as the Deputy Director of Intelligence. They told me that there was no way I was going to leave that place free and that it was futile trying to resist. They told me even the State House was concerned that they had not disposed of me (I understood State House to mean President Daniel arap Moi). They also showed me blank detention forms signed by J. Mathenge, the Permanent Secretary in the Office of the President in charge of internal security and provincial administration.

Opiyo told me I had four options to choose from:

1.   Being tortured to death;
2.   Being detained without trial;
3.   Being charged with treason and sentenced to hang;
4.   Admitting a charge of sedition and being jailed for a few years.

None of the options were appealing to me but I also realized I was going to die in those dungeons. I told them I would not choose any of the options. I was then sent into the water again. However, after about three hours I was removed, dressed, blindfolded and driven away. I later found myself at Kilimani Traffic Police Headquarters where a confession was read to me and I was told to sign. I refused. The man who read the confession to me, Superintendent Huko, then said if I refused he would just hand me back to my people at Nyayo House. That is when I realized I had been held at Nyayo House all those days.

When I was taken back to Nyayo House, I was immediately led into a room that had some hooks in the ceiling. My legs were chained and I was suspended upside down with my hands tied. The officers then began beating me. This was the most uncomfortable position I had been in. I began feeling an intense headache as I was beaten. I promised to sign the confession.

On April 28, I was taken back to the Traffic Headquarters, which also house the firearms bureau, and I signed the confession. I was then given conditions, including mitigation—if I failed to adhere to this they would lead me back to Nyayo House for further torture. I just wanted to leave that place and agreed to accept anything. I was thus taken to court on April 29, 1986, at 4:52 P.M. where I was convicted of a sedition charge and sentenced to four years' imprisonment. I was taken to Nairobi Remand and Allocation Prison at Industrial Area.

On April 30, 1986, I wrote my appeal against conviction and sentence which the prison authorities submitted to the court on May 2, 1986. On receiving my appeal, the court authorities alerted the Special Branch, and on May 5, 1986, Peter Kimundi, a senior assistant commissioner of police, came to prison to intimidate me to withdraw the appeal. I refused. He left, assuring me that the appeal will not be listed, let alone heard.

I was transferred to Kamiti Maximum Security Prison on May 21, 1986, and on June 16, 1986, Opiyo visited Kamiti to threaten me to withdraw the appeal. According to Opiyo, if I did not withdraw the appeal, it would be delayed until I finished serving the four years or they would even consider enhancing my sentence. "You should not forget that the offense for which you were convicted carries a maximum of ten years' imprisonment," he told me.

Life in the Kenyan prisons, especially at Kamiti Maximum Security Prison—where I spent two years and eight months—becomes very difficult to describe. It is a disgraceful, inhuman and degrading situation. A warder does not hesitate to slap a prisoner or batter him with a bludgeon for petty reasons or amusement. For the ranks of corporal and above, the weapon used for illegal chastisement is the swagger stick.

Disobedience of lawful orders might include attempting to wash hands before a meal, hesitating to squat on one's haunches when one is taking a meal or being counted, failing to address the warder as afande (meaning my master) or asking to be escorted to dispensary when one is sick. Brutality and other forms of sadism are seen as the real medicine for a prisoner, whether convicted or not. The daily life of a prisoner in

Kenya is characterized by battery and insults. Sometimes prisoners are beaten to death. The four-year sentence I served at Kamiti Maximum Security Prison was permanently characterized by these.

According to the Prisons Act, every prisoner shall be entitled to a sufficient quantity of plain, wholesome food. The Minister for Home Affairs can make rules with regard to the provision of a suitable diet and dietary scales. This is only on paper. The diet in prison is simple, filthy and monotonous.

For breakfast, take a cauldron of boiling water, put in some stale maize flour, stir crudely for two to three minutes and dredge out the stiff porridge before being completely cooked, and, hey presto, you can serve the prisoner with half a liter of it for his breakfast. For lunch, again take a cauldron of boiling dirty water, put in stale maize flour, mingle crudely and when half-cooked, half-mingled, take out a paste and that is wholesome ugali for prisoners. Chop a few bundles of rotten yellow-leaf sukumawiki (kale) leaves, stems, roots and all, pour on these plenty of boiling water so that the sukumawiki scatters and floats in it, and there you have wholesome vegetables for the prisoners. This is then served with sixty grams of half-cooked ugali. It is instructive to note that for 1,700 prisoners at Kamiti, thirty kgs of stale sukumawiki gets cooked. For supper, you have ugali prepared as above, and some beans, stones and weevils, all boiled for some time and two drums of water added. The utensils which the meals are served with are enough to de-appetize.

As for clothing, prisoners continue wearing what colonialists declared fit for native *kaffirs*: shorts and collarless shirts made of cheap cotton calico without underpants. The attire is known in the prison nomenclature as *kunguru*.

This demeaning approach to the welfare of prisoners, does not allow for the provision of beds; they should sleep on the floor—cold and hard—with no mattress, of course, and only two very light blankets infested with lice and bedbugs. These blankets are always very dirty and dusty and prisoners are not allowed to wash them; they are always passed from one prisoner to another with no regard to the prisoners' health.

There are innumerable sadistic practices perpetrated against prisoners—like the searches. Under the guise of carrying out searches, prisoners are subjected to unimaginable indignity.

I was finally released from prison on December 29, 1988, having served my term. Thereafter I was denied employment. My attempt to enroll for postgraduate diploma in computer science at the Institute of

Computer Science of the University of Nairobi was also blocked because I had failed to get a clearance from the Special Branch.

In November 1989, I, with three friends, registered a consultancy firm specializing in promoting community-initiated projects (food production, income-generating projects etc). Within six months of establishing the firm we were already deeply involved with women's groups, youth groups, church groups, ranchers and fishermen. Even the Fisheries Department in the Ministry of Regional Development had asked our firm to conduct seminars for fishermen on their behalf.

In April 1990, I was questioned over three articles I had written which appeared in local papers. These were in *Business Contact* of April/May 1989, an article entitled "Cost-sharing in Education: Kenya's Melic that is Parents' Melancholy"; in *The Standard* of December 23, 1989, an article entitled "Education and Exams"; and in the *Nairobi Law Monthly*, no. 22 of March 1990, a letter entitled "Assault of Some of the Fundamental Rights and Liberties."

On July 10, 1990, following the July 7 pro-democracy protests, my colleague Dr. Adhu Awiti and his wife were arrested after a search lasting eight hours. Having failed to find seditious publications, the state went ahead to charge the couple with possession of a voter's card. Meanwhile, I was tipped that security personnel were looking for me. I immediately went into hiding on July 11, 1990, before fleeing to Dar es Salaam three weeks later.

I had been in Tanzania for only one month, where I was registered with United Nations High Commissioner of Refugees office as an asylum seeker, when I was tipped off about a plan by the Kenyan security officials to abduct me. I slipped into Uganda where the UNHCR office has refused to accord me protection insisting that I should go back to Tanzania. I am therefore without legal status.

APPENDIX B
COURT RECORDS OF KISUMU CHILDRENS' TRIALS

WINAM R. M.'S COURT KISUMU
CRIMINAL CASE NO. 745 OF 1990

Charge: Taking part in a riot contrary to Section 80 of the Penal Code.

1. Baraka Origindo Saoke, Francis Mutange Lubanda found guilty after trial, fined 800 shillings [$31] in default. Two months imprisonment. Did not appeal.
2. Arthur Oumaayaro pleaded guilty, sentenced to suffer six strokes of the cane because he is a juvenile.
3. Andrew Omdo Omuto found guilty after trial, fined 800 shillings in default two months imprisonment. Did not appeal.
4. Ongeti Alfonce Onyango found guilty after trial, fined 800 shillings in default, two months imprisonment. Did not appeal.
5. Leonard Wala Owino found guilty after trial, fined 800 shillings in default, two months imprisonment. Did not appeal.
6. Richard Duma Owena pleaded guilty after trial. Sentenced to suffer six strokes of the cane because he is a juvenile.
7. Paul Odungu Muija found guilty after trial, fined 800 shillings in default, two months imprisonment.
8. Maurice Nyanfowa, Calleb Okeyo Omulo found guilty after trial fined 800 shillings in default, two months imprisonment. Did not appeal.
9. Joel Onyango Omulo, found guilty after trial fined 400 shillings [$15] in default, one month imprisonment. Did not appeal.
10. George Ouma Oye pleaded guilty after trial. Sentenced to suffer six strokes of the cane, because he is a juvenile.
11. Harison Omolo Mbaja pleaded guilty after trial. Sentenced to suffer six strokes of the cane, because he is a juvenile.
12. George Wanyama Osanyo found guilty after trial, fined 800 shillings in default, two months imprisonment. Did not appeal.
13. Joseph Drayo Ogola found guilty after trial, fined 800 shillings in default two months imprisonment. Did not appeal.
14. David Okoth Jekome, found guilty after trial, fined 800 shillings in default two months imprisonment. Did not appeal.

15.   Benson Oluala found guilty after trial, fined 800 shillings in default, two months imprisonment. Did not appeal.
16.   David Ocheve Lusasa, discharged under Section 35(1) C.P.C.
17.   Paul Omandi Omwand, Discharged under Section 35(1) C.P.C.
18.   Paul Owiti Ndonga, discharged under Section 35 (1) C.P.C.
19.   Ezekiel Chongelwa Mbese, absent on plea.

WINAM R. M.'S COURT KISUMU
CRIMINAL CASE NO. 744 OF 1990

Charge: Taking part in a riot contrary to Section 80 of the Penal Code.

1.   Nicholas Lukasa Ado found guilty after trial, fined 800 shillings in default, two months imprisonment. Did not appeal.
2.   Samson Adongo Ogony found guilty after trial, fined 800 shillings in default, two months imprisonment. Did not appeal.
3.   Fitalis Ondewe Wandewe found guilty after trial, fined 800 shillings in default, two months imprisonment. Did not appeal.
4.   George Ochieng Frack, sentenced to suffer six strokes of the cane because he is a juvenile.
5.   Seth Ginards Senerwe found guilty after trial, fined 800 shillings in default, two months imprisonment. Did not appeal.
6.   Puis Musiasi Angolo found guilty after trial, fined 800 shillings in default, two months imprisonment. Did not appeal.
7.   Peter Otieno Omwanya found guilty after trial, fined 800 shillings in default, two months imprisonment. Did not appeal.
8.   Kennedy Adede Jumba sentenced to suffer six strokes of the cane because he is a juvenile.
9.   Laban Osulu Dende found guilty after trial, fined 800 shillings in default, two months imprisonment. Did not appeal.
10.   John Odongo Omboga found guilty after trial, fined 800 shillings in default, two months imprisonment. Did not appeal.
11.   Ojwang Orono found guilty after trial, fined 800 shillings in default, two months imprisonment. Did not appeal.
12.   Caleb Agwenge Otieno found guilty after trial, fined 800 shillings in default, two months imprisonment. Did not appeal.
13.   Henry Obondo Owera found guilty after trial, 800 shillings in default, two months imprisonment. Did not appeal.
14.   Caleb Otieno Magondo found guilty after trial fined 800 shillings in default, two months imprisonment. Did not appeal.

15.   John Onyango Owino found guilty after trial, fined 800 shillings in default, two months imprisonment. Did not appeal.

16.   Lakayo Otieno Oyudo, found guilty after trial, fined 800 shillings in default, two months imprisonment. Did not appeal.

17.   Richard Ochieng Odendo, found guilty after trial, fined 800 shillings in default, two months imprisonment. Did not appeal.

18.   Jeremiah Odhiambo Sigh pleaded guilty after trial. Sentenced to suffer six strokes of the cane, because he is a juvenile.

19.   Lucas Odhiambo Obondo

20.   Lawrence Otieno Oyudo

21.   Samson Moth Ondik

22.   Pamela Akinyi Apiny

23.   John Ogumbe Obule

24.   Frederick Otieno Obule

25.   Henry Vincent Adede

26.   Norbert Olongo Ochodo

27.   David Onyango Mwai

28.   Joseph Omolo Atet

29.   Maurice Onyango Agach

30.   James Shikuku Owini

31.   Hilary Mukwenyi Aketi found guilty after trial fined 800 shillings in default, two months imprisonment. Did not appeal.

32.   Antony Oduori Keya found guilty after trial, fined 800 shillings in default, two months imprisonment. Did not appeal.

33.   Zakaria Mboya Ogire found guilty after trial fined 800 shillings in default, two months imprisonment. Did not appeal.

34.   James Oduori pleaded guilty. Sentenced to suffer six strokes of the cane because he is a juvenile.

35.   George Onyango Ogongo found guilty after trial, fined 800 shillings in default, two months imprisonment. Did not appeal.

36.   Stephen Owuor Nyapollo found guilty after trial, fined 800 shillings in default, two months imprisonment. Did not appeal.

37.   Julius Odongo Ouria found guilty after trial, fined 800 shillings in default, two months imprisonment. Did not appeal.

WINAM R. M.'S COURT KISUMU
CRIMINAL CASE NO. 743 OF 1990

Charge: *Taking part in a riot contrary to Section 80 of the Penal Code.*

1. George Oduori Ojwang, found guilty after trial, fined 800 shillings in default two months imprisonment on June 7, 1990. Did not appeal.
2. Peter Otieno Obwaw, found guilty after trial, fined 800 shillings in default two months imprisonment on June 7, 1990. Did not appeal.
3. Stanley Otieno Omolo pleaded guilty, fined 800 shillings two months imprisonment.
4. Emmanuel Waine Olwa pleaded guilty, sentenced to suffer six strokes of the cane because he is a juvenile.
5. Morris Oracha Odhola, pleaded guilty, fined 800 shillings two months imprisonment.
6. Fredrick Odhiambo William pleaded guilty, fined 800 shillings two months imprisonment.
7. David Hamisi pleased guilty, sentenced to suffer six strokes of the cane because he is a juvenile.
8. James Were Alou, pleaded guilty fined 800 shillings two months imprisonment.
9. Michael Otieno Okumu pleaded guilty, sentenced to suffer six strokes of the cane because he is a juvenile.
10. Simon Otieno Murage, pleaded guilty fined 800 shillings two months imprisonment.
11. Stephen Okilo pleaded guilty, sentenced to suffer six strokes of the cane because he is a juvenile.
12. Isaac Owiti pleaded guilty fined 800 shillings two months imprisonment.
13. Joseph Atambo pleaded guilty, sentenced to suffer six strokes of the cane because he is a juvenile.
14. Peter Okende Jerry pleaded guilty, fined 800 shillings two months imprisonment.
15. Peter Ambuyo Mbita found guilty after trial, fined 800 shillings in default two months imprisonment on June 7, 1990. Did not appeal.
16. William Ochieng Amata, discharged under Section 35(1) of P.E.
17. Bernard Opiyo Ojwang found guilty after trial fined 800 shillings in default, two months imprisonment. Did not appeal.

18.   Joseph Olengo found guilty after trial, fined 800 shillings in default, two months imprisonment. Did not appeal.
19.   Tom Chakaya found guilty after trial, fined 800 shillings in default, two months imprisonment. Did not appeal.
20.   Okutale Max Achia found guilty after trial, fined 800 shillings in default, two months imprisonment. Did not appeal.

APPENDIX C
CASES OF SEDITION AND BREACH OF THE PEACE
JANUARY 1990–JULY 1991

Date	*Circumstances*
February 14, 1990	Sheikh Abdulaziz Rimo, Malindi, charged with "uttering seditious words" in a sermon on August 25, 1989. He was brought to court on February 14, 1990, after being held in police custody for an unknown period of time. He pleaded guilty to the charges and was unrepresented. The prosecution alleged that Sheikh Rimo had said he had no respect or confidence in the government and it should be overthrown. He was sentenced to six years.
March 29, 1990	Rev. Lawford Ndege Imunde charged with printing and being in possession of a seditious publication, a desk diary. He was held for two weeks in police custody and pleaded guilty to charges he later denied. He was unrepresented, but sought representation for appeal after he received a six year sentence. In March 1991, he was released by the Court of Appeal.
April 3, 1990	Three 17-year-old students charged with reproducing a seditious publication titled "I support Mwakenya and Kenya patriotic follow-up" in an exercise book. The offense was allegedly committed between January 1, 1987 and February 2, 1990. The students were unrepresented, and placed under a three year probation.
May 17, 1990	Daniel Nyoike Waweru charged with creating a disturbance likely to cause a breach of the peace.

It was alleged that in Langata police canteen, Mr. Waweru shouted that he wanted a new government with two political parties. He was released on 5,000 shilling ($192) bond with a surety of similar amount. He denied the charge.

May 20, 1990   Ainea Katizi Luvusi charged with creating a disturbance by shouting that Kenya should have more political parties.

May 22, 1990   Four people in Kiambu District charged with flashing the two-finger salute. It was reported: "Three of them were picked up from a bar at Kikuyu Trading Center and frogmarched to Kikuyu police station under tight security."

May 30, 1990   John Maina Kamangara, a politician seeking the Nakuru North parliamentary seat, charged with behaving in a manner likely to cause a breach of the peace. He reportedly shouted: "Now that the official candidate [for the Nakuru North parliamentary seat] has arrived, they [the government officials] will process things faster." The prosecution objected to bond saying: "The circumstances under which the offence was committed were serious and threatened public order, peace and security."

June 7, 1990   Sammy Maina, former Nairobi KANU branch organizing secretary, charged with breach of the peace. He reportedly shouted at the Rongai District Officer that the present government would not last more than five years. On June 12, he was charged with sedition as it was alleged the words were uttered with "seditious intention." Bail was denied by the magistrate who said: "The alleged utterances could not be taken lightly since they threatened the security of the state."

June 11, 1990   Peter Oketch Magolo, game ranger at Tsavo East National Park in Taita-Taveta district, charged with making seditious documents. Bail application opposed on the grounds that Mr. Magolo would "interfere with investigations."

June 1990   Councillor Njunguna Njui from Kabaju in Subukia-Nakuru charged with behaving in a manner likely to cause a breach of the peace. Plea taken *in camera*.

July 1990   Daniel Nyoike Waweru charged with behaving in a manner likely to cause a breach of the peace by shouting in a bar that he wanted a new government and two political parties. He was released on a bond of 5,000 shillings ($192).

July 6, 1990   Eighteen shop attendants and street vendors charged with offenses ranging from possessing seditious publications/music cassettes, offering them for sale, reproducing them, and uttering words with seditious intention. The accused included Jo Mwangi Mathai, producer at Nairobi's Matunda music stores, and five of his employees: Anne Wairimu Wachira, Catherine Wairimu Mathu, Charity Wanjuku Muriuku, Peter Maina Ngatia, Simon Wambugu Maina. The vendors charged were: John Swaleh Mbuui, Bernard Wanjohi, Paul Nganga Mwangi, Samuel Ondiek Mukua, Johnstone Njoroge Kimuhu. The cassettes included: Mucemanio wa Nyamu (meeting of the beasts), Matiba Saga, Patriotic Contributions, Dr. Ouko, Thiina wa Muoroto (the problems of Muoroto). The magistrate said: "These songs allegedly contained material calculated to raise discontent or disaffection amongst Kenyans."

July 7, 1990   Ten hawkers charged with offering for sale seditious publications/music cassettes at Nakuru

bus park. They were: John Kinuthia, John
Maina, Ruth Wanjiru, David Kuria, David
Ndeitu, Jane Wambui, Stephen Kimili, Joseph
Gitau and two others. The cassettes included
Mahoya ma Bururi (Prayers for the Nation), and
Patriotic Contributions. Mirugi Kariuki appeared
for the accused.

July 1990   Joseph Gerishon Ndereba, lecturer, charged with
                     behaving in a manner likely to cause a breach of
                     the peace by shouting: "Matiba was tipped to be
                     the next president, Rubia the vice-president and
                     Odinga the prime minister." The magistrate
                     denied bail: "From the content of the charge, I
                     feel that the prosecution need enough time to
                     investigate the allegations without interference."

July 8, 1990   A street preacher in Nyeri was arrested for
                     allegedly delivering a sermon touching on state
                     security. It was reported: "Eye-witnesses said
                     that the preacher had told his audience that he
                     was not afraid of being arrested, detained or
                     tortured."

July 11, 1990   Paul Muchemi Kamau was charged with creating
                     a disturbance in a manner likely to cause a
                     breach of the peace. He reportedly shouted at
                     KANU youthwingers that the party only had one
                     day to go and the wingers would have nothing to
                     eat. He was fined 5,000 shillings ($192) or three
                     months in jail.

July 11, 1990   James Mwaniki Githogori charged with creating
                     a disturbance likely to cause a breach of the
                     peace: he removed a portrait of President Moi
                     from the wall of a hotel.

July 11, 1990   Six people (two women and four men) charged
                     with possessing seditious cassettes. (Nyeri)

July 12, 1990   George Njuguna Kori, a Nakuru councillor, charged with conspiring to take part in a riot with seditious intention.

July 12, 1990   Ten people were arrested in the Sipili trading center in Laikipia District as they were "suspected of inciting people to riot." It was claimed they were flashing the two-finger salute.

July 13, 1990   Two people allegedly in possession of two seditious music cassettes were remanded in custody pending consent from the attorney general to prosecute them.

July 14, 1990   Peter Ndungu Wainaina charged with creating a disturbance likely to cause a breach of the peace. It was reported that he flashed the two-finger salute and called youthwingers "frogs." (Nakuru)

July 14, 1990   Sixteen people were charged with shouting and throwing stones at youthwingers. (Nakuru)

July 14, 1990   Three people charged with creating a disturbance likely to cause a breach of the peace. (Nyeri)

July 14, 1990   Peter Kariuki Muchiri charged with causing a breach of the peace by saying that the Nyayo government was dead. Nyeri principal magistrate, Babu Achieng, ordered that Mr. Muchiri be examined by a psychiatrist to establish his mental state.

July 15, 1990   A man was arrested for flashing the two-finger salute. (Mombasa)

July 17, 1990   Seven people charged with creating a disturbance likely to cause a breach of the peace. They were: Ephraim Njoroge, Peter Muigai Evans, Simon Ngugi Mwangi, Geoffrey Maina

Richard, Wilson Kariuki Muttika, Joseph Mwai Wachira, Patrick Njau. It was alleged that Messrs. Muttika and Wachira had shouted in a hotel that some Kikuyu MPs were selling the Kikuyu tribe. Mr. Njau was accused of throwing stones at the police. Mr. Njoroge was charged with looting. Mr. Evans denied the charge of creating a disturbance.

July 17, 1990   Peter Njunguna charged with behaving in a manner likely to cause a breach of the peace by shouting that he supported a multiparty system of government and was ready to die for it. It was alleged that he said he did not recognize President Moi. (Nairobi)

July 18, 1990   Fifty-two people charged with creating a disturbance during the July 7 riots. They were remanded in custody. (Nyeri)

July 18, 1990   Four people charged with creating a disturbance in a manner likely to cause a breach of the peace. They were: Henry Munyu Njenga, John Njoroge Thiongo, Newton Nyaga Muthi, Joseph Mjugu Ndungu.

July 19, 1990   James Kisenge Musyoka charged with sedition. He was accused of obtaining 180 copies of the seditious publication *MwaKenya*.

July 21, 1990   Samuel Kama Njogu charged with being in possession of a seditious publication, *Beyond* magazine, and two seditious music cassettes, Patriotic Contributions and The Problems of the Muroto People. (Nakuru)

July 21, 1990   Moses Kiragu charged with inciting violence. He was accused of pointing at a portrait of President Moi and calling him "a stupid person." He was released on a 5,000 shilling ($192) bond. (Eldoret)

July 21, 1990   Joseph Njeru Gichuki charged with inciting violence by flashing the two-finger sign. (Eldoret)

July 21, 1990   Peter Githuku charged with pointing at the portrait of President Moi and saying he was "nobody." (Eldoret)

July 21, 1990   Stephen Kihumba Kiguri charged with ordering people to flash the two-finger slaute and demanding for the immediate release of Kenneth Matiba and Charles Rubia. (Kitale)

July 21, 1990   James Mbunga and John Mburu Meshack Mjeru charged with flashing the two-finger salute.

July 21, 1990   Adrian Induri Shkiari charged with creating a disturbance. It was claimed he shouted abusive words about President Moi and wished Dr. Josephat Karanja were president. (Nyahururu)

July 24, 1990   Joseph Mwangi and Benjamin Njunguna Muroki were each fined 10,000 ($385) shillings for flashing the two-finger sign and shouting that they "did not give a damn" even if they were taken wherever Matiba and Rubia were taken. The prosecutor, Chief Inspector Giichia, said Mr Muroki was openly shouting support for Messrs. Matiba and Rubia. (Nairobi)

July 25, 1990   Six persons charged with possession of seditious cassettes. They were released on bond of 50,000 shillings ($1,923) each. (Nyeri—Principal Babu Achieng)

July 26, 1990   Four people charged with sedition. They were: George Anyona, Ngotho Kariuki, Edward Okungo Oyugi and Augustus Njeru Kathanga. The charges included holding a seditious meeting intended to overthrow the government and possession of the publication *Africa Confidential*.

July 27, 1990   Gitobu Imanyara charged with publishing a seditious publication the *Nairobi Law Monthly* (issue "The Historic Debate—Law, Democracy and Multi-party Politics in Kenya"). He was released on bail of 200,000 shillings ($7,692) and similar sureties. (Nairobi—Chief Magistrate's Court)

July 27, 1990   Gilbert Mutava and Tabitha Mueni charged with creating a disturbance in a manner likely to cause a breach of the peace. They were accused of provoking KANU and saying that they were supporters of Matiba. It was claimed they said: "What is KANU? We are for Matiba." The magistrate denied bail, saying: "I do not think it's safe to release the accused persons on bond at this time." (Kitui—Resident Magistrate's Court)

July 31, 1990   Wachira Kingau Ngethe charged with creating a disturbance in a manner likely to cause a breach of the peace. It was alleged he shouted that "it was police officers and not Mr. Matiba's supporters who broke into shops and looted during the recent spate of riots." He was represented by Mirugi Kariuki, and released on a bond of 5,000 shillings ($192). (Nakuru—Chief Magistrate's Court)

August 1, 1990   Caleb Ooro Odero, secondary school teacher in South Nyanza District, charged with possessing five seditious publications: Mao Tse Tung, Manifesto of the Communist Party, Critique of the Gorgotha Progam, the State Card, and Communique of the Second Plenary Session of the Ninth Central Committee of the Communist Party of China. He was released on a bond of 10,000 shillings ($385). (Homa Bay)

August 1, 1990   Jacob Thingau charged with possessing a banned publication *Mzalendo MwaKenya* (Patriotic

MwaKenya). Reports in the national press said he was held in custody for fourteen months. He was sentenced on March 12, 1991, to one month in jail, having changed his plea from not guilty to guilty after the court allowed the police to continue their investigations. (Nairobi—Chief Magistrate's Court)

August 1, 1990   Peter Karanja Karingiu and Michael Juma Hamisi were charged with creating a disturbance in a manner likely to cause a breach of the peace. They allegedly said that the current government would not last a year and that security personnel shot innocent people during the July riots. They were released on a personal bond of 10,000 shillings ($385).

August 1, 1990   Two men charged with creating a disturbance by allegedly saying the Kenyan government would not last more than five years.

August 3, 1990   Irungu Muturi charged with creating a disturbance by telling a youthwinger to flash the two finger sign. He was fined 10,000 shillings ($385). (Nairobi—Chief Magistrate's Court)

August 8, 1990   Joe Omwaka Ager, a former manager with British Airways in Kenya and Uganda, charged with possessing a seditious publication, *Africa Confidential*, which contained an article entitled "Kenya—The Security Home Boys." He was denied bail and lost his job because he was held in police custody for thirty days. (Nairobi—Chief Magistrate's Court)

August 10, 1990   Hima Kumalija, a Tanzanian, charged with possessing a seditious publication, *Africa Confidential*, which contained an article entitled "Kenya—The Security Home Boys." He was released on 50,000 shilling ($1,923) bond.

August 11, 1990   Florence Nyaguthie Murage, an administration
                         officer with the University of Nairobi, charged
                         with possession of a seditious publication, *Africa
                         Confidential*, which contained an article entitled
                         "Kenya—The Security Home Boys". (Nairobi—
                         Chief Magistrate's Court)

August 14, 1990   Thomas Kipkurui Murgor, son of former
                         Assistant Minister for Agriculture William
                         Murgor, charged with breach of the peace. He
                         allegedly shouted: "A multiparty system is best,"
                         which implied that he was against the present
                         Kenyan government. He was also accused of
                         flashing the two-finger salute. (Eldoret)

August 22, 1990   Philip Githaiga Gachoka, former election
                         manager of Kenneth Matiba, charged with
                         possessing a seditious document, *MwaKenya*. He
                         was represented by Paul Muite who said that Mr.
                         Gachoka had been subjected to degrading
                         treatment—he was blindfolded, bundled into a
                         car and had not been allowed to change his
                         clothes for five days. Mr. Muite said that when
                         his client had been interrogated, he was not
                         asked about the seditious document, and that
                         Special Branch officers dwelt on political matters
                         not associated with the charges. Mr. Gachoka was
                         denied bail. (Nairobi—Chief Magistrate's Court)

August 22, 1990   Police in Murang'a questioned five people
                         suspected to have been behind seditious
                         pamphlets scattered in the town on August 19,
                         1990. Senior Superintendent of Police, Philip
                         Kindiga, said three suspects were arrested by
                         members of the public while another two were
                         found by police reading the papers. He said
                         those arrested by the public were reportedly
                         forcing people to read the papers.

August 23, 1990   David Karobi Musa and Danile Kimani Mwangi
                         appeared before Murang'a resident magistrate,
                         Kathoka Ngoma, charged with having copies of
                         a seditious newsletter *Mzalendo MwaKenya* dated
                         August 17, 1990. He was unrepresented in court,
                         did not apply for bond.

August 28, 1990   Caleb Mokaya Gichana charged with possessing
                         seditious document *MwaKenya*. The charge said
                         he was at Buru Buru police station in Nairobi on
                         August 22, 1990 with the document. He was first
                         arrested on August 11, 1990 with George Anyona
                         and three others, when he had been held for ten
                         days before being discharged without any case
                         being brought against him. Since that time, Mr.
                         Gichana had been summoned several times to
                         appear at the Central Investigation Department
                         by a Mr. Kingori to sign documents and accept
                         to be a prosecution witness against Anyona's
                         case. Mr. Gichana had been arrested again on
                         August 22, 1990 at 6:00 A.M. and taken to
                         various police stations. During the previous five
                         days he had been constantly asked why he would
                         not sign documents to be a witness against
                         Anyona. Mr. Gichana lost his job as a school
                         teacher when he was in police custody for ten
                         days. He was not told of the charges against him
                         until August 27, 1990. He was denied bail.
                         (Nairobi—Chief Magistrate's Court)

September 6, 1990   Sammy Kinyanjui Waithera and Harrison
                         Githaiga Gicheru were charged with writing
                         seditious letters to the chief of general staff and
                         the Nairobi city engineer. Mr. Gicheru was
                         accused of writing to the commander of the
                         armed forces on May 29 inviting him to meet
                         the new "president," Mr. Kinyangui. He was also
                         charged with inviting the city engineer to a rally
                         where "President Kinyangui" and "His Highness

King" Harrison Githaiga would address a meeting. (Nakuru)

September 6, 1990   Geoffrey Waweru Thuo charged with possessing a copy of the proscribed *Financial Review* magazine. He denied the charge and was released on bail.

September 12, 1990   Mary Slessor Ager, schoolteacher, charged with possessing a seditious document, *Africa Confidential*, which contained the article "Kenya—The Home Security Boys." Her husband, Joe Omwaka, faced a similar charge. Both were granted bail.

September 14, 1990   Robert Muthami Murage charged with possessing seditious music cassettes. (Nairobi)

September 20, 1990   Ernest Mukikema charged with breach of the peace. It was alleged he shouted that Bishop Alexander Muge was killed for nothing and that President Moi would be toppled by September 17, 1990. (Kisumu)

September 22, 1990   Charles Kuria Wamwere charged with belonging to a clandestine movement, the Kenya Patriotic Front. He was unrepresented, and jailed for four years. (Nairobi—Chief Magistrate's Court)

October 13, 1990   Gilbert Gichini, a 68-year-old Nakuru businessman, charged with possessing prohibited publications, two copies of the *Financial Review* and a publication entitled *A Decade Under Mao Tse Tung*. He was also accused of possessing government property. Mr. Gichini denied the charges. (Nakuru)

October 19, 1990   Chris Kamuyu, Dagoretti MP, charged with possessing proscribed magazines, nine copies of the *Financial Review* and a copy of the June 1989 issue of *Development Agenda*. He was denied bail.

October 19, 1990

Koigi wa Wamwere, Mirugi Kariuki, Rumba Kinuthia and Geoffrey Kariuki were brought to court on charges of treason and sedition. Four other accused, including three relatives of Rumba Kinuthia, faced charges of misprision of treason: Joseph Kinuthia, Mary Kinuthia, Margaret Kinuthia and James Mwaura. These charges were withdrawn against Mary Kinuthia and Margaret Kinuthia after they had been held in custody for two months. The court heard allegations of torture and obstruction to legal representation and medical attention on November 2.

October 19, 1990

Charles Rukwaro was jailed for six months, without option of a fine, for possessing two copies of the *Financial Review*.

January 1, 1991

John Githingi Ruriga charged with creating a disturbance likely to cause a breach of the peace. He was arrested for wearing a badge with a two-finger logo. The police inspector who arrested Mr. Ruriga said that the accused was followed by "a number of people who were murmuring" and therefore his wearing of the badge was inciting members of the public.

July 11, 1991

George Anyona, Ngotho Kariuki, Edward Okong'o Oyugi and Augustus Njeru Kathanga found guilty of the sedition charges (detailed above, July 26, 1990) and each sentenced to seven years imprisonment for holding a seditious meeting, with eighteen months running concurrently for Anyona and Kathangu for being in possession of seditious and proscribed publications. The trial lasted six months, making

it Kenya's longest sedition trial. All four accused
alleged torture and ill-treatment.

APPENDIX D
CONSTITUTIONAL AMENDMENTS

1.   *The Constitution of Kenya (Amendment) Act, No. 28 of 1964*
     declared Kenya a Sovereign Republic with the president as head
     of state and government. The powers of the president were
     amplified to include:

     i.   Privileges and prerogatives of the British Crown;
     ii.   Power to appoint public officials;
     iii.   The discretion in (ii) was absolute as regards the attorney
            general, the comptroller and auditor general, the
            permanent secretaries and the police commissioner;
     iv.   The position of commander-in-chief of the armed forces.

2.   *The Constitution of Kenya (Amendment) Act, No. 2 of 1964*
     further strengthened the presidency by:

     •   abolishing the revenue basis of the regions by making
            them dependent on central government budgeting;
     •   giving the President further powers in the appointment
            of judges, including the power to appoint the chief justice
            without consulting the regions. He could also instigate an
            inquiry into the conduct of any judge by setting up a
            special tribunal for the purpose.

3.   *The Constitution of Kenya (Amendment) Act, No. 14 of 1965*
     changed the constitutional provisions relating to the amendment
     of the constitution.

     •   Former provisions meant that 90 percent of the Senate
            vote and 75 percent of the Lower House were necessary
            to effect an amendment. Now only 65 percent of the vote
            in both houses was needed to amend the constitution.
     •   Provisions relating to the invocation of emergency
            powers were relaxed. (A simple majority in either house
            was now all that was required to authorize a declaration
            of emergency.)

Circumstances Leading to the Expansion of Emergency Powers:
"Certain members of the ethnic Somali community had tried to secede and the government, taking advantage of the scare caused by the crisis, prevailed upon the parliament to broaden the powers of the President in reference to emergencies."

4.   *The Constitution of Kenya (Amendment) Act, No. 16 of 1966* introduced provisions regulating the tenure of members of parliament viz:

   •   any member of parliament sentenced by a court of law to a term of more than six months in jail automatically lost his/her seat;
   •   any member of parliament who failed to attend parliament for eight consecutive sittings without the permission of the Speaker lost his/her seat (unless pardoned by the President).

5.   *The Constitution of Kenya (Amendment) No. 2 Act, No. 17 of 1966* required any parliamentarians who had earned their seats on a party ticket and later resigned from that party, to stand down from office and seek fresh support from the electorate. This was prompted by the acrimonious exchanges between the radicals and the moderates within KANU after which, President Kenyatta proposed fundamental changes to the constitution (at the Limuru KANU conference). Immediately afterwards, twenty-eight members of parliament announced that they were forming a new political party. Oginga Odinga and Achieng Oneko later resigned from KANU and joined the twenty-eight MPs in Kenya People's Union. To unite the fractured KANU, a further amendment to the constitution was proposed.

6.   *The Constitution of Kenya (Amendment) No. 3 Act, No. 18 of 1966*

   •   removed parliamentary control over the exercise of emergency powers. The president could, by a notice in the gazette, bring into operation Part III of the Preservation of the Public Security Act.

- The duration of an emergency was extended from seven to twenty-eight days. Detention orders could now operate indefinitely.

7. *The Constitution of Kenya (Amendment) No. 4, Act No. 40 of 1966*

- The senate was abolished and merged with the Lower House.
- Forty-one new constituencies were created for the former senators (meaning that these senators became members of parliament without being elected in those regions that they were said to represent).
- The dissolution of the first parliament was postponed from 1968 to 1970.

8. *The Constitution of Kenya (Amendment) Act, No. 14 of 1967*
All the MPs who had resigned from KANU prior to Constitutional Amendment No. 14 (see above) lost their parliamentary seats. They then sought a declaratory order from the High Court that the fifth amendment did not affect them and that therefore they were still members of parliament. With matters still pending in court the government rushed an amendment through parliament ostensibly to clarify the fifth amendment but in reality it was to nullify the claims made by these MPs. It was provided that the fifth amendment applied to members who had resigned prior to the amendment.

9. *The Constitution of Kenya (Amendment) Act, No. 16 of 1968*
addressed the question of regionalism.

10. *The Constitution of Kenya (Amendment) Act, No. 45 of 1968*
changed the method of presidential elections. The existing methods of electing the president by a general election or by parliament acting as an electoral college were challenged as inadequate, susceptible to indiscipline and not assuring the president of continued loyalty. To remedy these so-called defects the new amendment provided that every party taking part in a general election had to put forward a presidential candidate. All

candidates for parliamentary seats therefore shared a ticket with
a presidential candidate.

Implications

- undermined legislative authority over the presidency;
- abrogated the provisions for independent parliamentary
  candidatures;
- removed from parliament and vested in the president
  parliament's power to nominate/elect twelve additional
  members.

11.   *The Constitution of Kenya (Amendment) Act, No. 3 of 1969*

- consolidated the existing amendments;
- vested increased powers in the president—he now had the
  power to appoint the electoral commission;
- declared itself to be "the Constitution of Kenya and to be
  the authentic version thereof."

12.   *The Constitution of Kenya (Amendment) Act, No. 2 of 1974*
made Kiswahili the official language of the National
Assembly.

13.   *The Constitution of Kenya (Amendment) No. 2 Act, No. 10 of 1974*
changed the voting age from 21 to 18.

14.   *The Constitution of Kenya (Amendment) Act, No. 1 of 1975*
repealed the constitution of Kenya (Amendment) Act No. 2 of
1974 (see above). It provided for the use of both English and
Kiswahili in the National assembly:

- parliamentary proceedings would be in Kiswahili;
- all bills, financial results and all written laws to be in
  English.

15.   *The Constitution of Kenya (Amendment) No. 2 Act, No. 14 of 1975*
added to the President's prerogative of mercy cases of
disqualifications from participating in parliamentary elections on

account of having been convicted of an election offense under the Election Offenses Act.

Background to the Amendment
Paul Ngei, President Kenyatta's longtime friend, was found guilty of an election offense during the hearing of an election petition. That meant that his election to parliament was invalid and further that he was disbarred from presenting himself for election in the subsequent by-election. So that Ngei could participate, the constitution was hastily amended to give the president power to pardon offenders under election law. Ngei was pardoned, stood for the elections and was re-elected.

The bill was introduced in parliament on December 9, 1975, and was debated and passed within a day. It was given presidential assent on December 11, 1975, but its date of commencement was backdated to January 1, 1975 so that Ngei's election offense, which had been committed earlier in the year, could be pardoned.

16. *The Constitution of Kenya (Amendment) Act, No. 13 of 1977*
established the Kenyan Court of Appeal as the highest court in the land. Previously, before the collapse of the East African Community collapses in 1977, the highest court had been the East African Court of Appeal.

17. *The Constitution of Kenya (Amendment) Act, No. 1 of 1979*

   •   provided that English could be used as an alternative to Kiswahili in parliamentary debate;
   •   that, in future, proficiency in both English and Kiswahili would be a prerequisite to qualifying for election to parliament.

18. *The Constitution of Kenya (Amendment) No. 2 Act, No. 5 of 1979*
It is a requirement in Kenya that those public officials who wish to contest parliamentary elections must first resign from their jobs. This amendment provided that the minister could give an order (published in the *Kenya Gazette*) specifying when such public officials had to resign so as to be eligible for election (provided

the minister did not require a person to vacate office more than six months prior to the preliminary elections).

19.   *The Constitution of Kenya (Amendment) Act, No. 7 of 1982*

- it converted the de facto one party system into a de jure one-party system;
- created office of the Chief Secretary.

20.   *The Constitution of Kenya (Amendment) Act, No. 7 of 1984*

- Abolished all appeals arising out of decisions of the High Court in the course of hearing election petitions. In the memorandum of objects and reasons, this would "rectify the anomalous position under case law whereby interlocutory decisions of the High Court as an election court hearing election petitions can not be appealed to the Court of Appeal whereas final decisions are not."
- Made provision for Judges of Appeal to be able to sit in the High Court to complete cases commenced before them prior to their appointment to the Court of Appeal.
- Changed the composition of the Public Service Commission by increasing membership from seven to a total of seventeen (including the chair and the deputy chair). Provision was also made for the Public Service Commission to appoint officers to local authorities.

21.   *The Constitution of Kenya (Amendment) Act, No. 6 of 1985*

- addressed citizenship;
- any person born in Kenya after December 11, 1963, would be a Kenyan citizen if at the time of his birth one of his parents was a citizen of Kenya.

22.   *The Constitution of Kenya (Amendment) Act, No. 14 of 1986*

- abolished the position of Chief Secretary;
- parliamentary constituencies were increased from 158 to 188;

- removed the security of tenure formerly enjoyed by the offices of the attorney general, comptroller and auditor general.

23. *The Constitution of Kenya (Amendment) Act, No. 20 of 1987*
related to a court's discretion in granting of bail. This amendment followed the High Court's ruling in *Margaret Magiri Ngui v. The Republic.* The facts were as follows:

- By a 1982 amendment to the Criminal Procedure Code, it was provided that murder, treason, robbery with violence or attempted robbery with violence, were not bailable offenses. Yet Section 72 of the constitution provided for bail in all cases (irrespective of the charge). The applicant in this case was awaiting trial as a suspect in a robbery case. Her application for bail was dismissed by the Magistrate's Court. She then appealed to the High Court, contending that Section 123 of the Criminal Procedure Code under which her application had been thrown out, was unconstitutional. The High Court accepted her argument. This amendment was effected to overrule the High Court decision by imposing restrictions on bail—it made the granting of bail discretionary.
- Since this amendment was effected, the practice of the courts has been that anyone charged with a politically sensitive offense, like sedition, is rarely granted bail.

24. *The Constitution of Kenya (Amendment) Act No. 4 of 1988*

- removed the tenurial security of judges;
- increased the length of time over which a suspect on a capital charge—murder, treason, robbery with violence, suspected robbery with violence—could be held without being taken to court (from 24 hours to 14 days).
- The provision increasing the length of time the government may hold a suspect in incommunicado detention and is now used in all cases where the state wishes to punish a person without appearing to.

APPENDIX E
TESTIMONY OF A SOMALI REFUGEE
WHO CAME BY SEA AND ARRIVED IN KENYA
IN FEBRUARY 1991

I arrived in Kenya at Kiunga port with a family of thirteen people, including children and close relatives. We have been stranded in this location for three weeks waiting for transport to take us to Mombasa refugee camp. This was mainly due to official stonewalling by local authorities.

Given the circumstances, I took my family back to Ras Kiamboni to find direct sea transport to Mombasa port. After ten days of waiting for transport without success, I realized that my wife, who was in her last days of pregnancy, could not waste any more time. I was forced to come back to Kiunga where health services were available to her to deliver in safer circumstances.

On April 8, my wife had a baby girl, and we had to wait for another three weeks until she could cope with rough road transportation. In the meantime, a lot of dealings were going on so that the Kenyan authorities would allow us to proceed to Mombasa before the rainy season closes all access roads to Kiunga. In order to get the permission to leave, we had to bribe the local authorities.

On April 25, we left Kiunga on top of a fish lorry and spent four nights in Majengo before we could reach Mokowe, the land access to Lamu island. At Mokowe, the police rounded us up and escorted us to Kanu hall in Lamu. That was May 1. When we were brought to Kanu hall, we found almost fifty other people already there. These were mainly small fishing boat owners and their staff who were kept there against their will, accused of transporting refugees.

I spent twenty-one days in the Kanu hall with my family in miserable living conditions. The hall—where more than seventy were kept—had not water or sanitation facilities. Being the rainy season, the roof was also continuously leaking. To add insult to injury, at the back of the hall there was a slaughter house, and when there was a high tide its dirt washed into the premises of the hall.

On several occasions, I put my case to the District Commissioner of Lamu, Mr. Makumi, the District Officer 1 (DO1), Mr Hassan, and the District Officer 2 (DO2), Mr. Ogola, to take me and my family to the refugee camp in Mombasa with my own means. I asked them to treat me like other refugees so I could free myself from all this uncertainty.

On May 21, all the occupants of the Kanu hall were rounded up. The DO2, together with two naval officers, asked those who wished to go back to Somalia to raise their hands. Only twelve people out of seventy-two raised their hands. Those people were told to pack their personal belongings and leave with a police escort. The remaining group was asked to explain why they did not wish to be ferried back to Somalia. Abdullahi Ugas, a former MP and general manager, started to explain why he had to abandon his home country for the time being, but he was interrupted by the DO2. The meeting was abandoned, with strict orders for us to keep seated.

Earlier in the day, the District Commissioner (DC), Mr. Makumi, told the staff of the MV *Koyama* that the ship would be towed by the Kenyan navy to Somalia. Mr. Ali, the ship's accountant, expressed his misgivings and asked who would be accountable in case of an accident. The DC fired back that he would not be accountable for any tragedy outside his jurisdiction, and the operation would be enforced by the police.

At 7:00 P.M., the DO2, Mr Ogola, accompanied by the OCS [Officer in Charge of Station], Mr Kabogo and 120 policemen forced us into the Kanu hall and informed us that we would be transported to Somalia against our will. My wife shouted: "You are killing me and my family." The children were so restless. I tried to explain to both the DO2 and the OCS that I did not deserve such horrible treatment and that they should have killed us straight away, instead of delegating murder. I was shocked to see both of them shaking their heads. Then they ordered thirty policemen to beat us—we were slapped and kicked in the stomach. My family members were brutalized. Even my daughter and the breast-feeding mother were not spared. Our personal belongings were thrown on the dirty ground of the hall. I had to comply with the orders.

The police boat ferried us all to MV *Koyama*. They distributed a loaf and a packet of biscuits to each passenger. Another group of refugees, who had been on board a ferry for sixteen days, were also brought in. The MV *Koyama* was small, about twenty-five meters long and seven meters wide, with a steering cabin with four beds for the staff. During that night, most of us could not sleep as the rain poured on the deck and the waves started shaking the vessel. The number of occupants exceeded 130, and the cabin could only shelter fifteen persons maximum.

A captain came and tried to get the engine alive. When I questioned him about our plight he responded that he was implementing orders from the security council of Lamu district.

On May 22, the efforts of the navy at repairing the engine did not succeed. They towed the MV *Koyama* and a fishing boat with a dead engine from Lamu waters to Magakoni naval base. As we were almost five sea miles away, the fishing boat capsized, and it took two hours to get us moving again amid the rough sea. As we reached the base at 3:00 P.M., we were surprised to find another three fishing boats full of refugees waiting there. These refugees were also jammed into MV *Koyama*, especially women and children. They had been told earlier in the day that they would be transferred to Lamu on their way to Mombasa refugee camp. This official misinformation had kept them in Fasa and Kilangistini islands for over forty days.

On May 23, the navy tried to get the engine of MV *Koyama* back in order, but in vain. Some bread was distributed—one loaf for each refugee and a can of corned beef for every six persons. As the rains poured, many of the refugees from Fasa and Kilangistini islands asked for shelters on top of the navy patrol ships, Madararka and Mamba. They were accepted—forty-eight on the Madararka and thirty-four on the Mamba, the majority women and children.

On May 24, all the small fishing boats left on their way back to Somalia, passing through the sheltered waters between the islands. The patrol ship Madararka towing the defective fishing boat, and the patrol ship Mamba towing the MV *Koyama* started their trip toward the border area at 6:00 A.M. At 4:00 P.M., the towing rope of MV *Koyama* was cut loose, and the vessel drifted across the border where it collided with a coral atoll. This immediately caused the death of sixteen refugees. Among these were my beloved wife, Hawa Mohamed Abdi Geer, aged 31, and mother of eight children, our daughter Samiya, aged 14, her brother, Burhan Mohamed Abdi, aged 13, Dr. Ahmed Hassan Dhore, aged 46, and father of five children. My new-born child, Somaya Mohamud Ali, passed away in Kiunga health center ten days after the accident as a result of head injuries. I do not know the names of the other victims.

As the patrol ships stood in rough waters about six sea miles from the coast, the fishing boats could not move close enough to rescue the remaining refugees, who were now stranded on the boat. The next day the captains of the patrol ships loaded three male adults, three female adults and three children, together with two navy men aboard a navy rubber boat. Despite the strong protests of the refugees, the operation continued. The rubber boat turned upside down 200 yards away from its starting point. They were lucky enough to have a woman national swimmer who did not panic but brought the rubber boat back to normal and loaded the people back to the boat. The rest, still stranded on the boat, were later taken ashore by a fishing boat.

The captain of the Madararka patrol ship lectured the forty-eight refugees—they would now all be loaded on the defective fishing boat, the one which had once capsized near Lamu and was already half full with sea water, and then towed to the coast. Three male adults and forty-five women and children were forced with brutal tactics to descend from the ship to the boat. As the towing started, both the fishing boat and the navy rubber boat capsized. As the navy men were wearing floating vests, they put the rubber boat back to normal. But instead of rescuing lives, they focused on picking gold valuables from the struggling victims and pickpocketed from the dead.

These are twenty-one of the victims: 1) Anab Mohamud Ismail, 33, pregnant wife and mother of the following three children; 2) Nimo Yusuf Mohamed, age 7; 3) Said Yusuf Mohamed, age 3; 4) Kin Yusuf Mohamed, age 1; 5) Abdiweli Abdillahi Mohamed, age 7; 6) Hasan Abdillahi Mohamed, age 5; 7) Leyla Hasan Jama, age 19; 8) Ayan Ahmed Yusuf, age 5; 9) Yasin Ahmed Yusuf, age 2; 10) Farhiya Dahir Abdi, age 6; 11) Amina Ali Jibril, age 20; 12) Ismahan Hasan H Muse, 24, mother of the following two children; 13) Mukhtar Adan Jama, age 8; 14) Suad Adan Jana, age 5; 16) Fadumo Herso Mohamed, 34, mother of the following three children; 17) Ashia Abdinasir Jama, age 8; 18) Mohamed Ismail Abdulle, age 6; 19) Fartun Abdi Ossoble, age 4; 20) Amina Artain Hussen, age 30; 21) Ibad Artan Husen, age 27. Most of the bodies of the dead victims, washed ashore on both sides of the border, were buried in Ras Kiambone, four kilometers north of the Kenyan border.

The community of Ras Kiambone in Somalia assisted the victims by providing funeral services free of charge, and showing the evidence to the police of Kiunga in Kenya, 14 kilometers south of the Somali border, until the Kenyan police stopped them from giving further evidence.

The response of Lamu district authorities to the fatal incident centred on issuing a false statement, disinforming the Kenyan government and the whole world. The official statement of Lamu police department told of a Somali ship, named *Tahlil*, which left Kisimayo port on May 23, and capsized in the border area on May 26, with special emphasis on the brave role of the Kenyan navy. The death toll was set at thirty-three and it said that survivors were treated in Kiunga health center.

On May 27, I went to the Kenyan police at Kiunga to report my case personally, but the inspector refused to take any statement from me—his reason being that the accident took place outside the Kenyan border. Other survivors of the capsized fishing boat within the Kenyan border had no better treatment. Some leaks from the Kiunga police indicate that special orders were issued from Lamu district authorities: statements from accident survivors have to be expelled straight afterwards; 2) stopping all survivors from passing through to other parts of Kenya, even if they have legitimate documents of passage; 3) airplanes with the intention of lifting Somalis are denied the right to land in Kiunga.

You may ask what motivates the gentlemen of Lamu district to play it rough that way? Why is the record of Lamu district as recipient of Somali refugees so miserable, although the President of the Republic of Kenya appeals almost twice every month since last February, sympathizing with the tough times in Somalia? Why the Somali boat owners were harassed since February as they ferried refugees? Why have the refugees in Kiunga been transported to the Mombasa refugee camp only since the influx of refugees?

Personally, I think it is greed, overpowering all the humanitarian aspects of sound judgement. The harassment of boat owners and illegal confiscation of property dates back to early February this year. The official explanation of such behaviour was that they would be kept from sea so they would not bring in more refugees. All the boat owners were deported without any official documents from Lamu district—they were given no papers for their property. The DO2, Mr. Ogola, tried to convince me that all the boat owners were free to go back to Somalia without the boats and come back when the war is over, come back with a letter from his office. We are told we can recover everything after the war is over.